Quotient Space Based Problem Solving: A Theoretical Foundation of Granular Computing

Quotient Space Based Problem Solving: A Theoretical Foundation of Granular Computing

Ling Zhang and Bo Zhang

AMSTERDAM • BOSTON • HEIDELBERG • LONDON
NEW YORK • OXFORD • PARIS • SAN DIEGO
SAN FRANCISCO • SINGAPORE • SYDNEY • TOKYO

Morgan Kaufmann is an imprint of Elsevier

ELSEVIER

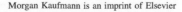

Morgan Kaufmann is an imprint of Elsevier
The Boulevard, Langford Lane, Kidlington, Oxford OX5 1GB, UK
225 Wyman Street, Waltham, MA 02451, USA

First edition 2014

Notice

No responsibility is assumed by the publisher for any injury and/or damage to persons or property as a matter of
products liability, negligence or otherwise, or from any use or operation of any methods, products, instructions or
ideas contained in the material herein. Because of rapid advances in the medical sciences, in particular, independent
verification of diagnoses and drug dosages should be made

British Library Cataloguing in Publication Data
A catalogue record for this book is available from the British Library

Library of Congress Cataloging-in-Publication Data
A catalog record for this book is availabe from the Library of Congress

ISBN: 978-0-12-410387-0

For information on all Morgan Kaufmann publications
visit our web site at store.elsevier.com

ELSEVIER Book Aid International

Working together
to grow libraries in
developing countries

www.elsevier.com • www.bookaid.org

Contents

Preface

The term problem solving is used in many disciplines, sometimes with different perspectives. As one of the important topics in artificial intelligence (AI) research, it is a computerized process of human problem-solving behaviors. So the aim of problem solving is to develop techniques that program computers to find solutions to problems that can properly be described.

In the early stage of AI, symbolists play a dominant role. They believe that all human cognitive behaviors, including problem solving, can be modeled by symbolic representation and reasoning and do not advocate the use of strict mathematical models. The most general approach to tackle problem-solving processes is "generation and test". Applying an action to an initial state, a new state is generated. Whether the state is the goal state is tested; if it is not, repeat the procedure, otherwise stop and the goal is reached. This principle imitates human trial-and-error behaviors in problem solving sufficiently. The principle has widely been used to build AI systems such as planning, scheduling, diagnosis, etc. and to solve a certain kind of real problems. Therefore, the heuristic and scratch method is misunderstood as a unique one in AI for many people. We believe that more and more modern sciences such as mathematics, economics, operational research, game theory and cybernetics would infiltrate into AI when it becomes mature gradually. Over the years, we devoted ourselves to introducing mathematics to AI. Since 1979 we have introduced statistical inference methods to heuristic search, topological dimension reduction approach to motion planning, and relational matrix to temporal planning. Due to the introduction of these mathematical tools, the efficiency and performance of AI algorithms have been improved significantly. There are two main trends in AI research recently. One is attaching importance to the usage of modern scientific methods, especially mathematics; the other is paying attention to real-world problem solving. Fortunately, our efforts above are consistent with these new trends.

Based on these works, we explored further the theoretical framework of problem solving. Inspired by the following basic characteristics in human problem solving, that is, the ability to conceptualize the world at different granularities, translate from one abstraction level to the others easily and deal with them hierarchically, we establish an algebraically quotient space model to represent the multi-granular structures of the world so that it's easy for computers to deal with them hierarchically. Certainly, this model can simulate the above characteristics of human problem-solving behaviors in a certain extent. We expect more human characteristics to merge into the model further. The system is used to describe the hierarchical and multi-granular structure of objects being observed and to solve the problems that are faced in inference, planning, search, etc. fields. Regarding the relation between computers and human problem solvers, our standpoint is that the computer problem solver should learn some things from human beings but due to the difference between their physical structures they are distinguishing.

Already 20 years has passed since the English version of the book published in 1992. Meanwhile, we found that the three important applied mathematical methods, i.e., fuzzy mathematics, fractal geometry and wavelet analysis, have a close connection with quotient space based analysis. Briefly, the representational method of fuzziness by membership functions in fuzzy mathematics is equivalent to that based on hierarchical coordinates in the quotient space model; fractal geometry rooted in the quotient approximation of spatial images; and wavelet analysis is the outcome of quotient analysis of attribute functions. The quotient space theory of problem solving has made new progress and been applied to several fields such as remote sensing images analysis, cluster analysis, etc. In addition, fuzzy set and rough set theories have been applied to real problems for managing uncertainty successively. The computational model of uncertainty has attracted wide interest. Therefore, we expanded the quotient space theory to non-equivalent partition and fuzzy equivalence relation. We explored the relation between quotient space theory and fuzzy set (rough set) theory. The quotient space theory is also extended to handling uncertain problems. Based on these works, we further proposed a new granular computing theory based on the quotient space based problem solving. The new theory can cover and solve problems in more domains of AI such as learning problems so as to become a more general and universal theoretical framework. The above new progress has been included in the second version of the book.

The quotient space based problem solving that we have discussed mainly deals with human deliberative behaviors. Recently, in perception, e.g., visual information processing, the multi-level analysis method is also adopted. So the quotient space model can be applied to these fields as well. But they will not be involved in the book.

There are seven chapters and two addenda in the book. In Chapter 1, we present a quotient space model to describe the world with different grain-sizes. This is the theoretical foundation throughout the book and is the key to problem solving and granular computing. The principle of "hierarchy" as an important concept has been used in many fields such as control, communication theory. In Chapter 2, we discuss the principle starting with the features of the human problem-solving process and pay attention to its mathematical modeling and relation to computational complexity. In Chapter 3, we discuss synthetic methods that involve the inverse of top-down hierarchical analysis, that is, how to combine the information from different viewpoints and different sources. Since synthetic method is one of main measures for human problem solving we present a mathematical model and induce the corresponding synthetic rules and methods from the model. Although there have been several inference models in AI, the model presented in Chapter 4 is a new network-based one. The new model can carry out inference at different abstraction levels and integrates deterministic, non-deterministic and qualitative inferences into one framework. And the synthetic and propagation rules of network inference are also introduced. In Chapter 5, the application of quotient space theory to spatial planning is presented. It includes robot assembly sequences and motion planning. For example, in motion planning instead of widely adopted geometry-based planning we pay attention to a topology-based one that we propose, including its principles and applications. The statistically heuristic search algorithms are presented in Chapter 6, including theory, computational complexity, the features and realization of the algorithms, and their relation to hierarchical problem-solving principles and multi-granular computing. In Chapter 7, the original equivalence relation based theory is expanded to including tolerant relations and relations defined by closure operations. Also, a more general quotient space approximation principle is presented. Finally, the basic concepts and theorems of mathematics related to the book are introduced in addenda, including point set topology and statistical inference.

The authors gratefully acknowledge support by National Key Basic Research Program (973 Program) of China under Grant Nos. 2012CB316301, 2013CB329403, National Natural Science Foundation under Grant No. 60475017. Many of the original results in the book were found by the authors while working on these projects.

CHAPTER 1

Problem Representations

Chapter Outline

1.1 Problem Solving

The term problem solving was used in many disciplines, sometimes with different perspectives (Newell and Simon, 1972; Bhaskar and Simon, 1977). As one of the main topics in artificial intelligence (AI), it is a computerized process of human problem-solving behaviors. It has been investigated by many researchers. Some important results have been provided (Kowalski, 1979; Shapiro, 1979; Nilson, 1980). From an AI point of view, the aim of the problem solving is to develop theory and technique which enable the computers to find, in an efficient way, solutions to the problem provided that the problem has been described to computers in a suitable form (Zhang and Zhang, 1992; 2004).

Problem-solving methods and techniques have been applied in several different areas. To motivate our subsequent discussions, we next describe some of these applications.

1.1.1 Expert Consulting Systems

Expert consulting systems have been used in many different areas to provide human users with expert advice. These systems can diagnose diseases, analyze complex experimental data and arrange production schedule, etc.

In many expert consulting systems, expert knowledge is represented by a set of rules. The conclusion can be deduced from initial data by successively using these rules.

1.1.2 Theorem Proving

The aim of theorem proving is to draw a potential mathematical theorem from a set of given axioms and previously proven theorems by computers. It employs the same rule-based deduction principle as in most expert systems.

1.1.3 Automatic Programming

Automatic programming, automatic scheduling, decision making, robotic action planning and the like can be regarded as the following general task. Given a goal and a set of constraints, find a sequence of operators (or actions) to achieve the goal satisfying all given constraints.

All the problems above can be regarded as intelligent problem-solving tasks. In order to enable computers to have the ability of finding the solution of these problems automatically, AI researchers made every effort to find a suitable formal description of problem-solving process. It is one of the central topics in the study of problem solving.

In the early stage of AI, symbolists play a dominant role. They believe that all human cognitive behaviors, including problem solving, can be modeled by symbols and symbolic reasoning. The most general approach to tackle problem solving is generation and test. Applying an action to an initial state, a new state is generated. Whether the state is the goal state is tested; if it is not, repeat the procedure, otherwise stop and the goal is reached. This principle imitates human trial-and-error behaviors in problem solving sufficiently. The principle has widely been used to build AI systems. The problem-solving process is generally represented by a graphical (tree) search or an AND/OR graphical (tree) search.

1.1.4 Graphical Representation

A graphically causal model (Pearl, 2000) is an abstract model that describes the causal mechanisms of a system. So some problem-solving processes can be regarded as inference over the graphically causal model. For example, automatic reasoning, theorem proving and the like can be considered as searching a goal node in the model. And robotic action planning, automatic programming, etc., can be formalized as searching a path in the model; and the path being found is the solution of the problem and called a solution path.

Let us take the robot's indoor path-planning problem as an example. Assuming that the initial position of the robot is in room X and the goal position is in room Y, the aim is to find a path from room X to room Y. Fig. 1.1 shows the graphical representation of the problem-solving process. The nodes shown in Fig. 1.1 represent subsets of potential solutions. For example, the node denoted by A represents all potential paths from room X to room Y by going through room A; while the node C all potential paths by going through rooms A and C; and so on. The arcs linking two nodes are planning rules for finding a path from one room to another. The path that links X and Y is the solution path.

1.1.5 AND/OR Graphical Representation

Some problem-solving processes may be represented more conveniently by the so-called AND/OR graph. In this representation, a complex original problem is divided into a conjunction of several subproblems. These subproblems are simpler than the original one and can generally be solved in isolation. The subproblems can be further decomposed into still more simple sub-subproblems until they can be easily solved.

In fact, the problem-solving processes above are regarded as an AND/OR graph search. The graph is similar to the general graph except that there are two kinds of links. One, called OR link, is the same as that in the general graphs. The other, called AND link, is special to the AND/OR graphical representation.

All nodes in an AND/OR graph represent subproblems to be solved or subgoals to be reached. The situation is the same as in the general graph. But in AND links, although the individual subproblems are represented by separate nodes, they all must be solved before

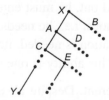

Figure 1.1: The Graphical Representation of a Problem

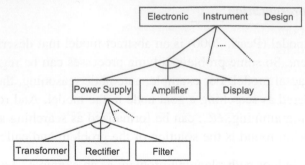

Figure 1.2: AND/OR Graphical Representation of a Problem

their parent problem is considered solved. The curved arcs between links are drawn to show this fact (see Fig. 1.2).

A solution to the problem represented by a general graph is a terminal node of the graph. However, the complete solution in an AND/OR graphical representation is represented by an AND/OR subgraph, called a solution graph (see Chapter 6 for more details).

As an example shown in Fig. 1.2, the initial problem is to design an electronic instrument. The task can be divided into several subtasks called component designs, such as power supply, amplifier and display component design. Furthermore, each subtask can be divided into several sub-subtasks called part designs. For example, power supply design consists of transformer, rectifier and filter designs, etc.

Although a wide range of problems can be described by the above representations, there is still a big gap between the formal description and human behavior in problem solving so that generally the computer solver cannot find the solution in an efficient way as a human does.

One of the basic characteristics in human problem solving is the ability to conceptualize the world at different granularities and translate from one abstraction level to the others easily, i.e. deal with them hierarchically (Hobbs, 1985). It is the hierarchy that underlies the human power in problem solving. Suppose that a manager sitting in his office drafted a production plan for his factory. In his early mental planning stage, only a coarse-grained model of the factory is needed. The factory in his mind may be encoded as a 'block diagram' consisting of several workshops while ignoring all details within the workshops. When a plan has briefly been sketched out, he must enter a more fine-grained model to consider the details within the workshops, i.e., he needs a fine coding of the factory. In some planning stage, if global information is needed, he will immediately switch to the coarse-grained representation again. This ability is one of the human intelligence.

For a computer, things are quite different. Despite all data about a factory, such as machines, workers, tools, buildings, etc., having been stored in its memory, it is still unknown how to generate different representations from these data, how to choose a properly representational form based on different computational requirements, how to transform a coarse-grained model into a fine one or vice versa. Neither general graphical nor AND/OR graphical representation can tackle such problems as they lack a mechanism for representing the world at different granularities. Therefore, we have to provide a precise formalization of the notion of problem representations at different granularities in order for computers to imitate the above human abilities.

1.2 World Representations at Different Granularities

1.2.1 The Model of Different Grain-Size Worlds

From the above discussion, it seems important to develop a new theory and technique which will in some way enable computers to represent the world at different granularities.

Suppose that a problem-solving space, or a problem space for short, is described by a triplet (X, f, T).

X denotes the problem domain, or universe. In the preceding example, when drafting a production plan, the factory as a whole is the domain in question.

$f(.)$ indicates the attributes of domain X or is denoted by a function $f : X \rightarrow Y$, where Y may be a real set, a set of n-dimensional space R^n, or a general space, $f(x)$ is either single-valued or multi-valued. For each element $x \in X$, $f(x)$ corresponds to a certain attribute of the x, and is called an attribute function. In the example above, value of output, work-force and profit are the attributes that depict the factory.

T is the structure of domain X, i.e. the relations among elements in X. For example, the relations among workshops, workers, machines and managers, etc. Structure T is the most complex and various part of the triplet description. One main category includes the Euclidean distance in Euclidean space, the inner product in inner product space, the metric in metric space, the semi-order in semi-order space, topology in topological space, directed graphs and undirected graphs, etc. The other is the structure that arose from some operations such as linear space, group, ring, field and lattice in algebra and logic inference. Certainly, the above two categories may be combined to form a new structure, for example, normed space, normed ring, etc.

Given a problem space (X, f, T), solving a problem implies the analysis and investigation of X, f and T. But the problems are how to choose a suitable granularity of X, what relationships exist among different grain size worlds, etc.

Suppose that X indicates a domain with the finest grain-size. By simplifying X we have a more coarse-grained domain denoted by $[X]$. So the original problem space (X, f, T) is

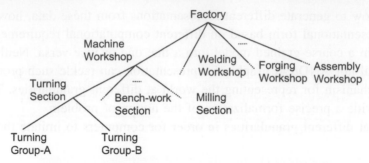

Figure 1.3: The Hierarchical Structure of a Factory

transformed into a new one $([X], [f], [T])$ with a new abstraction level. In the above 'factory' example, if groups are elements of domain X, then, in a simplified domain $[X]$, its elements may be sections, each consists of several groups, i.e., the elements with common or similar functions in X as shown in Fig. 1.3.

The hierarchical structure shown in Fig. 1.3 is quite similar to the concept of quotient set in mathematics (Eisenberg, 1974).

Assume that X is a domain, R is an equivalence relation on X, and $[X]$ is a quotient set under R. Regarding $[X]$ as a new domain, we have a new world which is coarser than X. We say that X is classified with respect to R.

Before the discussion of the domain partition, we first introduce some concepts and propositions of set theory.

Definition 1.1

Assume that X and Y are two sets, $R \subset X \times Y$ is a product set of X and Y on $X \times Y$. For $\forall (x, y) \in X \times Y$, have $(x, y) \in R$. We say that x and y have relation R denoted as xRy, or R is a relation on $X \times Y$. When $X = Y$, R is called a relation on X.

Definition 1.2

Assume that X is a set, R is a relation on X and satisfies

(1) Reflexivity: xRx,
(2) Symmetry: if xRy, then yRx,
(3) Transitivity: If xRy and yRz, then xRz,

R is called an equivalence relation on X denoted by xRy or $x \sim y$.

Definition 1.3

For $x \in X$, $[x] = \{y | x \sim y\}$ is called an equivalence class of x.

Definition 1.4

$[X] = \{[x]|x \in X\}$ is a quotient set of X under R.

Namely, quotient set $[X]$ becomes a new set by regarding $[x]$ as its elements.

From the previous discussion, it is known that the different grain-size world and the concept of quotient set in mathematics are unified or quotient sets can be regarded as a mathematical model of domains of the different grain-size world.

Different grain-size world model: To investigate problem (X, f, T) from different granularities (angles, or abstraction levels) means inspecting the corresponding problem $([X], [f], [T])$, where $[X]$ is a quotient set of X under equivalence relation R, $[f]$ and $[T]$ are the quotient attribute and quotient structure on $[X]$, respectively. $([X], [f], [T])$ is a quotient space of (X, f, T). Different quotient sets of X correspond to different quotient spaces which compose different grain-size worlds of problem (X, f, T). **Quotient space theory** is used to investigate the representations and properties of domains, attributes and structures of a problem space under different granularities, and their interdependent and transformational relations.

Definition 1.5

If $\{A_\alpha\}$ is a partition of $X \Leftrightarrow$ (1) $X = \bigcup_\alpha A_\alpha$, (2) if $\alpha \neq \beta$ then $A_\alpha \cap B_\alpha = \varnothing$, where A_α is a subset of X.

Proposition 1.1

If R is an equivalence relation on X, then $\{[x]|x \in X\}$ is a partition of X. Conversely, giving a partition $\{A_\alpha\}$ on X, an equivalence relation R on X is uniquely defined. A set $\{[x]|x \in X\}$ of equivalence classes of X corresponding to R is $\{A_\alpha\}$.

From the above proposition, it is known that different grain-size representations of a problem correspond to different equivalence relations or different partitions. In a factory, if we consider machining as an equivalence class called a workshop, then turning, milling and bench work sections belong to the same workshop. They are included in the same equivalence class, whereas in a fine-grained model, turning, milling and bench work may be regarded as different elements (see Fig. 1.3).

1.2.2 The Definition of Quotient Space

In summary, when a problem (X, f, T) and an equivalence relation R are given, we define a quotient space $([X], [f], [T])$ as follows:

$[X]$: a quotient set corresponding to R
$[f]$: if $f : X \rightarrow Y$, define $[f] : [X] \rightarrow Y$ (see Section 2.3 for more details)
$[T]$: if T is a topology, then $[T]$ is defined as $\{u|p^{-1}(u) \in T, u \in [X], p : X \rightarrow [X]\}$

Then, we have a new problem $([X], [f], [T])$, that is, a new abstraction level of the original problem (X, f, T). Each R corresponds to a certain grain-size world.

1.3 The Acquisition of Different Grain-Size Worlds

What are the principles of partitioning or granulation of the worlds? Certainly, some of them are domain-dependent. Some are not. We now discuss the general principles.

Granulation problem can be performed in three different ways.

First, the granulation is directly executed on domains (or universes). A domain is partitioned into regions with different sizes, and then we have a new grain-size world.

Second, the granulation is first performed on attribute values f. And then the domain is accordingly partitioned based on the granulation of f.

Third, the granulation is carried out on structure T. The domain is then partitioned based on the granulation of T.

1.3.1 The Granulation of Domain

1 Function Based Granulation

Elements of a domain are classified according to their functions, i.e., the elements with the same (or similar) function are classified into one category. For example, the granulations of an instrument and a factory are shown in Figs 1.2 and 1.3, respectively.

2 Constraint-Based Granulation

Given n constraints $C_1, C_2, ..., C_n$, and a domain X, we may partition X according to $C_i, i = 1, 2, ..., n$. That is, for constraint C_1, X is divided into two classes. One satisfies C_1. The other does not. Then, the two classes are further divided into two sub-classes, respectively, according to C_2 and so on. So we have a 2-ary tree structure of X.

Obviously, for each C_i, X can be divided into more than two classes, which satisfy C_i in various degrees. We then end up with a general tree structure of X.

In reality, this kind of granulations is used extensively.

Example 1.1

Suppose that we design a building which must satisfy a lot of constraints, such as two floors, three bedrooms, the area of dining room must be greater than 10 square meters, etc. First, we have a building sketch which only satisfies some main constraints. Then, the sketch is refined. Finally, we have a complete design. From the hierarchical point of view, the building sketch can be regarded as an equivalence class consisting of all sorts of buildings that satisfy the main constraints. Then the equivalence class is gradually partitioned into the final design via the refining of the sketch.

3 Granulation by Combination

From a known quotient space X_1, its supremum X_2 and infimum X_3 quotient spaces may be obtained. Then, we have three quotient sets with different granularities. Through intersection and union operations over the three quotient sets, we have a new quotient set and its corresponding quotient space (see Section 1.4 for more details).

1.3.2 The Granulation by Attributes

Partition attribute values first, then the corresponding partition of the domain is obtained.

1 Granulation by Attribute Values

Assume that $f : X \rightarrow Y$ is an attribute function. If f is single-valued, then X can be partitioned in accordance with attribute values Y. Usually, we are familiar with Y, for example, Y is a real number or a Euclidean space E^n. We can classify X by using Y as follows.

Assume that $\{Y_i\}$ is a partition of Y. Define:

$$X_i = \{x|\, f(x) \in Y_i\}$$

$\{X_i\}$ is a partition of X.

Example 1.2

X is a set of examinees attending the nation-wide university's entrance examination. For each examinee $x \in X$, $F(x)$ indicates his total test scores (TTS). Let $f : X \rightarrow Y = [0, 700]$. Divide Y into $Y_1 = [0, 420)$, $Y_2 = [420, 460)$, $Y_3 = [460, 550)$, and $Y_4 = [550, 750]$, where 520 is the minimal TTS required for admission to key universities, 460 is the minimal TTS for general universities, 420 is the minimal TTS for institutes.

Define: $X_i = f^{-1}(Y_i)$, $i = 1, 2, 3, 4$.

X_4 is the set of examinees admitted to key universities, X_3 is the set of examinees admitted to general universities, etc. In a word, based on the partition of a subset [0,700] of real numbers, we have a corresponding partition of examinees.

Granulation by attribute values is extensively used in rough set theory (Pawlak, 1982). Assume that (X, f), denoted by (U, A) in rough set, is a data table (information system), where $f = (f_1, f_2, ..., f_n)$. A_i is the quotient set corresponding to f_i. Granulation by attribute values is sometimes called the quantification of attribute values.

Define $X_i = f_i^{-1}(Y_i), i = 1, 2, ..., n$. X_i is a quotient set of X, where $f_i, i = 1, 2, ..., n$ is the granulation of f. If X is simultaneously granulated by f_1 and f_2, the corresponding quotient space obtained is denoted by X_{12}. X_{12} is the supremum of X_1 and X_2. Using all combinations of the quantification of attribute values, the corresponding quotient spaces (sets) gained are all possible quotient spaces that can be obtained by the granulation based on the attribute values. One of the main goals in rough set analysis is to choose a proper one from among all the possible quotient spaces so that the recognition or classification task can be effectively achieved.

Example 1.3

Assume that X is a set of freshmen. The constitution of the freshmen can be described by several attributes such as f_1 height, f_2 weight, f_3 sight, etc. Sometimes, we are only concerned with some of them and classify the freshmen based on these attributes. This classification is regarded as a projection-based method.

Example 1.4

A data table (X, A) is given below.

A X	f_1	f_2	f_3	f_4
1	5	1	3	2
2	3	1	2	1
3	3	1	3	1
4	2	1	3	0
5	2	0	1	0
6	3	0	3	0

Based on attribute values we have the following quotient spaces.

$$X_1 = \{(1), (2, 3, 6), (4, 5)\}$$
$$X_2 = \{(1, 2, 3, 4), (5, 6)\}$$
$$X_3 = \{(5), (2), (1, 3, 4, 6)\}$$
$$X_4 = \{(4, 5, 6), (2, 3), (1)\}$$

and have

$$X_{12} = X_1 \wedge X_2 = \{(1), (2, 3), (4), (5), (6)\}$$
$$X_{123} = X_1 \wedge X_2 \wedge X_3 = X$$

where $\wedge$ denotes the supremum operation.

If all quotient spaces in a semi-order lattice, which order is decided by the inclusion relation of subsets of attributes, are given, the so-called 'attribute reduction' in rough set theory is to find the simplest supremum within the semi-order lattice, where the 'simplest' means the minimal number of attributes.

In rough set theory, given a quotient space (knowledge base) and a set S, if S can be entirely represented by the union of elements in the quotient space, S is called crisp or discernible, otherwise, indiscernible. The indiscernible set can be represented by the upper and lower approximation sets.

'Fuzziness' is an inevitable outcome of his/her observation when he/she watches the world at a coarse grain-size. So the concept of fuzziness is closely related to granularity and can be described by quotient spaces with different granularities. Using the elements of a set of quotient spaces to depict 'fuzziness', the cost is greatly reduced since the potential of quotient spaces is much less than that of the original space. The description of fuzziness by membership functions in fuzzy set theory (Zadeh, 1965) is very expensive. The description of fuzziness in rough set theory is less expensive but still much more expensive than the quotient space description.

When 'fuzziness' appears in our observation, this means that we are lacking detail. If we use an elaborate tool to describe a 'fuzzy' object in detail, it seems unreasonable. Thus, the representation of fuzziness by membership functions in fuzzy set theory is not necessarily an effective method.

2 Projection-Based Partition

Assume that f is multi-dimensional. Let its n attribute components be $f_1, f_2, ..., f_n$, X is classified with respect to $f_{i+1}, f_{i+2}, ..., f_n$ values, while ignoring their attribute components $f_1, f_2, ..., f_i$. This method is said to be a projection-based method.

The geometrical interpretation of the projection-based method is that observing the same object from different view-points. For example, the three perspective drawings of a mechanical part are based on the projection-based method.

1.3.3 Granulation by Structures

1 Coarse Topology

Problem (X, f, T) is given. Assume that T_1 is a topology on X denoted by $T_1 < T \Leftrightarrow T_1 \subset T$.

Definition 1.6

Given (X, f, T), T_1 and $T_1 < T$. Define an equivalence relation R on X as $xRy \Leftrightarrow \forall u(x)$, $y \in u(x)$ *and* $\forall u(y), x \in u(y)$, where $u(x)(u(y))$ is an open neighborhood of $x(y)$ on T_1.

From quotient set X_1 defined by R, we have a quotient space (X_1, f_1, T_1). Since structure T_1 is coarser than T, (X_1, f_1, T_1) is a quotient space of (X, f, T). Through coarsening structure T, we have a new coarse space which may not necessarily be obtained from domain granulation or granulation by attributes.

Example 1.5

A topologic space (X, T), where

$$X = \{1, 2, 3, 4\}$$
$$T = \{\varnothing, (1), (2), (1, 2), (1, 2, 4), (2, 3, 4), (2, 3), (3), (1, 2, 3), (3, 4), X\}$$

Let $T_1 = \{\varnothing, (2), (1, 2), (2, 3), (2, 3, 4), X\}$, $T_1 < T$.

Then, we have X_1 and quotient space (X_1, T_1), where $X_1 = X$.

Since the quotient topology $[T]$ of X_1 is T, (X_1, T_1) cannot be obtained from domain granulation.

An example is given below to show how to use the structure-based granulation to problem solving.

Example 1.6

In a temporal world model presented by Allen (1981, 1983, 1984), there are 13 temporal relations between two events, i.e., $(<, m, o, fi, di, s, =, si, d, f, oi, mi, >)$. For two events $I_1 = [a_1, b_1]$ and $I_2 = [a_2, b_2]$, their 13 temporal relations are defined as follows.

$$
\begin{aligned}
&I_1(<)I_2 && a_1 < b_1 < a_2 < b_2 \\
&I_1(m)I_2 && a_1 < b_1 = a_2 < b_2 \\
&I_1(o)I_2 && a_1 < a_2 < b_1 < b_2 \\
&I_1(fi)I_2 && a_1 < a_2 < b_1 = b_2 \\
&I_1(di)I_2 && a_1 < a_2 < b_2 < b_1 \\
&I_1(s)I_2 && a_1 = a_2 < b_1 < b_2 \\
&I_1(=)I_2 && a_1 = a_2, b_1 = b_2 \\
&I_1(si)I_2 && a_1 = a_2 < b_2 < b_1 \\
&I_1(d)I_2 && a_2 < a_1 < b_1 < b_2 \\
&I_1(f)I_2 && a_2 < a_1 < b_1 = b_2 \\
&I_1(oi)I_2 && a_2 < a_1 < b_2 < b_1 \\
&I_1(mi)I_2 && a_2 < b_2 = a_1 < b_1 \\
&I_1(>)I_2 && a_2 < b_2 < a_1 < b_1
\end{aligned}
$$

Assume that X is a set of events in question. All time intervals that events happened in are regarded as attribute functions, the 13 temporal relations as structure T. Then, temporal planning is transformed into solving problem (X, f, T).

Coarsening structure T, e.g., 13 temporal relations are simplified to eight relations T_1 as follows.

$$T_1 = \{(<), (m), (mi), (>), (di, si, fi, =), (oi, f), (o, s), (d)\}$$

Quotient structure T_1 is obtained from structure T by merging both $a_1 < a_2$ and $a_1 = a_2$ into $a_1 \leq a_2$, and both $b_1 > b_2$ and $b_1 = b_2$ into $b_1 \geq b_2$.

Define quotient set $X_1 : xRy \Leftrightarrow R(x, y) = \{=\}$, where $R(x, y)$ is a set of temporal relations between events x and y.

Quotient space (X_1, f_1, T_1) is coarser than the original space (X, f, T). In Chapter 6, we will show the problem solving based on the coarsening structure and by using the corresponding falsity preserving, etc. properties to reduce the computational complexity in problem solving.

2 Classification with Overlapped Elements

In some cases, some $x \in X$ may belong to more than one class. For example, in an electronic instrument, one part may be contained in two different components. That is, the classification has overlapped elements or the contours of classes are blurred. We have:

Definition 1.7

Assume that X is a domain, $A_i, i \in I$ is a subset of X, where I is a set of subscripts. If $X = \underset{i \in I}{\cup} A_i$, regarding A_i as a set of new elements, then $< X >= \{A_i\}$ is a new abstraction level.

It should be noted that $A_i \cap A_j = \varnothing, i \neq j$, doesn't always hold here. In order to distinguish the classification with overlapped elements, we use angle brackets $< >$ instead of square brackets $[\ ]$. Here the symbol A_i is used for representing both subsets of X denoted by $A_i \subset X$, and elements of $< X >$ denoted by $A_i \in < X >$.

In Chapter 2, we will discuss one specific case, i.e., tolerant relations, of classification with overlapped elements.

1.4 The Relation Among Different Grain Size Worlds

Generally, we treat a problem under various grain sizes. Thus, it is necessary to establish the relationship between the worlds at different granularities.

1.4.1 The Structure of Multi-Granular Worlds

Semi-Order Lattice

Definition 1.8

Assume that $\mathfrak{R}$ is all equivalence relations on X and $R_1, R_2 \in \mathfrak{R}$. If $x, y \in X$, $xR_1y \Rightarrow xR_2y$, then R_1 is said to be finer than R_2, and denoted by $R_2 < R_1$.

Proposition 1.2

Under the relation '<' defined in Definition 1.8, the family of quotient sets corresponding to $\mathfrak{R}$, or simply $\mathfrak{R}$, is a complete semi-order lattice.

Note: Definition of complete semi-order lattice (Davey and Priestley, 1992) is the following.

A semi-order relation '$\leq$' is defined on X (X may be infinite). $\forall A \subset X$, if A has the supremum and infimum, i.e., there exist $x_0, x_0 \in X$, for $\forall x \in A, x \leq x_0$ if $\forall x \in A, x \leq y$, then $x_0 \leq y$ (supremum) and there exist $x_1, x_1 \in X$, for $\forall x \in A, x_1 \leq x$ if $\forall x \in A, y \leq x$, then $y \leq x_0$ (infimum), then $(X, \leq)$ is called a complete semi-order lattice.

Proof:

For a family $\{R_\alpha, \alpha \in I\} \subset \mathfrak{R}$ of relations, define $\overline{R} : x\overline{R}y \Leftrightarrow \forall \alpha, xR_\alpha y$.

$\underline{R} : x\underline{R}y \Leftrightarrow$ there exists a finite sequence $x = x_0, x_1, \cdots, x_n = y$ and $R_{\alpha_1}, R_{\alpha_2}, \cdots, R_{\alpha_n}$ such that $x_i R_{\alpha_i} x_{i+1}, i = 0, 1, \cdots n-1$, simply $[x = x_0, x_1, \cdots, x_n = y]$.

Now we prove that $\overline{R}$ is the supremum of $\{R_\alpha\}$ below.

First, we show that $\overline{R}$ is an equivalence relation. Its reflexivity and symmetry are obvious.

We show its transitivity. Assume $x\overline{R}y, y\overline{R}z \Rightarrow \forall \alpha, xR_\alpha y, yR_\alpha z \Rightarrow \forall \alpha, xR_\alpha z \Rightarrow x\overline{R}z$. Assume that R satisfies $\forall \alpha, R_\alpha < R$. Then, $xRy \Rightarrow \forall \alpha, xR_\alpha y \Leftrightarrow x\overline{R}y$, i.e., $\overline{R} < R$. Thus, $\overline{R}$ is the supremum.

Now we prove that $\underline{R}$ is the infimum of $\{R_\alpha\}$ below.

First, we show that $\underline{R}$ is an equivalence relation. From the definition of $\underline{R}$, its reflexivity and symmetry are obvious.

From $x\underline{R}y, y\underline{R}z \Rightarrow \exists x = x_0, x_1, \cdots, x_n = y, [x = x_0, x_1, \cdots, x_n = y]$ and

$\exists y = y_0, y_1, \cdots, y_m = z, [y = y_0, y_1, \cdots, y_m = z]$, we have

$[x = x_0, x_1, \cdots, x_n = y = y_0, y_1, \cdots, y_m = z]$, i.e., $x\underline{R}z$. $\underline{R}$ has transitivity. Thus, $\underline{R}$ is an equivalence relation.

Now we show that $\underline{R}$ is the infimum. Assume that R is any lower bound of $\{R_\alpha\}$, i.e., for $\forall \alpha, R < R_\alpha$. Assume $x\underline{R}y$, i.e., $\exists x = x_0, x_1, \cdots, x_n = y$ such that $R_{\alpha_i}, x_i R_{\alpha_i} x_{i+1}$, $i = 0, 1, \cdots, n-1$. From $\forall i \ x_i R_{\alpha_i} x_{i+1}$ and $R < R_{\alpha_i}$, we have $x_i R x_{i+1}, i = 0, 1, \cdots, n-1$.

From its transitivity, we have that $x = x_0$ and $y = x_n$ are R equivalent, i.e., $x\underline{R}y \Rightarrow R < \underline{R}$. Again, $\forall \alpha, xR_\alpha y \Rightarrow x\underline{R}y$, then $\underline{R}$ is the infimum.

Finally, $\mathfrak{R}$ is a complete semi-order lattice.

Obviously, when $R_1 < R_2$, $[X]_{R_1}$ is a quotient set of $[X]_{R_2}$, where $[X]_R$ is a quotient set of X corresponding to equivalence relation R. The proposition shows that given a domain X, all its quotient sets compose a complete semi-order lattice based on the inclusion relations of the sets. We can implement various supremum and infimum operations over the lattice.

In Fig. 1.3, if under the equivalence relation R_0, the whole factory is regarded as an equivalence class, i.e., all elements of X are equivalent, then R_0 is the coarsest relation among $\boldsymbol{R}$. If the factory is decomposed into several equivalence classes such as machining, assembly and welding workshops, etc., we have a new equivalence relation R_1. Similarly, each workshop can be further divided into fine-grained cells, and so on. Finally, we have R_n such that $x \sim y \Leftrightarrow x = y$. This means that R_n is the finest relation among $\boldsymbol{R}$. And we have

$$R_0 < R_1, ..., < R_n$$

Generally, assume that G is a tree with n levels shown in Fig. 1.4. Let X be all leaves of G and $p \in G$ be a node of G. (p) denotes all leaves of the subtree rooted at p. Let A_i be a set of nodes at depth i. Then each A_i corresponds to a partition of X, i.e., for $p \in A_i$, (p) is an equivalence class and corresponds to an equivalence relation R_i.

Obviously, $R_0 < R_1, ..., < R_n$.

Conversely, a sequence of monotonic relations $R_0 < R_1, ..., < R_n$ can be represented by a tree with n levels.

If a function $f(x)$ is assigned to each leaf $x \in G$, then a heuristic search of G can be regarded as a hierarchical inference over a sequence of monotonic equivalence relations, that is, a heuristic tree search can be transformed into a hierarchical problem solving. We will further discuss it in Chapter 6.

1.4.2 The Structural Completeness of Multi-Granular Worlds

In Section 1.4.1, we show the structural completeness of a family of quotient sets, i.e., given domain X, all equivalence relations defined on X compose a complete semi-order lattice. This is a structural completeness theorem of a family of quotient sets. We'll extend

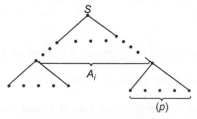

Figure 1.4: The Hierarchical Relation of a Tree

the theorem to a family of quotient spaces, i.e., the structural completeness theorem of multi-granular worlds.

We'll discuss the properties of three different complete lattice structures in a family of quotient spaces. And we'll show that the three complete lattice structures correspond to the closures of three main operations on quotient-based granular computing, respectively.

Definition 1.9

(X, T) is a topologic space. $\mathfrak{R}$ is a set of all equivalence relations on X. For $R_1, R_2 \in \mathfrak{R}$, if $x, y \in X$, $xR_1y \to xR_2y$, R_1 is said to be finer than R_2 denoted by $R_2 < R_1$.

Basic Theorem (Completeness Theorem)

Under the relation '<' defined in Definition 1.9, the family of quotient spaces corresponding to $\mathfrak{R}$, or simply $\mathfrak{R}$, composes a complete semi-order lattice.

Compared to other methods such as rough set theory, quotient space theory pays more extension to the concept of 'structures'. So it is needed to investigate families of all quotient spaces composed from topologic space (X, T) and to establish the corresponding structural theorem. We will establish three different complete lattice structures of families of quotient spaces and their properties, relations and applications below.

1.4.2.1 The Basic Theorem of Families of Quotient Spaces

A topologic space (X, T) is given. Let $\mathfrak{A}$ be a set of all possible quotient sets on X, and X_i denotes its element.

$(X_i, [T_i])$ is a quotient space, where $[T_i]$ is a quotient topology on X_i induced from topologic space (X, T). In the following discussion, in order to differentiate from other topologies, symbol $[T]$ with square brackets [ ] is used to denote a quotient topology induced from a corresponding quotient set.

$U = (\mathfrak{A}, \mathfrak{R}) = \{(X_i, [T_i]), X_i \in \mathfrak{A}, [T_i] \in \mathfrak{R}\}$, where $\mathfrak{R}$ is a set of all quotient topologies induced from quotient sets.

Definition 1.10

Assume $(X_i, [T_i]), (X_j, [T_j]) \in (\mathfrak{A}, \mathfrak{R})$. If X_i is a quotient set of X_j, then $(X_i, [T_i]) < (X_j, [T_j])$.

Theorem 1.1

Under the Definition 1.10, $U = (\mathfrak{A}, \mathfrak{R})$ composes a complete semi-order lattice.

From the basic theorem, we have the theorem above.

If the topology on quotient sets is unrestricted, i.e., it is not limited to the quotient topology induced from quotient set, the theorem does not necessarily hold. This means that the supremum (or infimum) of a family of topologies is not a quotient topology induced from quotient set. Namely, there exists a subset of U such that it does not have the supremum (infimum) within U. The following example shows the fact.

Example 1.7

Topologic space (X, T) is given, where $X = \{1, 2, 3, 4\}$ and $T\{\varnothing, (1, 2), (3, 4), X\}$. Let $X_1 = \{(1), (2, 3, 4)\}$ and $X_2 = \{(2), (1, 3, 4)\}$. We have $[T_1] = \{\varnothing, X\}$ and $[T_2] = \{\varnothing, X\}$, the induced quotient topologies from X_1 and X_2, respectively. Thus, their supremum topology $T^* = [T_1]$.

In the other hand, the supremum of X_1 and X_2 is $X_3 = \{(1), (2), (3, 4)\}$. The induced topology from X_3 is $[T_3] = \{\varnothing, (1, 2), (3, 4), X\}$. Thus, $[T_3] = T^*$.

Definition 1.11

A topologic space (X, T), if T_1 is another topology on X and $T_1 < T$, T_1 is called a 'lower topology' of T.

Definition 1.12

Assume $W = (\mathfrak{A}, \mathfrak{M}) = \{([X], T[X]) | [X] \in \mathfrak{A}, T([X]) < [T], T([X]) \in \mathfrak{M}\}$, where $[T]$ is a quotient topology on $[X]$ induced from (X, T). $\mathfrak{M}$ is a set of all lower topologies of T on X. Define a semi-order '$<$' on $W = (\mathfrak{A}, \mathfrak{M})$ as follows: $(X_1, T_1), (X_2, T_2) \in (\mathfrak{A}, \mathfrak{M})$, if $X_1 < X_2$ and $T_1 < T_2$, then $(X_1, T_1) < (X_2, T_2)$.

First, two lemmas are introduced below (Eisenberg, 1974).

Lemma 1.1

Assume that $\forall a \in I, f_a : (X_a, T_a) \rightarrow Y$. There exists a maximal (finest) topology among all topologies that makes each f_a continuous on Y.

Lemma 1.2

Assume that $\forall a \in I, f_a : X \rightarrow (Y_a, T_a)$. There exists a minimal (coarsest) topology among all topologies that makes each f_α continuous on X.

Definition 1.13

Given $X_\alpha \in \mathfrak{A}$. Let $T(X_a) = \{T' | \exists \{(X_i T_i), i \in I\} \subset U\}$, where X_a is the supremum (infimum) of $\{X_i, i \in I\}$, T' is the supremum (infimum) of $\{T_i, i \in I\}$. Define

$$V = \{(X_\alpha, T_\alpha) | X \in \mathfrak{X}, T_\alpha \in T(X_\alpha)\}$$

Definition 1.14

$A = \{(X_a, T_a), a \in I\}$ is any subset from W. Let X' be the supremum of $\{X_\alpha\}$. Construct a mapping $p_a : X' \to (X_a, T_a), a \in I$, where p_α is a nature projection. From Lemma 1.2, it is known there is a minimal topology T' on X' such that it makes all mappings continuous. Define (X', T') as the supremum of quotient spaces on A.

Definition 1.15

$A = \{(X_a, T_a), a \in I\}$ is any subset from W. Let $\underline{X}$ be the infimum of $\{X_a\}$. Construct a mapping $p_a : \underline{X} \to (X_a, T_a), a \in I$, where p_a is a nature projection. From Lemma 1.1, it is known that a maximal topology $\underline{T}$ on $\underline{X}$ exists such that it makes all mappings continuous. Define $(\underline{X}, \underline{T})$ as the infimum of quotient spaces on A.

It's noted that for any subset on V, based on Definitions 1.13 and 1.14 we can also define its corresponding supremum and infimum quotient spaces, respectively.

Theorem 1.2

Under the supremum and infimum operations defined by Definitions 1.13 and 1.14, V (or W) composes a complete semi-order lattice.

Proof:

First, we prove that W is a complete semi-order lattice.

$A = \{(X_a, T_a), a \in I\}$ is any subset from W, X' is the supremum of $\{X_\alpha\}$, and $p_a : X' \to (X_a, T_a), a \in I$ is a nature projection. From Lemma 1.2, a minimal topology T' exists on X' such that it makes all mappings continuous. Since p_α is continuous, $(p_\alpha)^{-1}$ is an open mapping, i.e., open sets are mapped as open sets. We have that all open sets on $\forall a, (X_a, T_a)$ are mapped as open sets on (X^1, T'). From Definition 1.12, we have $\forall a \in I, T_a < T'$. T' is the upper bound of $(T_a, a \in I)$. Since T' is the coarsest topology, we have that $(X, T') \in W$ is the supremum of A.

Similarly, for any subset B, there exists its infimum. Therefore, W is a complete lattice.

Similarly, we can prove that V is a complete semi-order lattice.

Obviously, V is a sub-lattice of W and a complete lattice obtained by the supremum and infimum operations over elements of U. And W is a complete lattice composed by elements of U and all lower topologies of the induced quotient topologies on U.

1.4.2.2 The Properties and Relations of U, V and W

Complete semi-order set U is a basic quotient space structure in quotient space-based theory. Given a space (X, T), using the induced quotient topology we can construct all quotient spaces of U. Conversely, a quotient space constructed by the induced quotient topology must be an element (space) of U. In other words, with respect to the operation of constructing quotient spaces by the induced quotient topology, U is closed. The completeness of U provides a theoretical foundation for the constructing quotient space method by induced quotient topology.

The combination method of quotient spaces is the main one in quotient space theory. V is the maximal complete lattice that can be produced by using the supremum and infimum operations over the induced quotient topologies of U. This is just a combination method of quotient spaces and similar to the method that quotient topologies are produced by topological bases. The supremum and infimum operations over induced quotient topologies of U are closed on V, which ensures the completeness of the family of quotient spaces that is produced by the combination method.

If the quotient spaces are not only constructed by domain granulation (quotient sets) but also by topology granulation in U, then we have W, the complete lattice composed by all possible quotient spaces from the above method and from the supremum and infimum operations over the quotient spaces.

In order to discuss the relation among U, V and W, we introduce the concept of 'minimal open set' below.

Definition 1.16

Given a topologic space (X, T). For any open set B, if a non-empty bipartition $B = B_1 \cup B_2$ exists such that one of them is an open set at most, B is called a minimal open set.

Lemma 1.3

For any open set A, it either a discrete topology or a minimal open set.

Proof:

Otherwise, assume that A is not a minimal open set. For $\forall x \in A$, constructing a non-empty bipartition $A = \{x\} \cup (A/\{x\})$ of A, since any singleton $\{x\}$ of A is an open set, A is a discrete topology.

Obviously, $U \subset V \subset W$. We'll prove below that in general the relation among U, V and W is a proper subset one. For example, in Section 1.4.2.1, quotient space (X_3, T') is in V but not in U, so U is a proper subset of V.

Theorem 1.3

Given a topologic space (X, T). The necessary and sufficient condition of $U=V$ should satisfy one of the following conditions.

(1) $|X| < 3$
(2)   T is a trivial topology
(3)   T is a discrete topology.

Proof:

If $|X| < 3$, obviously, $U = V$.

$\Leftarrow$ Sufficient condition: Since (X, T) is a trivial (or discrete) topology, i.e., all quotient topologies on any quotient set $[X]$ are trivial or discrete, $U = V$.

$\Rightarrow$ Reduction to absurdity: Assume that T is neither a trivial nor a discrete topology. We show below that $V \neq U$. Let $T = (B_\alpha, \alpha \in I)$. From Lemma 1.3, for each B_α, a non-empty bipartition of B_α exists and one of its bipartition is an open set at most, i.e., a minimal open set. The open set is left, otherwise B_α is divided into a set of singletons. After the treatment, T is denoted as $\{B_\alpha\}$, where B_α is either a singleton or a minimal open set.

If T has only one component B_α, then T is a trivial topology. This is a contradiction.

If each B_α is a singleton, then T is a discrete topology. This is also a contradiction.

Thus, there exist some B_α's such that $|B_\alpha| > 1$. Let B_1 be the one having the minimal cardinality among B_α's. Now we discuss the following two cases.

(1) $B_1 = X$ and any proper subset on X is not a minimal open set, then $B_i, i \neq 1$ must be a singleton. Let $C = \cup B_j, j \neq 1, D = X/C$. Since $|X| > 2$, there must exist a set in C and D with cardinality > 1. If $|C| > 1$, construct a partition $C = C_1 \cup C_2, C_i \neq \varnothing, i = 1, 2$ of C. We have a partition $X_1 = \{C_1, C_2 \cup D\}, X_2 = \{C, D\}$. Set D is not open, otherwise, from Lemma 1.3, D is a singleton. This is a contradiction. Set $C_2 \cup D$ is not open as well, otherwise, $C_2 \cup D$ is a minimal open set. This is also a contradiction.

Then, we have induced quotient topologies $[T_1] = \{\varnothing, C_1, X\}, [T_2] = \{\varnothing, C, X\}$ and the supremum topology $T^* = \{\varnothing, C_1, C, X\}$.

On the other hand, we have the supremum $X_3 = \{C_1, C_2, D\}$ of X_1 and X_2. Since $[T_3] = \{\varnothing, C_1, C_2, C, X\}$ is the induced quotient topology from X_3, $T_3 \neq T^*$, then $U \neq V$. This is a contradiction.

If C is a singleton, there exists a non-empty bipartition $X/C = \{A_1, A_2\}$ on X/C. Construct $X_1 = (C \cup A_1, A_2), X_2 = (C \cup A_2, A_1)$. Then, $A_i, C \cup A_i, i = 1, 2$ are not open. Otherwise, assume that A_1 is an open set. From Lemma 1.3, A_1 is either a discrete topology or a minimal open set. But the former is impossible since C is a singleton. The latter is impossible as well since A_1 is a proper sunset of X. This is a contradiction. Therefore, $A_i, i = 1, 2$ are not open sets.

Similarly, $C \cup A_i, i = 1, 2$ are not open sets either.

We have $[T_1] = \{\varnothing, X\}, [T_2] = \{\varnothing, X\}$. Then $T = \{\varnothing, X\}$.

On the other hand, $X_3 = \{A_1, A_2, C\}$, we have $T_3 = \{\varnothing, C, X\}, [T_3] \neq T^*$

Then, $U \neq V$. This is a contradiction.

(2) $B \neq X, |B| > 1$. Letting $B = A_1 \cup A_2, A_i \neq \varnothing, i = 1, 2$, there exists a A_i at least such that it is not an open set. Construct a partition $X_1 = \{A_1, X/A_1\}$, $X_2 = \{A_2, X/A_2\}$.

    (2.1) If both A_1 and A_2 are not open sets, the induced quotient topology from X_1 and X_2 is $[T_1], [T_2] = \{\varnothing, X\}$. The supremum of $[T_1], [T_2]$ is $T^* = \{\varnothing, X\}$.
        On the other hand, $X_3 = \{A_1, A_2, X/(A_1 \cup A_2)\}$ is the supremum of X_1, X_2. The induced quotient topology is $[T_3] = \{\varnothing, B, \cdots, X\}, [T_3] \neq T^*$.

    (2.2) If one of $A_i, i = 1, 2$ is an open set, in assuming that A_1 is an open set, then X/A_1 is not open. Otherwise, $A_2 = (X/A_1) \cap B$ is open. This is a contradiction. Therefore, we have $[T_1] = \{\varnothing, A_1, X\}, [T_2] = \{\varnothing, X\}$ (or when X/A_2 is an open set, we have $\{\varnothing, X/A_2, X\}$). Its supremum is $T^* = \{\varnothing, A_1, X\}$ (or $\{\varnothing, A_1, X/A_2, X\}$ when X/A_2 is open). Since $[T_3] = \{\varnothing, A_1, B, \cdots, X\}$ is the induced quotient topology of $X_3 = \{A_1, A_2, X/(A_1 \cup A_2)\}$, we have $[T_3] \neq T^*$. Finally, $U \neq V$. This is a contradiction.
        Using Theorem 1.3, we can make the following conclusion: a space may belong to lattice W but not to V.

Example 1.8

Given $X = \{1, 2, 3, 4\}$, T is a discrete topology. From Theorem 1.3, we have U and V corresponding to (X, T). Letting $T_1 = \{\varnothing, (1), (1, 2), (1, 2, 3), X\}$, we have $T_1 < T$. Thus, $(X, T_1) \in \mathbf{W}, (X, T_1) \notin \mathbf{V}$, V is a proper subset of W.

The three semi-order lattices given in the section correspond to three different multi-granular worlds. The completeness of the lattices provides a theoretical foundation for the translation, decomposition, combination operations over the multi-granular worlds.

1.5 Property-Preserving Ability

1.5.1 Falsity-Preserving Principle

We have discussed the relation between the domains $[X]$ and X. For a problem space $(X, f, T,)$, structure T is very important. When a domain X is decomposed, its structure will change as well. Generally, it is simplified. The main point is whether some properties (or attributes) in X that we are interested in are still preserved after the simplification.

Generally speaking, there is a wide variety of structures. It is difficult to make a general discussion. We'll focus our attention on two common cases, i.e., topologic structure and semi-order structure. Although semi-order is one of topologic structures, due to its particularity we still discuss them separately.

1.5.1.1 Structure and Quotient Structure Analysis

(1) Topologic Space (X, f, T)

We first introduce some basic concepts of topology below. Readers who are not familiar with them are referred to (Eisenberg, 1974; Sims, 1976).

Definition 1.17

Assume that X is a set. T is a family of subsets on X. If T satisfies

(1) $\emptyset, X \in T$
(2) If $u_1, u_2 \in T$, then $(u_1 \cap u_2) \in T$
(3) If $u_\alpha \in T, \alpha \in I$, then $\bigcup_{\alpha \in I} u_\alpha \in T$, where I is an index set, the potential of I is arbitrary.

T is a topology on X. (X, f, T) is a topologic space. For $u \subset X$, if $u \in T$, then u is said to be an open set.

Example 1.9

Let $X = \{a,b,c,d\}$ and $T = \{\emptyset, \{a,b,c\}, \{c,d\}, \{c\}, \{a,b,c,d\}\}$. T is a topology on X.

If a topology is given on X, then the inner-relational structure T among the elements of X will be defined. Since the relationship among the elements in many domains can be described by topologic structure, topology is a useful tool in problem solving and granular computing. In fact, different topologies can be defined on the same domain X, i.e., the topology of X is not unique.

Definition 1.18

Assume that (X, f, T) is a topologic space. B is a family of sets on X and satisfies

(1) $u \in B \Rightarrow u \in T$
(2) $\forall w \in T$, there exists a subset $B_1 \subset B$ of B such that $w = \bigcup_{u_\alpha \in B_1} u_\alpha$

B is called a base of (X, f, T).

In Definition 1.18, the condition (1) shows that B is composed by open sets and (2) shows that any open set on X can be represented by the union of some sets of B.

Example 1.10

Assume that X is a one-dimensional Euclidean space. Letting $B = \{(a,b)|a < b, a, b \in X\}$, then B is a base of X, where (a, b) denotes an open interval.

For a domain X, when its base is confirmed, its corresponding topology is uniquely decided. Contrary, although topology T is decided on X, it can have different bases.

Assume that R is an equivalence relation on X. From R, we have a quotient set $[X]$. A topology $[T]$ on $[X]$ induced from T is defined as follows.

$$[T] = \{u | p^{-1}(u) \in F, u \subset [X]\}$$

$[T]$ is said to be a quotient topology. $([X], [T])$ is a quotient topologic space. In addition, $p: X \rightarrow [X]$ is a natural projection that is defined as follows:

$$p(x) = [X]$$
$$p^{-1}(u) = \{x | p(x) \in u\}$$

Quotient structures have a clear geometric interpretation. If an element of $[X]$ is regarded as a subset of X, then a subset of $[X]$ is a set of X. When a subset of $[X]$ is an open set of X, then the subset is defined as an open set on $[X]$, and vice versa. In other words, an open set of $[X]$ is merged by elements of $[X]$ and is also an open set of X.

Example 1.11

Let $X=\{1,2,3,4,5\}$, $T = \{\varnothing, X, \{2,3\}, \{4,5\}, \{1,2,3\}, \{2,3,4,5\}\}$. T is a topology on X.

Assuming $R : a_1 = \{1,2\}, a_2 = \{3\}, a_3 = \{4,5\}$, we have $[X] = \{a_1, a_2, a_3\}$.

From the above definition, we obtain

$$a_3 = \{4,5\} \in T, \quad \therefore \{a_3\} \in [T]$$
$$\{a_1, a_2\} = \{1,2,3\} \in T, \quad \therefore \{a_1, a_2\} \in [T]$$
$$\{a_1, a_2, a_3\} = \{1,2,3,4,5\} \in T, \quad \therefore \{a_1, a_2, a_3\} \in [T]$$
$$\varnothing \in [T]$$

Thus, $[T] = \{\varnothing, \{a_3\}, \{a_1, a_2\}, [X]\}$

Example 1.12

(X,T) is a two-dimensional Euclidean plane E^2. Topology T is defined by Euclidean distance.

If choosing equivalence relation R as follows:
$p_1 = (x_1, y_1), p_2 = (x_2, y_2) \in E^2, p_1 \sim p_2 \Leftrightarrow x_1 = x_2$, then we have a corresponding quotient space $([X],[T])$ that is homeomorphous to E^1.

The geometric intuition of the above equivalence transformation is the following. If all points of the line that are perpendicular to x axis at point x_1 are regarded as an equivalence class, then we have a quotient space $([X],[T])$, where each element of $[X]$ corresponds to a point of x axis, and quotient topology $[T]$ corresponds to Euclidean distance on x axis.

Example 1.13

In an electronic instrument, if its elements such as resistors, capacitors and integrated circuits, etc., compose a domain *X*, then the circuit consisting of these elements is a structure *T* of *X*. If some elements of *X* with similar function are classified and designated as components, for example, power supply, amplifier, etc., and the components are regarded as new elements, we then have a new domain [*X*]. The block diagram consisting of these components is a structure [*T*] of [*X*]. It turns out a simplified 'circuit' of the original one.

From topology (Eisenberg, 1974), it's known that some properties of the original topologic space (*X, T*) can still be preserved in its quotient space ([*X*],[*F*]). We have:

Proposition 1.3

Natural projection *p* from (*X, T*) to ([*X*], [*T*]) is a continuous mapping. If $A \subset X$ is a connected set on *X*, then *p*(*A*) is a connected set on [*X*].

This means that in some cases the connectivity is invariant under the grain-size change.

In reality, the solution to some problems can be found by considering the connectivity of a set. From Proposition 1.3, it shows that if there is a solution path (connected) in the original domain *X*, then there exists a solution path in its properly coarse-grained domain [*X*]. Conversely, in a coarse-grained domain, if a solution path does not exist, there is no solution path in its original domain. These properties are very useful in practice.

Taking motion planning of a robotic arm as an example, when its environment is rather complicated, the complexity would result in it being computationally intractable if one tries to find a collision-free path for the arm with the geometric details of the environment all at once. Based on topological approaches, the geometric space can be divided into several homotopically equivalent regions. That is, each region has the same topologic structure. We view each as an equivalence class, ignoring all the geometric details within the regions. Then, the original geometric space will be transformed to a network with a finite number of nodes which consist of these regions. From topology, it's known that the connectivity of the network is the same as that of the original space, although the original space has been greatly simplified. In other words, the network, called characteristic net, is a quotient space of the original space, which preserves the connectivity as the original one.

Instead of one step planning, the motion planning may be hierarchically decomposed into two steps. First, it identifies quickly the possible collision-free paths on the characteristic network. Then, it refines the path within the original space based on some given requirements. From Proposition 1.3, it's known that since the regions which have no collision-free paths have been pruned off in the first step, the complexity of the motion planning in the second step is greatly reduced. So, the total complexity of motion planning is improved. A more detailed discussion of the approach will be presented in Chapter 5.

(2) Semi-Order Space (X, T)

(X, T) is a semi-order space, if there exists a relation $<$ among a part of elements on X such that

$$(1)\ x < y, y < x \Rightarrow x = y$$
$$(2)\ x < y, y < z \Rightarrow x < z$$

where x, y and z are elements of X.

If only condition (2) holds, (X, T) is called a pseudo semi-order space.

In order to establish some relations between semi-order spaces at different grain sizes, we expect to induce a structure $[T]$ of $[X]$ from T of X such that $([X], [T])$ is also a semi-order space and for all $x \in X$, if $x < y$ then $[x] < [y]$. Namely, it is desired that the order relation is preserved invariant under the grain-size change, or order-preserving for short.

It needs several steps to reach the goal.

(1) Transform (X, T) into some sort of topologic space,
(2) Construct a quotient topologic space $([X], [T])$ from (X, T), and
(3) Induce a semi-order from $([X], [T])$ such that the original order relations are preserved in the quotient space.

Definition 1.19

Assume (X, T) is a semi-order space, for $x \in X$, we define a set $u(x) = \{y | x < y, y \in X\}$.

Let $B = \{u(x) | x \in X\}$. The topology T_r with B as its base is said to be a right-order topology of X. Hence, a semi-order space is transformed to a topologic space (X, T_r).

Assume that $[X]$ is a quotient set of X. $([X], [T_r])$ is a quotient space with respect to (X, T_r).

One of the main properties of the right-order topology is stated as follows.

Property 1.1

(X, T) is a semi-order space. T_r is a right-order topology induced from T. Then, $\forall x \in X$, there exists a minimal open set $u\ (x)$ containing x, where $u(x) \in T_r$.

Conversely, if there is a topology T satisfying T_0-separation axiom such that for all $x \in X$ there exists a minimal open set $u(x) \in T$, then a semi-order T_s on X can be induced from T by the following approach. And T is just the right-order topology of T_s, i.e.,
$T_s : x, y \in X, x < y \Leftrightarrow y \in u(x)$, where $u(x)$ is a minimal open set containing x.

Note that a topologic space (X,T) is said to be T_0-separation, if for all $x, y \in X$, either there exists a neighborhood $u(x)$ of x such that $y \notin u(x)$ or there exists a neighborhood $u(y)$ of y such that $x \notin u(y)$.

Definition 1.20

Assume (X, T) is a topologic space, we define a relation $<$ by T as follows. For $x, y \in X, x < y \Leftrightarrow \forall u(x), y \in u(x)$, where $u(x)$ is an open neighborhood of x. The topology T_s corresponding to relation '$<$' obtained above is called the induced (pseudo) semi-order from T.

The relation '$<$' defined by Definition 1.20 always satisfies the transitivity but generally does not satisfy the condition: $x < y, y < x \Rightarrow x = y$.

Definition 1.21

(X,T) is a topologic space. If the relation '$<$' defined by Definition 1.18 satisfies the condition: $x < y, y < x \Rightarrow x = y$, topology T is said to be compatible with relation '$<$'.

If a relation '$<$' is compatible with T of (X,T), then relation '$<$' is a semi-order and X is a semi-order set under relation '$<$'. (X,T_s) is a semi-order space corresponding to (X,T). Sometimes, it is also denoted by (X,T) for short.

Suppose that (X,T) is a semi-order space. $[X]$ is a quotient set of X with respect to R. T_r is a right-order topology induced from T. If topology $[T_r]$ of quotient topologic space $([X],[T_r])$ is compatible with the relation '$<$' defined by Definition 1.20, R is said to be compatible with T, or simply, R is compatible, $([X],[T_r]_s)$ (or $([X],[T_r])_s$) is a semi-order space under relation '$<$' and is denoted by $([X],[T])$ for short. It is a quotient structure induced from the semi-order space (X,T) and has the order-preserving ability. If R is not compatible with relation '$<$', $([X],[T_r]_s)$ is a pseudo semi-order space.

Example 1.14

(X,T_r) is a semi-order space as shown in Fig. 1.5. Let equivalence relation R_1 be $a_1 = \{1,3\}, a_2 = \{2\}$ and $a_3 = \{4,5\}$.

Whether there exists a quotient semi-order in $[X]_1$; the answer is the following.

(1)   right-order topology T_r induced from T

$$u_1 = \{1,2,3,4,5\}$$
$$u_2 = \{2,5\}$$
$$u_3 = \{3,4,5\}$$
$$u_4 = \{4,5\}$$
$$u(5) = \{5\}$$

Thus, $T_r = \{\varnothing, X, \{5\}, \{2,5\}, \{4,5\}, \{3,4,5\}, \{2,4,5\}\{2,3,4,5\}\}$

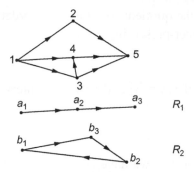

Figure 1.5: Compatible Relation Graph

(2) quotient topology $[T_r]$ on $[X]_1$ induced from T_r

$$a_3 = \{4,5\} \in T \Rightarrow \{a_3\} \in [T_r]$$
$$\{a_2, a_3\} = \{2,4,5\} \in T \Rightarrow \{a_2, a_3\} \in [T_r]$$
$$\{a_1, a_2, a_3\} = X \in T \Rightarrow [X]_1 \in [T_r]$$

Thus $[T_r] = \{\varnothing, \{a_3\}, \{a_2, a_3\}, [X]_1\}$

(3) semi-order $[T]_s$ induced from $[T_r]$
From Definition 1.19, we obtain

$$[T]_s : a_1 < a_2, a_1 < a_3, a_2 < a_3$$

Obviously, R is compatible with T. $[T]_s$ is a semi-order on $[X]_1$ and
$p: (X, F) \to ([X], [F]_s)$ has the order-preserving ability.
If $R_2 : b_1 = \{1,4\}, b_2 = \{3,5\}$ and $b_3 = \{2\}$, then

$$[T_r] : \{\varnothing, [X]_2\}$$
$$[T]_s : b_1 < b_2, b_1 < b_3, b_2 < b_3, b_2 < b_1, b_3 < b_1, b_3 < b_2$$

Hence, $[F]_s$ is not a semi-order on $[X]_2$. R_2 is not compatible with T.

Now, we consider some useful properties of $([X], [T])$ and (X, T) below.

Proposition 1.4

Suppose that R is compatible with T. If $x, y \in (X, T)$ and $x < y$, then $[x] < [y]$, where $[x], [y] \in ([X], [T])$.

Proof:

Assume $x < y$. Let $a = [x]$. $u(a)$ is whichever open neighborhood of a on $[X]$. Since $p : X \to [X]$ is continuous, $p^{-1}(u(a))$ is an open set on X, i.e., a neighborhood of x.

And $x < y \Rightarrow y \in p^{-1}(u(a)) \Rightarrow p(y) \in u(a) \Rightarrow [y] \in u(a)$, we have $[x] < [y]$.

Proposition 1.4 indicates that the quotient (pseudo) semi-order space constructed by the preceding approach has the order-preserving ability.

Proposition 1.5

Assume that R is compatible. If $x, y \in [x]$ and $x < y$, then interval $[x, y] = \{z | x < z < y, z \in X\} \subset [x]$.

Proof:

From $x < z < y$ and Proposition 1.4, we have $[x] < [z] < [y]$. Since $[x] = [y] \Rightarrow [x] < [z], [z] < [x]$, from the compatibility of R, we have $[z] = [x] \Rightarrow z \in [x] \Rightarrow [x, y] \subset [x]$.

Definition 1.22

(X, T) is a semi-order set. $A \subset (X, T)$ is connected $\Leftrightarrow \forall x, y \in A, \exists x = z_1, z_2, \ldots, z_n = y$, such that z_i and z_{i+1}, $i = 1, 2, \ldots, n\text{-}1$, are compatible.

Definition 1.23

(X, T) is a semi-order set. $A \subset (X, T)$ is a semi-order closure $\Leftrightarrow$ if $x, y \in A$, and $x < y$, then interval $[x, y] \subset A$.

Corollary 1.1

In assuming that R is compatible, each component of $[X]$ must consist of several semi-order closed, mutually incomparable, and connected sets.

Note that sets A and B are mutually incomparable, if for $\forall x \in A, y \in B$, x and y are incomparable.

Proof:

$[X]$ is divided into the union of several connected components, obviously, these components are mutually incomparable. We'll prove that each component is semi-order closed below.

Assume that A is a connected component of $[X]$. If A is not semi-order closed, then $\exists x_1, x_2 \in A$ and $y \notin A$ such that $x_1 < y < x_2$. Since R is compatible, $p: X \to [X]$ is order-preserving. We have

$$p(x_1) < p(y) < p(x_2) \Rightarrow [x] < [y] < [x]$$
$$\Rightarrow [y] = [x]$$

That is, $y \in [x]$. Since $y \notin A$, y must belong to another connected component B of $[X]$. Thus, $x_1 \in A$ is comparable with $y \in B$. This contradicts with that components A and B are incomparable.

Corollary 1.2

If X is a totally ordered set and R is compatible, then each equivalence class of $[X]$ must be an interval $<x,y>$, where interval $<x,y>$ denotes one of the following four intervals: $[x, y], [x, y), (x, y], (x, y)$.

Especially, when $X = R^1$ (real number set), Corollary 1.2 still holds.

From the above corollaries, it's known that when partitioning a semi-order set with respect to R, only the corresponding equivalence classes satisfy some structure as shown in the above corollaries so that R is compatible. In order to rationally partition a semi-order set, strong constraints have to be followed.

Proposition 1.6

(X, T) is a semi-order set, then $((X, T)_r)_s = (X, T)$.

From the previous discussion, it concludes that a quotient semi-order set $([X], [T])$ can be induced from a semi-order set (X, T) so long as R is compatible. And $([X], [T])$ has order-preserving ability.

When X is a finite semi-order set, it can be represented by a directed acyclic network G. And $x < y \Leftrightarrow$ there exists a directed path in G from x to y. When X is a finite set, X can be represented by a spatial network. We present a simple method for constructing a quotient (pseudo) semi-order on $[X]$ below.

Given (X, T) and an equivalence relation R, we have a quotient set $[X]$. Define a relation '$<$' on $[X]$ as $\forall a, b \in [X], \exists x_1 \in a, x_2 \in b, x_1 < x_2 \Rightarrow a<'b$. Finding the transitive closure of relation '$<$', have a pseudo semi-order $[T]'$ and quotient space $([X],[T]')$.

Proposition 1.7

$[T]' = [T_r]_s$ holds, where $[T]'$ as defined above. (See Section 1.6 for the proof of Proposition 1.7.)

Using the above-mentioned method to Example 1.4 and 1.5, we still have the solutions as shown in Fig. 1.5.

Using Proposition 1.7, when X is a finite set, the directed graph corresponding to (pseudo) semi-order on $[X]$ can easily be defined as follows: $\forall a, b \in [X], a \rightarrow b \Leftrightarrow \exists x, y \in X, x \in a, y \in b, x < y$, where $a \rightarrow b$ means there exists a directed edge between a and b. The (pseudo) semi-order corresponding to the directed graph is just the quotient structure on $[X]$.

1.5.1.2 Falsity (Truth)-Preserving Principle

The order-preserving ability among different grain-size worlds has an extensive application. For example, the relation among elements of domain X is represented by some semi-order structure. A starting point $x \in X$ is regarded as a premise and a goal point $y \in X$ as a conclusion. Whether the directed path from point x to point y exists corresponds to whether conclusion y can be inferred from premise x. If X is complex, introducing a proper partition R to X, then we have $[X]$. A quotient (pseudo) semi-order $[T]_s$ on $[X]$ can be induced. Due to the following proposition, the original directed path finding from x to y on X is transformed into that from $[x]$ to $[y]$ on $[X]$.

Proposition 1.8

(X,T) is a semi-order set. R is an equivalence relation on X. For $x, y \in X$, if there exists a directed path from x to y on (X,T), there also exists a directed path from $[x]$ to $[y]$ on $[X]$.

The proposition shows that if the original problem (domain) in hand is too complex, by a proper partition, the original domain is transformed into a coarse one. If there does not exist a solution in the coarse world, then the original problem does not have a solution as well. Since the coarse world is generally simpler than the original one, the problem solving will be simplified.

Note that in Proposition 1.4, even R is incompatible, the order-preserving ability still holds.

From the previous discussion, it is known that an 'inference' can be transformed into a spatial search from a premise to a conclusion, i.e., a path-search in a topologic space. And if an original problem (X, f, T) is too complex, then the problem can be transformed into its quotient space $([X], [f], [T])$ which is generally simpler than the original one. The order-preserving and the falsity (truth)-preserving ability that we will mention below clarify the main characteristics of the multi-granular world; which provide a theoretical foundation for multi-granular computing (inference).

Theorem 1.4 Falsity-Preserving Principle

If a problem $[A] \rightarrow [B]$ on quotient space $([X], [f], [T])$ has no solution, then problem $A \rightarrow B$ on its original space (X, f, T) has no solution either. In other words, if $A \rightarrow B$ on (X, f, T) has a solution, then $[A] \rightarrow [B]$ on $([X], [f], [T])$ has a solution as well.

Proof:

If problem $A \rightarrow B$ has a solution, then A and B belong to the same (path) connected set C of (X, f, T). Let $p : X \rightarrow [X]$ be a natural projection. Since p is continuous, $p(C)$ is (path) connected on $([X], [f], [T])$. $p(A) = [A]$ and $p(B) = [B]$ belong to the same (path) connected set of $([X], [f], [T])$. The problem $[A] \rightarrow [B]$ has a solution.

Falsity-preserving ability within a multi-granular world is unconditional but truth preserving is conditional.

Theorem 1.5 Truth-Preserving Principle I

A problem $[A] \rightarrow [B]$ on $([X], [f], [T])$ has a solution, if for $[x]$, $p^{-1}([x])$ is a connected set on X, problem $A \rightarrow B$ on (X, f, T) has a solution.

Proof:

Since problem $[A] \rightarrow [B]$ on $([X], [f], [T])$ has a solution, $[A]$ and $[B]$ belong to the same connected component C. Letting $D = p^{-1}(C)$, we prove that D is a connected on X.

Reduction to absurdity: Assume that D is partitioned into the union of mutually disjoint non-empty open close sets D_1 and D_2. For $\forall a \in C$, $p^{-1}(a)$ is connected on X, then $p^{-1}(a)$ only belongs to one of D_1 and D_2. $D_i, i = 1, 2$, composes of elements of $[X]$. There exist C_1, C_2 such that $D_1 = p^{-1}(C_1), D_2 = p^{-1}(C_2)$. Since $D_i, i = 1, 2$, are open close sets on X and p is a natural projection, C_1, C_2 are non-empty open close sets on $[X]$. While C_1 and C_2 are the partition of C, then C is non-connected. This is a contradiction.

Theorem 1.6 Truth-Preserving Principle II

(X_1, f_1, T_1) and (X_2, f_2, T_2) are two quotient spaces of (X, f, T). $T_i, i = 1, 2$ are semi-order. (X_3, f_3, T_3) is the supremum space of (X_1, f_1, T_1) and (X_2, f_2, T_2). If problems $A_1 \rightarrow B_1$ and $A_2 \rightarrow B_2$ have a solution on (X_1, f_1, T_1) and (X_2, f_2, T_2), respectively, then problem $A_3 \rightarrow B_3$ on (X_3, f_3, T_3) have a solution, where $A_3 = A_1 \cap A_2$, $B_3 = B_1 \cap B_2$.

How to make use of the falsity- and truth-preserving principles will be discussed in Chapters 5 and 7.

1.5.1.3 Computational Complexity Analysis

Using the falsity- and truth-preserving principle, the computational cost of the multi-granular computing (or inference) can greatly be reduced. For example, by choosing a proper quotient space and using the falsity-preserving principle, the part of the space without solution can be removed for further consideration so that the computing is accelerated. Similarly, by choosing a proper quotient space and using the truth-preserving principle I, the problem solving on the original space can be simplified to that on its quotient space. In general, the size of the quotient space is much smaller than that of the original one so the computational cost is reduced. Concerning the truth-preserving principle II, assume that n and m are the potentials of X_1 and X_2, respectively. The potential of X_3 is nm at most. Let $g(\cdot)$ be the computational complexity. When the problem is solved on X_3 directly, $g(\cdot) = g(nm)$. If using the truth-preserving principle II, the problem is solved on X_1 and X_2, separately, the computational complexity is $g(n) + g(m)$. This is equivalent to reducing the complexity from $O(N)$ to $O(\ln N)$.

Note that T_3, a topology on (X_3, f_3, T_3), is not necessarily an induced quotient topology $[T_3]$ of X_3, generally $T_3 < [T_3]$. Namely, (X_3, f_3, T_3) is only an element of complete semi-order lattice V but U.

1.5.2 Quotient Structure

In the previous section, we discussed two specific spaces, i.e. topologic and semi-order spaces, the general topologic structure will be shown below.

Definition 1.24

Given a problem space (X, f, T), and $A \subset X$ has some attribute H, if we introduce a structure $[T]$ into $[X]$ such that $p(A)$ on $([X], [f], [T])$ has the same attribute H, then $[T]$ is said to be a quotient structure with attribute H, where $p : X \to [X]$ is a natural projection.

If (X, T) is a topologic space and $([X], [T])$ is its quotient topologic space, $[T]$ is a quotient structure with the connectivity (H) within $A \subset X$.

If (X, T) is a semi-order space and its quotient space $([X], [T]_s)$ defined in Section 1.5.1.1 (2), $[T]_s$ is a quotient structure with order preserving ability.

When we have natural projection $p : X \to [X]$ and quotient space $[X]$, the operators, concepts, functions, etc. defined on X can formally be removed to $[X]$ easily. For example, assuming $g : X \to X$ is a function, define a corresponding function $G : [X] \to [X]$ on $[X]$ such that $G([x]) = [g(x)]$. Generally, all attributes of g on (X, f, T) are not necessarily kept in that of $[g]$ on $[X]$ completely. This means that in the coarse-grained world some information might lose due to the abstraction, if the missing attributes are not interested, that does not matter very much. But for the attributes that we needed, they should be preserved by choosing a proper partition.

In conclusion, we know that for different purposes, from a computational object (X, f, T), different quotient sets $[X]$ may be constructed and in the same quotient set different quotient structures $[T]$ may be induced, i.e., choosing a proper granularity. This is the key to multi-granular computing.

Finally, the classification with overlapped components will be discussed in Section 3.4.8.

1.6 Selection and Adjustment of Grain-Sizes

The ability to select a proper grain-size world for a given problem is fundamental to human intelligence and flexibility. The ability enables us to map the complex world around us into a simple one that is computationally tractable. At the same time, the attributes in question of the world are still preserved. As mentioned before, it is not necessarily true that any classification can achieve the goal.

How to select a proper grain-size is a domain-dependent problem mainly. We'll discuss some general principles below via semi-order spaces.

It has been shown that the compatibility of R and T is the foundation for assuring that $([X], [T])$ is also a semi-order space. We will discuss below how to adjust R such that it is compatible with T.

1.6.1 Mergence Methods

Assume that (X, T) is a semi-order space, where X is a finite set, R is an equivalence relation on X and is incompatible with T. $[X] = \{a_i\}$ is a quotient space corresponding to R. We will discuss how to adjust R by mergence methods.

We define a new partition $b_i = \{a_t | a_t < a_i$ and $a_i < a_t\}, i = 1, 2, \cdots$, where '$<$' is a topology $[T]_s$ on $[X]$ induced from T. Obviously, $\{b_i, i = 1, 2, ...\}$ is a partition of X. Let R_1 be an equivalence relation corresponding to partition $\{b_i\}$.

Proposition 1.9

R_1 defined above is compatible with T. If an equivalence relation R' satisfies (1) R' and T are compatible, (2) if $R' < R$, then $R' < R_1$, i.e., R_1 is the finest one, where $R' < R \Leftrightarrow$ if xRy, then $xR'y$.

Proof:

T_r on (X, T) is a right-order topology induced from T. $[X]$ is a quotient space corresponding to R. $[T_r]$ is a quotient topology on $[X]$. $[X]_1$ and $[X]'$ are quotient spaces corresponding to R_1 and R', respectively.

For $a' \in [X]_1$, if $a, b \in a', a, b \in [X]$, from the definitions of $[X]_1$ and $[X]$, we have $a < b, b < a(R)$, i.e., any neighborhood of a must contain b and is also the neighborhood of b. Conversely, any neighborhood of b must contain a and is also the neighborhood of a. Thus, the neighborhood systems of a and b are the same. Their common neighborhood system is just the neighborhood system of a' on $[X]_1$. In other words, if elements on $[X]$ having a common neighborhood system are classified as one category, then $[X]$ is revised as $[X]_1$.

Now we prove that R_1 is compatible. Assuming $a' < b'$ and $b' < a'(R_1)$, from the above discussion, a' and b' on $[X]_1$ have a common neighborhood system.
$\forall a \in a', b \in b', a, b \in [X]$, a and b have a common neighborhood system. From the definition of $[X]_1$, a and b belong to the same category on $[X]_1$. Thus, $a' \sim b'(R_1)$, i.e., R_1 is compatible.

Finally, we prove that R_1 is the finest one. Assume that R' is any partition and $R' < R$.

We will prove below that $R' < R_1$. Let $[X]'$ be a quotient space corresponding to R' and its projection be $p : [X] \to [X]'$. For $x, y \in [X]$ and $x \sim y(R_1)$, let $p(x) = a, p(y) = b$, $a, b \in [X]'$.

Assume that $u(a)$ is any neighborhood of a on $[X]'$. Since $R' < R$, regarding $u(a)$ as a set on $[X]$, it is open, i.e., $p^{-1}(u(a))$ is open on $[X]$. Since $p(x) = a$, $x \in p^{-1}(u(a))$, i.e., $x \in p^{-1}(u(a))$ is a neighborhood of x. On the other hand, since $x \sim y(R_1)$, x and y have the same neighborhood system, i.e., $p^{-1}(u(a))$ is also a neighborhood of y. Thus, $y \in p^{-1}(u(a))$. We have $b = p(y) \in p(p^{-1}(u(a))) \subset u(a)$, i.e., $a < b(R')$.

Similarly, $b < a(R')$, i.e., $a \sim b(R')$.

Finally, $R' < R_1$.

Example 1.15

Assume that (X, T) is a semi-order set as shown in Fig. 1.5. Let $R : a_1 = \{1, 4\}, a_2 = \{3, 5\}, a_3 = \{2\}$. From Example 1.14, we have that $[T_r] : \{\varnothing, [X]\}$ is a topology on $[X]$ corresponding to R, i.e., a_1, a_2 and a_3 have the same neighborhood system on $[X]$. Based on the mergence method, we have a revised partition $R_1 : a = \{1, 2, 3, 4, 5\}$. The example shows that undoubtedly by the mergence method, an incompatible equivalence relation can be transformed into a compatible and the finest one. But in some cases, the revised grain-size is too coarse. In the example, R_1 only has one equivalence class, this is an extreme case. This is not our expectation.

In order to overcome the shortage of the mergence method, the space $[X]$ may be refined such that the revised equivalence relation R_2 is compatible. Of course, such R_2 exists, since X itself has already satisfied the compatible requirement, but it is too fine. So the point is to find the coarsest one among all refined spaces, i.e., the refinement method has minimality. This is the decomposition method that we will discuss below.

1.6.2 Decomposition Methods

In the following discussion, we assume that (X, T) is a finite semi-order set, its topology is a right-order topology of T. $p : X \to [X]$ is a projection, where $[X]$ is a quotient space.

Definition 1.25

(X, T) is a (pseudo) semi-order set. For $A \subset X$, let

$C(A) = \{y|$ there exist $x_1, x_2 \in A, x_1 < y < x_2\}$.

$C(A)$ is called a (pseudo) semi-order closure of A on X.

Definition 1.26

(X, T) is a semi-order set. For $A, B \subset X$ and $A \subset B$, we define $\partial_B(A) = \{x | x \in A,$ if $y \in B$ and $x < y$, then $y \in A\}$. $\partial_B(A)$ is called a boundary point of A with respect to B, simply denoted as ∂A.

Assume that $[X]$ is a quotient space of (X, T), R is its corresponding equivalence relation. From Section 1.5, we have $T \rightarrow$ right-order topology $T_r \rightarrow$ quotient topology $[T_r] \rightarrow [T]_s$. $[T]_s$ is called a pseudo semi-order on $[X]$. When R is compatible, $[T]_s$ is a semi-order. If $a < b$ on $[X]$ under the topology $[T]_s$, where $a, b \in [X]$, then it is denoted as $a < b(R)$.

Definition 1.27

R is an equivalence relation on (X, T) and its corresponding quotient space is $[X]$. For $a, b \in [X]$, if $a < b, b < a(R)$, then a and b are pseudo-equivalent and denoted by $a \approx b$.

Definition 1.28

If $[X]$ is a quotient spare corresponding to R, for $\forall a \in [X]$ letting $<a> = \{b | b \approx a\}$, $<a>$ is called a pseudo-equivalence class corresponding to a.

Lemma 1.4

If A is a pseudo-equivalence class on $[X]$, then $C_{[X]}(A) = A$, or simply $C(A)$ if it does not cause any confusion.

Proof:

Otherwise, $\exists a \in C(A)/A$. From $a \in C(A)$ and the definition of $C(A)$, we can see that $\exists a_1, a_2 \in A$ such that $a_1 < a < a_2(R)$. Since a_1 and a_2 are pseudo-equivalent $\Rightarrow$ $a_2 < a_1(R)$. We have $a < a_1$, then, a and a_1 are pseudo-equivalent, i.e., $a \in A$. This is in contradiction to $a \notin A$.

Lemma 1.5

(X, T) is a semi-order set. $[X]$ is a quotient set of X. For $\forall a \in [X]$, there exists a minimal open set $u(a)$ containing a. $[T_r]$ is a topology on $[X]$. Set $u(a)$ can be constructed as follows.

Let $D_0 = a, B_1 = \bigcup_{x \in D_0} u(x)$, where $u(x)$ on (X, T_r) is a minimal open set containing x. T_r is a right-order topology of T.

Let $C_1 = p(B_1), D_1 = p^{-1}(C_1)$, $p : X \rightarrow [X]$ is a projection.

Generally, we define $C_i = p(B_i), D_i = p^{-1}(C_i), B_{i+1} = \bigcup_{x \in D_i} u(x)$.

Since $[X]$ is finite, there exists a minimal integer n such that $C_n = C_{n+1}$.

Let $u(a) = C_n$. Set $u(a)$ is just a minimal open set on $([X], [T_r])$ containing a.

Proof:

First, we show that C_n is an open set.

$$D_n = p^{-1}(C_n) \subset B_{n+1} \Rightarrow pp^{-1}(C_n) \subset p(B_{n+1}) = C_{n+1}$$
$$\Rightarrow p^{-1}p(B_{n+1}) = p^{-1}(C_{n+1}) = p^{-1}(C_n)$$

Since $B_{n+1} \subset p^{-1}p(B_{n+1})$, have $B_{n+1} \subset p^{-1}(C_n)$. Thus, $p^{-1}(C_n) = B_{n+1}$.

Since B_{n+1} is an open set, C_n is open.

Assuming that $w(a)$ is an arbitrary open set containing a, then $C_0 = a \subset w(a)$.

By induction, assume that $C_i \subset w(a)$.

From the continuity of p, $D_i = p^{-1}(C_i) \subset p^{-1}(w(a))$.

$p^{-1}(w(a))$ is an open set $\Rightarrow B_{i+1} = \underset{x \in D_i}{\cup} u(x) \subset p^{-1}(w(a)) \Rightarrow C_{i+1} = p(B_{i+1}) \subset pp^{-1}(w(a)) \subset w(a)$.

From induction, we have $C_n \subset w(a)$. Therefore $C_n = u(a)$ is a minimal open set containing a.

Lemma 1.6

R is an equivalence relation in semi-order space (X, T). Let $a, b \in [X]$ $a < b(R)$, there exist $x_i, x_i' \in X, i = 1, 2, \cdots, m$ such that $x_i \sim x_i', x_i' < x_{i+1}, x_1 \in a, x_m' \in b$.

Proof:

Letting $u(a)$ be a minimal open set containing a, since $a < b(R)$, have $b \in u(a)$.

From Lemma 1.5, we have $C_0 = a \subset C_1 \subset \cdots \subset C_n = u(a)$.

Assuming that $b \in C_m = p(B_m)$, we have $\exists x_m' \in b, x_m \in B_m$, i.e., $x_m \sim x_m'$.

Since $B_m = \underset{x \in D_{m-1}}{\cup} u(x)$, have $\exists x_{m-1} \in D_{m-1}, x_{m-1} < x_m$.

Moreover, $D_{m-1} = p^{-1}(C_{m-1}) \Rightarrow \exists x_{m-1}' \in C_{m-1}$ such that $x_{m-1} \sim x_{m-1}'$.

By induction, for $\forall i < m$, have $x_i' \in C_i$, $x_i \sim x_i'$ and $x_i < x_{i+1}'$, $i = 1, 2, ..., m$.

Namely, $x_1' \sim x_1 < x_2' \sim x_2 < x_3' \sim \cdots < x_m' \in b$.

We will prove Proposition 1.10 by using Lemma 1.6 below.

Proposition 1.10

Assume that $a, b \in [X]$, then $a<'b \Leftrightarrow a < b$, where $<'$ is a pseudo semi-order on quotient space $([X], [T]')$.

Proof:

Assume that $a, b \in [X], a<'b \Rightarrow \exists a = a_1, a_2, ..., a_m = b, a_i \rightarrow a_{i+1}, i = 1, ..., m - 1,$
$\Rightarrow \exists x_i, x_i' \in X, i = 1, 2, \cdots, m,$ have $x_i \sim x_i', x_i' < x_{i+1}, x_i, x_i' \in a_i, x_m' \in b.$

Letting $p : (X, T) \rightarrow ([X], [T_r]_s)$ be a natural projection, from the order-preserving ability of p, have $p(x_1) \sim p(x_1') < p(x_2) \sim \cdots < p(x_m') \Rightarrow p(x_1) < p(x_m') \Rightarrow a < b.$

Conversely, assume $a, b \in [X], a < b$. From Lemma 1.6, $\exists x_i, x_i' \in X, i = 1, 2, \cdots, m,$ such that $x_i \sim x_i', x_i' < x_{i+1}, x_i, x_i' \in a_i, x_m' \in b \Rightarrow a_i \rightarrow a_{i+1}, i = 1, ..., m - 1.$ From the definition of '$<$', we have $a<'b$.

Decomposition Method

When R and T are not compatible, we will show below how to decompose R such that the decomposed R' is compatible with T.

(X, T) is a semi-order space and $[X]$ is a quotient space. Let $A = \emptyset$.

(1) If $[X] = \emptyset$, then stop and A is what we want. Otherwise, go to (2).
(2) For $a \in [X]$, let $X_0 = X$. If $C_{X_{i-1}}(a) = a$, letting $A = A \cup \{a\}$ and
$X_i = a \cup \{x | x \in X_{i-1}/a\}$, then $X_{i-1} \leftarrow X_i$ and $[X] \leftarrow [X]/a$, go to (1). Otherwise, go to (3).
(3) Decomposing a, have $a_1 = \partial_{C_{X(i-1)}(a)}(a)$. Let $a_2 = a/a_1$.
    (3.1) If $a_2 = \emptyset$, we have the decomposition $A = A \cup \{a_1\}$. Letting
        $X_i = a_1 \cup \{x | x \in X_{i-1}/a_1\}$, then
        $X_{i-1} \leftarrow X_i$ and $[X] \leftarrow [X]/a$, go to (1).
    (3.2) If $a_2 \neq \emptyset$, letting $X_i = a_1 \cup \{x | x \in X_{i-1}/a \text{ or } x \in a_2\}$ and $A = A \cup \{a_1\}$, then
        $X_{i-1} \leftarrow X_i$ and $a \leftarrow a_2$, go to (3).
Finally, we have a space denoted as $\overline{[X]}$. Its corresponding equivalence relation is $\overline{R}$. $\overline{R}$ is what we want. $\overline{[X]}$ is called a normed decomposition space of $[X]$. We will prove below that $\overline{R}$ is compatible with X and has minimality.
Before the proof of the above basic property, we will show some properties of semi-order closures.

Definition 1.29

(X, T) is a semi-order space. For $A \subset X$, if $C_X(A) = A$, A is called semi-order closed on (X, T), or semi-order closed for short.

The properties of $C_X(A)$ are as follows.

Property 1.2

(X, T) is a semi-order space. For $A \subset X$, $C_X(A)$ is semi-order closed.

Proof:

Assuming $y \in C_X(C_X(A))$, there exist $x_1, x_2 \in C_X(A)$ and $x_1 < y < x_2$, i.e.,
$x_3, x_4, x_5, x_6 \in A, x_3 < x_1 < x_4, x_5 < x_2 < x_6$. We have
$x_3 < x_1 < y, y < x_2 < x_6, x_3 < y < x_6, y \in C_X(A)$. Thus, $C_X(A)$ is semi-order closed.

Property 1.3

(X, T) is a semi-order space. Assuming $A \subset X$, then $\partial_{C(A)}A$ is semi-order closed.

Proof:

Assuming $x_1 < y < x_2, x_1, x_2 \in \partial_{C(A)}A$, have $y \in C(A)$. $\forall z \in C(A)$ and $y < z$, have
$x_1 < y < z$. From $x_1 \in \partial_{C(A)}A$, have $y, z \in A$. And from the definition of boundary points,
have $y \in \partial_{C(A)}A$, i.e., $\partial_{C(A)}A$ is semi-order closed.

Property 1.4

If A is semi-order closed with respect to X, then $\partial_{C(A)}A = A$.

Proof:

Obviously, $A \subset C(A)$.

Assuming $x \in C(A)$, there exists $x_1 < y < x_2, x_1, x_2 \in A$. Since A is semi-order closed,
$y \in A$ and $C(A) = A$. From the definition of $\partial_{C(A)}A$, have $\partial_{C(A)}A = \partial_A A = A$.

Proposition 1.11

(X, T) is a semi-order space. For $a \subset X$, a is a semi-order closed. Letting its quotient space
be $X_1 = a \cup \{x | x \in X/a\}$, then (X_1, T_1) is also a semi-order space, where T_1 is a quotient
structure (topology) corresponding to X_1.

Proof:

Assume $y_1, y_2 \in X_1, y_1 < y_2 < y_1$. If $y_1, y_2 = a$, have $y_1 = y_2 = a$ on X_1. If $y_1 = a, y_2 \neq a$,
from Lemma 1.5, have $\exists y_3, y_4 \in X, y_1 \sim y_3 < y_2 < y_4 \sim y_1$. From a is semi-order closed,
have $y_2 \in a$. This is a contradiction.

If $y_1 \neq a, y_2 = a$, from Lemma 1.5, have $\exists y_3, y_4 \in a, y_1 < y_3 \sim y_2, y_2 \sim y_4 < y_1$. Thus,
$y_4 < y_1 < y_3$ and $y_1 \in a$. This is a contradiction.

We have that X_1 is a semi-order space.

Theorem 1.7

(X, T) is a semi-order set. $[X]$ is a quotient space. $[\overline{X}]$ is a normed decomposition of $[X]$. Then $([\overline{X}], \overline{T})$ is a semi-order space, where $\overline{T}$ is a quotient structure corresponding to $[\overline{X}]$.

Proof:

$[\overline{X}] = \{a(1), \cdots, a(n)\}$ is the decomposed partition of $[X]$.

Let $X_0 = X, X_i = \{a(1), ..., a(i)\} \cup \{x | x \in X / \{a(1), ..., a(i)\}\}, i = 1, ..., n$. From Property 1.3, each $a(i)$ is semi-order closed on X_{i-1}. From Proposition 1.10, we have that (X_i, T_i) is a semi-order space. Letting $i = n$, have $X_n = [\overline{X}]$. Namely, quotient space $([\overline{X}], \overline{T})$ is a semi-order one.

Lemma 1.7

$[X]$ is a quotient space of semi-order set (X, T). Let $a \in [X]$. Assume that $a = \{a(1), \cdots, a(n)\}$ is its normed decomposition space. Then when $j < i$, we have $a(i) < a(j)$.

Proof:

First, we prove that $\forall x \in a(2)$, $\exists z \in a$ and $y \notin a$ such that $z \in a(1), x < y < z$. From the definition of $a(i)$, $\forall x \in a(2)$ there must exist $y, x < y, y \in C(a)$, but $y \notin a$. Otherwise, from the definition of $a(i)$, $x \in a(1)$. This is a contradiction. And from $y \in C(a)$, we have $\exists z \in a$ and $y < z$. Then, $z \in a(1)$. Otherwise, $z \in a/a(1)$. This is in contradiction with $x \in u(2)$. From the definition of quotient structures, we have $a(2) < a(1)$.

Similarly, for $i > j$, we have $a(i) < a(j)$.

Theorem 1.8

R is an equivalence relation on semi-order set (X, T). $[X]$ is a quotient space. Let $\overline{R}$ be an equivalence relation corresponding to the normed decomposition space of $[X]$. We have

(1) $R < \overline{R}$ and $\overline{R}$ are compatible.
(2) $\overline{R}$ has minimality, i.e., for $\forall R'$, if $R < R' < \overline{R}$ and R' are compatible, then $R' = \overline{R}$.

Proof:

From the procedure of the normed decomposition and Theorem 1.7, $\overline{R}$ is compatible. Now, we prove that $\overline{R}$ is the minimum.

Assume that $R < R' < \overline{R}$ and R' are compatible. If $R' \neq \overline{R}$, obviously, for $x_1, x_2 \in [\overline{X}]$, x_1 and x_2 belong to the same equivalence class on $[X]'$ but are not equivalent on $[\overline{X}]$. Since x_1 and x_2 are equivalent on $[X]'$ and $R < R'$, then x_1 and x_2 are also equivalent on R.

Assume that $x_1, x_2 \in a \in [X]$ denoted $x_1 = a(i), x_2 = a(j)$, where $a(i)$ and $a(j)$, $i > j$, are obtained from the normed decomposition of a. From Lemma 1.7, there exists $x \in a(i), y \notin a, z \in a(j), x < y < z$. Now we regard $[X]'$ as a quotient space of X. Let $p : X \rightarrow [X]'$.

From the compatibility of R', we have $p(x) < p(y) < p(z)$. Thus, x, y and z belong to the same equivalence class of $[X]'$ denoted by b. Then, $b \cap a \neq \emptyset$.

Since $y \notin a \Rightarrow b \cap a^c \neq \emptyset$, where a^c is the complement set of a, this contradicts with $R < R'$.

Thus, $a(i) = a(j)$, this is in contradiction with the assumption that x_1 and x_2 are not equivalent in $[\overline{X}]$.

Finally, $R' = \overline{R}$.

Example 1.11

A semi-order set X as shown in Fig. 1.6. Let $R : a_1 = \{1, 2\}, a_2 = \{3, 4\}, a_3 = \{5, 6\}$. Since R is not compatible, decompose R as follows.

For $a_1 = \{1, 2\}$, since $C_X(a_1) = a_1$, we have $a_1 = \{1, 2\}$. Let $X_1 = \{\{1, 2\}, 3, 4, 5, 6\}$.

For $a_2 = \{3, 4\}$, since $C_{X_1}(a_2) = a_2$, we have $a_2 = \{3, 4\}$. Let $X_2 = \{\{1, 2\}, \{3, 4\}, 5, 6\}$.

For $a_3 = \{5, 6\}$, since $C_{X_2}(a_3) = X_2 \neq a_3$, we have $a_{31} = \partial_{X_2}(a_3) = \{6\}$. Then a_3 is decomposed into $a_{31} = \{6\}$ and $a_{32} = \{5\}$.

We have $X_3 = \{\{1, 2\}, \{3, 4\}, \{5\}, \{6\}\}$. X_3 is a semi-order space. Its corresponding equivalence relation $\overline{R}$ is the decomposed one of R and compatible.

The decomposition procedure is shown in Fig. 1.6.

Now, we have the necessary and sufficient condition for the compatible equivalence relation R as follows.

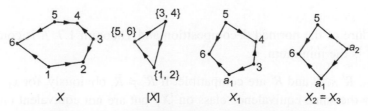

Figure 1.6: The Decomposition of Granularity

Theorem 1.9

R is an equivalence relation corresponding to semi-order set (X, T). $[X] = \{a_1, a_2, \cdots, a_n\}$ is its corresponding quotient space. $C_{Y_i}(a)$ is a (pseudo) semi-order closure of a on Y_i. Then, R and T are compatible $\Leftrightarrow$ $\forall i, C_{Y_i}(a_i) = a_i$.

Proof:

Obviously, if Y_1 is a quotient space of Y, then $\forall A \subset Y_1, C_Y(A) \subset C_{Y_1}(A)$.

$\Leftarrow$: Assume $\forall i, C_{Y_i}(a_i) = a_i$. Decompose $[X]$ according to the following order $a_1, a_2, \cdots, a_n$. Obviously, if it is $a_i's$ turn for decomposition, assuming that X_i is the decomposed space and Y_i is a quotient set of X_i, then $C_{X_i}(a_i) \subset C_{Y_i}(a_i) = a_i$. And $a_i \subset C_{X_i}(a_i)$, then $C_{X_i}(a_i) = a_i$, i.e., a_i needs not be decomposed. R is compatible.

$\Rightarrow$: If R is compatible, then $\forall i$, we leave the decomposition of a_i to the end. From the compatibility of R, $a_j, j \neq i$ needs not be decomposed. Therefore, $X_i = \{a_t | t \neq i\} \cup \{x | x \in a_i\} = Y_i$. Since a_i needs not be decomposed as well, then $C_{X_i}(a_i) = C_{Y_i}(a_i) = a_i$.

1.6.3 The Existence and Uniqueness of Quotient Semi-Order

Assume that (X, T) is a semi-order space. From the previous discussion, we have the following results.

1. If equivalence relation R and semi-order structure T on X are compatible, we offer a method that induces a quotient semi-order of $[X]$ such that its projection has the order-preserving ability.
2. If equivalence relation R and semi-order structure T on X are incompatible, we show there are modification methods such that the modified R is compatible.
    (1) By mergence method, we have an equivalence relation $\underline{R}$ and satisfies
        (a) $\underline{R} < R$, (b) $\underline{R}$ is compatible , and (c) $\underline{R}$ is the maximum (finest).
    (2) By decomposition method, we have an equivalence relation $\overline{R}$ and satisfies
        (a) $R < \overline{R}$, (b) $\overline{R}$ is compatible, and (c) $\overline{R}$ is the minimum.

Therefore, under the maximal (minimal) sense, the modification above is unique.

The idea of the construction of quotient semi-order that we offered is the following.

First, a right-order topology T_r is induced from T. From T_r, a quotient topology $[T_r]$ on $[X]$ is induced. Finally, from $[T_r]$, a quotient (pseudo) semi-order on $[X]$ is induced. Now, the point is whether there exists another method for inducing quotient semi-order. If the method exists, the induced quotient semi-order is as the former, i.e., the uniqueness of quotient semi-order. Moreover, when R and T are incompatible, we show that the method above cannot induce quotient semi-order on $[X]$. Then, whether there is another method that can induce quotient semi-order on $[X]$ such that its projection is order-preserving. That is, the existence of quotient semi-order.

The following two propositions answer the above uniqueness and existence problems.

Proposition 1.12

R is an equivalence relation on semi-order set (X, T). R and T are compatible. Let $[T]$ be the quotient semi-order obtained from the above method. $[T]'$ is any quotient semi-order that has the order-preserving projection $p : X \rightarrow [X]$, then $[T]' < [T]$.

Proof:

Assuming $a, b \in [X]$, then $a < b([T])$. From Lemma 1.5, we have

$$\exists x_i, x_i' \in X, i = 1, 2, \cdots, n \text{ such that } x_i, x_i' \in a, x_n \in b, x_i \sim x_i'(R) \quad \text{and} \quad x_1' < x_2 \sim x_2' < x_3 \sim x_3'$$
$$< \cdots < x_n = b.$$

Let $p : X \rightarrow ([X], [T]')$. From the assumption that p is order-preserving, have $p(x_i') < p(x_{i+1}), i = 1, 2, \cdots, n - 1$ and $p(x_i') = p(x_i)$.

Thus, $a = p(x_1) < p(x_2) < \cdots < p(x_n) = b$, i.e., there exists $a < b$ on $[T] \Rightarrow [T] < [T]$.

Proposition 1.13

If R and T are incompatible, there is no quotient semi-order such that $p : X \rightarrow [X]$ is order-preserving.

Proof:

Assume that R and T are incompatible and there exists a quotient semi-order on $[X]$ that has the order-preserving ability. Since the incompatibility of R and T, $\exists a < b, b < a([T])$, $a \sim b$ does not hold. From $a < b, b < a([T])$, $\exists x_i, x_i'$ satisfy $x_i' \in a, x_m \in b, x_m' \in b, x_n \in a, m < n$ and $x_1' < x_2 \sim x_2' < x_3 \sim x_3' < \cdots < x_m \sim x_m' < x_{m+1} < \cdots < x_n$.

From the order-preserving ability of $[T]'$, we have $p(x_i') < p(x_{i+1})$ and $p(x_i') = p(x_i), i = 1, 2, \cdots, n - 1$. Thus, $a < p(x_2) < \cdots < b < \cdots < p(x_n) = a$.

Since $[T]'$ is semi-order, $b = a$. This is in contradiction with that $b \sim a$ does not hold.

1.6.4 The Geometrical Interpretation of Mergence and Decomposition Methods

The structure of a finite semi-order space may be represented by a directed acyclic graph geometrically. For a semi-order space (X, T), when the quotient structure $[T]$ of its quotient space $([X], [T])$ is represented by a directed graph, if there is no directed loop in the graph, then the corresponding structure is semi-order; otherwise, it is not semi-order.

There are two methods to 'remove' the loops on the graph. One is to merge all notes on a loop into a new note and carry on until the graph becomes an acyclic one. Then the quotient structure obtained is a semi-order structure. This is the mergence method. The other one is to choose an arbitrary note on a loop and cut the loop open from the note, carry on until the graph becomes an acyclic one. This is just the idea of decomposition. Due to the different cutting sequences, the acyclic graph obtained may be different. So the semi-order structure obtained by the decomposition method is not unique. We can prove the structure is local minimum but not a global one.

1.7 Conclusions

In this chapter, we present a quotient space representation method for problem solving. Based on the method, a problem is represented by a triplet (X, f, T). Compared to general graph and AND/OR graph representations, it enables us to describe different structures, attribute functions and operations on a domain. Especially, it offers a tool for depicting different grain-size worlds. In the following chapters, we will show the application of the representation.

When (X, T) is a topologic or a semi-order space, we discuss how to construct the quotient topology and quotient (pseudo) semi-order on its corresponding quotient space $[X]$ and after the construction what kind of quotient structures that we can have.

We show the three different kinds of complete semi-order lattices we can have and how they correspond to different construction methods. We also investigate the relation among three lattices. These results offer the mathematical tools and methods for granular analysis and computing later on.

Hierarchy and Multi-Granular Computing

2.1 The Hierarchical Model

The concept of hierarchy has long been used in many fields, e.g., information, control, and management sciences. Recently, AI researchers also use it extensively in, for example, hierarchical planning, hierarchical learning, etc.

In this book, the word 'hierarchy' has two meanings. First, it means a sort of architecture or organization in natural and man-made systems. Second, it represents the hierarchical analysis methodology in human problem-solving activities. In the book, we mainly focus on the second meaning.

For example, in a national administration, the whole nation is divided into several provinces. Each province is further divided into several counties and so on.

A man-made control system is generally divided into several levels. The whole system is decomposed into several subsystems. Each subsystem has its own functions, and is controlled by higher-level controllers. The subsystem may further be split into smaller ones. This is the well-known 'hierarchical control' as the system has a hierarchical structure.

The above two examples are typical hierarchical organizations.

In human problem solving, instead of considering all the details of the problem at once, the original complex problem is first simplified by ignoring some details. The simplified model is then gradually refined until the problem is finally solved. That is, we solve the problem from top to bottom, from the coarse grain to the fine one, or from global to local gradually. This is called hierarchical problem solving. The examples are given below.

Example 2.1

To make a nation-wide economic development plan, a plan for each department, such as power supply, transportation, etc., is usually worked out first. Then the plans for factories and enterprises are worked out on the basis of the departments' plans. Similarly, when making a long-term 5-year plan, we generally work out annual plans first, and then monthly plans and so on. The plan is refined gradually according to the chronological order.

Example 2.2

In troubleshooting, a complex electronic instrument is tested. One always examines its components such as power supply, display unit, etc., first, and then go deep into the elements of each component until some faults are detected.

A similar process can be seen in many engineering designs.

Example 2.3

Suppose that someone is looking into the structure of the age distribution of a city, he/she would prefer first grouping the citizens in terms of junior, adult, senior or the like to going through the statistics of the recent census. This means that he/she is consciously using the concept of hierarchy. Each group may contain a lower level of hierarchy, e.g., the senior group may be divided into smaller groups like 'below 60', 'above 60', and so on. We can see that grouping is done at different levels (higher or lower) and we sometimes refer to them as abstraction levels.

Why has a nation to be organized as a hierarchical structure? The fact is that it is impossible for the head of the state to look after all his citizens directly. The same is true for the case of armed forces. A general cannot command each soldier directly. The soldiers have to be grouped into divisions, regiments and battalions, etc. In man-made machines, as mentioned above, it is not true that the central controller deals with every single element directly.

It is generally recognized that the hierarchical structure can enhance the efficiency. This is just the hierarchical problem-solving strategy that humans use for dealing with complex problems. We call the strategy multi-granular computing.

There are two cases for using the strategy. First, we sometimes only need to know the general properties of the domain rather than the details. Thus, just one proper granularity (or abstraction level) is needed. For example, we expect to survey the distribution of a disease over some region. It is unlikely to investigate each citizen in the region. Generally, a region is divided into several typical areas. Taking samples from these areas, a statistical distribution of the disease over that region will be obtained. The other case is that since the problem in question is quite complex, it is hard to handle the whole problem at once. Then the problem is decomposed into several different grain-size worlds (abstraction levels). From the analysis of the coarse granular levels (higher abstraction levels), some primary results are obtained. Then, going deeper into the fine granular levels (lower abstraction levels), more information is gained under the guidance of the results already collected, until the problem is finally solved.

It seems that the multi-granular computing is aimed at improving efficiency, or in terms of computer science, reducing the computational complexity. Whether or not the strategy can reduce the computational complexity, in what conditions the goal can be reached, etc., we will discuss them in this chapter.

Generally, there are two kinds of partition paradigms in multi-granular computing. One is called branching. A problem is divided into several sub-problems. And each sub-problem is divided into sub-sub-problems and so on. When the decomposition does not have overlapped parts, it is a tree structure. Otherwise, it is a graph. The other is called nested. A problem is divided into several levels with different details. For example, we investigate the transportation problem in some area, in a map with 1:40,000,000 scale, the main cities, rivers and railways, etc., are indicated. Further, in a map with 1:15,000,000 scale, more details such as counties, highways, etc., are shown. The maps with different scales compose a nested structure.

Obviously, the branching structure can be represented by the mathematical model presented in Chapter 1. For a nested structure, in some coarse granularity, some details are missing. The missing parts can be classified into an equivalence class. When entering into a fine one, some missing parts appear. Then, they are further classified. Hence, the nested structure can be represented by the quotient structure model as well.

The above hierarchical structures can be obtained in two ways, one from prior knowledge, and the other from data. Many machine learning and data mining methods (Mitchell,

1997; Hand et al., 2001) can be used to get the structures behind data that are not involved in the book.

2.2 The Estimation of Computational Complexity

The aim of this section is to estimate the computational complexity, based on the mathematical model presented in Chapter 1, when the multi-granular computing is used (Zhang and Zhang, 1990d, 1992).

2.2.1 The Assumptions

A problem space is assumed to be a finite set. Symbol $|X|$ denotes the number of elements in X. Sometimes, we simply use X instead of $|X|$ if no confusion is made.

If we solve the problem X directly, i.e., finding a goal in X, the computational complexity is assumed to be $f(X)$. Then, the complexity will be changed to $f_1(X)$ by using the multi-granular computing. Now, the point is in what conditions that we may have the result $f_1(X) \leq f(X)$.

Before the discussion, we make the following assumption for $f(\cdot)$.

Hypothesis A

Assume that $f(\cdot)$ only depends on the number of elements in X, and independent of its structure, or other attributes. Both domain and range of $f(\cdot)$ are assumed to be $[0, \infty)$, i.e., a non-negative real number. Namely,

(1) $f : R^+ \to R^+$ is a monotonically increasing function on $R^+ = [0, \infty)$.
(2) $\forall x \in R^+$, we have $f(x) \leq x$.

$f(\cdot)$ is called a computational complexity function on X, or complexity function for short.

Now, we solve X by using the multi-granular computing strategy. That is, X is classified with respect to R_1. Its corresponding quotient space is denoted by X_1. Then the original problem on X is converted into the corresponding problem on X_1. Since some information will lose on X_1 due to the abstraction, generally, we can't find the goal of X directly from its quotient space X_1. Instead, we can only have a useful clue to the final solution of X from X_1. Thus, in order to describe the relation between the results obtained from the quotient and its original spaces, we introduce a new function as follows.

Definition 2.1

Assume that X_1 is a quotient space of X and f is a complexity function of X. Suppose that the complexity function of X_1 is less than $f(|X_1|)$ and the number of elements which might contain the goal is estimated at g at most. Define a goal estimation function $g(\cdot)$ as follows:

$$g : R^+ \rightarrow R^+, g(|X_1|) = g$$

Assume that $g(\cdot)$ is a monotonically increasing function and $g(x) \leq x, \forall x \in R^+$.

We have a sequence $X_1, X_2, \cdots, X_t, X_{t+1} = X$ of quotient spaces with t levels, where X_i is a quotient space of X_{i+1}, $i = 1, 2, \cdots, t$. After the multi-granular computing with t levels, the total complexity function is assumed to be $f_t(X)$. We next estimate the $f_t(X)$.

2.2.2 The Estimation of the Complexity Under Deterministic Models

Our goal is to estimate the asymptotic property of complexity function under the multi-granular computing. For simplicity, let $|X| = e^n$, i.e., X has e^n elements. The other variables are limited to the order of $\ln n$, $(\ln n)^\alpha$, and n^α, where $\alpha > 0$.

Local Partition Method

Definition 2.2

Assume $|X| = e^n$. The complexity function $f(|X|)$ is called divergent if for any given $b > 0$, have $\lim\limits_{n \to \infty} \frac{f(|X|)}{n^b} = \infty$.

$g(x) \equiv 1$ Case

Suppose that X_1 is a quotient space of X. We seek the goal of X from X_1. When solving the problem on X_1, the computational complexity only depends on the number of elements in X_1. After the amount $f(|X_1|)$ of computation, we find element $a_1 \in X_1$ which might contain the goal. Due to $g(x) \equiv 1$, there is only one such element, a_1. Again, assume that each equivalence class has the same number of elements.

Then, we seek the goal within the equivalence class a_1 (a_1 is an element in X_1) in X.

When $|X_1| = e^{n_1}$, from $X = e^n$ we have $|a_1| = e^{n-n_1}$. Thus, the total computational complexity for solving X by the multi-granular computing with two levels is

$$f_1(X) = f(X_1) + f(a_1) = f(e^{n_1}) + f(e^{n-n_1}) \tag{2.1}$$

Regarding a_1 as a set of X, if set a_1 is too large, then a_1 is further partitioned. Assume that Y_2 is a quotient set of set a_1 and $|Y_2| = e^{n_2}$. The total complexity for solving X by the multi-granular computing with three levels is

$$\begin{aligned} f_2(X) &= f(X_1) + f(Y_2) + f(a_2) \\ &= f(e^{n_1}) + f(e^{n_2}) + f(e^{n-n_1-n_2}) \end{aligned} \tag{2.2}$$

where, $a_2 \in Y_2$ is an element of Y_2 which might contain the goal.

From induction, the total complexity for solving X by the multi-granular computing with t levels is

$$f_t(X) = f(e^{n_1}) + f(e^{n_2}) + \cdots + f(e^{n_t}) \tag{2.3}$$

where

$$n = \sum_{i=1}^{t} n_i$$

If in each level, its elements are classified into c equivalence classes without exception, where $c > 0$ is an integer, i.e., $e^{n_i} = c$, $\forall i$. Since $n = \sum_{i=1}^{t} n_i$, we have $e^n = c^t = (e^a)^t = e^{at}$, where $c = e^a$. Then, we have $at = n$, $t = \frac{n}{a}$. Substituting $t = \frac{n}{a}$ into (2.3), we have $f_t(X) = tf(c) = c_1 n$, i.e., $f_t(X) \sim O(n)$.

We have the following proposition.

Proposition 2.1

If a unique element which contains the goal can be found at each granular level, i.e., $g(x) \equiv 1$, there exists a hierarchical partition method for X such that X can be solved in a linear time ($\sim O(n)$), in spite of the form of complexity function $f(X)$ ($f(X)$ might be divergent).

Example 2.4

We are given 3^n coins, one of which is known to be lighter than the rest. Using a two-pan scale, we must find the counterfeit coin as soon as possible.

To solve the problem, we may weigh a pair of coins (one in each pan) at a time. That is, we find the counterfeit one from 3^n coins directly. The mean computational complexity, the average number of weighing, is $O(3^n)$. By the multi-granular computing, 3^n coins may first be divided into three groups equally. Then a quotient space $X_1 = \{A, B, C\}$ is gained. Obviously, we can find which group will contain the counterfeit coin in one test. That is, by weighing A and B, the suspect will be in C in case the scale balances, the suspect will be in either A or B (the lighter one) in case the scale tips. In our terminology, in the first weighting, $f(X_1) = 1$ and $g(x) \equiv 1$.

The same procedure can be used for the suspect class, the outcome of the first weighting. The same process continues until the counterfeit coin is found. From (2.3) by letting $f(c) = 1, t = n$, we have $f_t(X) = n$. That is, the counterfeit coin can be found in n tests.

Proposition 2.2

If the complexity function of X is $f(e^n) = n^\alpha$, then

(1) when $\alpha > 1, f(X) > f_t(X)$,
(2) when $\alpha = 1, f(X) \sim f_t(X)$,
(3) when $\alpha < 1, f(X) < f_t(X)$.

From Proposition 2.1, the proposition is obtained directly.

The proposition indicates that as long as the complexity $f(X)$ is greater than a linearly growing function, it can be reduced by the multi-granular computing:

$g(x) > 1$ case

Quotient space X_1 is obtained after partitioning X. Through the amount $f(|X_1|)$ of computation, it is found that $g(X_1)$ elements in X_1 might contain the goal of X. These elements are assumed to be $a_1, a_2, \cdots$. The total complexity for solving X by the multi-granular computing with two levels is

$$
\begin{aligned}
f_1(X) &= f(X_1) + f(a_1) + f(a_2) + \cdots \\
&= f(X_1) + g(X_1)f\left(e^{n-n_1}\right) \\
&= f(e^{n_1}) + g(X_1)f\left(e^{n-n_1}\right)
\end{aligned}
$$

Each a_i is partitioned. The corresponding quotient space is denoted by X_2, $|X_2| = e^{n_2}$. The complexity for solving X by the multi-granular computing with three levels is:

$$
\begin{aligned}
f_2(X) &= f(X_1) + g(X_1)\left[f(X_2) + g(X_2)f\left(e^{n-n_1-n_2}\right)\right] \\
&= f(e^{n_1}) + g(X_1)f(e^{n_2}) + g(X_1)g(X_2)f\left(e^{n-n_1-n_2}\right)
\end{aligned}
$$

From induction, the total complexity for solving X by the multi-granular computing with t levels is:

$$
\begin{aligned}
f_t(X) = {}&f(e^{n_1}) + g(X_1)f(e^{n_2}) + g(X_1)g(X_2)f(e^{n_3}) + \cdots \\
&+ g(X_1)g(X_2)\cdots g(X_t)
\end{aligned}
\tag{2.4}
$$

where e^{n_i} is the number of elements in the i-th granular level (abstraction level), $g(X_i)$ is the goal estimation function on X_i.

From (2.4), we estimate the order of $f_t(X)$. If $g(X) \equiv c > 1$, we have

(1) If $f(X)$ is divergent, for any t, then $f_t(X)$ must be divergent;
(2) If $f_t(X) = n^{\alpha}$, letting $t = t_0$ (constant), then $f_t(X) \sim n^{\alpha}$;
(3) If $f_t(X) = n^{\alpha}$, letting $t = \ln(n)$, then $f_t(X) \sim n^b, (b > a)$;
(4) If $f_t(X) = n^{\alpha}$, letting $t = n^d (d > 0)$, then $f_t(X)$ is divergent.

We only give the proof of case (3) below.

From assumption that $f(X) = n^a$ and $t = \ln(n)$, substituting the above values into Formula (2.4), we have

$$f_t(X) \sim \left(\frac{n}{\ln n}\right)^a \left[1 + c + \cdots + c^{(\ln n-1)}\right] + c^{\ln n} \sim \left(\frac{n}{\ln n}\right)^a \left(\frac{c^{\ln n} - 1}{c - 1}\right) + c^{\ln n} \qquad (2.5)$$

Letting $c^{\ln n} = n^\beta, (\beta > 0)$, and substituting into Formula (2.5), we obtain

$$f_t(X) \sim \left(\frac{n}{\ln n}\right)^a \cdot n^\beta + n^\beta \sim n^{a+\beta} = n^b, b > a.$$

From the results above, we have the following proposition.

Proposition 2.3

If $g(X) \equiv c > 1$, based on the above partition model, we cannot reduce the asymptotic property of the complexity for solving X by the multi-granular computing paradigm. The result is disappointing. It is just the partitioning strategy we adopted that leads to the result. Based on the above strategy, in the first granular level if elements $a_1, a_2, \cdots a_m$ are suspected of containing the goal, then each $a_i, i = 1, 2, ..., m$, is further partitioned, respectively. Assume that each a_i still has m suspects. The process goes on, after n granular levels (abstraction levels), we will have m^n suspects, so the divergence happens. This partitioning method is called local partition.

In order to overcome the shortage of local partition, the second alternative can be adopted. When $a_1, a_2, \cdots a_m$ are found to be suspects, all $a_i, i = 1, 2, ..., m$, are merged into one equivalence class a. Then, we partition the whole merged class a rather than each a_i. This strategy is called global partition.

Global Partition Method

Assume that in a granular level there exist bx elements that are suspected of containing the goal, where x is the total number of elements in that level. That is, $g(x) = bx, 0 < b < 1$.

Suppose that X is partitioned with respect to R. Its corresponding quotient space is X_1. Letting $|X| = x$, $|X_1| = x_1$, we have the complexity function:

$$f_1(X) = f(x_1) + f\left(bx_1\frac{x}{x_1}\right) = f(x_1) + f(bx)$$

Here each equivalence class in X_1 is supposed to have the same number of elements of X.

Now, by partitioning bx_1 elements, i.e., all suspects in X_1, we have a quotient space X_2. Letting $|X_2| = x_2$, we have

$$f_2(X) = f(x_1) + f(x_2) + f\left(bx_2\frac{bx}{x_2}\right) = f(x_1) + f(x_2) + f(b^2x)$$

From induction, it follows that

$$f_t(X) = f(x_1) + f(x_2) + \cdots + f(b^t x) \tag{2.6}$$

When $b^t x \leq 1$, the goal is found.

Suppose that $x = e^n$. By letting $t = n$, we have $b \leq \frac{1}{e}$, i.e., $b^n x \leq 1$.

Generally, letting $b^t x = b^t e^n = 1$, we have $t \ln b + n = 0$.

Since $b < 1$, we have $t = \frac{n}{|\ln b|}$.

Assume $x_i = c$ (constant), from Formula (2.6) it follows that $f_t(X) = tf(c) = c_1 n \sim O(n)$.

We have the following proposition.

Proposition 2.4

If we can have $g(x) = bx, b < 1$, by the global partition method, when $t \geq n/|\ln b|$, then the complexity for solving X is $O(n)$ regardless of whether the original complexity function $f(\cdot)$ is divergent or not.

The proposition shows that different partition strategies may have different results. So long as in each granular level there is enough information such that $g(x) = bx, b < 1$, then when $t \geq n/|\ln b|$, the linear complexity can be reached by the global partition method. In the following example, since $b = \frac{2}{3} < 1$, from Proposition 2.4, it is known that so long as $t \geq n/|\ln \frac{2}{3}| \sim 2.47n$, we can get the linear complexity.

Example 2.5

We are given 3^n coins, one of which is known to be heavier or lighter than the rest. Using a two-pan scale, we must find the counterfeit coin and determine whether it is light or heavy as soon as possible.

First, coins are divided into three groups (A, B, C) equally. By weighing A and B (one in each pan), the suspect will be in C in case the scale balances, the suspect will be in A or B in case the scale tips.

In terms of our quotient space model, we have

$$X_1 = \{A, B, C\}, x_1 = |X_1| = 3, g(x) \leq \frac{2}{3}x, b = \frac{2}{3} < 1$$

From Proposition 2.4, so long as the number t of granular levels is greater than $2.47n$, the counterfeit coin can be found.

In fact, it can be proved that the counterfeit coin may be found from $\frac{3^n - 1}{2}$ coins in n tests.

It is shown that the computational complexity by the multi-granular computing also depends on the way in which the domain X is partitioned.

2.2.3 The Estimation of the Complexity Under Probabilistic Models

In the previous section, two partition methods are given. One is to partition each class that might contain the goal. It is called the local partition method. The method requires that only the unique element that might contain the goal is identified at each partition so that the computational complexity can be reduced. The other one is to partition the whole set of classes that might contain the goal. This is called the global partition method. In order to reduce the complexity by the method, $g(x) \leq bx, b < 1$ must be satisfied at each partition. These results are unsatisfactory. So we need a more reasonable model, i.e., probabilistic models.

From Definition 2.1, it's known that goal estimation function $g(\cdot)$ is:

$$g : R^+ \to R^+, g(|X_1|) = g$$

If $g(|X_1|) = g$, it means that the number of elements in X_1 which might contain the goal is g at most. Generally, it is not the case that each element contains the goal with the same probability. Thus, it can reasonably be described by probabilistic models.

Definition 2.3

Assume that $p(x)$ is a probabilistic distribution function that exactly x elements of set A might contain the goal. Let $g(A) = \int_{A_1} xp(x)dx$, where $A_1 = \{1, 2, \cdots, |A|\}$. Then, $g(A)$ is a goal estimation function under the statistical model.

Example 2.6

We are given 3^n coins, one of which is known to be heavier or lighter than the rest. Using a two-pan scale, we divide the coins into three groups equally: A, B, C. First, group A is compared with B. A or B will contain the counterfeit coin in case the scale tips and C will contain the counterfeit one in case the scale balances. In terms of distribution function $p(x)$, we have:

$$p(x) = \begin{cases} 1/3, x = 1 \\ 2/3, x = 2 \\ 0, x = 3 \end{cases}$$

Here, 3^n coins are assumed to be divided into three groups at random. Thus, the counterfeit coin falls in each group with same probability $\frac{1}{3}$. We have:

$$g(X_1) = \int_{X_1} xp(x)dx = 1 \times \frac{1}{3} + 2 \times \frac{2}{3} + 3 \times 0 = \frac{5}{3}$$

where $X_1 = \{1, 2, 3\}$.

$g(X_1) = \frac{5}{3}$ is the result we have in only one weighting. The number of weightings can be increased. For example, when the scale tips in the first weighting, then A and C (one in each pan) are weighed. The counterfeit coin is in B in case the scale balances and the counterfeit coin is in A in case the scale tips. That is, $g(X_1) = 1$.

In other words, so long as increasing a certain amount of computation on X_1, the value of goal function $g(X_1)$ can always be reduced. Taking this into account, we have the following definition.

Definition 2.4

Assume that X_1 is a quotient space of X. $f(\cdot)$ is a computational complexity function of X. Besides the amount $f(X_1)$ of computation on X_1, an additional amount y of computation is added. Then, the goal distribution function is changed to $p(x, y)$. Let

$$g(X_1, y) = \int_{X_1'} xp(x, y)dx = 1 + \alpha(y)$$

where $X_1' = \{1, 2, 3, \cdots, |X_1|\}$.

$(f(X), g(X_1, y))$ is called a probabilistic model for estimating the computational complexity of X with the multi-granular computing.

Certainly, the computational complexity above depends on the forms of $f(X)$ and $\alpha(y)$.

Now, we only discuss two specific kinds of $\alpha(y)$, i.e., $\alpha(y) \sim e^{-y}$ and $\alpha(y) \sim y^\alpha (\alpha < 0)$.

$$1. \; \alpha(y) \sim e^{-y}, \text{ i.e., } y = |\ln \alpha|(\alpha > 0) \text{ case}$$

We know that when y increases, then $g(X_1, y)$ decreases. From Formula (2.4), $f_t(X)$ decreases as well. Certainly, the reduction of computational complexity is at the cost of additional computation y. But the point is how to choose an appropriate y and t such that the total computational complexity will be decreased. The following proposition gives a complete answer.

Proposition 2.5

Assume $y = |\ln \alpha|$. If the number of granular levels is $t \sim O(n)$, the computational complexity is the minimal by using the multi-granular computing with t levels. And its asymptotic complexity is $O(n \ln n)$, where the number of elements in X is assumed to be e^n.

Proof:

Assume that the local partition approach is adopted and $t \sim O(n)$.

Let $g(X_i, y_i) = 1 + \alpha_i(y_i)$, where $g(X_i, y_i)$ is the goal estimation function in the i-th granular level (abstraction level), when the additional computation is y_i.

Proposition 2.4 shows that if $g(x) \geq c > 1$, by local partition method the computational complexity cannot be reduced. In order to reduce the complexity, it is demanded that $g(X_i, y_i) \to 1$, i.e., $\alpha_i \to 0$.

Now, let

$$\alpha_i = \left(\frac{1}{i}\right)^c, c > 1, i = 1, 2, \cdots, t. \prod_{i=1}^{t} g(X_i, y_i) = \prod_{i=1}^{t}(1 + \alpha_i) = \prod_{i=1}^{t}(1 + i^{-c}) < c_1 < \infty$$

(2.7)

Substituting (2.7) into (2.4), we have $f_t(X) \sim O(n)$.

On the other hand, the total amount of additional computation is:

$$\sum_{i=1}^{t} \left(\prod_{j=1}^{t} g\left(X_j, y_j\right) \right) y_i \leq c_1 \sum_{i=1}^{t} y_i = c_1 \sum_{i=1}^{t} |\ln \alpha_i| \sim O(n \ln n) \quad \text{since } t \sim O(n)$$

The total computational complexity is $F_t(X)$.

$$F_t(X) \sim O(n) + O(n \ln n) \sim O(n \ln n)$$

We'll show below that if t is not equal to $\sim O(n)$, the asymptotic complexity of $F_t(X)$ will be greater than or equal to $O(n \ln n)$. There are three cases.

(1) If $f(X) \sim O(e^n)$, letting $t \sim O(n^b), 0 < b < 1$, then $F_t(X)$ is divergent.
    Assume that X_i is a quotient space at the i-th granular level. Let $|X_i| = x_i$. Due to the local partition, we have $x_1 \cdot x_2 \cdot x_3 \cdots x_t = x = e^n$.
    By letting each x_i be d, obtain $d^t = e^n$, i.e., $d = \sqrt[t]{e^n} = e^{n/t}$.
    From $t \sim O(n^b)$, we have $d \sim O(e^{n^{(1-b)}})$.
    Again, from $f(X) = O(e^n)$, we have $f(d) \sim O(d) \sim O(e^{n^{(1-b)}})$.
    Substituting the above result into Formula (2.4), it follows that $F_t(X)$ is divergent.

(2) If $f(X) \sim O(n^a)$, when $a > 1$, letting $t = O(n^b), 0 < b < 1$, the order of $F_t(X)$ will not be less than $O(n \ln n)$.
    Similar to the inference in (1), we have $x_i = e^{n^{(1-b)}}$. By letting $\alpha_i = i^{-1}(e > 1)$, we

obtain $\prod_{i=1}^{t} g(X_i, y_i) < c_1 < \infty$. Substituting the result into Formula (2.4), we obtain:

$$f_t(X) = \left(n^{1-b}\right)^a + g_1\left(n^{1-b}\right)^a + g_1 g_2 \left(n^{1-b}\right)^a + \cdots + \prod_{i=1}^{t} g_i,$$

where $g_i = g(X_i, y_i)$

Thus,

$$f_t(X) \sim O\left(n^b n^{a(1-b)}\right) = O\left(n^{a(1-b)+b}\right), \text{ since } t \sim O(n^b)$$

On the other hand, the additional amount $h_i(X)$ of computation is

$$h_i(X) \leq c_1 \sum_{i=1}^{t} |\ln \alpha_i| \leq O(n^b \ln n)$$

Finally,

$$F_t(X) \sim O\left(n^{a(1-b)+b}\right) + O(n^b \ln n). \tag{2.8}$$

Letting the order of $F_t(X)$ in Formula (2.8) be less than $O(n \ln n)$, it's known that the necessary and sufficient condition is:

$$a(1-b) + b \leq 1 \Leftrightarrow a(1-b) \leq 1 - b \Leftrightarrow a \leq 1$$

This is in contradiction with $a > 1$. Thus, the order of $F_i(X)$ is not less than $O(n \ln n)$.

(3) If $t \sim O(n^b), b > 1$, the order of $F_i(X)$ is $O(n^b)$ at least, or greater than $O(n \ln n)$. From Formula (2.4), it's known that $f_t(X) \geq tf(X_i)$. Thus, $f_t(X) \geq O(n^b)$. Since $b > 1$, the order of $f_t(X)$ is greater than $O(n \ln n)$. Still more, the order of $F_t(X)$ is greater than $O(n \ln n)$.

From the results of (1), (2) and (3), we conclude that the order of complexity is minimal by using the multi-granular computing with $t \sim O(n)$ levels.

$$2. \ \alpha(y) \sim y^d (d < 0), \text{ i.e., } y = \alpha^h (h < 0) \text{ case}$$

Proposition 2.6

Assume that $y = \alpha^h (h < 0)$ and $f(X) \sim e^n$. If $t \sim O(n^b)$, then we have:

(i)   when $0 < b < 1$, $F_t(X)$ is divergent;
(ii) when $b \geq 1$, if $\alpha_i = i^{-c}, c > 1$, then $F_t(X) \sim O(n^{b(1-ch)})$;
(iii) when $b = 1$, if $t \sim O(n), F_t(X)$ is minimal and its order is $O(n^{1-ch})$.

Proof:

When $t \sim O(n^b), 0 < b < 1$, from Proposition 2.5 (1), it's known that $F_t(X)$ is divergent.

When $t \sim O(n^b), b \geq 1$, letting $a^i = i^{-c}, c > 1$, from Formula (2.4), we have:

$$f_t(X) \sim O(n^b)$$

The additional amount $h_i(X)$ of the computation is

$$h_t(X) \leq c_1 \sum_{i=1}^{t} y_i = c_1 \sum_{i=1}^{t} i^{-ch} \sim O\left(n^{b(1-ch)}\right), \text{ since } t \sim O(n^b)$$

Thus,

$$F_t(X) \sim O\left(n^{b(1-ch)}\right) + O(n^b)$$

Since

$$h < 0, \text{ have } F_t(X) \sim O\left(n^{b(1-ch)}\right)$$

From the result above, it's known that the order of $F_t(X)$ is minimal, when $b=1$, by using the multi-granular computing with $t \sim O(n)$ levels.

Proposition 2.7

Assume that $f(X) \sim O(n^a), a > 1$ and $y = \alpha^h (h < 0)$. Let $\alpha_i = i^{-c}, (c > 1)$. When $t \sim O\left(n^{\frac{a}{a+c_1}}\right)$, where $c_1 = -ch$, the order of $F_t(X)$ is minimal and equals $O\left(n^{\frac{a(1+c_1)}{a+c_1}}\right)$. It is less than the order of $f(X)$.

Proof:

If $t \sim O(n^b), 0 < b < 1$, from Proposition 2.6, we have $f_t(X) \sim O(n^{a(1-b)+b})$.

If the additional amount $h_t(X)$ of computation satisfies

$$h_t(X) \leq c_2 \sum_{i=1}^{t} y_i \sim \sum_{i=1}^{t} (i)^{-ch} = \sum_{i=1}^{t} i^{c_1} \sim \int_0^t x^{c_1} dx \sim O\left(n^{b(1+c_1)}\right)$$

Where, $c_1 = -ch, c_2 = \prod_{i=1}^{t}(1 + \alpha_i)$, finally, we have

$$F_t(X) \sim O\left(n^{a(1-b)+b}\right) + O\left(n^{b(1+c_1)}\right) \tag{2.9}$$

In order to have the minimal order of $F_t(X)$

$$\Leftrightarrow a(1 - b) + b = b(1 + c_1) \Rightarrow b = a/(a + c_1)$$

Substituting b by $a/(a + c_1)$ in Formula (2.9), we have $F_t(X) \sim O\left(n^{\frac{a(1+c_1)}{a+c_1}}\right)$.

Due to $a > 1 \Rightarrow a + ac_1 < a^2 + ac_1 \Rightarrow \frac{a(1+c_1)}{a+c_1} < a$, we have

$$F_t(X) \sim O\left(n^{\frac{a(1+c_1)}{a+c_1}}\right) < f(X) \sim O(n^a)$$

Here, $t \sim O\left(n^{\frac{a}{a+c_1}}\right)$, let $t \sim O(n^b)$.

When $b \geq 1$, the order of $F_t(X)$ is minimal at $b = 1$ and equal to $O(n^{1+c_1})$.

When $0 < b < 1$, letting $b = \frac{a}{a+c_1}$, the order of its corresponding $F_t(X)$ is minimal and

equal to $O\left(n^{\frac{a(1+c_1)}{a+c_1}}\right)$. Since $c_1 > 0$, $\frac{a(1+c_1)}{a+c_1} < (1+c_1)$. So the order $O\left(n^{\frac{a(1+c_1)}{a+c_1}}\right)$ is less than

$O(n^{1+c_1})$.

Finally, when $0 < b$, letting $b = \frac{a}{a+c_1}$, the order of $F_t(X)$ is minimal and equal to

$$O\left(n^{\frac{a(1+c_1)}{a+c_1}}\right).$$

Proposition 2.8

If $f(X) \sim O(n^a)$, $a > 1$ $y = \alpha^h (h < 0)$ and $y = \alpha^h (h < 0)$, by letting $\alpha_i = (i)^{-c}$, $0 < c < 1$,
then $F_t(X)$ is divergent.

Proof:

From $\alpha_i = (i)^{-c}$, $0 < c < 1$, we have

$$\prod_{i=1}^{t} g_i = \prod_{i=1}^{t} \left(1 + (i)^{-c}\right) = B$$

$$\ln B = \sum_{i=1}^{t} \ln\left(1 + (i)^{-c}\right) \sim \sum_{i=1}^{t} (i)^{-c} \sim \int_{1}^{t} \frac{dx}{x^c} \sim t^{1-c}$$

From $t \sim O(n^b) \Rightarrow B \sim O(e^{n^{b(1-c)}})$, we obtain B is divergent so that $F_t(X)$ is divergent.

Proposition 2.9

If $f(X) \sim O(n^a)$, $a > 1$, $y = \alpha^h$, $(h < 0)$ and $t \sim O(n^b)$, then

(1) when $a > 2$, by letting $\alpha_i = \frac{1}{i}$, the order of $F_t(X)$ is less than that of $f(X)$.
(2) when $a \leq 2$, by letting $\alpha_i = \frac{1}{i}$, the order of $F_t(X)$ is not less than that of $f(X)$.

Proof:

From $\alpha_i = \frac{1}{i}$, we have

$$\prod_{i=1}^{t} g_i = \prod_{i=1}^{t} (1 + i^{-1}) = B$$

Taking the logarithm on both sides of the above formula, we have

$$\ln B = \sum_{i=1}^{t} \ln \left(1 + (i)^{-1}\right) \sim \sum_{i=1}^{t} (i)^{-1} \sim \int_{1}^{t} \frac{dx}{x} = \ln t$$

Thus, $B \sim O(t) \sim O(n^b)$

Substituting into Formula (2.4), we have

$$f_t(X) \sim O(tBf(X_1)) \sim O\left(n^b n^b n^{a(1-b)}\right) \sim O\left(n^{a(1-b)+2b}\right)$$

The order of the additional computation is $\sim O(n^{b(1-h)})$, since $c=1$, hence

$$F_t(X) = O\left(n^{a(1-b)+2b}\right) + O\left(n^{b(1-h)}\right)$$

For the order of $F_t(X)$ to reach the minimal,

$$\Leftrightarrow a(1 - b) + 2b = b(1 - h) \Leftrightarrow b = \frac{a}{a - 1 - h} \Rightarrow F_t(X) \sim O\left(n^{\frac{a(1-h)}{a-1-h}}\right)$$

For the order of $F_t(X)$ to be less than that of $f(x)$,

$$\Leftrightarrow \frac{a(1 - h)}{a - 1 - h} < a \Leftrightarrow a(a - 2) > 0$$

Since $a > 1$, have $a > 2$. When $a > 2$, the order of $F_t(X)$ is less than that of $f(x)$. When $a \leq 2$, the order of $F_t(X)$ is not less than that of $f(x)$.

In summary, although the complexity estimation models we use are rather simple, the results of our analysis based on these models can completely answer the questions we raised at the beginning of this chapter. That is, in what conditions the multi-granular computing can reduce the computational complexity; under different situations, in what conditions the computational complexity can reach the minimal. These results provide a fundamental basis for multi-granular computing.

The results we have already had are summarized in Table 2.1, but only dealing with $f(\cdot) \geq O(n^a), a > 1$.

Applications

From the conclusions we made in Propositions 2.5–2.9, it is known that there indeed exist some proper multi-granular computing methods which can make the order of complexity

Table 2.1: The order of Computational Complexity at Different Cases

α_i	$f(x)$	$y = y(\alpha)$	t	$F_t(\cdot)$	Compared to $f(\cdot)$
$\alpha_i = i^{-c}$ $c > 1$	$f(\cdot) \geq O(n^a)$ $a > 1$	$y = \|\ln \alpha\|$	$O(n)$	$O(n \ln n)$	$<$
	$f(\cdot) = O(n^a)$ $a > 1$	$y = \alpha^h$ $h < 0$	$O(n^b)$	$b \geq 1$ $O(n^{b(1+c_1)})$ $c_1 = -ch$ $b = 1$ $O(n^{(1+c_1)})$	
				$0 < b < 1$ $b^* = \frac{a}{a+c_1}$ $O\left(n^{\frac{a(1+c_1)}{a+c}}\right)$	$<$
$\alpha_i = \frac{1}{i}$	$a > 2$	$y = \alpha^h$ $h < 0$	$O(n^b)$	$b^* = \frac{a}{1-h}$ $O\left(n^{\frac{a(1-h)}{a-1-h}}\right)$	$<$
	$1 \leq a \leq 2$				$\geq$

Where b^* is the optimal value of b.

$F_t(X)$ less than that of the original one $f(x)$. To the end, the condition needed is that the corresponding $\alpha(y_i) \to 0$ when the additional amount y_i of computation at each granular level increases. Namely, y_i should grow at a negatively polynomial rate with $\alpha(y_i)$, i.e., $\alpha^h(y_i), h < 0$. The problem is if there exists such a relation between y_i and $\alpha(y_i)$ objectively. We next discuss the problem.

Assume that $g(X_i, y_i) = 1 + \alpha(y_i)$ is the goal estimation function under the nondeterministic model with additional computation y_i. In order for $\alpha(y_i) \to 0$, if $t \sim O(n)$, then $|X_i| < c$ (constant) and the corresponding distribution function $p(x, y)$ at $x \neq 1$ has to be arbitrarily small. This is equivalent to the goal falling into a certain element with probability one when the additional computation y_i gradually increases. In statistical inference, it is known that so long as the sample size (or the stopping variable in the Wald sequential probabilistic ratio test) gradually increases the goal can always be detected within a certain element with probability one. Therefore, if regarding the sample size as the additional amount of computation, there exist several statistical inference methods which have the relation $y \sim O(|\ln \alpha|)$, where the meaning of α is the same as that of the α in the formula $g(X_i, y_i) = 1 + \alpha(y_i)$. Then, from Proposition 2.5, it shows that if a proper statistical inference method is applied to multi-granular computing methods, the order of complexity $F_t(X)$ can reach $O(n \ln n)$ regardless of the form of the original complexity $f(X)$.

Tree search is a typical example of multi-granular computing as mentioned in Chapter 1, where $t \sim O(n)$ and $|X_i| \leq m$, m is the branching factor of the tree. It is expected that tree search will benefit from introducing statistical inference methods to search. More details will be presented in Chapter 6.

2.2.4 Successive Operation in Multi-Granular Computing

From the probabilistic model, it shows that some elements in a certain granular level which contain the goal can only be found with certain probability. It implies that the elements we have already found might not contain any goal. Thus, the mistakes should be corrected as soon as they are discovered. By tracing back, we can go back to some coarse granular level and begin a new round of computation. In our terminology, it is called successive operation. In Chapter 6, we'll show that under certain conditions, by successive operation the goal can be found with probability one but the order of complexity does not increase at all.

2.3 The Extraction of Information on Coarsely Granular Levels

Solving a problem in space (X, T, f) means investigating the attribute function of each element and the relationships among elements of X, i.e., the structure T, through analyzing and reasoning on domain X. If the multi-granular computing is adopted, the same attribute function f and structure T will be gained by analyzing and reasoning on a certain coarse granular world $[X]$ of X. Thus, $[f]$ and $[T]$ in space $([X][T][f])$ must represent f and T to some extent, respectively. In Chapter 2, we have already discussed how $[T]$ is induced from T when T is a topology or a semi-order. The construction of $[f]$ will be discussed in this section.

Generally, constructing $[f]$ from f is a domain-dependent problem. For example, when diagnosing an electronic instrument, our aim is to find the faulty element (or elements) of the instrument. The domain X is all electronic elements in the instrument. The attribute function $f(x)$ is the functional parameters of each element in X. The aim of the diagnosis is to find which $f(x)$ (or $f(x)$'s) is abnormal. In the case of the multi-granular diagnosis, the diagnosis first begins from a certain coarse granular level consisting of some components, for example, $X_1 = \{$power-supply, amplifier, output-unit$\}$. Thus, the attribute function $[f]$ is represented by the functional parameters of these components, for example, the voltage of power supply, the amplification of amplifier, etc. How to choose these parameters in order to have more information regarding the fault of elements in X can be handled by an experienced troubleshooter easily. A knowledge-driven approach is generally adopted by many troubleshooters.

The construction of $[f]$ still has some general principles. We next discuss these principles.

From the analysis of computational complexity above, we know that the relation between the goal estimation function and additional computation y is $g(X, y) = 1 + \alpha(y)$, where the form of $\alpha(y)$ affects the computational complexity directly. If constructing a hierarchical structure (or $[f]$) such that $y = |\ln \alpha|$, the complexity will be reduced to $O(n \ln n)$ by the multi-granular computing. Conversely, if constructing a hierarchical structure (or $[f]$) such that $y = \alpha^h (h < 0)$, generally, only the polynomial complexity can be obtained by using multi-granular computing. At worst, if an improper structure (or [*f*]) is constructed, the computational complexity may not be reduced.

The preceding discussion implies that the multi-granular computing does not necessarily bring up high efficiency. The key is to construct a proper hierarchical structure. Generally, in multi-granular computing we follow the following principle. When a new problem space $([X][T][f])$ is constructed from the original one (X, T, f), we expect to get from the former as more useful information regarding the latter as possible while keeping the new problem space simple.

Here, we propose a general principle for constructing quotient space. It is called 'homomorphism principle'.

Homomorphism Principle

If there is a solution of problem p in space (X, T, f), i.e., p is true, then a solution of corresponding problem [*p*] in $([X][T][f])$ also exists, i.e., [*p*] is also true. In other words, if there is no solution of [*p*] in $([X][T][f])$, then there is no solution of p in (X, T, f) either.

It seems that the homomorphism principle above is used extensively in our everyday life. Some examples are given below.

Example 2.7

Making an annual production plan, one first makes quarterly plans then monthly plans within each quarter and daily plans, etc., hierarchically.

Obviously, if there is an annual plan satisfying some given conditions, there exist quarterly plans, monthly plans and daily plans which satisfy the given conditions.

Conversely, if there is no quarterly plan, monthly plan or daily plan which satisfies the conditions, the annual plan cannot be worked out.

Example 2.8

In a find-path planning of an indoor robot, if the robot environment is rather complicated, it would be difficult to find a collision-free path at once by considering all the details of the whole environment. The path planning might have two levels. The first one, referred to as INTERROOM plan, is the planning of navigation from room to room without considering any details within the rooms. The second level, called INROOM plan, is the level of planning robot movements within the rooms.

It is obvious that if we cannot find a path from room to room, the entire path planning must fail.

We have seen that by the 'homomorphism principle', if we fail to find a solution in some parts of a coarse space, the corresponding parts of the original fine space have no solution either and can be pruned off. Clearly, through each granular level computing the search space is narrowed down. We now come to the key issue in our multi-granular computing. Whether the computational complexity can be reduced depends on how much search space is narrowed down through each granular level computing and how much additional computation is needed in order to have such a reduction. This is just the consideration that we need in constructing [f].

2.3.1 Examples

Before going deeply into the approaches to constructing [f], let us now examine some examples.

Example 2.9

In a national economy developing plan, if factories, mines and enterprises are elements of domain X, and $f(x), x \in X$, x indicates the annual output value of these units. By hierarchical partition, some factories or enterprises compose a department A. The annual output value $[f](A)$ of each department A, certainly, is defined as

$$[f](A) = \sum_{x \in A} f(x)$$

If $f(x), x \in X$ indicates the productivity of each factory, the productivity for A is defined as

$$[f](A) = \{f(x), \text{ the mean value at } x \in A\}$$

Example 2.10

When throwing a ball upwards, $f(x) = (s(x), v(x))$ represents the attributes of the ball's motion at moment $x \in [t_0, t_2]$, where $s(x)$ is the distance of the ball from the ground, $v(x)$ is its velocity and $[t_0, t_2]$ is a time interval.

If we are only interested in the qualitative attributes of the motion, i.e., whether the ball goes upwards or downwards, or static, then time interval $X = [t_0, t_2]$ is partitioned into five parts as follows.

$$A_0 = \{t_0\}, A_1 = (t_0, t_1), A_2 = \{t_1\}, A_3 = (t_1, t_2), A_4 = \{t_2\}$$

where, $v(t_1) = 0$.

Let $[f](A_i) = (s_i, v_i), i = 0, 1, 2, 3, 4$

where, $s_i \in \{0, +\}$, $v_i \in \{-, 0, +\}$, and $s_i = 0$ denotes that the ball is on the ground, $s_i = +$ above the ground, $v_i = +$ goes upwards, $v_i = -$ goes downwards, and $v_i = 0$ static. It is easy to have

$$[f](A_0) = (0, +), [f](A_1) = (+, +), [f](A_2) = (+, 0), [f](A_3) = (+, -), [f](A_4) = (0, 0)$$

Note that the range of function $[f]$ is defined on some quotient set $[Y]$ rather than $Y(f : X \to Y)$. That is, partitioning Y into several equivalence classes and giving each equivalence class a symbolic name, the range of $[f]$ is just a set of these names. Sometime, it's called a qualitative description of $[f]$.

In summary, assume that $f(x)$ $(f : X \to Y)$ is known. $f(x)$ represents some attribute of element $x \in A$. The point is how to choose the value of $[f](A)$ that can properly mirror the feature of the whole set A representing by the attribute $f(x)$ and satisfies the homomorphism principle above. Generally, $[f](A)$ may be a value from Y or $[Y]$.

More generally, given some local information of a set, we want to find the global information such that it can depict the features of the whole set. For example, the feature extraction of images in pattern recognition is somewhat similar to the above problem, where $f(x)$ (color, gray-level) is extracted from each pixel x, while $[f]$ represents the feature of regions or the whole image. We next present some common approaches to constructing function $[f](A)$.

2.3.2 Constructing [f] Under Unstructured Domains

Starting from the domains X where elements are independent or near-independent of each other, we call it unstructured domains.

In terms of statistics, this amounts to 'mutually independent' assumption for random variables. In topological terminology, it is equivalent to 'discrete topology.' So unstructured is a special structure.

1. (X, f, T) is a space, where T is a discrete topology and $f : X \to R^n$, R^n is an n-dimensional Euclidean space. Assume that R is an equivalence relation on X. The corresponding quotient space is $[X]$. $[f]$ is an attribute function on $[X]$.

   (1) Statistical method

   Since X is unstructured, $[f](A)$ depends on $\{f(x) | x \in A\}$ completely. From statistics, attribute $\{f(x) | x \in A\}$ of X can be regarded as a set of mutually independent random variables. Thus, attribute $[f](A)$ of $[X]$ can be defined as some kind of statistics.

   (2) Inclusion principle

   If $f(A) = \{f(x) | x \in A\}$, define $[f](A)$ as a specific point within $C_0(f(A))$ where $C_0(B)$ is a convex closure of B. For example,

$[f](A) = $ the mean of $f(x)$ on A,

$$[f](A) = \sup_{x \in A} f(x)$$

$$[f](A) = \inf_{x \in A} f(x)$$

$[f](A) = $ the center of gravity of $C_0(f(A))$, etc.

In Section 2.3.1, many examples for extracting $[f](A)$ belong to the inclusion principle.

  (3) Combination principle

If A is a finite set, $[f]$ can be defined as follows

$[f](A) = g(f(x), x \in A)$, where g is an arbitrary combination function, for example, $[f](A) = \sum_{x \in A} f(x)$.

2. $f : X \to Y$ is a set-valued function, i.e., $\forall x \in X, f(x)$ is a subset of Y.

  (1) Intersection or union method

$$[f](A) = \bigcap_{x \in A} f(x) \text{ or } [f](A) = \bigcup_{x \in A} f(x)$$

If Y is a complete semi-order lattice, then $\bigcap_{x \in A} f(x)$ and $[f](A) = \inf_{x \in A} f(x)$ or $\bigcup_{x \in A} f(x)$ and $[f](A) = \sup_{x \in A} f(x)$ are equivalent. The method is equal to the inclusion principle in 1.

An example is given below.

Assume that $A = \{$a set of quadrilaterals on a plane$\} = \{a_1, a_2, a_3, a_4, \ldots\}$

$a_1 = \{$a set of squares$\}$, $a_2 = \{$a set of rectangles$\}$,

$a_3 = \{$a set of diamonds$\}$, $a_4 = \{$a set of parallel quadrilaterals$\}$,...

Let

$f(a_1) = \{$four edges are equal, four angles are equal, the sum of all inner angles is $2\pi,\ldots\}$,

$f(a_2) = \{$two mutually opposite edges are equal, four angles are rectangle, the sum of all inner angles is $2\pi,\ldots\}$,

$f(a_3) = \{$four edges are equal, two mutually opposite angles are equal, the sum of all inner angles is $2\pi,\ldots\}$,

$f(a_4) = \{$two mutually opposite edges are equal, two mutually opposite angles are equal, the sum of all inner angles is $2\pi,\ldots\}$,....

Now, we can use $f(a_i), \ i = 1, 2, \ldots$ to define $[f](A)$, for example,

$$[f](A) = \bigcap_{a_i \in A} f(a_i).$$

  (2) Quotient space method

Assume that $f : X \to Y$ is an attribute function on X, $[Y]$ quotient space is constructed from Y, and $[X]$ is a quotient space of X.

For $A \in [X]$, define $[f](A)$ as
$$[f](A) = p(f(A)), \text{ where } f(A) \subset Y, p : Y \to [Y].$$

Thus, $p(f(A))$ represents the image of $f(A)$ on $[Y]$ via natural projection p. The range of $[f](A)$ is $[Y]$.

From Example 2.10 in Section 2.3.1, we know that when throwing a ball upwards, $f(x) = (s(x), v(x)), f : X \to R^+ \times R$, where $R^+ = [0, \infty), R = (-\infty, \infty)$.

In qualitative analysis, R^+ is partitioned into $b_1 = \{0\}$ and $b_2 = (0, \infty)$, simply, b_1 denotes as '0' and b_2 as '+', respectively. R is partitioned into $C_1 = (-\infty, 0), C_2 = \{0\}$, and $C_3 = (0, \infty)$, simply, C_1 as '0', C_2 as '$-$', and C_3 as '+', respectively. Defining $[f](A_i) = p(f(A_i))$, we then have the same results as shown in Example 2.10 of Section 2.3.1. Using the elements (or subsets) in quotient space $[Y]$ to describe $[f]$ is a useful method in qualitative reasoning especially. We'll discuss the problem in Chapter 4.

2.3.3 Constructing [f] Under Structured Domains

Under the structured domains, the values of $f(x)$ that correspond to different element x are interdependent and are related to structure T. So from structure T, we can have some knowledge about $f(x)$. Generally, structure T may be classified into three main classes below.

(1) T is a topologic structure. For example, X is an n-dimensional Euclidean space. Then the Euclidean distance is its topologic structure T. Generally speaking, any metric space is an instantiation of topologic structures.
(2) Defining a semi-order relation on X, we have a semi-order structure T. Anyway, we can introduce a corresponding semi-order to any system which can be represented by a directed acyclic graph. Hence, semi-order relation represents a wide range of structures in real world.
(3) The structure of X can be induced by some operations defined on X. For example, given a unary operator $p : X \to Y$, i.e., $p(x) = y$, it implies that a relation between elements x and $y = p(x)$ is established. Linking these two elements by a directed edge, we define a directed graph corresponding to operator p. And, the directed graph determines a corresponding pseudo semi-order relation as well. If p is a multivariate operator on X, $p(x_1, x_2, ..., x_n) = y$, it can also be represented by a graph. For example, each x_i, $i = 1, 2, ..., n$ connects to y with a directed edge. And the n directed edges connected to y are linked by a curved arc. Then, we have a graph corresponding to p and it is somewhat similar to an AND/OR graph or a hyper-graph. From the graph, we can define its structure, T. So the relation among elements can be defined by multivariate operation p as well.

This section only tackles the problem of constructing $[f]$ under topologic structures. For semi-order structures, see discussion in Chapter 3.

Assume that (X, T) and (Y, T_1) are two topologic spaces. $f : (X, T) \rightarrow (Y, T_1)$ is an attribute function on X. The continuity of f is a key issue in analyzing the properties of (X, T). For example, we are given a premise s_0, in order to affirm if the conclusion s_N holds or not, our objective is to determine if there exists a sequence $s_0 \rightarrow s_1 \cdots \rightarrow s_N$ of reasoning steps from s_0 to s_N. If so, the conclusion s_N holds, otherwise, s_N does not hold. This is similar to the concept of 'path-connected' in topology. We show the concept as follows. If $x_0, x_N \in A$, there exist $x_1, x_2, ..., x_n = x_N$ such that each line segment $[x_i, x_{i+1}]$, $i = 0, 1, ..., n - 1$ belongs to A, then x_0 and x_N are said to be path-connected in A. Therefore, by introducing a proper topology T into X, the problem that if s_0 can infer s_N is transformed to that of whether s_0 and s_N belong to the same path-connected component. In Section 2.5, we'll discuss the problem in more details.

Generally, X is rather complicated. It is not easy to judge whether any two given points belong to the same path-connected component. By using transformation function $f : X \rightarrow Y$, the problem can be transferred into an easier one if the structure of Y is simpler than X. Obviously; we expect that if set $A \subset X$ is a connected, the transformed set $f(A) \subset Y$ is still connected. From topology, we know that if $A \subset X$ is a connected set, the image $f(A)$ of A is also a connected set in Y when f is continuous. Once again it shows that the continuity of function f is a very significant property.

By partitioning (X, T) we have a quotient space $([X], [T])$. From f we induce a function $[f] : [X] \rightarrow Y$ on $[X]$. Obviously, we expect that $[f]$ would still be continuous. Unfortunately, it is not true generally. Even so we expect that $[f]$ still remains some weaker continuity than the strict one in favor of the analysis.

1.   Constructing $[f] : [X] \rightarrow Y$

First, we introduce some concepts below.

Definition 2.5

Assume that (X, d) is a metric space. Let $d(A) = \sup\limits_{x, y \in A} d(x, y)$, $A \subset X$.

$d(A)$ is said to be a diameter of A.

Definition 2.6

R is an equivalence relation on (X, d). Let $d(R) = \sup\limits_{a \in [X]} d(a)$, where $[X]$ is a quotient space corresponding to R. $d(R)$ is said to be fineness of R. Intuitively, $d(R)$ can be regarded as 'the maximal diameter' of equivalence classes corresponding to R.

Definition 2.7

Assume that $f : (X, d) \rightarrow (Y, d_1)$, R is an equivalence relation on (X, d), and $[X]$ is a quotient space under R. Let $d(R, f) = \sup\limits_{a \in [X]} d_1(f(a))$. $d(R, f)$ is said to be fineness of R with respect to f.

Definition 2.8

Assume that $f : (X, d) \rightarrow (Y, d_1)$. Let $M = \sup\limits_{\substack{x,y \in X \\ x \neq y}} \frac{d_1(f(x), f(y))}{d(x,y)}$. M is called the ratio of expansion and contraction of f, or simply REC.

Definition 2.9

Assume that $f : (X, T) \rightarrow (Y, d)$, where (Y, d) is a metric space. Given a positive constant α, if $\forall x \in X$ there exists an open set $u(x)$ such that $f(u(x)) \subset B(f(x), \alpha)$. f is said to be α-continuous on X, where $B(f(x), \alpha) = \{y | d(f(x), y) < \alpha\}$.

Proposition 2.10

Assume that $f : (X, d_1) \rightarrow (Y, d_2)$ is a continuous function, $[X]$ is a quotient space of X. Define $[f] : [X] \rightarrow (Y, d_2)$ as $\forall a \in [X], [f](a) \in f(a)$, where $f(a) = \{f(x) | x \in a\}$.

Suppose that M is a REC of f and the fineness of $[X]$ is l. Given $\alpha > 2Ml$, we obtain that $[f] \circ p$ is a α-continuous function on X, where $p : X \rightarrow [X]$ is a natural projection function.

Proof:

$\forall x \in X$, $\forall \varepsilon > 0$, from the continuity of f, there exist $\delta(x)$ and $B(x, \delta(x))$ such that $f(B(x, \delta(x))) \subset B(f(x), \varepsilon)$.

Since the fineness of $[X]$ is l, we can write the diameter of $p(B(x, \delta(x))) \leq 2l + \delta(x)$.

From the REC M of f, we have the diameter of $f(p^{-1}(p(B(x, \delta(x))))) \leq M(2l + \delta(x))$

From the definition of $[f]$, we obtain

$$[f](a) \in f(p^{-1}(p(B(x, \delta(x))))), a \in p(B(x, \delta(x)))$$

That is

$$[f] \circ p(B(x, \delta(x))) \subset B(f(x), M(2l + \delta(x)))$$

Given $\alpha > 2Ml$, by letting $\delta(x)$ be small enough such that $\alpha > M(2l + \delta(x))$, we have that $[f] \circ p$ is α-continuous at x. $[f] \circ p$ is α-continuous on X.

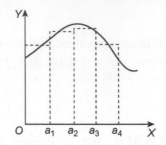

Figure 2.1: α-Continuous Function

Example 2.11

As shown in Fig. 2.1, $f : X \rightarrow Y$ is a continuous function.

Assume that $|f| \leq M$. Axis X is partitioned into several intervals equally, each interval a_i with length $\leq l$. If using a step function as follows

$f_1(x) = y_i$, $\forall x \in a_i$, $y_i \in \{f(x)|x \in a_i\}$, from Proposition 2.10, we can see that f_1 is $2Ml$-continuous on X.

Proposition 2.10 indicates that under quotient space transformation the continuity of the transformed function does not always hold but α-continuity, a weak continuity, is preserved. It implies that if viewing from a coarse granular level, the properties of the original function become rough (fuzzy). Intuitively, it may be likened to copperplate etching technique. The coarser the etching grain-size of a copper plate the rougher its image.

Generally speaking, instead of some attribute f in the original space, a new attribute α_f can be used for describing the corresponding one in its quotient space. In order to transform the original attribute function f into α_f, it is needed to redefine the function. As we know, the original function $f(x)$ is defined on 'all neighborhoods of x' or 'a neighborhood existed in x', we now need to redefine α-$f(x)$ on 'a fixed α-neighborhood of x' or 'some fixed neighborhood of x'. This idea has also been used in the mathematical morphology method of pattern recognition (Serra, 1982).

We might as well try to analyze two basic operations in mathematical morphology from our granular computing point of view.

Definition 2.10

Assume that X is a domain. $A \subset X$, $\forall x \in X$, a corresponding subset $B(x)$ is given on X. $B(x)$ is called a structural element with respect to x. Define

$$\text{Dilation}(A) = \{x|B(x) \cap A \neq \varnothing\}, \text{ or simply } D(A).$$
$$\text{Erosion}(A) = \{x|B(x) \subset A\}, \text{ or simply } E(A).$$

$D(A)$ is called a dilation of A with respect to $B(x)$. $E(A)$ is called an erosion of A with respect to $B(x)$.

Dilation and erosion are two basic operations in mathematical morphology. Any morphological transformation can be obtained through union, intersection and deference of these two operations.

In topology, the minimal closed set containing A is called a closure of A denoted by $\overline{A}$ and is defined as:

$$\overline{A} = \{x \,|\, \forall v(x) \text{ such that } v(x) \cap A \neq \varnothing\}$$

where, $v(x)$ is an open set containing x.

Accordingly, given a set A, the maximal open set being contained by A is called an inner-kernel of A and denoted by $\overset{\circ}{A}$. Mathematically, the definition is as follows:

$$\overset{\circ}{A} = \{x \,|\, \text{there exists } v(x) \text{ such that } v(x) \subset A\}$$

Either closure or inner-kernel operation can be used for defining a topologic structure of a space. Hence, closure and inner-kernel operations are two basic operations in topology.

It is clear that both $\overline{A}$ and $D(A)$ are quite similar. So long as replacing '$\forall v(x)$ ' (in the definition) by a fixed subset $B(x)$, the concept $\overline{A}$ becomes $D(A)$. So the concept $D(A)$ is equivalent to 'α-closure'. The same is true for the relation between $\overset{\circ}{A}$ and $E(A)$. Thus, $E(A)$ is equivalent to 'α-inner kernel'.

We know that $D(A)$ and $E(A)$ are the rough descriptions of closure $\overline{A}$ and inner-kernel $\overset{\circ}{A}$ in the coarse granular level, respectively. The aim of mathematical morphology is to extract some essential characteristics of images while ignoring their details. This is identical with the 'α-**' concept. As J. Serra pointed out 'The images under study exhibit too much information and the goal of any morphological treatment is to manage the loss of information through the successive transformations' (Serra, 1982). The multi-granular computing is similar to the above idea.

The concept of 'α-**' is an outcome of hierarchy. The similarity between the concept of 'α-**' and the concept of dilation (or erosion) in mathematic morphology indicates that our quotient structure model can be extended to more general cases.

When space X is transformed to its quotient space $[X]$, i.e., $x \to p(x)$, where p is a natural projection, the attribute '**' becomes 'α-**'. Similarly, when $x \to B(x)$, where $B(x)$ is a subset of X, the $\overline{A}$ (or $\overset{\circ}{A}$) becomes $D(A)$ (or $E(A)$). In this case, if X is an original space, $\{B(x) \,|\, x \in X\}$ can be regarded as a 'quotient space' of X by considering each $B(x)$ as an element.

Definition 2.11

Assume that (X, d) is a metric space. If X cannot be represented by the union of two non-empty sets A and B that satisfy the following condition (2.9)

$$\overline{B}\left(A, \frac{l}{2}\right) \cap \overline{B}\left(B, \frac{l}{2}\right) = \varnothing, \tag{2.9}$$

where

$$B\left(A, \frac{l}{2}\right) = \left\{y \mid \exists x \in A, d(x, y) < \frac{l}{2}\right\}, \ \overline{B}\left(A, \frac{l}{2}\right) \ \text{is the closure of} \ B\left(A, \frac{l}{2}\right),$$

then X is said to be l-connected.

Property 2.1

Assume that $f : (X, d) \to (Y, d_1)$, R is an equivalence relation on X, and $d(R) = l$. The ratio of expansion and contraction (or REC) of f is M. We have:

$$d(R, f) \leq Ml$$

Proof:

From the definitions of l, M and $d(R, f)$, we have the proof directly.

Theorem 2.1

Assume that $f : (X, d) \to (Y, d_1)$ is continuous, X is connected, R is an equivalence relation on X, and $d(R) = l$. The REC of f is M. Define

$$[f] : [X] \to Y, \ \forall a \in [X], [f](a) \in \{f(x) \mid x \in a\}$$

That is, we take on $f(x)$ at any point $x \in a$ as the value of $[f]$ at point $a \in [X]$. Thus, $[f]([X])$ is $2Ml$-connected.

Proof:

Let $d = 2Ml$. From Property 2.1, we have $d(R, f) \leq Ml = \frac{d}{2}$.

Reduction to absurdity, assume that $[f]([X])$ is not d-connected. Letting $D = [f]([X])$, there exist non-empty sets A and B that satisfy (Fig. 2.2):

$$D = A \cup B \quad \text{and} \quad \overline{B}\left(A, \frac{d}{2}\right) \cap \overline{B}\left(B, \frac{d}{2}\right) = \varnothing.$$

$$\text{Let} \ A_1 = [f]^{-1}(A), A_2 = p^{-1}(A_1) \subset X$$
$$B_1 = [f]^{-1}(B), B_2 = p^{-1}(B_1) \subset X$$

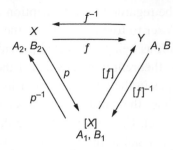

Figure 2.2: *I*-Connected Graph

We first show that

$$\forall x \in A_2 \Rightarrow f(x) \in B\left(A, \frac{d}{2}\right)$$

Since

$$x \in A_2 \Rightarrow [x] \in A_1$$

$$\Rightarrow [f]([x]) = f(x_1) \in A, x_1 \in [x] \Rightarrow d_1(f(x), [f]([x])) = d_1(f(x), f(x_1)) \le \frac{d}{2}$$

That is,

$$f(x) \in \overline{B}\left(A, \frac{d}{2}\right) \Rightarrow f(\Lambda_2) \in \overline{B}\left(A, \frac{d}{2}\right)$$

Similarly

$$\forall x \in B_2 \Rightarrow f(x) \in \overline{B}\left(B, \frac{d}{2}\right) \Rightarrow f(B_2) \in \overline{B}\left(B, \frac{d}{2}\right)$$

Since $\overline{B}(A, \frac{d}{2}) \cap \overline{B}(B, \frac{d}{2}) = \varnothing \Rightarrow A_2 \cap B_2 = \varnothing$ and $X = A_2 \cup B_2 \Rightarrow A_2 = B_2^c$, by letting $X = A_2 \cup B_2 \Rightarrow A_2 = B_2^c$, again from $D = A \cup B \Rightarrow X = D_1 \cup D_2$ and $B_2 \subset f^{-1}f(B_2) \subset f^{-1}\left(\overline{B}(B, \frac{d}{2})\right) = D_2$, we have $B_2 \cap D_1 = \varnothing$.

Similarly, we have $A_2 \cap D_2 = \varnothing$.

From $X = A_2 \cup B_2 \Rightarrow A_2 = D_1, B_2 = D_2$. $\overline{B}(A, \frac{d}{2})$ and $\overline{B}(B, \frac{d}{2})$ are closed sets and f is continuous, we know that D_1 and D_2 are closed on X. Therefore, $\Rightarrow X = A_2 \cup B_2$, where A_2 and B_2 are non-empty closed sets and $A_2 \cap B_2 = \varnothing$. Thus, X is not connected, which contradicts the assumption that X is connected.

Consequently, $[f]([X])$ is d-connected.

The concept of d-connected can be regarded as a description of the degree of connectivity of a set. The smaller the d, the closer to true connectivity the d-connectivity is. In other words, regarding any two sets on X as being connected provided their distance is less than d, then we have d-connected. The theorem indicates that if the REC of f is fixed, the roughness of connectivity of images in the coarse granular level is inversely proportional to the fineness of R. That is, the finer the partition, the less rough (finer) the connectivity of images in the coarse granular level. Conversely, keeping the fineness of R fixed, the roughness of connectivity is proportional to the REC of f. That is, the larger the REC the rougher the connectivity of the mapped images. The above intuition can accurately be proved by our quotient space model.

Obviously, the concept of d-connectivity is an instantiation of the concept of 'α-**' that we mentioned before. After the partition, some information must be lost in coarse granular levels. Generally, it is hard to preserve the original attributes (e.g., continuity, connectivity, etc.) of the original space. By introducing the concept of 'α-**' attributes, weaken attributes, the original attributes will remain valid in a relaxed sense. This will provide a useful clue to the analysis of coarse granular levels.

For some concept such as connectivity in topology, a set either is connected or not. Either of the two facts must be true. By introducing 'd-connectivity', the different degrees of connectivity can be described. This is just like the concept of membership functions in fuzzy mathematics. The concept of 'α-**' attributes that we presented here virtually relates our methodology to that of fuzzy mathematics. It makes granular computing more powerful.

2. Constructing $[f] : [X] \to [Y]$

In the preceding section, we know that the value of $[f]$ can also be represented in quotient space $[Y]$ of Y. We next present its properties.

Assume that (X, T) and (Y, T_1) are topologic spaces, $f : (X, T) \to (Y, T_1)$ is a one-to-one corresponding function, R is an equivalence relation on X. $[X]$ is a quotient space of X with respect to R.

Definition 2.12

Define an equivalence relation R_1 on Y such that:

$$\forall x, y \in Y, x R_1 y \Leftrightarrow f^{-1}(x) R f^{-1}(y)$$

That is, x and y are equivalent on Y if and only if the original images of x and y are equivalent on X. R_1 is said to be an equivalence relation on Y induced from R via f or an induced equivalence relation from R.

Conversely, if R_1 is an equivalence relation on Y, define an equivalence relation on X such that

$$\forall x, y \in X, xRy \Leftrightarrow f(x)R_1 f(y)$$

R is said to be an equivalence relation on X induced from R_1 via f or an induced equivalence relation from R_1, where f is not necessarily one-to-one correspondent.

Lemma 2.1

Assume that (X, T) and (Y, T_1) are topologic spaces, $f : (X, T) \rightarrow (Y, T_1)$, R is an equivalence relation on X, R_1 is an equivalence relation on Y induced from R. Let $[X]$ and $[Y]$ be quotient spaces corresponding to R and R_1, respectively. Define

$$\forall a \in [X], [f] : [X] \rightarrow [Y], [f](a) \in p_1(f(a))$$

where $p : X \rightarrow [X]$ and $p_1 : Y \rightarrow [Y]$ are natural projections. Then, for $\forall A \subset [Y]$, we have $f^{-1}(p_1^{-1}(A)) = p^{-1}p(f^{-1}(p_1^{-1}(A)))$.

Proof:

Obviously, $f^{-1}(p_1^{-1}(A)) \subset p^{-1}p(f^{-1}(p_1^{-1}(A)))$.

Conversely,

$$\forall x \notin f^{-1}(p_1^{-1}(A)) \Rightarrow y = f(x) \notin p_1^{-1}(A)$$
$$\Rightarrow \forall y_1 \in p_1^{-1}(A), \ y_1 \text{ and } y \text{ are not } R_1 \text{ equivalent.}$$
$$\Rightarrow \forall x_1, f(x_1) = y_1 (y_1 \in p_1^{-1}(A)), \ x_1 \text{ and } x \text{ are not } R \text{ equivalent.}$$
$$\Rightarrow x \notin p^{-1}p(f^{-1}(p_1^{-1}(A)))$$
$$\Rightarrow p^{-1}p(f^{-1}(p_1^{-1}(A))) \subset f^{-1}(p_1^{-1}(A))$$
$$\Rightarrow f^{-1}(p_1^{-1}(A)) = p^{-1}p(f^{-1}(p_1^{-1}(A)))$$

We have that $f^{-1}(p_1^{-1}(A))$ is a set composed by elements of $[X]$, where the element of $[X]$ is a subset of X.

Theorem 2.2

Assume that (X, T) and (Y, T_1) are topologic spaces, R is an equivalence relation on X, R_1 is an equivalence relation on Y induced from R, $[X]$ and $[Y]$ are quotient spaces with respect to R and R_1, respectively, $f : X \rightarrow Y$ is a continuous function. Let $[f]$ be $\forall a \in [X], [f][a] \in p_1(f(a))$, where $p : X \rightarrow [X]$ and $p_1 : Y \rightarrow [Y]$ are projection functions. Thus, $[f] : ([X], [T]) \rightarrow ([Y], [T_1])$ is continuous.

Proof:

For $\forall a \in [X]$, assume that v is an arbitrary neighborhood of $[f](a)$. Let $u = f^{-1}(v)$. Regarding v as a set of Y, it is open. Since f is continuous, we know that u is an open set on X. From Lemma 2.1, we can see that u is a set on $[X]$. Thus, together with the definition of quotient topology, it implies that u is a neighborhood of a. From the definition $[f](u) \subset p_1(f(u)) = p_1(f(f^{-1}(v))) \subset p_1(v) = v$, we have that $[f]$ is continuous at a. That is, $[f] : [X] \to [Y]$ is continuous.

Corollary 2.1

If R_1 is an equivalence relation on Y and R is an equivalence relation on X induced from R_1. $f : X \to Y$ is continuous. Then $[f] : ([X], [T]) \to ([Y], [T_1])$, for $\forall a \in [X], [f][a] \in p_1(f(a))$ is continuous.

Theorem 2.2 presents another approach for constructing function $[f]$. It has a wide-ranging application, for example, qualitative reasoning in AI. We next analyze the Example 2.11 in Section 2.3.1.

When an object is thrown upwards, its state at moment x can be represented by $f(x) = (s(x), v(x))$, where $s(x)$ and $v(x)$ indicate its distance from the ground and velocity at moment x, respectively. Now only the qualitative properties of its state are paid attention to. The range $[0, \infty)$ of $s(x)$ is partitioned into two classes $\{0\}$ and $(0, \infty)$. While the range $(-\infty, \infty)$ of $v(x)$ is divided into three classes $\{0\}$, $(-\infty, 0)$, and $(0, \infty)$. $f(x)$ is regarded as a continuous function on $X = [t_0, t_2] \to Y = R^+ \times R$. The preceding partition corresponds to an equivalence relation R_1 on Y. From Theorem 2.2, in order to construct $[f]$, we need an equivalence relation on X induced from R_1.

R^+ is partitioned into $\{0\}$ and $(0, \infty)$, R' is its induced equivalence relation on X. Then, R': $\{t_0, t_2\} = f_1^{-1}(\{0\}), (t_0, t_2) = f_1^{-1}((0, \infty))$.

R is partitioned into $(-\infty, 0)$, $\{0\}$ and $(0, \infty)$, R'' is its induced equivalence relation on X. Then,

$$R'': (t_1, t_2) = f_2^{-1}((-\infty, 0)), \quad [t_0, t_1) = f_2^{-1}((0, \infty)), \quad \{t_0, t_2\} = f_2^{-1}(\{0\}),$$

where f_1^{-1} indicates the inverse transformation of the first component of f,

f_2^{-1} indicates the inverse transformation of the second component of f.

The combination equivalence relation of R' and R'' is R_0 and

$$R_0 : \{t_0\}, \{t_1\}, \{t_2\}, (t_0, t_1), (t_1, t_2)$$

Let $[X]$ and $[Y]$ be quotient spaces with respect to R_0 and R_1, respectively. From Theorem 2.2, we know that $[f] : [f](a) \in p_1(f(a)), a \in [x]$, where $p_1 : Y \to [Y]$ is a projection function, and $[f]$ is a continuous function of $([X], [T]) \to ([Y], [T_1])$.

If the first component $\{0\}$, $(0, \infty)$ of $[Y]$ is named as '0', '+'; the second component $(-\infty, 0)$, $\{0\}$ and $(0, \infty)$ of $[Y]$ as '−', '0' and '+', we have $[f]((t_1, t_2)) = (+, -)$,

$[f]({t_1}) = (+, 0)$, etc. These results are consistent with that shown in Example 2.11 of Section 2.3.1.

From our quotient space model, a strong property of $[f]$ is discovered, that is, $[f]$ is a $([X], [T]) \rightarrow ([Y], [T_1])$ continuous function, if it is constructed in the way that we already showed. In the light of the result, we can see that this is one of the possible ways for partitioning X (or Y).

2.3.4 Conclusions

In this section, we have discussed how to establish a function $[f]$ on $[X]$ induced from f. When X is an unstructured domain, we presented four basic methods for constructing $[f]$, that is, statistics, closure, quotient space and combination methods. If X is a structured domain, only topologic structures and continuous function f are involved. When $[f]$ is a $[X] \rightarrow Y$ function, we introduced the concepts of $\alpha\_$continuity and $\alpha\_$connectivity and established the corresponding properties of $[f]$. When $[f]$ is a $[X] \rightarrow [Y]$ function, we presented an approach for constructing function $[f]$ which guarantees its continuity.

So far we have established all three elements of problem space $([X], [T], [f])$. Further discussion will be presented in Chapters 3 and 4.

2.4 Fuzzy Equivalence Relation and Hierarchy

In Chapter 1, we use the concept of quotient set in mathematics for establishing a multi-granular space. Our discussions have so far been limited to the partition of a domain so that each element belongs definitely to one and only one equivalence class. In reality, this is not always the case. Sometimes, the boundaries between two equivalence classes are not clear-cut. Two classes may have overlapped elements or their boundaries are fuzzy, i.e. the classification is fuzzy (Cheeseman, 1986; Nutter, 1987).

In clear-cut classification, we use equivalence relation R for establishing our model. A natural question is whether fuzzy equivalence relation can be used for constructing fuzzy classification model. We next try to do so. First, we introduce some concepts in fuzzy mathematics.

2.4.1 The Properties of Fuzzy Equivalence Relations

Definition 2.13

X is a domain. $\underset{\sim}{A}$ is a fuzzy set on X, that is, for $x \in X$ there must exist a fixed number $\mu_A(x) \in [0, 1]$ called a membership degree of x with respect to A. The mapping $\mu_A :$ $X \rightarrow [0, 1]$ or $x \mapsto \mu_A(x)$ is called a membership function of $\underset{\sim}{A}$.

More simply, any function $\mu : X \rightarrow [0, 1]$ defines a fuzzy subset on X. If $F(X)$ is a set of all fuzzy subsets on X, then $F(X)$ is a functional space consisting of all functions $\mu : X \rightarrow [0, 1]$.

Definition 2.14

$X \times X$ is a product space of X and X. For $\underset{\sim}{R} \in F(X \times X)$, $\underset{\sim}{R}$ is a fuzzy subset of $X \times X$, if it satisfies

(1) $\forall x \in X, \underset{\sim}{R}(x, x) = 1$
(2) $\forall x, y \in X, \underset{\sim}{R}(x, y) = \underset{\sim}{R}(y, x)$
(3) $\forall x, y, z$, we have $\underset{\sim}{R}(x, z) \geq \sup_{y}(\min(\underset{\sim}{R}(x, y), \underset{\sim}{R}(y, z)))$

$\underset{\sim}{R}$ is called a fuzzy equivalence relation on X.

If the value of $\underset{\sim}{R}(x, y)$ only takes on 0 or 1, $\underset{\sim}{R}$ is just the common equivalence relation that we have discussed in the preceding sections. Thus, $\underset{\sim}{R}(x, y)$ can be regarded as depicting the degree to which x and y are equivalent.

We now discuss the relationship between fuzzy equivalence relation and hierarchy.

Proposition 2.11

Assume that $\underset{\sim}{R}$ is a fuzzy equivalence relation on X. If we define

$$\forall x, y \in X, x \sim y \Leftrightarrow R(x, y) = 1,$$

then '$\sim$' is just a common equivalence relation on X. The corresponding quotient space is denoted by $[X]$.

Proof:

The reflexivity and symmetry of $\underset{\sim}{R}$ are obvious. We now prove its transitivity.

From $x \sim y, y \sim z \Rightarrow \underset{\sim}{R}(x, y) = 1$ and $\underset{\sim}{R}(y, z) = 1$, we have

$$\underset{\sim}{R}(x, z) \geq \min(\underset{\sim}{R}(x, y), \underset{\sim}{R}(y, z)) = 1 \Rightarrow x \sim z$$

Theorem 2.3

$\underset{\sim}{R}$ is a fuzzy equivalence relation on X. $[X]$ is a quotient space as defined in Proposition 2.11. Define $\forall a, b \in [X]$,

$$d(a, b) = 1 - \underset{\sim}{R}(x, y), \forall x \in a, y \in b \tag{2.10}$$

Then, $d(.,.)$ is a distance function on $[X]$.

Proof:

First, we show that $\forall y \in X, x_1, x_2 \in a \in [X]$, have $\underset{\sim}{R}(x_1, y) = \underset{\sim}{R}(x_2, y)$.

From the condition (3) in the definition of $\underset{\sim}{R}$, have

$$\underset{\sim}{R}(x_1, y) \geq \min(\underset{\sim}{R}(x_1, x_2), \underset{\sim}{R}(x_2, y)) = \min(1, \underset{\sim}{R}(x_2, y)) = \underset{\sim}{R}(x_2, y).$$

Similarly, $\underset{\sim}{R}(x_2, y) \geq \underset{\sim}{R}(x_1, y)$.

Then, $\underset{\sim}{R}(x_2, y) = \underset{\sim}{R}(x_1, y)$.

Therefore, $\forall y_1, y_2 \in b,\ x_1, x_2 \in a$ and $\underset{\sim}{R} = (x_1, y_1) = \underset{\sim}{R}(x_2, y_2)$.

Thus, $\forall a.b \in [X]$, a unique non-negative value $d(a, b)$ can be determined by Formula (2.10).

We show below that $d(.,.)$ is a distance function on $[X]$.

If $d(a, b) = 0$, i.e., $d(a, b) = 1 - \underset{\sim}{R}(x, y) = 0, x \in a, y \in b$, we have

$$\underset{\sim}{R}(x, y) = 1, \Rightarrow x \sim y, \text{ i.e., } a = b.$$

Secondly, from $\underset{\sim}{R}(x, y) = \underset{\sim}{R}(y, x)$, we have that d is symmetry.

Finally,

$$\forall x \in a, y \in b, z \in c, \text{ from } \underset{\sim}{R}(x, z) \geq \min(\underset{\sim}{R}(x, y), \underset{\sim}{R}(y, z))$$

$$\Rightarrow 1 - \underset{\sim}{R}(x, z) \leq 1 - \min(\underset{\sim}{R}(x, y), \underset{\sim}{R}(y, z))$$

$$\Rightarrow d(a, c) \leq (1 - \underset{\sim}{R}(x, y)) + (1 - \underset{\sim}{R}(y, z)) = d(a, b) + d(b, c)$$

That is, d satisfies the triangle inequality and $d(.,.)$ is a distance function. $([X], d)$ is a metric space.

The theorem shows that a fuzzy equivalence relation on X corresponds to a metric space on $[X]$. Then, a distance function on $[X]$ can be used to describe the relation between two elements on X. The nearer the distance between two elements the closer their relation is. This means that any tool for analyzing metric spaces can be used to fuzzy equivalence relations.

Definition 2.15

$\underset{\sim}{R}$ is a fuzzy equivalence relation on X. Metric space $([X], d)$ defined in Theorem 2.3 is called a quotient structure space with respect to $\underset{\sim}{R}$.

Definition 2.16

R is a fuzzy equivalence relation on X. Let

$$R_\lambda = \{(x,y) \mid \underset{\sim}{R}(x,y) \geq \lambda\}, 0 \leq \lambda \leq 1,$$

R_λ is a common equivalence relation on X, and is called a sectional relationship of $\underset{\sim}{R}$.

Let $X(\lambda)$ be a quotient space with respect to $\underset{\sim}{R}$.

From the definition, we have the following property.

$0 \leq \lambda_2 \leq \lambda_1 \leq 1 \Leftrightarrow R_{\lambda_2} < R_{\lambda_1} \Leftrightarrow X(\lambda_2)$ is a quotient set of $X(\lambda_1)$.

A family $\{X(\lambda) \mid 0 \leq \lambda \leq 1\}$ of quotient spaces composes an order-sequence under the inclusion relation of quotient sets. $\{X(\lambda) \mid 0 \leq \lambda \leq 1\}$ forms a hierarchical structure on X. Thus, a fuzzy equivalence relation on X corresponds to a hierarchical structure on X.

Theorem 2.3 states that from a fuzzy equivalence relation on X, a distance function can be defined on some quotient space $[X]$. Next, in Proposition 2.12, we will show conversely that from a distance function defined on $[X]$, a fuzzy equivalence relation on X can be obtained. That is, a fuzzy equivalence relation on X is equivalent to a distance defined on $[X]$.

First we introduce some basic concepts.

Definition 2.17

R is an equivalence relation on X. If $D \subset R$ satisfies: for $\forall a \in R$ there exist $x_1, x_2, ..., x_m \in X$ such that $(x_i, x_{i+1}) \in D, i = 1, 2, ..., m - 1$ and $a = (x_1, x_m)$, then D is said to be a base of D.

Conversely, given $D \subset X \times X$ and it satisfies for $\forall x \in X$, have (1) $(x, x) \in D$, and (2) $(x, y) \in D \Rightarrow (y, x) \in D$. Again define $R = \{(x, y) \mid$ there exist $x = x_1, x_2, ..., x_m = y$ such that $(x_i, x_{i+1}) \in D, i = 1, 2, ..., m - 1\}$.

R is an equivalence relation on X, and is called an equivalence relation induced from D, or an equivalence relation with as D its base.

We next show that R defined above is, indeed, an equivalence relation.

The reflexivity and symmetry of R are obvious.

Assume $a = (x, y) \in R, b = (y, z) \in R$, i.e., there exist $x = x_1, x_2, ..., x_m = y$ such that $(x_i, x_{i+1}) \in D, i = 1, 2, ..., m - 1$, and $y = y_1, y_2, ..., y_n = z, (y_j, y_{j+1}) \in D, j = 1, 2, ..., n - 1$.

Let $z_i = x_i, i = 1, 2, ..., m - 1, z_{m-1+i} = y_i, i = 1, 2, ..., n$.

We have $z_1 = x, z_{m+n-1} = z$, and $(z_i, z_{i+1}) \in D, i = 1, 2, ..., n + m - 2$.

Consequently, $(x, z) \in R$, i.e., R has transitivity.

R is an equivalence relation.

Example 2.13

Assume that X is a network. B is a set of edges. R is an equivalence relation with B as its base. The quotient space corresponding to R is a space with connected components of X as its elements.

Next, we discuss below that in what conditions a normalized distance can produce a corresponding fuzzy equivalence relation.

Definition 2.18

For a normalized metric space (X, d), i.e., $\forall a, b \in [X]$, $d(a, b) \leq 1$, if any triangle composed by any non-collinear three points on X is an isosceles triangle, and its congruent legs are the longest side of the triangle, the distance in the space is called the isosceles distance.

Proposition 2.12

$d(., .)$ is a normalized distance function on $[X]$, the quotient space of X. Assume that

$$B_\lambda = \{(x, y) | d(x, y) \leq \lambda, \lambda \geq 0\}$$

D_λ is an equivalence relation with B_λ as its base. Let $R_\lambda = D_{1-\lambda}$. Then $\{R_\lambda | 0 \leq \lambda \leq 1\}$ define a fuzzy equivalence relation $\underset{\sim}{R}$ on X uniquely, and with R_λ as its cut relation.

Proof:

Let $S(\lambda)$ be a quotient space corresponding to D_λ. From the definition of D_λ, we have $0 \leq \lambda_1 < \lambda_2 \leq 1$, $S(\lambda_2)$ is a quotient space of $S(\lambda_1)$. Thus, $\{S(\lambda) | 0 \leq \lambda \leq 1\}$ forms an ordered chain, under the inclusion relation of quotient spaces.

Then, R_λ satisfies that $0 \leq \lambda_1 < \lambda_2 \leq 1$, $R_{\lambda_1} < R_{\lambda_2}$. Therefore, $\{R_\lambda | 0 \leq \lambda \leq 1\}$ defines a fuzzy equivalence relation $\underset{\sim}{R}$ on X uniquely, and with R_λ as its cut relation.

Proposition 2.13

If d is a normalized distance corresponding to a fuzzy equivalence relation, then it is an isosceles distance.

Proof:

Reduction to absurdity, otherwise, assume that there exist $x, y, z \in X$ such that $d(x, z) > \max(d(x, y), d(y, z))$. Thus,

$$R(x, z) = 1 - d(x, z) < 1 - \max(d(x, y), d(y, z)) = \min(1 - d(x, y), 1 - d(y, z))$$

$$= \min(R(x, y), R(y, z))$$

$\underset{\sim}{R}$ does not satisfy the condition (3) in the definition of fuzzy equivalence relation.

Theorem 2.4

$[X]$ is a quotient space of X. $d(.,.)$ is a normalized isosceles distance function on $[X]$. By letting $\forall x, y \in X, R(x, y) = 1 - d(x, y)$, then $R(x, y)$ is a fuzzy equivalence relation on X.

Proof:

Obviously, $R(x, y)$ satisfies the conditions (1) and (2) in the definition of fuzzy equivalence relation. We show that it also satisfies the condition (3).

$\forall x, y, z \in X$, from d is an isosceles distance, $d(x, z) \leq \max(d(x, y), d(y, z))$. Thus, $1 - d(x, z) \geq 1 - \max(d(x, y), d(y, z)) = \min((1 - d(x, y)), (1 - d(y, z)))$, i.e., $R(x, z) \geq \min(R(x, y), R(y, z))$.

Carrying out the operation sup over y in the right hand side of the above formula, we have that $R(x, y)$ satisfies condition (3) in the definition of fuzzy equivalence relation.

From Theorems 2.3 and 2.4, it's known that a fuzzy equivalence relation on X is one-to-one correspondent to a normalized isosceles distance function on some $[X]$. The relationship shows that it is possible to use metric space as a tool for investigating fuzzy equivalence relations, or we can carry out study of fuzzy equivalence relations under the quotient space theoretical framework (X, T, f), where T is a topology induced from a fuzzy equivalence relation.

Moreover, from Proposition 2.12, it is known that a normalized distance $\underline{d}$ may produce a fuzzy equivalence relation $\underset{\sim}{R}$ on X. Theorem 2.3 and Proposition 2.13 show that $\underset{\sim}{R}$ can also produce a normalized isosceles distance d_1. But $d \neq d_1$ generally, since d is not necessarily an isosceles distance. Turning d into d_1 is equivalent to changing a relation with only reflexive and symmetric properties to an equivalence relation, by a transitive operation.

It has been proved that a fuzzy equivalence relation on X corresponds to a unique hierarchical structure of X. Conversely, their relation is also true, as we will show in the following theorem.

Theorem 2.5

Assuming that $\{X(\lambda)|0 \leq \lambda \leq 1\}$ is a hierarchical structure of X, there exists a fuzzy equivalence relation $\underset{\sim}{R}$ on X with cut relation R_λ, and $X(\lambda), \lambda \in [0, 1]$ is the quotient space corresponding to R_λ.

Proof:

From the above assumption, $\{X(\lambda)\}$ is a hierarchical structure of X, and each $X(\lambda)$ is a quotient space of X. Let $R_\lambda, 0 \leq \lambda \leq 1$ be an equivalence relation corresponding to $R_\lambda, 0 \leq \lambda \leq 1$. $\forall x, y \in X$, define

$$R(x,y) = \begin{cases} \inf\{\lambda|(x,y) \notin R_\lambda\} \\ 1, \forall \lambda, (x,y) \in R_\lambda \end{cases}$$

$\forall x, y, z \in X$, let $R(x,y) = a_1, R(x,z) = a_2, R(y,z) = a_3$.

$\forall \varepsilon > 0$, we have $a_1 - \varepsilon < d_1 \leq a_1, a_2 - \varepsilon$

$< d_2 \leq a_2, d_3 < a_3 - \varepsilon < d_3 \leq a_3.\ (x,y) \in R_{d_1}, (x,z) \in R_{d_2}, (y,z) \in R_{d_3}$.

If $d_2 \geq \min(d_1, d_3)$, then

$R(x,z) \geq d_2 \geq \min(R(x,y) - \varepsilon, R(y,z) - \varepsilon)$

$\geq \min(R(x,y), R(y,z)) - \varepsilon$.

If $R(x,z) \geq d_2 \geq \min(R(x,y) - \varepsilon, R(y,z) - \varepsilon)$

$\geq \min(R(x,y), R(y,z)) - \varepsilon$, in assuming that

$d_3 \leq d_1$, from $(x,y) \in R_{d_1}, (y,z) \in R_{d_3}$, we have $(x,y) \in R_{d_3}$.

That is, $x \sim y, y \sim z\,(R_{d_3})$, then $x \sim z\,(R_{d_3})$.

Namely, $R(x,z) \geq d_3 = \min(d_1, d_3) \geq \min(R(x,y), R(y,z)) - \varepsilon$.

Letting $\varepsilon \to 0$, carrying out the *sup* operation over y in the right hand side of the above formula, we have $R(x,z) \geq \sup_y(\min(R(x,y), R(y,z)))$.

Finally, $R(x,y)$ is a fuzzy equivalence relation on X with R_λ as its cut relation.

All the above results that we have can be summarized in the following basic theorem.

Basic Theorem

The following three statements are equivalent.

(1)   A fuzzy equivalence relation on X;
(2)   A normalized isosceles distance on some $[X]$;
(3)   A hierarchical structure of X.

Through the theorem, it follows that a fuzzy granular computing can be transformed into a computing on structure $([X], d)$. Therefore, quotient space theory is also available in fuzzy case.

Example 2.14

A hierarchical structure of X is as follows.

$X(1) = \{\{1, 2, ..., 15, 16\}\}$,
$X(2) = \{\{1, 13, 6, 8\}, \{2, 5, 7, 14, 16\}, \{3, 11\}, \{4, 9, 12, 10, 15\}\}$,
$X(3) = \{\{1, 13, 6\}, \{8\}, \{2, 5, 7\}, \{14, 16\}, \{3, 11\}, \{4, 9, 12\}, \{10, 15\}\}$,
$X(4) = \{\{1\}, \{13, 6\}, \{8\}, \{2, 5\}, \{7\}, \{14, 16\}, \{3, 11\}, \{4\}, \{9, 12\}, \{10, 15\}\}$.

Find their corresponding fuzzy equivalence relations.

Solution:

Let $X'(1) = X(1), X'(0) = X(4)$.

For $X(2)$, let $X'\left(\frac{1}{2}\right) = X(2)$.

For $X(3)$, since $X(2) < X(3) < X(4) = X'(0), X(2) = X'\left(\frac{1}{2}\right)$, letting

$$a_3 = \frac{0 + \frac{1}{2}}{2} = \frac{1}{4}, \text{ i.e., } X'\left(\frac{1}{4}\right) = X(3). \text{ We have } \left\{X'(1), X'\left(\frac{1}{2}\right), X'\left(\frac{1}{4}\right), X'(0)\right\}$$

Then, distance $d(.,.)$ as follows.

The distances between 6 and 13, 2 and 5, 14 and 16, 9 and 12, 3 and 11, 10 and 15 are 0, respectively.

The distances between 1 and 13 (or 6), 7 and 2 (or 5), 4 and 9 (or 12) are $\frac{1}{4}$, respectively.

The distances between 8 and 1 (6 or 13), 14 (or 16) and 2 (5 or 7), 10 (or 15) and 4 (9 or 12) are $\frac{1}{2}$, respectively.

The distances between the other two elements are 1.

Letting $\underset{\sim}{R}(x, y) = 1 - d(x, y)$, fuzzy equivalence relation $\underset{\sim}{R}$ corresponding to $\{R_\lambda\}$ is the result that we want.

From the basic theorem and the above example, it is known that $\underset{\sim}{R}$ corresponding to a hierarchical structure $X(\lambda)$ of X is not unique. In other words, quotient space $X(\lambda)$ based on cut relation R_λ that corresponding to $\underset{\sim}{R}$ represents the essence of $\underset{\sim}{R}$. In fuzzy mathematics, this is called clustering structure $X(\lambda)$ of fuzzy equivalence relations. This means that if two fuzzy equivalence relations $\underset{\sim}{R}_1$ and $\underset{\sim}{R}_2$ have the same clustering structure $X(\lambda)$, then they are the same in essence. Their difference is superficial. So a hierarchical structure representation of X is more efficient than a fuzzy equivalence representation on X.

2.4.2 The Structure of Fuzzy Quotient Spaces

The Structure of Fuzzy Quotient Spaces

Definition 2.19

Assume that R is a fuzzy equivalence relation on X. From the basic theorem, there is a normalized isosceles distance $d(.,.)$ on quotient space $[X]$ of X corresponding to R. For $\forall a \in [X]$, define $\mu_a(b) = 1 - d(a, b), \forall b \in [X]$. Thus, each μ_a defines a fuzzy set on $[X]$.

The space composed by these fuzzy sets corresponds to fuzzy quotient space $\{\mu_a | a \in [X]\}$ of fuzzy equivalence relation R. These fuzzy sets compose a fuzzy knowledge base.

Definition 2.20

Assume that R_1 and R_2 are two fuzzy equivalence relations. If for $\forall (x, y) \in (X \times X)$, there exists $R_2(x, y) \leq R_1(x, y)$, then R_2 is called finer than R_1, and denoted by $R_1 < R_2$.

Theorem 2.6

Under the '$<$' relation defined in Definition 2.20, the whole fuzzy quotient spaces on X compose a semi-order lattice.

Proof:

Given a set $\{R_\alpha, \alpha \in I\} \subset \mathcal{R}$, define $R^- : R^-(x, y) = \inf_a \{R_a(x, y)\}$ and $R_- : R_-(x, y) = \sup\{\lambda | \exists x = x_0, x_1, ..., x_m = y, R_{\alpha_1}, ..., R_{\alpha_m}$, satisfy $R_{\alpha_i}(x_{i-1}, x_i) \geq \lambda$, $i = 1, 2, ..., m\}$

We show below that R^- is the supremum of $\{R_\alpha\}$. First, we show that it is a fuzzy equivalence relation.

The reflexivity and symmetry of R^- are obvious. Now, we show its transitivity.

Assume that $\forall x, y, z, R_\alpha, R_\alpha(x, z) \geq \sup_y (\min(R_\alpha(x, y), R_\alpha(y, z)))$. From the definition of operation 'inf', we have

$$\forall x, y, z, R_\alpha, \text{ have } R_\alpha(x, z) \geq \sup_y (\min(\inf_\alpha(R_\alpha(x, y)), \inf_\alpha(R_\alpha(y, z))))$$
$$\geq \sup_y (\min(R^-(x, y), R^-(y, z))) R_\alpha(x, z)$$
$$\geq \sup_y (\min(R^-(x, y), R^-(y, z)))$$

Carrying out the operation 'inf' in regard to α over the left hand side of the above formula, we have $R^-(x, z) \geq \sup_y(\min(R^-(x, y), R^-(y, z)))$. Then, R^- is a fuzzy equivalence relation.

Now, assume that R^* is an upper bound of $\{R_a\}$, i.e., $\forall x, y, a, R^*(x, y) \leq R_a(x, y)$. Carrying out the operation 'inf' in regard to α over the right hand side of the above formula, we have $R^*(x, y) \leq \inf_\alpha(R_\alpha(x, y)) = R^-(x, y)$. Thus, R^- is the supremum of $\{R_\alpha\}$.

Now, we show that R_- is the infimum of $\{R_\alpha\}$. First, we show that it is a fuzzy equivalence relation.

The reflexivity and symmetry of R_- are obvious. Now, we show its transitivity.

For any x, y, z, assume $R_-(x,y) = a_1, R_-(x,z) = a_2, R_-(y,z) = a_3$. For $\varepsilon > 0$, there exist d_1, d_2, d_3 such that $a_1 - \varepsilon < d_1 \leq a_1, a_2 - \varepsilon < d_2 \leq a_2, a_3 - \varepsilon < d_3 \leq a_3$, and there exist $x = x_0, x_1, ..., x_m = y; y = y_0, y_1, ..., y_n = z; R_{\alpha_1}, ..., R_{\alpha_m}; R_{\beta_1}, ..., R_{\beta_n}$ such that $R_{\alpha_i}(x_{i-1}, x_i) \geq d_1$, $i = 1, 2, ..., m; R_{\beta_j}(y_{j-1}, y_j) \geq d_3, j = 1, ..., n$.

In assuming that $d_1 \geq d_3$, and letting $x_{j+m} = y_j, R_{\alpha_{(j+m)}} = R_{\beta_j}, j = 1, ..., n$, we have $x = x_0, x_1, ..., x_{m+n}$ and $R_{\alpha_i}(x_{i-1}, x_i) \geq d_3, i = 1, ..., n + m$.

From the definition of R_-, we have

$$R_-(x, z) \geq d_3 = \min(d_1, d_3) \geq \min(R_-(x, y), R_-(y, z)) - \varepsilon$$

Carrying out the operation 'sup' in regard to y over the right hand side of the above formula, and letting $\varepsilon \to 0$, we then have $R_-(x, z) \geq \sup_y(\min(R_-(x, y), R_-(y, z)))$. That is, R_- satisfies the transitivity, and R_- is a fuzzy equivalence relation.

Finally, we show that R_- is the infimum of $\{R_\alpha\}$.

Assume that R_* is a lower bound of $\{R_\alpha\}$. For any $R_\alpha, x, y, R_*(x, y) \geq R_\alpha(x, y)$. Assume $R_-(x, y) = a$. From the definition of R_-, for any $\varepsilon > 0$, there exist $R_{\alpha_1}, ..., R_{\alpha_m}$ such that $R_{\alpha_i}(x_{i-1}, x_i) \geq a - \varepsilon, i = 1, ..., m$.

Construct a cut relation $R_{*_{a-\varepsilon}}$. Since $R_{\alpha_i}(x_{i-1}, x_i) \geq a - \varepsilon$, x and y are equivalent under the cut relation $R_{*_{a-\varepsilon}}$, i.e., $R_*(x_{i-1}x_i) \geq a - \varepsilon$. Letting $\varepsilon \to 0$, we have $R_*(x, y) \geq a = R_-(x, y)$. Thus, $R_* < R_-$, i.e., R_- is the infimum of $\{R_a\}$.

So far we have proved that via fuzzy equivalence relation, the common quotient space theory can be extended to the fuzzy issues. First, we show that the following four statements are equivalent: (1) a fuzzy equivalence relation R on X, (2) a normalized isosceles distance d on quotient space $[X]$ of X, (3) a hierarchical structure $\{X(\lambda)\}$ of X, (4) a fuzzy knowledge base of X. Secondly, we show that the whole fuzzy equivalence relations on X compose a semi-order lattice. These results provide a powerful tool for quotient space based fuzzy granular computing.

2.4.3 Cluster and Hierarchical Structure

In real problems, fuzzy equivalence relation $\underset{\sim}{R}$ can be used for cluster analysis. So a cluster analysis is equivalent to a hierarchical structure of X corresponding to $\underset{\sim}{R}$.

Since a fuzzy equivalence relation equals to a normalized isosceles distance on a quotient space of X, distance D_λ can be used for distance analysis, i.e., the quotient space method based on equivalence relation $D_\lambda, B_\lambda = \{(x, y)|d(x, y) \leq \lambda\}$ as its base, can be used for cluster analysis. The method is the same as the 'the maximal tree' method of cluster analysis in fuzzy mathematics.

Example 2.15

$\underset{\sim}{R}$ is a fuzzy similar relation on X, $X = \{1, 2, ..., 14\}$. $\underset{\sim}{R}$ is represented by a symmetric matrix as follows.

r_{ij}	1	2	3	4	5	6	7	8	9	10	11	12	13	14
1	1													
2	0	1												
3	0	0	1											
4	0	0	0.4	1										
5	0	0.8	0	0	1									
6	0.5	0	0.2	0.2	0	1								
7	0	0.8	0	0	0.4	0	1							
8	0.4	0.2	0.2	0.4	0	0.8	0	1						
9	0	0.4	0	0.8	0.4	0.2	0.4	0	1					
10	0	0	0.2	0.2	0	0	0.2	0	0.2	1				
11	0	0.5	0.2	0.2	0	0	0.8	0	0.4	0.2	1			
12	0	0	0.2	0.8	0	0	0	0	0.4	0.8	0	1		
13	0.8	0	0.2	0.4	0	0.4	0	0.4	0	0	0	0	1	
14	0	0.8	0	0.2	0.4	0	0.8	0	0.2	0.2	0.6	0	0	1

Letting $d(i, j) = 1 - r_{ij}$, we construct a quotient space based on distance as follows.

$$X(0) = \{1, 2, ..., 14\}$$

$$X(0.2) = \{\{1, 13\}, \{2, 5, 7, 11, 14\}, \{3\}, \{4, 9, 10, 12\}, \{6, 8\}\}$$

$$X(0.5) = \{\{1, 6, 8, 13\}, \{2, 5, 7, 11, 14\}, \{3\}, \{4, 9, 10, 12\}\}$$

$$X(0.6) = \{\{1, 2, ..., 14\}\}$$

$$X(0.8) = \{\{1, 2, ..., 14\}\}$$

$$X(1) = \{\{1, 2, ..., 14\}\}$$

We have $X(1) < X(0.5) < X(0.2) < X(0)$ and $X(1) = X(0.8) = X(0.6)$.

From metric spaces to survey quotient space $X(\lambda)$, roughly speaking, the element of $X(\lambda)$ is regarded as a point that consists of all points which distance is $\leq \lambda$. Since a fuzzy equivalence relation is equivalent to a hierarchical structure, we can survey the fuzziness from the hierarchical point of view. For example, when using a ruler to measure lengths, if the minimal unit of the rule is 'meter', for an object with length 12 meters, then 12 meters is a certain concept, since it is neither 11 nor 13 meters. But in the finer level, 'centimeter' level, its length becomes about 1200 cm, then 1200 cm is an uncertain (fuzzy) concept, since it might be either 1201 or 1199 cm, etc. So the concepts between crisp and fuzzy are relative. Multi-granular computing can handle the relations between crisp and fuzzy, certain and uncertain efficiently. More details will be discussed in Section 2.5.

2.4.4 Conclusions

In order to extend quotient space theory to fuzzy spaces, there are three different ways. First, the fuzzification of domains, i.e., domain X is composed by fuzzy objects. Second, the fuzzification of structures, i.e., the structure is a fuzzy topology. Third, a fuzzy quotient space theory is established by expanding to fuzzy equivalent relations. In the section, we only discuss the third way. We have its basic property as follows. A fuzzy equivalence relation on X is equivalent to a normalized isosceles distance on some quotient space $[X]$ and also equivalent to a unique hierarchical structure of X. These results closely integrate the quotient space theory with fuzzy mathematics.

2.5 The Applications of Quotient Space Theory
2.5.1 Introduction

In this section, we will present a new constructional definition of fuzzy sets by using fuzzy equivalence relations, and discuss its properties. We will also discuss the isomorphism and similarity principles of fuzzy sets, the necessary and sufficient condition of the isomorphism and ε-similarity of two fuzzy equivalence relations. These principles and results can overcome the subjectivity of the concept of fuzzy sets defined by membership functions to a certain extent, and deepen the understanding of fuzzy set theory so that a more objectively fuzzy set theory can be established probably. More details can be seen in (Zhang and Zhang, 2003b, 2003d, 2005b, 2005c).

Zadeh (1965) presented a fuzzy set theory that is an efficient tool for describing uncertainty, and has wide applications, for example, fuzzy control, fuzzy reasoning, etc. But the concept of fuzziness defined by membership functions that many people pay close attention to is subjective. The definition of fuzziness that Zadeh proposed is the following.

Definition 2.21

X is a domain. If $\underline{A}$ is a fuzzy subset of X, for any $x \in X$, assigning a number $\mu_A(x) : X \to [0, 1]$ to x, $\mu_A(x)$ is called a membership of x with respect to $\underline{A}$.

Mapping $\mu_A(x) : X \to [0, 1]$, $x \to \mu_A(x)$ is called a membership function of $\underline{A}$.

It is noted that in the following discussion, domain X is assumed to be infinite (not limited to finite). For simplicity, the membership function is denoted by $A(x)$ rather than $\mu_A(x)$.

The main operations of fuzzy sets: given two fuzzy sets $A(x)$ and $B(x)$, the union, intersection, and complement operations are defined as follows:

$$(A \cup B)(x) = \max[A(x), B(x)], \quad (A \cap B)(x) = \min[A(x), B(x)], \quad \overline{A}(x) = (1 - A(x))$$

In practice such as fuzzy control, designers may choose the membership functions optionally in some degree, i.e., the membership functions of the same fuzzy variable may (slightly) be different, but the controllers designed from the different membership functions still have the same (or approximate) performances. The robustness of the fuzzy analysis method, based on (more or less) optionally chosen membership functions, has brought many people's attention. Some researchers (Liang and Song, 1996; Lin and Tsumoto, 2000; Mitsuishi et al., 2000; Verkuilen, 2001; Lin, 2001a) presented the probabilistic interpretation of membership functions. For example, Lin (2001a) interpreted memberships as probabilities. Each sample space has a probability, and each point is associated with one sample space. So the total space is like a fiber space. Each fiber space is a probability space. Liang and Song (1996) regarded the values of a membership function as independent and identically distributed random variables, and proved that the mean of the membership function exists for all the elements of the universe of discourse. He interpreted the meaning of a subjective concept of a group of people as the mean of a membership function for all people within the group. Mitsuishi et al. (2000) introduced a new concept of empty fuzzy set, in order to define the membership functions in the probabilistic sense. That is, although different persons may assign (slightly) different membership functions to a fuzzy concept, when solving a real problem (fuzzy control or fuzzy reasoning), in average they can get an approximate result. Unfortunately, these results were obtained based on a strong assumption, i.e., the values of a membership function are assumed to be independent and identically distributed random variables. Verkuilen (2001) introduced the concept of membership functions by the multi-scale method, and discussed its corresponding properties. Lin (1988, 1992, 1997) presented a topological definition, topological rough set, of fuzzy sets by using neighborhood systems, discussed the properties of fuzzy sets from their structure, and then presented a definition of the equivalence between two fuzzy membership functions, and the necessary and sufficient conditions of the equivalence between two membership functions. He also discussed the concept of granular fuzzy sets in Lin (1998, 2001b), and 'elastic' membership functions in Lin (1996, 2000, 2001b). Lin's works provide a structural interpretation of membership functions (fuzzy sets).

It can be seen that the membership function of a fuzzy set can be interpreted in two ways: one probabilistic, the other structural. We will show below that for a fuzzy set (concept), it may probably be described by different types of membership functions, as long as their structures (see the structural definition of fuzzy sets below) are the same, it still appears with the same characteristics. That is, although these membership functions are different in appearance, they are the same in essence. Therefore, the structural interpretation of fuzzy sets would be better than the probabilistic one. And it seems that in a given environment, most persons would have a similar structural interpretation for the same fuzzy concept. We will introduce a structural definition of fuzzy sets, and discuss its properties below, since the structural description is more essential to a fuzzy set.

2.5.2 The Structural Definition of Fuzzy Sets

2.5.2.1 The Structural Definition of Membership Functions

Definition 2.22

$R(x, y)$ is a fuzzy equivalence relation on X. A is a crisp set of X. Define a corresponding fuzzy set $\underline{A}$ such that its membership function $A(x)$ is as follows

$$A(x) = \sup\{R(x, y)|y \in A\} \tag{2.11}$$

$A(x)$ is called a structural definition of membership functions.

Therefore, $\underline{A}$ is a fuzzy set extended from a crisp set A by fuzzy equivalence relation R and with A as its core. The new definition is induced from a fuzzy equivalence relation, and represents the relationship between a crisp set and its corresponding fuzzy set so that it deepens the understanding of fuzzy sets.

The following example shows that two different equivalence relations may correspond to the same hierarchical structure.

Example 2.16

$X = \{1, 2, 3, 4\}$. Given two fuzzy equivalence relations R_1 and R_2 on X as follows.

Fuzzy equivalence relation R_1 : $R_1(1, 1) = R_1(2, 2) = R_1(3, 3) = R_1(4, 4) = 1, R_1(1, 2) = 0.8, R_1(3, 4) = 0.6$.

Its corresponding hierarchical structure is $X_1(1) = \{1, 2, 3, 4\}$, $X_1(0.8) = \{(1, 2), 3, 4\}$, $X_1(0.6) = \{(1, 2), (3, 4)\}$, and $X_1(0.5) = \{(1, 2, 3, 4)\}$.

Fuzzy equivalence relation R_2 is $R_2(1, 1) = R_2(2, 2) = R_2(3, 3) = R_2(4, 4) = 1, R_2(1, 2) = 0.9, R_2(1, 3) = R_2(1, 4) = R_2(2, 3) = R_2(2, 4) = 0.6$, and $R_2(3, 4) = 0.7$.

Its corresponding hierarchical structure is $X_2(1) = \{1, 2, 3, 4\}$, $X_2(0.9) = \{(1, 2), 3, 4\}$, $X_2(0.7) = \{(1, 2), (3, 4)\}$, and $X_2(0.6) = \{(1, 2, 3, 4)\}$.

Fuzzy equivalence relations R_1 and R_2 are different, but they have the same hierarchical structure $\{\{1,2,3,4\},\{(1,2),3,4\},\{(1,2),(3,4)\},\{(1,2,3,4)\}\}$. Certainly, there are countless fuzzy equivalence relations corresponding to the above hierarchical structure.

Definition 2.23

$\{X_1(\lambda), 0 \le \lambda \le 1\}$ and $\{X_2(\mu), 0 \le \mu \le 1\}$ are two hierarchical quotient structures on X. If there exists a one-one corresponding, strictly increasing, and onto mapping

$f : [0, 1] \rightarrow [0, 1]$ such that $X_1(\lambda) = X_2(f(\lambda)), 0 \le \lambda \le 1$, then $\{X_1(\lambda), 0 \le \lambda \le 1\}$ and $\{X_2(\mu), 0 \le \mu \le 1\}$ are called the same.

Definition 2.24

If R_1 and R_2 are two fuzzy equivalence relations corresponding to the same hierarchical structure, then R_1 and R_2 are called isomorphic.

Definition 2.25

Given a fuzzy subset $\underline{A}$ and its membership function $\mu_A(x)$. Defining an equivalence relation $R : x \sim y \Leftrightarrow \mu_A(x) = \mu_A(y)$ on X, we have a quotient space $[X]_A$ corresponding to R. Furthermore, define an order '<' on $[X]_A$ such that $[x] < [y] \Leftrightarrow \mu_A(x) \le \mu_A(y), x \in [x], y \in [y]$, space $([X]_A, <)$ obtained is a totally ordered quotient space corresponding to fuzzy set $\underline{A}$.

Definition 2.26

If two fuzzy subsets $\underline{A}$ and $\underline{B}$ correspond to the same totally ordered quotient space, then $\underline{A}$ and $\underline{B}$ are called isomorphic.

2.5.2.2 The Isomorphism Discrimination of Two Fuzzy Equivalence Relations

We will show below the properties of two equivalent fuzzy equivalence relations, and the necessary and sufficient condition of isomorphism for two fuzzy equivalence relations.

Proposition 2.14

If two fuzzy equivalence relations R_1 and R_2 on X are isomorphic, then we have the following properties.

1. For $x, y, u, v \in X$, $R_1(u, v) < R_1(x, y) \Leftrightarrow R_2(u, v) < R_2(x, y)$.
2. $\lim_{n \to \infty} R_1(x_n, y_n) = \lambda_1, \lim_{n \to \infty} R_1(u_n, v_n) = \lambda_2, \lambda_1 \ne \lambda_2$
   $\Leftrightarrow \lim_{n \to \infty} R_2(x_n, y_n) = \mu_1, \lim_{n \to \infty} R_2(u_n, v_n) = \mu_2, \mu_1 \ne \mu_2$
3. For $x, y, u, v \in X$, $R_1(u, v) = R_1(x, y) \Leftrightarrow R_2(u, v) = R_2(x, y)$.

For simplicity, in the following discussion, we use the symbol $R(x_n, y_n) \rightarrow$ instead of $\lim_{n \to \infty} R(x_n, y_n) \rightarrow$.

Proof:

1. Assume $R_1(u, v) < R_1(x, y)$. Let $\lambda_1 : R_1(u, v) < \lambda_1 < R_1(x, y)$. f is an isomorphic mapping.
   Letting $X_1(\lambda_1) = \{(x, y) | R_1(x, y) \ge \lambda_1\}$ and $X_2(f(\lambda_1)) = \{(x, y) | R_2(x, y) \ge f(\lambda_1)\}$, then x and y are equivalent in $X_1(\lambda_1)$, but u and v are not equivalent in $X_1(\lambda_1)$.

Since R_1 and R_2 are isomorphic, there exists a one-one, strictly increasing, and onto mapping $f : [0, 1] \to [0, 1]$. Letting $\mu_1 = f(\lambda_1), X_1(\lambda_1) = X_2(\mu_1)$, we have x and y equivalent in $X_2(\mu_1)$, but u and v are not equivalent in $X_2(\mu_1)$. Thus, $R_2(u, v) < \lambda_2$ and $R_2(x, y) \geq \lambda_2$, i.e., $R_2(u, v) < R_2(x, y)$.

Similarly, we have $R_2(u, v) < R_2(x, y) \Rightarrow R_1(u, v) < R_1(x, y)$.

2. Let $R_1(x_n, y_n) \to \lambda_1$ and $f(\lambda_1) = \mu_1$. We will show $R_2(x_n, y_n) \to \mu_1$.

   Otherwise, in assuming that $R_2(x_n, y_n) \to \mu_0 < \mu_1$, for $\mu_0 < \mu_2 < \mu_1$, let $f(\lambda_2) = \mu_2$. Since f is a one-one, strictly increasing and onto mapping, we have $\lambda_2 < \lambda_1$. In assuming $n_0, n > n_0$, we have $R_1(x_n, y_n) > \lambda_2$. Thus, $(x_n, y_n) \in X_1(\lambda_2) = X_2(\mu_2)$. Again, from $R_2(x_n, y_n) \to \mu_0 < \mu_2 < \mu_1$, we have $(x_n, y_n) \notin X_2(\mu_2)$. This is a contradiction. So $R_2(x_n, y_n) \to f(\lambda_1) = \mu_1$.

   Since f is a one-one mapping, we have

   $$R_1(x_n, y_n) \to \lambda_1, R_1(u_n, v_n) \to \lambda_2, \lambda_1 \neq \lambda_2$$
   $$\Leftrightarrow R_2(x_n, y_n) \to f(\lambda_1) = \mu_1, R_2(u_n, v_n) \to f(\lambda_2) = \mu_2, \mu_1 \neq \mu_2$$

3. Property 3 is the deduction of Property 1. Otherwise, there exist $R_1(x, y) = R_1(u, v)$ and $R_2(x, y) \neq R_2(u, v)$. But from Property 1, we have $R_1(x, y) \neq R_1(u, v)$. This is a contradiction. So Property 3 holds.

Definition 2.27

R_1 and R_2 are two fuzzy equivalence relations on X. Property 1 of Proposition 2.14 holds. Let S_1 and S_2 be the ranges of R_1 and R_2, respectively. Define $f : S_1 \to S_2$ as $\forall x, y \in X, f(R_1(x, y)) = R_2(x, y)$.

From Proposition 2.14, when Property 1 holds, Property 3 holds as well. From Definition 2.27, assume that $\forall x, y, u, v \in X, R_1(x, y) = R_1(u, v) = \lambda_1$. From Property 3, we have $R_2(x, y) = R_2(u, v) = \mu_1$. Then, $f(\lambda_1) = \mu_1$. Therefore, mapping f is defined as single valued and unique. From Property 1 of Proposition 2.14, f is a one-one and strictly increasing.

Proposition 2.15

R_1 and R_2 are two fuzzy equivalence relations on X, and satisfy Property 1 of Proposition 2.14. Let S_1 and S_2 be the ranges of R_1 and R_2, respectively. Then, the mapping f defined by Definition 2.27 can be extended to a one-one, strictly increasing, and onto mapping from $[0, 1] \to [0, 1]$.

Proof:

Letting $\overline{S}_1$ and $\overline{S}_2$ are closures of S_1 and S_2, respectively, set $[0, 1]/\overline{S}_i, i = 1, 2$, is open and may be represented by the union of at most countable many open intervals. Their starting and finishing points are $\{\lambda_1, \lambda_2, .., \lambda_n, ...\}$ and $\{\mu_1, \mu_2, .., \mu_n, ...\}$, respectively.

For any λ_i, there exists $R_1(x_n, y_n) \to \lambda_i$. Define $f(\lambda_i) : R_2(x_n, y_n) \to \beta \equiv f(\lambda_i)$.

We will show next that β must be some μ_j.

Otherwise, in assuming that $(\lambda_i, \lambda_{i+1}) \subset [0, 1]/\overline{S}_1$, there exists $R_2(u_n, v_n) \to \beta$ (monotonously decrease to β). From Property 1 and 2, we have $R_1(u_n, v_n) \to \lambda_i$ (monotonously decrease to λ_i). Then there exists n_0, when $n > n_0$, $\lambda_i \leq R_1(u_n, v_n) < \lambda_{i+1}$.

This contradict with $(\lambda_i, \lambda_{i+1}) \subset [0, 1]/\overline{S}_1$. Then, we have that $f(\lambda_i)$ is some μ_j.

Similarly, when $(\lambda_i, \lambda_{i+1}) \subset [0, 1]/\overline{S}_1$, we have $(f(\lambda_i), f(\lambda_{i+1})) \subset [0, 1]/\overline{S}_2$.

Now, f will be expanded to [0,1]. For $\lambda \in S_1$, let $f(\lambda) = \mu \in S_2$. When $\lambda \in \overline{S}_1/S_1$ let $R_1(x_n, y_n) \to \lambda_1$. And let $R_2(x_n, y_n) \to \mu = f(\lambda)$. When $\lambda \in ([0, 1]/\overline{S}_1)$ assume that $\lambda \in (\lambda_1, \lambda_2)$, $\lambda_1 \neq \lambda_2, \lambda_1, \lambda_2 \in \overline{S}_1$. Letting $f(\lambda_1) = \mu_1, f(\lambda_2) = \mu_2$ we have $\mu_1 \neq \mu_2$. When $\lambda = t\lambda_1 + (1 - t)\lambda_2$, $0 \leq t \leq 1$ define $f(\lambda) = t\mu_1 + (1 - t)\mu_2$.

Therefore, f is expanded to a one-one, strictly increasing, and onto mapping from $[0, 1] \to [0, 1]$.

Assume that $\{X_1(\lambda), 0 \leq \lambda \leq 1\}$ and $\{X_2(\mu), 0 \leq \mu \leq 1\}$ are hierarchical structures corresponding to R_1 and R_2, respectively, then $X_1(\lambda) = X_2(f(\lambda)), 0 \leq \lambda \leq 1$.

Theorem 2.7: The Discrimination Principle of Isomorphism

R_1 and R_2 are two fuzzy equivalence relations on X. The necessary and sufficient conditions of isomorphism of R_1 and R_2 are that the following two properties hold.

1. Property 1 of Proposition 2.14
2. Property 2 of Proposition 2.14

Proof:

$\Leftarrow$: Let f be the mapping defined in Definition 2.27. From Proposition 2.15, it's known that f can be expanded to [0,1], and is still a one-one, strictly increasing, and onto mapping. Thus, f is an isomorphic mapping of R_1 and R_2.

The expansion process is the following.

From Property 2 of Proposition 2.14, for point $\lambda \in \overline{S}_1/S_1$, let $R_1(x_n, y_n) \to \lambda$. Letting $R_2(x_n, y_n) \to \mu$, we define $f(\lambda) = \mu$. For $\lambda \in ([0, 1]/\overline{S}_1)$, i.e., λ is an external point of S, there exists an interval $(\lambda_1, \lambda_2) \subset ([0, 1]/\overline{S}_1)$ such that $\lambda \in (\lambda_1, \lambda_2), \lambda_1 \neq \lambda_2, \lambda_1, \lambda_2 \in \overline{S}_1$.

Letting $R_1(x_n, y_n) \to \lambda_1$ and $R_1(u_n, v_n) \to \lambda_2$, we have

$$R_2(x_n, y_n) \to \mu_1, R_2(u_n, v_n) \to \mu_2, \mu_1 \neq \mu_2$$

Letting $f(\lambda_1) = \mu_1, f(\lambda_2) = \mu_2$, and $\lambda = t\lambda_1 + (1-t)\lambda_2, 0 \leq t \leq 1$, define $f(\lambda) = t\mu_1 + (1-t)\mu_2$.

Therefore, f is expanded to a one-one, strictly increasing, and onto mapping from $[0,1] \rightarrow [0,1]$, i.e., an isomorphic mapping corresponding to R_1 and R_2.

$\Rightarrow$: From Proposition 2.14, Property 1 and 2 hold.

Proposition 2.16

The ranges of R_1 and R_2 are [0,1]. The isomorphism of R_1 and R_2 $\Leftrightarrow$ their corresponding function $f(R_1(x,y)) = R_2(x,y)$ is a strictly increasing and continuous function.

Proof:

$\Leftarrow$: Since f is a strictly increasing and continuous function, for any $x, y, u, v \in X$, $R_1(u,v) < R_1(x,y) \Leftrightarrow R_2(u,v) < R_2(x,y)$, and Property 2 of Proposition 2.14 holds. From Proposition 2.15, R_1 and R_2 are isomorphic.

$\Rightarrow$: Assume that R_1 and R_2 are isomorphic. From the Basic Theorem, it's known that their corresponding isomorphic mapping $f : [0,1] \rightarrow [0,1]$ is a one-one, strictly increasing, and onto mapping. So f is continuous.

Corollary 2.2

Assume $d(x,y)$ is a distance function on $X \subset R^n$. Two fuzzy equivalence relations on X are defined as follows.

$$\forall x, y \in X, R_1(x,y) = f_1(d(x,y)), \ R_2(x,y) = f_2(d(x,y))$$

where $f_i : [0,a] \rightarrow [0,1]$, $i = 1,2$ are strictly decreasing and continuous functions. Then, R_1 and R_2 are isomorphic.

Proof:

We have $R_2(x,y) = f_2(d(x,y)) = f_2(f_1^{-1}(R_1(x,y)) = f_3(R_1(x,y))$, where $f_3 = f_2 f_1^{-1}$, and f_1^{-1} is the inverse of f_1. Since f_1 and f_2 are strictly decreasing and continuous, f_1^{-1} is also strictly decreasing and continuous. Since f_3 is the combination of two strictly decreasing and continuous functions, f_3 is strictly increasing and continuous. Then, we have that R_1 and R_2 are isomorphic.

Corollary 2.3

Assume $d(x,y)$ is a distance function on $X \subset R^n$. Two fuzzy equivalence relations on X are defined as follows.

$$\forall x, y \in X, R_1(x,y) = f_1(d(x,y)), \ R_2(x,y) = f_2(d(x,y))$$

where $f_i : [0,a] \rightarrow [0,1]$, $i = 1,2$.

If $\forall x \in X, f'(x) < 0$, then R_1 and R_2 are isomorphic.

Example 2.17

Assume $X \subset R^m$. Let

$$R_1(x,y) = e^{-\sum_k |x_k - y_k|}$$

and $R_2 \;(x,y) = \left(1 - c \sum_k |x_k - y_k|\right)/(1\text{-}c)$

Choose a proper $0 < c < 1$ such that $0 \leq R_2(x,y) \leq 1$.

$$R_1(x,y) = e^{-d(x,y)}, \quad R_2(x,y) = (1 - cd(x,y))(1 - c)$$

We have $f_1(x) = e^{-x}$, $f_2(x) = (1 - cx)/(1 - c)$, $f_1'(x) = -e^{-x} < 0$, and $f_2'(x) = -c/(1 - c) < 0$. From Corollary 2.3, R_1 and R_2 are isomorphic.

2.5.3 The Robustness of the Structural Definition of Fuzzy Sets

2.5.3.1 The Isomorphism of Fuzzy Sets

Proposition 2.17

R_1 and R_2 are two isomorphic fuzzy equivalence relations on X. f is isomorphic transformation. A is a common set on X. For $\forall x \in X$, fuzzy subsets $A_1(x)$ and $A_2(x)$ are defined by R_1 and R_2, according to Definition 2.22. Then, $\underline{A}_1$ and $\underline{A}_2$ are isomorphic, and $A_2(x) = f(A_1(x))$, $\forall x \in X$.

Proof:

From Definition 2.22, we have

$$A_1(x) = \sup\{R_1(x,y)|y \in A\}, A_2(x) = \sup\{R_2(x,y)|y \in A\}$$

From $f(R_1(x,y)) = R_2(x,y)$ and that f is one-one and strictly increasing, there exists $y_n \in A, R_2(x,y_n) \to A_2(x)$ such that

$$A_2(x) = \sup\{R_2(x,y)|y \in A\} = \lim_{n \to \infty} R_2(x,y_n) = \lim_{n \to \infty} f(R_1(x,y_n))$$

Again, sine f is strictly increasing and continuous, we have $\lim_{n \to \infty} R_1(x,y_n) \leq A_1(x)$. Thus, $\lim_{n \to \infty} f(R_1(x,y_n)) \leq f(A_1(x))$ and $A_2(x) \leq f(A_1(x))$.

Similarly, we have $A_1(x) \leq f^{-1}(A_2(x)) \Rightarrow f(A_1(x)) \leq ff^{-1}(A_2(x)) = A_2(x)$, i.e., $f(A_1(x)) \leq A_2(x)$

Finally, $A_2(x) = f(A_1(x))$.

Proposition 2.18

R_1 and R_2 are two isomorphic fuzzy equivalence relations on X. A and B are two common sets on X. Fuzzy subsets $\underline{A}_1, \underline{A}_2$ and $\underline{B}_1, \underline{B}_2$ are defined by R_1 and R_2, according to Definition 2.22. Then, $\underline{A}_1 \cup \underline{B}_1$ and $\underline{A}_2 \cup \underline{B}_2$ (or $\underline{A}_1 \cap \underline{B}_1$ and $\underline{A}_2 \cap \underline{B}_2$) are isomorphic.

Proof:

$A_1(x), A_2(x), B_1(x)$ and $B_2(x)$ are membership functions corresponding to the four fuzzy subsets. The membership functions of $\underline{A}_1 \cup \underline{B}_1$ and $\underline{A}_2 \cup \underline{B}_2$ are denoted by $C_1(x)$ and $C_2(X)$, respectively. From Definition 2.22, we have $C_1(x) = \max[A_1(x), B_1(x)]$ and $C_2(x) = \max[A_2(x), B_2(x)]$.

In order to show that $C_1(x)$ and $C_2(X)$ are isomorphic, it is only needed to show $C_2(x) = f(C_1(X)), f(C_1(x)) = f(\max[A_1(x), B_1(x)])$. Since f is one-one and strictly increasing, from Proposition 2.15, we have

$$f(\max[A_1(x), B_1(x)]) = \max[f(A_1(x)), f(B_1(x))] = \max[A_2(x), B_2(x)] = C_2(x)$$

Therefore, $\underline{A}_1 \cup \underline{B}_1$ and $\underline{A}_2 \cup \underline{B}_2$ are isomorphic.

Similarly, $\underline{A}_1 \cap \underline{B}_1$ and $\underline{A}_2 \cap \underline{B}_2$ are isomorphic.

Proposition 2.19

R_1 and R_2 are two isomorphic fuzzy equivalence relations on X. A and B are two common sets on X. Fuzzy subsets $\underline{A}_1$ and $\underline{A}_2$ are defined by R_1 and R_2, according to Definition 2.22, then $\underline{A}_1^-$ and $\underline{A}_2^-$ are isomorphic, where $\underline{A}_1^-$ is the complement of $\underline{A}_1$, and its membership function is $\underline{A}_1^-(x) = 1 - \underline{A}_1(x)$.

Proof:

Since the corresponding totally ordered quotient space of the complement of $\underline{A}$ has the same elements with that of $\underline{A}$ and the only difference is their opposite order, $\underline{A}_1^-$ and $\underline{A}_2^-$ are isomorphic.

Theorem 2.8: Isomorphism Principle

R_1 and R_2 are two isomorphic fuzzy equivalence relations, and $A = \{A_1, \ldots, A_n\}$ is a set of common subsets on X. Define two sets $A = \{\underline{A}_1, \ldots \underline{A}_n\}$ and $B = \{\underline{B}_1, \ldots \underline{B}_n\}$ of fuzzy subsets from R_1 and R_2 respectively, and carry out a finite number of union, intersection and complement operations on them, we have two sets $C = \{\underline{C}_1, \ldots, \underline{C}_n\}$ and $D = \{\underline{D}_1, \ldots, \underline{D}_n\}$ of fuzzy subsets. Then, the two sets C and D of fuzzy sets are isomorphic.

Proof:

The conclusion can be obtained from Propositions 2.15 and 2.16.

The theorem shows that the corresponding totally ordered quotient space of a fuzzy subset is its essential property. For the isomorphic fuzzy subsets, although they might have different membership functions, after a finite number of operations (inference), the fuzzy subsets obtained are still isomorphic. Therefore, as long as the essential property of fuzzy subsets remains the same, the usage of different membership functions does not affect the final results.

Example 2.18

Sets $A=\{1,3\}$ and $B=\{1\}$ are taken from $X = \{1,2,3,4\}$. Fuzzy equivalence relations R_1 and R_2 as defined in Example 2.16.

Define fuzzy subsets $\underline{A}_1, \underline{A}_2$ and $\underline{B}_1, \underline{B}_2$ from R_1 and R_2, respectively. Their membership functions as follows.

$$A_1(x) : \{A_1(1) = 1, A_1(2) = 0.8, A_1(3) = 1, A_1(4) = 0.6\}$$
$$B_1(x) = \{B_1(1) = 1, B_1(2) = 0.8, B_1(3) = 0.5, B_1(4) = 0.5\}$$
$$A_2(x) = \{A_2(1) = 1, A_2(2) = 0.9, A_2(3) = 1, A_2(4) = 0.7\}$$
$$B_2(x) = \{B_2(1) = 1, B_2(2) = 0.9, B_2(3) = 0.6, B_2(4) = 0.6\}$$

Then we have

$$(A_1 \cap B_1)(x) = \{(A_1 \cap B_1)(1) = 1, (A_1 \cap B_1)(2) = 0.8, (A_1 \cap B_1)(3) = 0.5, (A_1 \cap B_1)(4)$$
$$= 0.5\}(A_2 \cap B_2)(x) = \{(A_2 \cap B_2)(1) = 1, (A_2 \cap B_2)(2) = 0.9, (A_2 \cap B_2)(3)$$
$$= 0.6, (A_2 \cap B_2)(4) = 0.6\}$$

Fuzzy sets A_1 and A_2 have different membership functions on X, but they are isomorphic since they correspond to the same totally ordered quotient space $\{(1,3), (2), (4)\}$.

Similarly, fuzzy sets $(\underline{A}_1 \cap \underline{B}_1)$ and $(\underline{A}_2 \cap \underline{B}_2)$ also have different membership functions, but they correspond to the same totally ordered quotient space $(\{(1), (2), (3,4)\})$ as well.

From the structural relation view point, both fuzzy subsets $\underline{A}_1$ and $\underline{A}_2$ indicate that elements 1 and 3 belong to their core A, and element 2 is closer to the core than element 4. Due to the different understanding of each person, their descriptions of the degree of closeness might be different, but the mutual relationships among elements should be the same.

The structural definition, given in Definition 2.22, of fuzzy sets is defined from fuzzy equivalence relations. This is very significant. For example, if using neighborhood systems to defined fuzzy sets directly, the isomorphism principle might not hold. The following is a counter-example.

Example 2.19

Assume that the structures of fuzzy subsets $\underline{A}$ and $\underline{B}$ are the following.

$$\underline{A} = \{(1,2),(3),(4)\}, \ \underline{B} = \{(1),(2),(3),(4)\}$$

Define their membership functions as follows

$A_1(x) = \{1,1,0.8,0.6\}$, $A_2(x) = \{1,1,0.8,0.7\}$, $B_1(x) = \{1,0.7,0.6,0.8\}$, and $B_2(x) = \{1,0.7,0.6,0.9\}$, where $A_1(x)$ and $A_2(x)$ are membership functions of $\underline{A}$, $B_1(x)$ and $B_2(x)$ are membership functions of $\underline{B}$.

Carry out set operations on $\underline{A}$ and $\underline{B}$ with membership functions $A_1(x)$, $B_1(x)$ and $A_2(x)$, $B_2(x)$, respectively, we have

$$\left(\underline{A} \cup \underline{B}\right)_1 (x) = \max\{A_1(x), B_1(x)\}$$

$$= \{1,1,0.8,0.8\}, \text{ its structure is } \{(1,2),(3,4)\}. \left(\underline{A} \cup \underline{B}\right)_2 (x)$$

$$= \max\{A_2(x), B_2(x)\} = \{1,1,0.8,0.9\}, \text{ its structure is } \{(1,2),(4),(3)\}$$

After the set operations, the results with respect to different membership functions are no long isomorphic. This shows that using fuzzy membership functions to define fuzzy sets, although it is a structural definition but cannot satisfy the isomorphism principle generally (Lin, 1997).

2.5.3.2 The ε -Similarity of Fuzzy Sets
The Definition of ε -Similarity of Fuzzy Sets

In the above section, we presented a structural definition of fuzzy sets, which answers the cause of the robustness of fuzzy analysis in some degree. But the conditions that two fuzzy equivalence relations are isomorphic are too strong. We present a weaker condition, i.e., ε-similarity of fuzzy sets, below.

Definition 2.28

Given two fuzzy equivalence relations R_1 and R_2, and $\varepsilon > 0$. If there exists fuzzy equivalence relation R_3 such that (1) R_3 and R_1 are isomorphic, (2) $\forall x,y \in X$, $|R_2(x,y) - R_3(x,y)| \leq \varepsilon$, then R_1 and R_2 are called ε-similarity.

Definition 2.29

Given two fuzzy equivalence relations R_1 and R_2, and $\varepsilon > 0$. If there exists fuzzy set $\underline{C}$ such that (1) $\underline{A}$ and $\underline{C}$ are isomorphic (or $\underline{B}$ and $\underline{C}$ are isomorphic), (2) $\forall x \in X$, $|\mu_C(x) - \mu_B(x)| \leq \varepsilon$ (or $\forall x \in X$, $|\mu_C(x) - \mu_A(x)| \leq \varepsilon$), then $\underline{A}$ and $\underline{B}$ are called ε-similarity.

Proposition 2.20

Assume that R_1 and R_2 are two ε-similarity fuzzy equivalence relations on X. A is a common set on X. Fuzzy subsets $\underline{A}_1$ and $\underline{A}_2$ are defined by R_1 and R_2, respectively, according to Definition 2.22, then $\underline{A}_1$ and $\underline{A}_2$ are called ε-similarity.

Proof:

Assume that $R_3 = R_1$, i.e., R_3 and R_1 are isomorphic, and $\forall x, y \in X$, $|R_2(x,y) - R_1(x,y)| \leq \varepsilon$.

For x, assume that $A_1(x) = R_1(a_1, x), A_2(x) = R_2(a_2, x)$. Thus

$$A_1(x) = R_1(a_1, x) \leq R_2(a_1, x) + \varepsilon \leq R_2(a_2, x) + \varepsilon = A_2(x) + \varepsilon$$

Similarly, $A_2(x) = R_2(a_2, x) \leq R_1(a_2, x) + \varepsilon \leq R_1(a_1, x) + \varepsilon = A_1(x) + \varepsilon$.

That is, $|A_1(x) - A_2(x)| \leq \varepsilon$. We have that $\underline{A}_1$ and $\underline{A}_2$ are ε-similarity.

Proposition 2.21

Assume that R_1 and R_2 are two ε-similarity fuzzy equivalence relations on X. A and B are two common sets on X. Fuzzy subsets $\underline{A}_1, \underline{B}_1$ and $\underline{A}_2, \underline{B}_2$ are defined from R_1 and R_2, according to Definition 2.22. Then, $\underline{A}_1 \cup \underline{B}_1$ and $\underline{A}_2 \cup \underline{B}_2$ (or $\underline{A}_1 \cap \underline{B}_1$ and $\underline{A}_2 \cap \underline{B}_2$) are ε-similarity.

Proof:

The membership functions corresponding to the four fuzzy sets are $A_1(x), A_2(x), B_1(x)$ and $B_2(x)$, respectively. The membership functions of $\underline{A}_1 \cup \underline{B}_1$ and $\underline{A}_2 \cup \underline{B}_2$ are denoted by $C_1(x)$ and $C_2(X)$, respectively. From Definition 2.22,

$$C_1(x) = \max[A_1(x), B_1(x)], C_2(x) = \max[A_2(x), B_2(x)]$$

Assume that $R_3 = R_1$, i.e., R_3 and R_1 are isomorphic, and $\forall x, y \in X, |R_2(x,y) - R_1(x,y)| \leq \varepsilon$.

Assume that $C_1(x) = A_1(x) = R_1(x, a_1) \leq R_2(x, a_1) + \varepsilon \leq A_2(x) + \varepsilon \leq C_2(x) + \varepsilon$.

Similarly, $C_2(x) \leq C_1(x) + \varepsilon$. Finally, we have $C_2(x) - \varepsilon \leq C_1(x) \leq C_2(x) + \varepsilon$, i.e., $\underline{A}_1 \cup \underline{B}_1$ and $\underline{A}_2 \cup \underline{B}_2$ are ε-similarity.

Similarly, $\underline{A}_1 \cap \underline{B}_1$ and $\underline{A}_2 \cap \underline{B}_2$ are ε-similarity.

Theorem 2.9: Similarity Principle

Assume that R_1 and R_2 are two ε-similarity fuzzy equivalence relations on X. $\{A_1, ..., A_n\}$ is a set of common sets on X. Using R_1 and R_2 to define a set of fuzzy sets, we have $\underline{A} = \{\underline{A}_1, ..., \underline{A}_n\}$ and $\underline{B} = \{\underline{B}_1, ..., \underline{B}_n\}$. And carrying out a finite number of set operations on A

and B, then we have sets $\underline{C} = \{\underline{C}_1, ..., \underline{C}_m\}$ and $\underline{D} = \{\underline{D}_1, ..., \underline{D}_m\}$ of fuzzy sets. Then, C and D are ε-similarity.

Proof:

Assume that R_3 and R_1 are isomorphic, and $\forall x, y \in X, |R_2(x, y) - R_3(x, y)| \leq \varepsilon$. Let $E = \{E_1, ..., E_n\}$ be a set of fuzzy sets defined by R_3. After a finite number of set operations, we have a set $F = \{F_1, ..., F_m\}$ of fuzzy sets. From the isomorphism principle, C and F are isomorphic.

On the other hand, using the same method of Proposition 2.21, we have $\forall i, |D_i(x) - F_i(x)| \leq \varepsilon$, i.e., D and C are ε-similarity, where $D_i(x)$ and $F_i(x)$ are membership functions of fuzzy sets D_i and F_i.

The Discrimination of ε-Similarity of Fuzzy Sets

Theorem 2.10

Assume that the ranges of R_1 and R_2 are [0,1]. Then, we have R_1 and R_2 are ε-similarity $\Leftrightarrow$ there exists a strictly increasing function F such that $\forall x, y \in X, |F(R_1(x, y)) - R_2(x, y)| \leq \varepsilon$.

Proof:

Let $R_3(x, y) = F(R_1(x, y))$. From Proposition 2.16, we have R_3 and R_1 are isomorphic. Then, from Definition 2.28, we have R_1 and R_2 are ε-similarity.

3 The Structural Property of ε-Similarity of Fuzzy Equivalence Relations

Assume that R_1 and R_2 are two equivalence relations. $\{X_1(\lambda)\}$ and $\{X_2(\mu)\}$ are their corresponding hierarchical structures. If R_1 and R_2 are ε-similarity, then there exists a strictly increasing function $F : \mu = F(\lambda)$ for $\forall \lambda_1$, $\exists \mu_1$ such that $X_2(\mu_1 - \varepsilon) < X_1(F(\lambda_1)) < X_2(\mu_1 + \varepsilon)$.

Conversely, for $\forall \mu_2$, $\exists \lambda_2$ such that $X_2(F(\lambda_2) - \varepsilon) < X_1(\mu_2) < X_2(F(\lambda_2) + \varepsilon)$.

The relation between $\{X_1(\lambda)\}$ and $\{X_2(\mu)\}$ can be shown in Fig. 2.3.

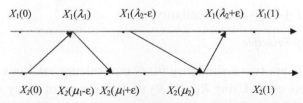

Figure 2.3: The ε-Similarity between Two Equivalence Relations

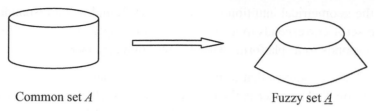

Common set A Fuzzy set $\underline{A}$

Figure 2.4: The Membership Functions of A and $\underline{A}$

Fig. 2.3 shows that the hierarchical structures corresponding to R_1 and R_2 cannot be merged into one structure, but for any quotient space $\{X_1(\lambda_1)\}$ within $\{X_1(\lambda)\}$, there exist two quotient spaces $X_2(\mu_1 - \varepsilon)$ and $X_2(\mu_1 + \varepsilon)$ in $\{X_2(\mu)\}$, one is in front of $\{X_2(\mu)\}$, and the other is behind $\{X_2(\mu)\}$. Conversely, for any $\{X_2(\mu_2)\}$ within $\{X_2(\mu)\}$, there exist two quotient spaces $X_1(\lambda_2 - \varepsilon)$ and $X_1(\lambda_2 + \varepsilon)$ in $\{X_1(\lambda)\}$, one is in front of $\{X_1(\lambda)\}$, and the other is behind $\{X_1(\lambda)\}$.

2.5.3.3 The Geometrical Meaning of the Structural Definition of Fuzzy Sets

In the structural definition of fuzzy sets, their membership functions are induced from equivalence relations. Now, we discuss the geometrical meaning of structures of fuzzy sets by using structures of fuzzy equivalence relations.

A fuzzy equivalence relation $R(x, y)$ is given. First, assume that fuzzy subset $\underline{A}$ is induced from a singleton $A = \{x_0\}$. The membership function of the fuzzy set defined by $A = \{x_0\}$ is $A_{x_0}(x) = R(x_0, x)$. From Basic Theorem, letting $d(x, y) = 1 - R(x, y)$, then $d(x, y)$ is a normalized isosceles distance of some quotient space $[X]$ of X. Under the distance, $\{S(x_0, \varepsilon), 0 \le \varepsilon \le 1\}$ is the neighborhood system of x_0, where $S(x_0, \varepsilon) = \{x | d(x_0, x) < \varepsilon, x \in X\}$ corresponds to the structure of fuzzy set $A_{x_0}(x)$.

According to Definition 2.25, a totally ordered quotient space $([X]_A, <)$ can be defined by the neighborhood system. The order of the quotient space is decided by the distance from point x_0.

Generally, for any set A, define a fuzzy set $\underline{A}$ based on Definition 2.22, and $A(x)$ is its membership function. Letting $d(A, x) = 1 - A(x)$, $d(A, x)$ is the distance from point x to set A in the sense of distance $d(x, y)$. If $S(A, \varepsilon) = \{x | d(A, x) < \varepsilon\}$ is a ε-neighborhood of A, then a corresponding totally ordered quotient space can be defined by the neighborhood system $\{S(A, \varepsilon), 0 \le \varepsilon \le 1\}$ of A, according to Definition 2.25, where the order of the quotient space is decided by the distance from a point to set A.

From the isomorphism principle in Section 2.5.2, it's known that the structure of the totally ordered quotient space, corresponding to a fuzzy subset, is the essential property of the fuzzy subset.

Fig. 2.4 shows the geometrical intuition of common set A, and its corresponding fuzzy set $\underline{A}$, where a crisp set A corresponds to a 'platform' with a vertical boundary face, while a fuzzy set $\underline{A}$ corresponds to a 'platform' with a slant boundary face.

From Definition 2.25, it's known that a fuzzy set $\underline{A}$ decides an order relation of some quotient space $[X]$ on X. The order is the essential property of $\underline{A}$, and provides the relationship of distances from a spatial point to the core A_0 of fuzzy set $\underline{A}$. In common membership functions, an absolute value is used to describe the relation between a fuzzy set and any element within the set. While in the structural definition of fuzzy sets, the relative order relationship among elements is used to describe the fuzziness. Using the structural definition, as long as people have the same understanding of the relative order relation (or ε-similarity) among elements, even different membership functions are used, the results they have are isomorphic (ε-similarity), and after a finite number of fuzzy set operations, the results are still isomorphic. We show an example below.

Example 2.20

Fuzzy equivalence relation R_1 is as Example 2.16. Letting $A = \{1\}$, define $\underline{A}$ and its corresponding membership function as

$$A_1(x) = \{A_1(1) = 1, A_1(2) = 0.8, A_1(3) = 0.5, A_1(4) = 0.5\}$$

Its corresponding totally ordered quotient space is $\{(1),(1,2),(1,2,3,4)\}$.

Letting R_2 be $A_2(x) = \{A_2(1) = 1, A_2(2) = 0.9, A_2(3) = 0.6, A_2(4) = 0.6\}$, then its corresponding totally ordered quotient space is $\{(1),(1,2),(1,2,3,4)\}$.

There are three elements $(1),(2),(3,4)$ in quotient space $[X]_A$. Their order relation is $(1)<(2)<(3,4)$. And the order relation is the essential property of fuzzy set $\underline{A}$.

2.5.4 Conclusions

In the section, from the quotient space theory, we present the structural definition of a fuzzy set based on fuzzy equivalence relations, and the isomorphism and similarity principles of fuzzy sets. These principles may interpret the cause of robustness of fuzzy analysis, and answer the question why the same (or similar) results can be had, even using different membership functions in real fuzzy analysis.

2.6 Conclusions

In this chapter, we have discussed the hierarchical analysis strategy in human problem-solving activities. We also show that by the strategy, the computational complexity can be reduced. Over the last decade, a number of physiological studies in brain have established several basic facts about the cortical mechanisms of visual perception. One of the main characteristics is the hierarchical architecture, for example, from the primary visual cortex (V1) to the inferotemporal cortex (IT), there is an increase in the size of the receptive fields (Serre et al., 2007). Namely, the visual information processing in human brain is also in a hierarchical way, i.e., from the fine level (primary cortex with small receptive fields) to the coarse level (inferotemporal cortex with large receptive fields) or vice versa. In a recent article, Yao et al. (2012) showed that 'hierarchy of information granules supports an important aspect of perception of phenomena...' So the issues discussed in the book are not only available to human deliberative behaviors but also to perception.

The hierarchical analysis strategy has also been adopted in machine learning, for example, deep learning, deep belief nets, etc. By using multilayer networks, more complex patterns can be learned effectively. Deep learning methods have been applied to pattern recognition and language processing, and have made some progress (Hinton et al., 2006; Benjio et al., 2007; Hu et al., 2012).

CHAPTER 3

Information Synthesis in Multi-Granular Computing

Chapter Outline

3.1 Introduction

In Chapter 1, we presented a mathematical model, quotient space based model, for multi-granular computing. We show that a problem can be described by a triplet (X, T, f). And we also discussed how corresponding quotient domain $[X]$, quotient structure $[T]$, and quotient attribute $[f]$ are constructed from original domain X, structure T and attribute f, respectively, i.e., a coarse grained space is constructed from a fine one.

In Chapter 2, we discussed one of the main characteristics of human problem solving, i.e., the multi-granular computing from coarse to fine, rough to detailed, and global to local hierarchically. Recall the example that we have mentioned, one always draws a draft of the whole building first, and then goes into its details, when designing a building. In our model, the analysis correspondingly goes from high to low abstraction levels through a hierarchical structure. The key issue of the computing is to establish the relationship between the quotient space and its original one.

However, the other scheme of multi-granular computing appears to be reverse, i.e., one usually learns things starting from local fragments, and gradually integrating them to form a global picture. On viewing an object from different abstraction levels, or different angles, integrate the fragmentary and one-sided observations into systematic and overall understanding. This process is called information synthesis, fusion, or combination.

Quotient Space Based Problem Solving. http://dx.doi.org/10.1016/B978-0-12-410387-0.00003-2

Let us examine some examples.

Example 3.1

Gathering a series of information from topographic survey, geological prospecting, and seismic method, etc., in some region, then to predict mineral deposit of the region, is an information synthesis problem.

Example 3.2

Having front, top and side views of an object A, to determine its shape in three-dimensional space is an information synthesis problem. Here, each of the three views of the object is regarded as one of its quotient space representations. It is known that 'projection' is one of the typical approaches to quotient space representations. If object A is quite simple, its shape can be uniquely decided by its three views. Otherwise, we need some additional information, for example, some auxiliary views, cross-section views, or comments.

Example 3.3

A doctor takes a patient's temperature and pulse, examines the beat of the patient's heart using his stethoscope, and asks some questions. Then, the doctor makes a diagnosis and prescription. The process can be viewed as making a global decision from local observations. Each observation is a local understanding of the whole patient's physical condition in some abstraction level.

From the three examples, we can see that these problems can be transformed to that of constructing a synthetic problem representation from its quotient space representations. The key issue of information synthesis is to establish the relationship between the original space and its quotient space representations.

The aim of this chapter is to establish a mathematical model for information synthesis. The model is then applied to uncertain reasoning, planning, and other multi-granular computing problems.

3.2 The Mathematical Model of Information Synthesis

Given an unknown problem space (X, T, f), we have the knowledge of its two abstraction levels denoted by (X_1, T_1, f_1) and (X_2, T_2, f_2), where X_1 and X_2 are quotient spaces of X. A natural question to ask is how to have a new understanding of X from the known knowledge.

Example 3.4

Assume that S is an object. Its front and top view are triangle $\triangle ABC$ and $\triangle A'B'D'$, respectively (see Fig. 3.1). How about its shape in three-dimensional space?

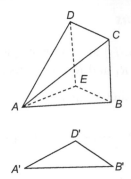

Figure 3.1: Two Projections of an Object

Only from its two projections (or two quotient spaces) in the example, we can't know its shape definitely, since there are infinite kinds of objects whose front and top views are identical with the two given triangles. If our domain is confined to be convex polyhedrons, S should be a kind of cone with A as its vertex, and its bottom consists of a convex polygon contained in quadrilateral BCDE, as shown in Fig. 3.1. If an additional constraint is given, for example, the volume of the object is maximal; the unique S can be identified.

Conversely, if less information is observed, for example, we only know that the front and top views of object S are arbitrary triangles, that is, the exact shape of the triangles is unknown, the constraints on the shape of S will be more relaxed.

In a word, if we are given the knowledge about A in some abstraction levels, generally, we can only have a new understanding about A at the level that is just one (finer) level below them. The complete details of A may not necessarily be known.

We may have the synthetic rules as follows.

Assume that (X_1, T_1, f_1) and (X_2, T_2, f_2) are the knowledge about $A = (X, T, f)$ in two different abstraction levels. The synthesis of (X_1, T_1, f_1) and (X_2, T_2, f_2) is defined as a new abstraction level of A, denoted by (X_3, T_3, f_3), which satisfies the following three basic synthetic principles.

(1) X_1 and X_2 are quotient spaces of X_3
(2) T_1 and T_2 are quotient structures of T_3 corresponding to X_3
(3) f_1 and f_2 are projections of f on X_1 and X_2, respectively.

Space (X_3, T_3, f_3) also needs to satisfy some optimal criteria generally.

We next discuss the synthesis of domain, structure and attribute function, respectively.

3.3 The Synthesis of Domains

Assume that (X_1, T_1, f_1) and (X_2, T_2, f_2) are quotient spaces of (X, T, f). X_1 and X_2 correspond to equivalence relations R_1 and R_2, respectively.

Define the synthetic space X_3 of X_1 and X_2 as follows, where R_3 is an equivalence relation corresponding to X_3

$$xR_3y \Leftrightarrow xR_1y \quad \text{and} \quad xR_2y$$

Example 3.5

X is the staff members of an organization.

Based on education received, the X is classified as follows, and is called a-classification.

$a_1 = \{$those with the educational level below middle school$\}$
$a_2 = \{$those with university educational level$\}$
$a_3 = \{$those with graduate school educational level$\}$.

X can also be classified in terms of age, and is called b-classification.

$b_1 = \{$whose age is younger than 25$\}$
$b_2 = \{$whose age is in between 25 and 35$\}$
$b_3 = \{$whose age is older than 35$\}$.

The synthesis of these two classifications is that x and y belong to the same synthetic class $\Leftrightarrow$ x and y belong to both the same a-class and the same b-class.

If there is no additional information, from these two partitions, we can only have education-level-based and age-based partitions. No more information such as sex can be known.

It is known that all equivalence classes on X form a semi-order lattice, under the set inclusion relation $R_1 < R_2 \Leftrightarrow$ if $xR_2y \Rightarrow xR_1y$.

In terms of the semi-order lattice, the synthesis of R_1 and R_2 can be defined as follows.

Definition 3.1

Assume that R_1 and R_2 are two equivalence relations on X. If R_3 is the least upper bound of R_1 and R_2 in the semi-order lattice, then R_3 is the synthesis of R_1 and R_2. Meanwhile, the synthesis can also be defined by partition. If $X_1 = \{a_i\}$ and $X_2 = \{b_i\}$ are two partitions with respect to R_1 and R_2, respectively, then the synthesis X_3 of X_1 and X_2 can be represented by

$$X_3 = \{a_i \cap b_j \mid a_i \in X_1, b_j \in X_2\}$$

We next show that the two definitions above are equivalent.

Proof:

If $x \sim y(X_3)$, then $\exists a_i, b_j, \ x, y \in a_i \cap b_j \Leftrightarrow x, y \in a_i$ and $x, y \in b_j$.

Where, symbol ' $\sim$ ' denotes an equivalence relation on X_3.

From Example 3.5, we have the synthesis of both educational-level- and age-based partitions as follows.

c_{11} ={those with the educational level below middle school and age below 25},

c_{12} ={those with the educational level below middle school and age being in between 25 and 35},

c_{13} ={those with the educational level below middle school and age being older than 35}....,

c_{33} ={those with graduate school educational level and age being older than 35}.

Obviously, space $X_3(c_{ij})$ defined above satisfies the synthetic principles. That is, both $X_1 = \{a_i\}$ and $X_2 = \{b_i\}$ are quotient spaces of $X_3(c_{ij})$. $X_3(c_{ij})$ is the finest space, which we can get from quotient spaces $X_1 = \{a_i\}$ and $X_2 = \{b_i\}$. It is also the coarsest one among the spaces which satisfy the synthetic principles. That is, it is the least upper bound. Since in some sense it is optimal, it is reasonable to regard $X_3(c_{ij})$ as a synthetic space of $X_1 = \{a_i\}$ and $X_2 = \{b_i\}$.

3.4 The Synthesis of Topologic Structures

We now discuss the synthesis of structures. As mentioned before, there are three kinds of common structures. That is, topologic, semi-order, and operation-based structures. In this section, we only discuss the synthesis of topologic structures.

Assume that (X_1, T_1, f_1) and (X_2, T_2, f_2) are quotient spaces of (X, T, f). Structure T_3, the synthesis of T_1 and T_2, is defined as follows.

Definition 3.2

The synthetic structure T_3 of T_1 and T_2 is the least upper bound of T_1 and T_2, in the semi-order lattice that consists of all topologic structures on X.

Obviously, T_3 satisfies the synthetic principles. That is, T_1 and T_2 are the quotient topologies of T_3 on quotient spaces X_1 and X_2, respectively. T_3 is the coarsest one, among the topologies whose quotient topologies are T_1 and T_2.

T_3 can be constructed as follows.

Let $B = \{w | w = u_i \cap v_i, u_i \in T_1, v_i \in T_2\}$. T_3 is the topology with B as its base, i.e., T_3 consists of all possible sets obtained from any union operations on the elements of B.

Example 3.6

$X = \{1, 2, 3, 4\}$, $T_1 = \{\varnothing, \{1\}, \{1, 2\}, \{1, 2, 3\}, X\}$ and $T_2 = \{\varnothing, \{1, 2\}, \{3, 4\}, X\}$ are given. Then $T_3 = \{\varnothing, \{1\}, \{1, 2\}, \{1, 2, 3\}, \{3\}, \{3, 4\}, \{1, 3\}, \{1, 3, 4\}, X\}$, where T_3 is the least upper bound of T_1 and T_2, i.e., the synthetic topology of T_1 and T_2.

3.5 The Synthesis of Semi-Order Structures

Semi-order is a common structure. Especially when X is a finite domain, many structures can be represented by a directed acyclic graph that can be described by a semi-order. So semi-order is one of the most popular structures.

3.5.1 The Graphical Constructing Method of Quotient Semi-Order

In Chapter 1, we have introduced a method for constructing quotient semi-order. The constructing process follows the line: semi-order $\rightarrow$ right-order topology $\rightarrow$ quotient topology $\rightarrow$ quotient quasi semi-order. Finally, the quotient semi-order on quotient space $[X]$ is defined by the quotient quasi semi-order. It has been proved that the approach is complete. That is, if there is a quotient semi-order in $[X]$ such that its natural projection p is order-preserving, then the quotient semi-order can be obtained by the approach. And in the 'minimum' sense, the quotient semi-order obtained is unique and optimal. But the approach, after all, is not straightforward, since the quotient semi-order must be defined by means of topology.

We next present a direct method for constructing quotient semi-order, when $[X]$ is finite.

Definition 3.3

(X, T) is a semi-order space. D is a subset of product space $X \times X$ and satisfies:

(1) $\forall (x, y) \in D \Rightarrow x < y(T)$,
(2) $\forall x, y \in X, x < y$, there exists a sequence $z_i = (x_i, x_{i+1})$, $i = 1, 2, ..., m - 1$ of finite elements in D such that $x = x_1, y = x_m$.

Then, D is called a semi-order base of T.

The condition (2) above can be restated as $\forall x, y \in X, x < y$, there exists a sequence $x_1, x_2, ..., x_m$ of finite points such that $x = x_1 < x_2 < ... < x_m = y$ and $(x_i, x_{i+1}) \in D, i = 1, 2, ..., m - 1$.

Example 3.7

(X, T) is a semi-order space as shown in Fig. 3.2. Then, a set $D = \{(1, 2), (1, 3), (2, 5), (3, 6), (2, 4), (4, 6), (5, 6)\}$ of its edges is a base of T.

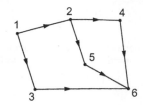

Figure 3.2: A Semi-Order Base

Proposition 3.1

(X, T) is a semi-order set consisting of a directed acyclic graph. The set D of directed edges of the directed graph is one of its semi-order bases.

Definition 3.4

(X, T) is a semi-order space consisting of a directed network, $[X]$ is a quotient space of X. Define a quasi semi-order on $[X]$ as follows:

$$\forall a, b \in [X], a < b \Leftrightarrow \exists x \in a, y \in b (x, y \in X) \quad \text{and} \quad x < y$$

Obviously, if there is no directed loop on the directed network corresponding to the quasi semi-order on $[X]$, then, in fact, the quasi semi-order is a semi-order. Thus, there exists a quotient semi-order on $[X]$. From the definition of quotient semi-order, it is easy to know that the quotient semi-order has order-preserving and is minimal.

Proposition 3.2

(X, T) is a semi-order space consisting of a directed network. $[X]$ is a quotient space of X. If the quasi semi-order on $[X]$ defined by Definition 3.4 is a semi-order, then the semi-order is the same as the quotient semi-order $[T]$ defined in Section 1.3.

From Definition 3.4, we know that constructing a directed network $([X], T_1)$ (it might have directed loops) from a directed network (X, T) is identical with the 'compression' operation of directed graph on graph theory.

If there are directed loops on $([X], T_1)$, compressing the nodes on each directed loop into one node, then we have a directed network without loops that just corresponds to the semi-order space with respect to $\underline{R}$ obtained by the mergence method in Section 1.4.

Example 3.8

(X, T) is a semi-order space as shown in Fig. 3.3(a). Let $R : \{1, 5\}, \{2, 4\}, \{3, 6\}$.

Compressing (X, T) into (X_1, T_1), as shown in Fig. 3.3(b), then we have a directed loop. Merging the directed loop into one node, we have a semi-order space (X_2, T_2), as shown in

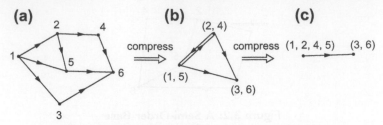

Figure 3.3: The Compression of a Directed Network

Fig. 3.3(c). The semi-order corresponding to (X_2, T_2) is just the quotient semi-order obtained by the mergence method.

Now, we find the least upper bound of quotient semi-order of space (X, T) with respect to R, by using the decomposition method presented in Section 1.4.

$[X] = \{a_1 = \{1, 5\}, a_2 = \{2, 4\}, a_3 = \{3, 6\}\}$ is a quotient space corresponding to R.

Decomposing a_1, we have $a_{11} = \{5\}, a_{12} = \{1\}$.

Decomposing a_2, we have $a_{21} = a_2 = \{2, 4\}$.

Similarly, $a_{31} = a_3 = \{3, 6\}$.

We have the least upper bound $\overline{X}$ of semi-order spaces with respect to $\overline{R}$, as shown in Fig. 3.4.

When $[X]$ is finite, it's known that a quotient semi-order can directly be constructed by using directed networks. Moreover, when $[X]$ is an infinitely countable set, the direct approach is still available.

3.5.2 The Synthesis of Semi-Order Structures

Assume that X_1 and X_2 are two quotient spaces of X. If there exist semi-orders on X_1 and X_2, then we have two semi-order spaces (X_1, T_1) and (X_2, T_2). Now, we find their synthetic semi-order space (X_3, T_3) that satisfies the synthetic principle, i.e., X_3 is the least

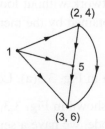

Figure 3.4: The Decomposition of a Directed Network

upper bound of X_1 and X_2, T_1 and T_2 are quotient semi-orders of T_3 on X_1 and X_2, respectively.

Now, the following two questions must be answered. In what condition does the synthetic semi-order space exist? If it exists, then how to construct such a space (X_3, T_3).

1. The synthetic procedure of semi-order spaces-topology based method

Semi-order spaces (X_1, T_1) and (X_2, T_2) are given. The synthetic procedure is as follows.

(1) Find the least upper bound of X_1 and X_2 denoted by X_3.
(2) Find the right-order topologies corresponding to T_1 and T_2, denoted by T_{1r} and T_{2r}, respectively.
(3) Find the synthetic topology T_{3r} of T_{1r} and T_{2r} on X_3. And topology T_{3r} is the least upper bound of T_{1r} and T_{2r} on X_3.
(4) Find the semi-order from T_{3r}, and denoted by T_3.

Finally, (X_3, T_3) is the synthetic semi-order space.

Example 3.9

Given (X_1, T_1) and (X_2, T_2) as shown in Fig. 3.5. Where

$$a_1 = \{1, 2, 3\}, a_2 = \{4, 5\}, a_3 = \{6, 7\}$$
$$b_1 = \{1, 2, 4\}, b_2 = \{3, 6\}, b_3 = \{5, 7\}$$

find the synthetic semi-order space (X_3, T_3).

(1) Find X_3, $X_3 = \{c_1, c_2, c_3, ..., c_6\}$, where
     $c_1 = \{1, 2\}, c_2 = \{3\}, c_3 = \{4\}, c_4 = \{5\}, c_5 = \{6\}, c_6 = \{7\}$.
(2) Find the right-order topologies T_{1r} and T_{2r} of T_1 and T_2, respectively. Their corresponding topologic bases are
     $B_1 = \{\{1, 2, ..., 7\}, \{4, 5\}, \{6, 7\}\}$
     $B_2 = \{\{1, 2, ..., 7\}, \{3, 6\}, \{5, 7\}\}$.
(3) Find the synthetic topology T_{3r}. Its corresponding topologic base is
     $B_3 = \{\{1, 2, ..., 7\}, \{4, 5\}, \{3, 6\}, \{5\}, \{6\}, \{7\}\}$.
(4) Find the semi-order T_3 induced from R_3. We finally have (X_3, T_3), as shown in Fig. 3.5.

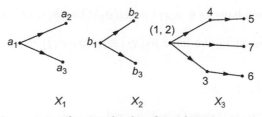

Figure 3.5: The Synthesis of Semi-Order Spaces

Obviously, the quotient semi-order structures of T_3 on X_1 and X_2 are just T_1 and T_2, respectively.

Theorem 3.1

X_1 and X_2 are quotient spaces of X. (X_1, T_1) and (X_2, T_2) are semi-order spaces. (X_3, T_3) is constructed by the preceding procedure. Then, (X_3, T_3) satisfies the following conditions.

(1) T_3 is a semi-order on X_3
(2) Mapping $p_i : (X_3, T_3) \rightarrow (X_i, T_i)$ is order-preserving
(3) T_3 is the coarsest one among semi-order structures which satisfy the conditions
     (1) and (2).

Proof:

Since X_3 is the least upper bound of X_1 and X_2. For $\forall x \in X_3$, there exist $a \in X_1$ and $b \in X_2$ such that $x = a \cap b$.

Let $u_1(a)$ $(u_2(b))$ be a minimum open set on $X_1(X_2)$ containing $a(b)$.

Obviously, $u(x) = u_1(a) \cap u_2(b)$ is a minimum open set on X_3 containing x, since topology T_{3r} is the least upper bound of T_{1r} and T_{2r}.

Assume that $x_1, x_2 \in X_3$, $x_1 < x_2 < x_1(T_3)$. We next show that $x_1 = x_2$.

Let $x_1 = a_1 \cap b_1$ and $x_2 = a_2 \cap b_2$, where $a_1, a_2 \in X_1$ and $b_1, b_2 \in X_2$. From $x_1 < x_2 < x_1(T_3) \Rightarrow u_1(x_1) = u_2(x_2)$, we have $u_1(a_1) \cap u_2(b_1) = u_1(a_2) \cap u_2(b_2)$.

Thus, $\{b_2\} \cap [u_2(b_1) \cap u_2(b_2)] \neq \varnothing$ and $u_2(b_1) \cap u_2(b_2)$ is an open set containing b_2. Then, $u_2(b_2) \subset u_2(b_1) \cap u_2(b_2) \Rightarrow u_2(b_2) \subset u_2(b_1)$.

Similarly, $u_2(b_1) \subset u_2(b_2) \Rightarrow u_2(b_1) = u_2(b_2)$

Since T_2 is a semi-order on X_2, we have $b_1 = b_2$.

Similarly, $a_1 = a_2 \Rightarrow x_1 = a_1 \cap b_1 = a_2 \cap b_2 = x_2$, i.e., T_3 is a semi-order on X_3.

Next, we show that $p_i : (X_3, T_3) \rightarrow (X_i, T_i)$ is order-preserving.

Assuming $x_1, x_2 \in X_3, x_1 < x_2 \Rightarrow \forall u(x_1)$, we have $x_2 \in u(x_1)$.

By letting $x_1 = a_1 \cap b_1$, we have $x_2 \in u(x_1) = u_1(a_1) \cap u_2(b_1)$, i.e., $x_2 \in u_1(a_1)$.

Carrying out operation p_1 on x_2, we have $p_1(x_2) \in p_1(u_1(a_1)) = u_1(a_1)$ since $u_1(a_1)$ is a set on X_1.

From $x_1 = a_1 \cap b_1$, $\Rightarrow p_1(x_1) = a_1$,

$\Rightarrow p_1(x_2) \in u_1(a_1) = u_1(p_1(x_1)) \Rightarrow p_1(x_1) < p_1(x_2)$.

That is, p_1 is order-preserving.

Similarly, p_2 is order-preserving.

Finally, we show that T_3 is the coarsest one.

Assume that $T_3{}'$ satisfies the conditions (1) and (2) of Theorem 3.1 and $T_3{}'$ is coarser than T_3.

Let $T_{3r}{}'$ and T_{3r} be the corresponding right-order topologies of $T_3{}'$ and T_3, respectively. Since $T_3{}'$ is coarser than T_3, we know that $T_{3r}{}'$ is coarser than T_{3r}. And both T_{1r} and T_{2r} are quotient topologies of $T_{3r}{}'$. This contradicts that T_{3r} is the coarsest one among topologies whose quotient topologies are T_{1r} and T_{2r}, or T_{3r} is the least upper bound of T_{1r} and T_{2r}.

Therefore, T_3 is the coarsest one among semi-order structures which satisfy the conditions (1) and (2).

From Theorem 3.1, it's known that T_3 is the coarsest one among semi-order structures which satisfy the conditions (1) and (2). This means that T_3 provides the maximum information regarding the relation among the elements on X_3, when the only known knowledge is (X_1, T_1) and (X_2, T_2). Therefore, T_3 is the 'optimal' synthetic structure.

2. The direct method for synthesizing semi-order spaces

In the above topology-based method, we first synthesize the right-order topologies corresponding to the given two semi-order structures T_1 and T_2, then find the synthetic semi-order. This is not a straightforward method. We now provide a new approach that constructs the synthetic semi-order from semi-order structures T_1 and T_2 directly.

Directed Method

(X_1, T_1) and (X_2, T_2) are semi-order spaces, (X_3, T_3) is their synthetic semi-order space.

(1) Find the least upper bound X_3 of spaces X_1 and X_2.
(2) For $\forall x_1, x_2 \in X_3$ let $x_1 = a_1 \cap b_1$ and $x_2 = a_2 \cap b_2$, where $a_1, a_2 \in X_1$ and $b_1, b_2 \in X_2$.

Define $x_1 < x_2 \Leftrightarrow a_1 < a_2$ and $b_1 < b_2$. Especially, if $b_1 = b_2$, then $x_1 < x_2 \Leftrightarrow a_1 < a_2$. The relation defined above is denoted by T_3'.

We now show that T_3' is just the same semi-order on X_3 as that obtained by the above topologic method.

Proposition 3.3

(X_1, T_1) and (X_2, T_2) are semi-order spaces. The structure T_3' on X_3 obtained from the direct method is identical with semi-order T_3 on X_3 constructed by the topologic method.

Proof:

$\forall x_1, x_2 \in X_3, x_1 = a_1 \cap b_1, x_2 = a_2 \cap b_2,$ where $a_1, a_2 \in X_1, b_1, b_2 \in X_2,$ and $x_1 < x_2(T_3')$

$$\Leftrightarrow a_1 < a_2(T_1) \quad \text{and} \quad b_1 < b_2(T_2)$$

$$\Leftrightarrow a_2 \in u_1(a_1) \quad \text{and} \quad b_2 \in u_2(b_1)$$

$$\Leftrightarrow a_2 \cap b_2 \in u_1(a_1) \cap u_2(b_1)$$

$$\Leftrightarrow x_2 = a_2 \cap b_2 \in u_1(a_1) \cap u_2(b_1) = u(x_1)$$

$$\Leftrightarrow x_1 < x_2(T_3),$$

We have $T_3' = T_3$.

Example 3.10

Spaces (X_1, T_1) and (X_2, T_2) are the same as that in Example 3.9, i.e.,

$$X_1 = \{a_1, a_2, a_3\}, a_1 = \{1, 2, 3\}, a_2 = \{4, 5\}, a_3 = \{6, 7\}$$
$$X_2 = \{b_1, b_2, b_3\}, b_1 = \{1, 2, 4\}, b_2 = \{3, 6\}, b_3 = \{5, 7\}$$
$$T_1 : a_1 < a_2, a_1 < a_3$$
$$T_2 : b_1 < b_2, b_1 < b_3$$

Find the synthetic space (X_3, T_3) by the direct method.

Solution:

$X_3 = \{c_1, c_2, ..., c_6\}$, where

$$c_1 = \{1, 2\} = a_1 \cap b_1, c_2 = \{3\} = a_1 \cap b_2$$
$$c_3 = \{4\} = a_2 \cap b_1, c_4 = \{5\} = a_2 \cap b_3$$
$$c_5 = \{6\} = a_3 \cap b_2, c_6 = \{7\} = a_3 \cap b_3$$

Find T_3 from the direct method.

Since $a_1 < a_2$ and $c_1 = a_1 \cap b_1, c_3 = a_2 \cap b_1$, we have $c_1 < c_3$.

Again $b_1 < b_3$ and $c_3 = a_2 \cap b_1, c_4 = a_2 \cap b_3$, we have $c_3 < c_4$.

...

Since b_2 and b_3 are incomparable and $c_5 = a_3 \cap b_2$, $c_6 = a_3 \cap b_3$, then c_5 and c_6 are incomparable as well.

Finally, we have (X_3, T_3) as the same as is shown in Fig.3.5.

Theoretically, since a semi-order structure can be transformed into a topologic structure, the former can be regarded as a special case of topologic structures. For example, the order-preserving property between a semi-order space and its quotient space, in essence, mirrors the continuity of projecting a topologic space on its quotient space. In addition, the 'coarsest' property of the synthetic semi-order represents the 'coarsest' property of the synthetic topology.

Although there is no difference between semi-order and topologic structures in theory, the former has widespread applications in reality. Especially, when domain X is a finite set, a semi-order can be represented by a directed network. Based on the network representation, a quotient semi-order can be obtained from its original semi-order directly. And a synthetic semi-order can also be obtained from semi-order structures directly; there is no need to transform it into topologic structures. This will make things convenient for the applications.

3.6 The Synthesis of Attribute Functions

For a problem space (X, T, f), given the knowledge of its two abstraction levels (X_1, T_1, f_1) and (X_2, T_2, f_2), we intend to have an overall understanding about (X, T, f).

Assume that the overall understanding of (X, T, f) is represented by (X_3, T_3, f_3). We are now going to discuss how to construct f_3 from f_1 and f_2 such that it satisfies the synthetic principles.

3.6.1 The Synthetic Principle of Attribute Functions

Given a problem space (X, T, f) and its quotient spaces (X_1, T_1, f_1) and (X_2, T_2, f_2). Let $p_i : (X, T, f) \to (X_i, T_i, f_i), i = 1, 2$, be nature projections. R_i is an equivalence relation with respect to quotient space X_i.

Fixing projection R_i, $p_i : X \to X_i$ is uniquely defined. When T is a topology, including a semi-order, fixing R_i, $p_i : T \to T_i$ is also uniquely defined.

Once the approach of constructing the global attributes of set A from its local information is determined, projection $p_i : f \to f_i$ is uniquely defined too.

Conversely, two spaces (X_1, T_1, f_1) and (X_2, T_2, f_2) are given. Let $p_i : (X, T, f) \to (X_i, T_i, f_i), i = 1, 2$. Their synthetic space (X_3, T_3, f_3) must satisfy the following three conditions at least

$$\begin{cases} p_i X_3 = X_i \\ p_i T_3 = T_i, i = 1, 2 \\ p_i f_3 = f_i \end{cases} \tag{3.1}$$

In general, the solution satisfying constraints (3.1) is not unique. In order to have a unique solution, additional optimization criteria have to be provided generally. In Section 3.3, the optimization goal of the synthetic space X_3 is represented by 'the least upper bound' criterion. In Section 3.4, the optimization goal of the synthetic topology is indicated by 'the coarsest' criterion.

We now present the synthetic principle of attribute functions as follows.

Given (X_1, T_1, f_1) and (X_2, T_2, f_2), find the synthetic space (X_3, T_3, f_3) satisfying the following conditions.

(1)

$$p_i f_3 = f_i, i = 1, 2 \tag{3.2}$$

where $p_i : (X_3, T_3, f_3) \rightarrow (X_i, T_i, f_i)$ $i = 1, 2$, is a natural projection.

(2)   Assume that $D(f, f_1, f_2)$ is a given optimization criterion. Then

$$D(f_3, f_1, f_2) = \min D(f, f_1, f_2) \text{ (or } \max D(f, f_1, f_2)) \tag{3.3}$$

where, the min (max) operation is carried on all attribute functions in X_3 which satisfy Formula (3.2).

We next show the rationality of the above synthetic principles.

The condition (1), i.e., $p_i f_3 = f_i, i = 1, 2$, is necessary. That is, the projections of f_3 on X_1 and X_2 must be identical with the given f_1 and f_2, respectively. As shown in Example 3.4, the corresponding projections of the object S synthesized from the given front and top views have to be identical to the given triangles ΔABC and $\Delta A'B'D'$ at least, respectively, as shown in Fig. 3.1.

In fact, the solution satisfying constraint (3.2) is not unique. This is not necessarily a bad thing. For example, when designing a mechanical part, we have to consider several requirements and each requirement can be regarded as a kind of constraint on its abstraction level. Generally, the design result satisfying these requirements is not unique. This means there is plenty of room for designers' imaginations. The design works will benefit from the variety of the results. But this is an obstacle to a computer while it is not intelligent enough. So in computer problem solving, some sort of optimization criteria are needed.

Condition (2) above is one such optimization criterion. As long as it is given, the computer will be able to find the optimal solution. For example, we design a container in order to satisfy the requirements shown in Fig. 3.1. That is, its front and top views are triangles $\triangle ABC$ and $\triangle A'B'D'$, respectively. For human designers, under such requirements, an infinite variety of designs can be envisioned. But, in order to have a solution by a computer, a specific criterion must be provided. For example, if taking the maximal volume of the container as a criterion then a cone ABCDE shown in Fig. 3.1 will be turned out.

Generally, the optimal synthetic criteria are domain-dependent and hard for computers to implement. In reality, we can only have some so-called satisfactory solutions. This is one of the main ideas in artificial intelligence.

In fact, in the real world, the situation is more complicated. For example, the information that we have in some abstraction level is not precise. Therefore, we have to handle the imprecise or incomplete information.

We are given spaces (X_1, T_1, f_1) and (X_2, T_2, f_2). Let (X_3, T_3, f_3) be a synthetic space.

Let Y_i be a space consisting of all attribute functions on X_i. Assume that there exists a metric d_i in each Y_i such that (Y_i, d_i), $i = 1, 2, 3$, $i = 1, 2, 3$, is a metric space.

Now, if the observation in level $X_i (i = 1, 2)$ is not precise, so Formula (3.2) may not hold accurately. Similar to the method of least-squares, we establish the following relation.

$$D(f, f_1, f_2) = d_1(p_1 f - f_1)^2 + d_2(p_2 f - f_2)^2 \tag{3.4}$$

where, $p_i X_3 \rightarrow X_i, i = 1, 2$, is a natural projection. And

$$D(f_3, f_1, f_2) = \min_f D(f, f_1, f_2), \tag{3.5}$$

where, the operation min is carried on all functions on Y_3.

If function f_3 satisfying Formula (3.5) is still not unique, an additional criterion is needed, for example, an additional function $D_1(f, f_1, f_2)$. By letting

$$D_2(f, f_1, f_2) = D(f, f_1, f_2) + D_1(f, f_1, f_2), \quad \text{then}$$
$$D_2(f_3, f_1, f_2) = \min_f D_2(f, f_1, f_2) \tag{3.6}$$

where, the operation min is carried on all functions on Y_3 as well.

Attribute function f_3 that obtained from f_1 and f_2 by Formulas (3.4) and (3.5), or by Formula (3.6), is a synthetic one.

As mentioned above, the optimization synthetic criteria are generally domain-dependent, and there is a great variety of methods for extracting global information from local ones, i.e., a variety of $D(f, f_1, f_2)$ functions. Therefore, it is hard to have a universal optimization criterion.

3.6.2 Examples

In this section, we will explain the computed tomography, CT for short, by our synthetic model in order to have a better understanding of the model.

Example 3.11

As shown in Fig. 3.6, *T* is a biological tissue under study, by placing an X-ray and photosensitive film DE alongside the tissue so that it lies perpendicular to the incident rays. When the X-ray traverses from left to right along the x-axis, an image on film DE of X-ray attenuation during this traverse is obtained. The image of the tissue's structure can be reconstructed by using a computer to analyze a set of these recorded images. This is the basic principle of computed tomography (Kak and Slaney, 2001).

When a beam of X-rays penetrates any structure shown in Fig. 3.6, attenuation occurs, the degree of the attenuation is related to: (a) the atomic number of the element of which the structure is composed, or the effective atomic number of a complex structure and (b) the concentration of the substances forming that structure. Thus, the density of electrons, or effective electron density, determines the degree to which a given beam of X-rays will be attenuated. Therefore, from the attenuation of the X-ray the structure of a tissue being tested can be known.

In Fig. 3.6, we now assume that $f(x, y)$ is the attenuation coefficient of that tissue at (x,y) in one of its cross-sections. When X-ray passes through the given structure, the density of the beam emerging from the other side of the structure will depend on $\int_l f(x, y) dl$. The one-dimensional image recorded in film DE is

$$g(x) = \int f(x, y) dy \tag{3.7}$$

when X-ray traverses along the x-axis.

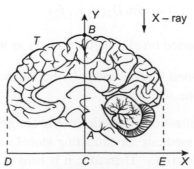

Figure 3.6: The Principle of CT

In terms of hierarchical model, the attenuation coefficient $f(x, y), (x, y) \in X$ can be regarded as an attribute function of a problem space (X, T, f), where (X, T) is a part of two-dimensional Euclidean space, e.g., a cross-section of a tissue as shown in Fig. 3.6.

From Formula (3.7), we can see that $g(x)$ is a projection of $f(x, y)$ on X. It forms a new space (X_1, T_1, f_1), where (X_1, T_1) is a quotient space of (X, T) by considering each line perpendicular to the x-axis as a point, i.e., an equivalence class. Thus, (X_1, T_1) is a line segment DE on the x-axis. The relation between attribute functions $f(x, y)$ and $g(x)$ is the following.

$$pf = g(x) = \int f(x, y) dy$$

where $p : (X, T) \rightarrow (X_1, T_1)$

For each line l_θ intersecting the x-axis with angle θ, we have a projection $g_\theta(s)$.

For all $0 \le \theta < \pi$, we have a set $\{g_\theta(s)\}$ of projections. Then, we obtain a set of quotient spaces denoted by $\{X_\theta, T_\theta, g_\theta\}, 0 \le \theta < \pi$.

The point is how to find $f(x, y)$ from a set $\{X_\theta, T_\theta, g_\theta\}, 0 \le \theta < \pi$ of quotient spaces. This is the same problem that CT intends to solve.

From the hierarchical model viewpoint, it is to find a synthetic space from a given set $\{X_\theta, T_\theta, g_\theta\}$ of quotient spaces. That is, given $\{g_\theta(s), 0 \le \theta < \pi\}$, we find a $f(x, y)$ such that it satisfies:

$$\forall \theta, p_\theta f(x, y) = g_\theta(s) \tag{3.8}$$

where $p_\theta : X \rightarrow X_\theta$ is a projection, X_θ is a domain of g_θ (s).

Letting $s = x \cos \theta + y \sin \theta, t = -x \sin \theta + y \cos \theta$, we have

$$g_\theta(s) = p_\theta f(x, y) = \int f(x, y) dt$$

$$= \int f(s \cos \theta - t \sin \theta, s \sin \theta + t \cos \theta) dt$$

In mathematics, it can be proved that a set of equations (3.8) has a unique solution. So there is no need of additional criteria in the synthetic model. The synthetic attribute function can be obtained by solving Formula (3.8) directly.

From the theorems of Fourier transform, we have the following theorem.

Theorem 3.2

The Fourier transform of the one-dimensional projection of a two-dimensional function is identical with the distribution on the central section of the Fourier transform of that function.

The theorem can be stated by the following mathematical formulas.

The Fourier transform of function $f(x, y)$ is as follows.

$$F(u, v) = \int\int_{-\infty}^{\infty} f(x, y)\exp[-j2\pi(ux + vy)]dxdy$$

The projection of $f(x, y)$ on X is

$$g_y(x) = \int_{-\infty}^{\infty} f(x, y)dy$$

The Fourier transform of $g_y(x)$ is

$$G_y(u) = \int_{-\infty}^{\infty} g_y(x)\exp(-j2\pi ux)dx$$

$$= \int\int_{-\infty}^{\infty} f(x, y)\exp(-j2\pi ux)dxdy = F(u, 0)$$

Let $u = r\cos\theta, v = r\sin\theta$, we have $F(u, v) = G(r, \theta)$.

By Fourier inverse transform of $F(u, v)$, we have

$$f(x, y) = \int\int_{-\infty}^{\infty} F(u, v)\exp[j2\pi(ux + vy)]dudv$$

Therefore, from a given set $\{g_\theta(s), 0 \le \theta < \pi\}$, we have a Fourier transform $F(u, v)$. Meanwhile, from the Fourier inverse transform of $F(u, v)$, we finally have $f(x, y)$. In CT, $f(x, y)$ corresponds to the image of the biological tissue being radiographed. Thus, the computed tomography is a special case of our synthetic problem, while there is no need for the optimal criteria.

Example 3.12

In reality, the reconstruction of $f(x, y)$ by the method indicated in Example 3.11 may not be feasible, since an infinite number of projections are needed. For this reason, Kashyap and Mittal (1975) presented a minimization approach to algebraic equations. We first briefly explain their approach in the way of our hierarchical model.

(1)   Discretization

Assume that the domain X of $f(x, y)$ is a square. Then, each edge of the square is equally divided into n intervals. We have a mesh consisting of $n \times n$ blocks. Regarding each block as a point, the value of $f(x,y)$ at its center is considered as the value of $f(x,y)$ in that block.

Regarding each block as an equivalence class, the mesh is a quotient space denoted by X. Taking the value of $f(x,y)$ at the central point of each block as the value of $f(x,y)$ in the block, which is called the inclusion principle, one of the basic approaches for constructing global information as mentioned in Chapter 2.

(2) Projection

f_{ij} indicates the value of $f(x,y)$ at the central point of the ij-th block (the block at the i-th row and the j-th column). Arranging f_{ij} according to the dictionary order of subscript (i,j), we have a n^2-dimensional vector f as follows.

$$f = (f_{11}, f_{12}, ..., f_{21}, f_{22}, ..., f_{n1}, f_{n2}, ..., f_{nn})$$

Then, (X, f) is a problem space after the discretization.

We draw a radial l_k that intersects the horizontal line at angle $\theta_k (k = 1, 2, ..., t)$. From vertexes A and B, we draw two lines perpendicular to l_k at points C and D, respectively. Then, line CD is divided into n intervals equally. From each end point of the intervals we draw a line perpendicular to l_k and have n regions of square X (Fig. 3.7). From left to right, the regions are denoted by $D(k, 1), D(k, 2), ..., D(k, n)$, respectively.

Let $X_k = \{D(k, i), i = 1, 2, ..., n\}$.

Obviously, X_k is a quotient space of X.

Define $g(D(k.l)) = \sum\limits_{(i,j) \in D(k,l)} f_{ij}$.

That is, $g(D(k, l))$ is the sum of f_{ij} over the range of region $D(k, l)$, or denoted by g_{kl} for short.

Define $g_k = (g_{k1}, g_{k2}, ..., g_{km})$.

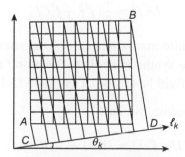

Figure 3.7: The Discrete Method of CT

Therefore, (X_k, g_k) is a quotient space of (X, f).

Given t projections $(X_k, g_k), k = 1, 2.., t$, we find their synthetic space (X, f). This is just the problem that CT intends to solve.

(3) Minimization

Changing the subscript of the vector f, we have $f = (f_j), j = 1, 2..., n^2$. Let $B = \{B_{ij}\}$ be a $tn \times n^2$ matrix. Then

$$
B_{(k-1)n+l,j} = \begin{cases} 1, & f_j \in D\left(k, l\right), k = 1, ..., t; i = 1, ..., n; j = 1, ..., n^2 \\ 0, & \qquad\qquad\qquad\qquad otherwise \end{cases}
$$

From the synthetic principles, f must satisfy the following formula.

$$
Bf = g \tag{3.9}
$$

where, $g = (g_{11}, g_{12}, ..., g_{1n}, g_{21}, g_{22}, ..., g_{t1}, g_{t2}, ..., g_{tm})$.

From linear algebra, we know that if $t = n$, then Equation (3.9) has a unique solution. The f obtained from Equation (3.9) is the synthetic attribute function, or the image of biological tissue being examined after discretization.

If $t > n$ generally, there is no solution to Equation (3.9). Similar to the method of least-squares, we construct a metric function $d(x, y)$, $x, y \in R^{t \times n}$ in $t \times n$ dimensional Euclidean space. Let

$$
D_1(f, g) = d(Bf, g)^2 \tag{3.10}
$$

The synthetic attribute function f is the one that makes the right hand side of Formula (3.10) minimum.

If $t < n$, Equation (3.9) has an infinite solution. It is necessary to introduce an optimal criterion such as

$$
D(f) = \frac{1}{2}(f'f + f'Cf) \tag{3.11}
$$

where C is a positive semi-definite matrix related to local smoothness, f' is a n^2-dimensional column vector. The synthetic attribute function f is the one that satisfies constraint (3.9) and makes the right hand side of Formula (3.11) minimum.

From Lagrange multiplier procedure, we have

$$
D_2(f, \lambda) = D(f) + \lambda(Bf - g) \tag{3.12}
$$

Finding the minimum of Formula (3.12), we have

$$\frac{\partial D_2}{\partial f} = f + fcf + B^T \lambda = 0 \tag{3.13}$$

Where, B^T is the transposed matrix of B. Formula (3.12) is simplified to

$$(I + C)f = -B^T \lambda$$

Since $(I+C)$ is not singularity, we have

$$f = -(I + C)^{-1} B^T \lambda$$
$$Bf = -B(I + C)^{-1} B^T \lambda$$

That is,

$$g = Bf = -B(I + C)^{-1} B^T \lambda$$

Since when $t<n$, B is not singularity, using pseudo-inverse we have

$$\lambda = -\left[B(I + C)^{-1} B^T\right]^{\#} g$$

where, '#' denotes the pseudo-inverse operation, B^T is the transpose of matrix B.

Finally, we have $f = Fg$, where $F = (I + C)^{-1} B^T [B(I + C)^{-1} B^T]^{\#}$. f is the synthetic attribute function, i.e., the function corresponding to the sectional images after discretization in computed tomography.

Next, we give a mathematical example which can be regarded as an application of the synthetic model.

Example 3.13

X is a linear normed space. Given a $f \in X$, since itself may be rather complicated, we project f on a simpler space, for example, a real number axis. Assume $A \in X^*$, where X^* is a conjugate space of X, i.e., X is a space consisting of all linear bounded functionals on X. For $\forall g \in A$, functional $g(f)$ is known. The problem is how to deduce f from $g(f)$. By the synthetic viewpoint, it means that constructing f from the known $\forall g \in A, g(f)$.

Let $L(A)$ be a linear sub-space on X^* containing A. Fixed f, $g(f)$ varying within $L(A)$, then $g(f)$ is a linear functional on $L(A)$, and is denoted by $\tilde{f} : \tilde{f}(g) = g(f)$. Assuming $L^*(A) \subset X^{**}, f \in L^*(A) \subset X^{**}$.

Assume further that $c : X \to X^{**}$ is a canonical mapping which embeds X within X^{**} and there exists c^{-1}. By letting $f_0 = c^{-1} f$, f_0 is just the synthesis of $g(f), \forall g \in A$.

Assume that X is a Euclidean space.

A set of equations is given below.

$$a_{11}x_1 + a_{12}x_2 + \ldots + a_{1n}x_n = b_1$$
$$a_{21}x_1 + a_{22}x_2 + \ldots + a_{2n}x_n = b_2$$
$$\ldots\ldots$$
$$a_{m1}x_1 + a_{m2}x_2 + \ldots + a_{mn}x_n = b_m$$

(3.14)

We can write Formula (3.14) in vectorial form $Ax = b$. Each row can be represented by $a_i x = b_i$, $i = 1, 2 \ldots m$.

Regarding vector $x = (x_1, \ldots, x_n)$ as a point in space E^n and $a_i x = b_i$ as a value of linear functional a_i at point x. Letting $A = (a_1, \ldots, a_m)$, $L(A)$ is a sub-space supported by m vectors.

If $L(A) = E^n$, Formula (3.14) has a unique solution, i.e., $x = A^{-1}b$. If $L(A)$ is a proper subset of E^n, Formula (3.14) has an infinite number of solutions. Then, we introduce an optimal criterion

$$D(x) = \sum_{i=1}^{m} (a_i x - b_i)^2$$

x_0 is the optimal solution with a minimal $D(x)$. From the geometrical point of view, x_0 on $L(A)$ has a shortest distance from x, and is regarded as the real value of x.

The example shows that solving a set of equations, or a constraint satisfaction problem, can be regarded as information synthesis.

In Chapter 4, uncertain reasoning will be studied by the synthetic model.

3.6.3 Conclusions

In this section, we present a synthetic model under the quotient space theory.

Spaces (X_1, T_1, f_1) and (X_2, T_2, f_2) are given. (X_3, T_3, f_3) is their synthetic space. We have

(1) The synthesis of domains: X_3 is the least upper space of X_1 and X_2
(2) The synthesis of topological structures: T_3 is the least upper topology of T_1 and T_2.
(3) The synthesis of attribute functions: f_3 satisfies the following condition
     $p_i f_3 = f_i, i = 1, 2$, where $p_i : X_3 \rightarrow X_i, i = 1, 2$, is a natural projection. If f_1 and f_2 have error, then the above formula will be replaced by the following formula.

$$D(f_3) = \min_f D(f) = \min \left[d_1 (p_1 f - f_1)^2 + \left(d_2 (p_2 f - f_2)^2 \right) \right]$$

Where $d_i(\cdot, \cdot)$ is a metric function on Y_i, Y_i is all attribute functions on X_i, and the min operation is carried out on all attribute functions f on X_3.

If the solution is not unique, a proper optimal criterion must be added in order to have an optimal solution.

The synthetic model can be applied to constraint satisfaction problems, reasoning processes, etc.

CHAPTER 4

Reasoning in Multi-Granular Worlds

Chapter Outline

4.1 Reasoning Models

The study of reasoning model draws its inspiration from the observation that reasoning is one of the main intelligent activities of human beings, and of the ways by which human thinking comes from one idea to a related idea. It has long been attempted to mimic such ability or the like for computers; the reasoning that modeled computationally is called automated reasoning. The study of automated reasoning is an area of artificial intelligence or computer science that helps to understand the characteristics of human reasoning. In the chapter, we will deal with the automated reasoning, or reasoning for short.

Quotient Space Based Problem Solving. http://dx.doi.org/10.1016/B978-0-12-410387-0.00004-4

There are several kinds of reasoning. Deductive reasoning or logic deduction, is the reasoning from one or more general premises to reach a logical conclusion. Traditional logic reasoning based on the first order predicate calculus is a simple model of human's reasoning process. This model is easy to mechanize and widely used in Al. For example, machine theorem proving based on resolution principle is one of the main areas in Al. In some expert systems, traditional logic reasoning has also been used. Logic reasoning is rigorous in mathematics and easy to be implemented by computers, yet it is far different from human everyday reasoning. Inductive reasoning is to formulate general statements or propositions based on previous limited observations of objects. Abductive reasoning is a form of inductive reasoning. It infers a hypothesis as an explanation of a set of observations. There are several (or infinite) explanations satisfying the observations generally, some other optimization condition is usually imposed in order to have the 'best' or 'simplest' one. In this chapter we mainly deal with deductive reasoning.

One of the major problems facing reasoning model designers is how to develop meaningful models to deal with uncertainty that is associated with the complexity of the real world. In real decision making, one can't have complete knowledge about the world, the causal relationship between events is not precisely known, and one's ability to deal with complex problems is limited — how would these uncertainties be taken care of by the model?

This chapter is an attempt to present a general reasoning framework for the manipulation and explanation of uncertainty in the multi-granular world, presented in Chapters 1—3. A new uncertain reasoning model will also be established in order to reflect some characteristics of human reasoning.

Study of the uncertain reasoning model blossomed in the mid-1970s and has enjoyed more than a decade of vigorous growth. Contributions to the growth have come from many researchers including Bayes' Statistics, Zadeh's Possibility Theory and Dempster-Shafer's Belief Functions, etc. We briefly introduce some well-known uncertain reasoning models as follows.

(1) Non-Monotonic Logic

Traditional logic is monotonic. Its monotonicity means that learning a new piece of knowledge cannot reduce the set of what is known. It is only available under certain and complete knowledge, but cannot handle various kinds of reasoning tasks such as default reasoning, abductive reasoning, and belief revision, etc. In these cases, as long as new knowledge is gained, the old assumption or conclusion may be revised even abandoned. So a non-monotonic logic model is needed (McDermott and Doyle, 1980).

In traditional logic, if A and B are theories, then we have

(1) Monotonicity. When

$$A \subseteq Th(A), \text{ if } A \subseteq B, \text{ then } Th(A) \subseteq Th(B)$$

(2) Idempotent

$$Th(Th(A)) = Th(A)$$

where $Th(A) = \{p : A |{-}p\}$ all theorems are inferred from A.

Non-monotonic logic is the extension of the traditional logic generally. In non-monotonic reasoning, adding a fact may lead to withdraw the negative conclusion. The well-known default reasoning (Reiter, 1980) and circumscription reasoning (McCarthy, 1980), etc., belong to the non-monotonic ones. For example, the aim of default reasoning is to handle the reasoning under incomplete knowledge and the exceptions expediently. One of its formalisms is $\frac{A:MB}{B}$, where 'MB' indicates that 'in the absence of information to the contrary, assume B', i.e., the default assumption. Certainly, default reasoning is non-monotonic, since when the default assumption is violated then the consequent will be retracted. These theories have been applied to some artificial intelligence systems such as Truth Maintenance System and KRL-Knowledge Representation Language, etc. (Bobrow and Winograd, 1977; Doyle, 1979).

In order to overcome the uncertainty produced by incomplete knowledge and limit-processing resources, the non-monotonic reasoning restricts the reasoning in the existing knowledge and system-processing capacity, so that the reasoning temporarily becomes certain. As long as new knowledge is gained, some conclusions will be withdrawn. This is the basic idea underlying the non-monotonic reasoning. The reasoning model embodies the phased, relative truth and changing process of human cognition.

(2) Reasoning with Uncertainty Measure

Another way to deal with the uncertain reasoning is intended to measure the degree of uncertainty quantitatively. Bayesian probabilistic model is the most commonly used method. In the reasoning with uncertainty measure, it's needed to solving the evidence synthesis and propagation problems during the reasoning process. Probability is a mature theory and can provide ready-made formulas and tools to the problems. So the probabilistic measure has widely been used in uncertain reasoning. But it has some disadvantages, for example, the cognitive complexity that followed from dealing with large numbers of conditional and prior probabilities.

In order to overcome the above deficit, some new mathematical models of uncertainty are proposed such as Dempster-Shaper belief theory (Shafer, 1976) and Zadeh possibility theory (Dubois and Prade, 2001). Taking D-S theory as an example, it first defines a basic probability assignment on a power set of a domain, then defines belief and plausibility functions based on the basic assignment. The difference between the two functions is designed to describe the degrees of ignorance about a domain. Therefore, the incompleteness of knowledge can be handled. The D-S synthetic rule is used for evidence synthesis in belief theory. But its computational complexity is very high when the domain is large. These theories are mainly still in the exploration stage and are not being widely applied.

Both probability and belief theory can be used to describe the uncertainty of truth of a proposition. But there is another kind of uncertainty. In the propositions, they have vague concepts that do not have clear intension and extension. Possibility theory provides a model for solving the issue. The fuzzy subsets and possibility distributions are used to represent fuzzy propositions. And fuzzy operations and relations are used to handle the evidence synthesis during reasoning. Fuzzy reasoning embodies the characteristics of human reasoning, i.e., the inaccuracy represented by fuzzy concepts and fuzzy causal relations. Some researchers strain at fuzzy reasoning due to the lack of its strict logical foundation.

(3) Qualitative Reasoning

When degrees of uncertainty are measured by numerical values quantitatively in reasoning, there are several disadvantages, for example, how to gain the numerical values to ensure the reasoning reliability and stability. Some researchers dislike such a way of the deterministic description of uncertainty and prefer the qualitative or symbolic description. Cohen (1985) proposed an endorsement theory. The degrees of belief are described by justifiable (symbolic) reasons rather than numerical values. Forbus (1981, 1984) presented a qualitative reasoning theory. The reasoning creates non-numerical descriptions of physical systems and their behavior, only preserving interested behavioral properties and qualitative distinctions. Its aim is to develop representation and reasoning methods that enable computers to reason about the behavior of physical systems, without precise quantitative information. It has become a topic of artificial intelligence and was successfully applied to many areas including autonomous spacecraft support, failure analysis and on-board diagnosis of vehicle systems, intelligent aids for human learning, etc. (Bredeweg and Struss, 2003).

(4) Empirical Methods

In the simple-Bayes model, it includes the assumptions: (1) faults or hypotheses are mutually exclusive and exhaustive, and (2) pieces of evidence were conditionally independent, given each fault or hypothesis. Unfortunately, the assumptions are often inaccurate in practice. Thus, in real AI expert systems, some empirical methods for uncertainty measure are used, for example, certainty factor (*CF*) in MYCIN system (Shortiffe, 1976) and likelihood reasoning model in PROSPECTOR system (Duda, 1978).

The *CF* model was created for the domain of MYCIN as a practical approach to uncertainty management in rule-based systems.

Certainty factor (*CF*) is defined as follows.

$$CF(H|E) = MB(H|E) - MD(H|E)$$

$$MB(H|E) = \begin{cases} 1, & p(H) = 1 \\ \dfrac{\max[p(H)|E), p(H)] - p(H)}{\max[1, 0] - p(H)}, & otherwise \end{cases}$$

$$MD(H|E) = \begin{cases} 1, & p(H) = 1 \\ \dfrac{\min[p(H)|E), p(H)] - p(H)}{\min[1, 0] - p(H)}, & otherwise \end{cases}$$

Where E is evidence, H is hypothesis, $p(H)$ is the prior-probability of H, $p(H|E)$ is the conditional probability of H given E, $MB(H|E)$ is the increment of belief of H given E, $MD(H|E)$ is the increment of disbelief of H given E. A $CF(H|E)$ between 0 and 1 means that a person's belief in H given E increases, while a $CF(H|E)$ between -1 and 0 means that a person's belief decreases. The evidence synthetic rules are the following.

The parallel-synthetic rule is $CF_3 = \begin{cases} CF_1 + CF_2 - CF_1CF_2 & CF_1CF_2 \geq 0 \\ CF_1 + CF_2 + CF_1CF_2 & CF_1CF_2 < 0 \\ \dfrac{CF_1 + CF_2}{1 - \min(|CF_1|, |CF_2|)} & otherwise \end{cases}$

The serial-synthetic rule is $CF_3 = \begin{cases} CF_1CF_2 & CF_3 > 0 \\ 0 & CF_3 \leq 0 \end{cases}$

4.2 The Relation Between Uncertainty and Granularity

Uncertainty originates in the lack of knowledge mainly. There are several kinds of uncertainty. All can be treated by quotient space model uniformly.

(1) Measurement Uncertainty

We say, 'His age is in the twenties', 'The length of the rope is about fifty meters'. Neither of the two statements is precise, since 'twenties' and 'about fifty meters' are not definite numbers. In daily life, we use these kinds of imprecise description widely. Now that much information we deal with is usually imprecise, what is the distinction between certainty (accuracy) and uncertainty (inaccuracy)?

Taking the 'length of a rope' as an example, we say, 'The length of the rope is about fifty meters'. Whether the statement is precise or not depends on the yardstick we use. If the yardstick we use is coarse, for example, taking 'ten meters' as a minimal measure unit, then 'five' is a precise number in the statement. When the yardstick is refined, for example, taking 'centimeter' as a measure unit, the same 'five' in 'five thousand centimeters' will be imprecise. In other words, as viewed from a low (fine) level, some information is imprecise. While viewed from a high (coarse) level, the same information may be precise. Therefore, whether the information is accurate or not depends on what abstraction level is thought about.

(2) Incomplete Knowledge

In a complex environment, it is hard to get complete information about a world. However, in what condition can sufficient information be obtained? For example, we have a map of nation-wide railway traffic. In the map, Shanghai City is just a point, if viewed for city bus route, there is no information at all. But the map is enough for investigating nation-wide railway transportation. Whether the map is completed or not also depends on the goal and level we are interested in. The information which is incomplete in some fine level may be complete and enough in some coarse level. Conversely, the information which is complete in low level may be redundant in high level. For example, in a map of nation-wide railway traffic, there is no need to depict the details within Shanghai City.

(3) Fuzzy Information

In daily life, people use fuzzy concepts extensively. They are not puzzled by these concepts. We say, 'Someone is young', 'It is cloudy, today', etc. 'Young' and 'cloudy', etc. are generally considered to be fuzzy concepts. Are they really fuzzy? It depends on in what abstraction level we use the information. If we use the concepts of 'young' and 'old' to depict the age of a certain person, certainly, they are 'fuzzy'. If the concepts are only used for describing the characteristics of different groups of people, they are clear and definite.

Given three concepts, for example youngsters, middle-aged persons and old men, denoted by *a, b,* and *c,* respectively. We have a domain $X = \{a, b, c\}$. The order is assumed to be $a<b<c$. If $f(x)$ is an attribute function on a, b and c, we finally have a problem space (X, f, T).

In the domain $X = \{a, b, c\}$, youngsters, middle-aged persons and old men are clearly distinguishable elements. Each has its own characteristic. For example, $f(a)=\{$ardent, full of vim and vigor,...$\}$, $f(b)=\{$experienced, mature,...$\}$, etc. The order relation among elements a, b and c, i.e., youngsters < middle-aged persons < old men, is domain-independent. But the relationship between these concepts and age is domain-dependent. For example, a sportsman who is only thirty years old may not be 'young', but an old man who is sixty years old is still 'young' in a senior citizen community. Conversely, for two sportsmen, so long as one is younger than the other, the age-relation between them, i.e., the former (age) < the latter, remains the same regardless of their real ages. The same is true of two persons in a senior citizen community. It implies that fuzziness occurs only when these concepts are transformed into the fine level-age level.

Therefore, a fuzzy concept may not necessarily be described by a membership function on its original domain. It can be represented in some quotient space. The same is true of uncertain and incomplete information.

Assume that $X, Y \subset X$ is a domain and for X/Y its attribute function $f(x)$ is unknown, i.e., function $f(x)$ is only defined on Y. Then, for $x \in X/Y, f(x)$ is undefined temporarily, whenever new information is gathered, it might be defined. We can still implement some operation on $f(x)$. For example, by the projection operation, we may have attribute function $[f]$ of $f(x)$ on its quotient space $[X]$, regardless of whether $f(x)$ has been defined completely or not. Sometime, in the reasoning process, it's needed to know the value of $f(x)(x \in X/Y)$. We may adopt the mean of $f(x)$ as its default value temporarily. If the default assumption is violated by new observation, then we may make a proper modification. This is just the basis of default reasoning. Thus, our hierarchical model can be used for representing different kinds of uncertainty.

In summary, we make the following assumptions.

Uncertainty Assumption

For some uncertain information A, there exists an abstraction level X_1 such that A is certain on that level. Conversely, some information A which is certain on level X_1 may be uncertain on a finer grained level X_2 to some degree.

From the analysis, it is known that certainty and uncertainty or fuzzy and crisp are relative. They are contrasted with different grain-sizes of the world. So in our reasoning model, uncertain information is represented by different grain-size worlds.

Besides uncertain information, the causal relations may also be uncertain in the reasoning process. We'll use probabilistic tool for representing these kinds of uncertainty.

4.3 Reasoning (Inference) Networks (1)

A great number of reasoning processes can be represented by a graph search.

First, let see an example.

Example 4.1

The jealous husbands problem is one of the well-known river-crossing puzzles. Three married couples denoted by {$A\ a,\ B\ b,\ C\ c$} must cross a river using a boat which can hold at most two people and subject to the constraints: (1) no woman can be in the presence of another man unless her husband is also present, (2) only three men $\{A,B,C\}$ and one woman $\{a\}$ master rowing technology. Under the constraints, we have two heuristic rules: (1) there cannot be both women and men present on a bank with women outnumbering men, since if there were, some woman would be husbandless, (2) only the following ways of river crossing exist: one or two men, woman a or with any other woman, or any couple. Where the married couples are represented by A (male) and a (female), B (male) and b (female), and C (male) and c (female), respectively.

Using the heuristics, we have a shortest solution to the problem shown in Table 4.1. There are 13 one-way trips. The river-crossing process can be represented by a graph as shown in Fig. 4.1.

That is, given a directed graph G, a premise A and a goal p in G, a reasoning process can be regarded as finding a path from A to p in the graph. Since a directed acyclic graph can be represented by a semi-order space (X,T,f), the reasoning mechanism can then be depicted as follows.

(1) $A \subset X$ is a premise, Let $\forall x \in A, f(x) = 1$, and a goal $p \in X$
(2) Reasoning rule: if b is a direct successor of a, then $f(b) = f(a)$.

If we find a p in (X,T,f) such that $f(p) = 1$, then p holds. Otherwise, p does not hold.

In order to change the certain reasoning model above into an uncertain reasoning model, the following two problems must be solved: (1) the representation of the uncertain premise; (2) the representation of the uncertain reasoning rule. As mentioned before,

Table 4.1: River-Crossing Process

Trip Number	Starting Bank	Travel	Ending Bank
Start	$A\,a\,B\,b\,C\,C$		
1	$A\,B\,C\,c$	$a\,b \rightarrow$	
2	$A\,B\,C\,c$	$\leftarrow a$	b
3	$A\,B\,C$	$a\,c \rightarrow$	b
4	$A\,B\,C$	$\leftarrow a$	$b\,c$
5	$A\,a$	$B\,C \rightarrow$	$b\,c$
6	$A\,a$	$\leftarrow B\,b$	$C\,c$
7	$B\,b$	$A\,a \rightarrow$	$C\,c$
8	$B\,b$	$\leftarrow C\,c$	$A\,a$
9	$b\,c$	$B\,C \rightarrow$	$A\,a$
10	$b\,c$	$\leftarrow a$	$A\,B\,C$
11	b	$a\,c \rightarrow$	$A\,B\,C$
12	b	$\leftarrow a$	$A\,B\,C\,c$
13		$a\,b \rightarrow$	$A\,B\,C\,c$
Finish			$A\,a\,B\,b\,C\,c$

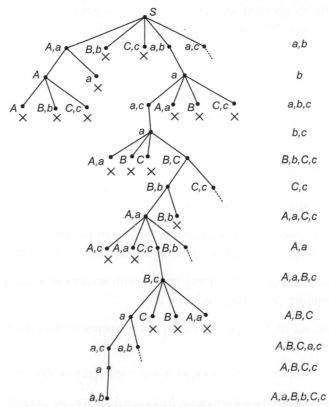

Figure 4.1: River-Crossing Graphical Representation

uncertain information can be described in different grain-size spaces, while uncertain reasoning rules can be represented by probability. We have the following uncertain reasoning model:

(1)   For $A \subset X$, we define a function $f : A \rightarrow [0, 1]$ on A

(2) D is a set of edges on a reasoning network. Define a reasoning function $g : D \rightarrow [0, 1]$

(3)   Reasoning rule: if b is a direct successor of a, for $e = (a, b), e \in D$, define an reasoning rule $f(b) = F(f(a), g(e))$

   F is an arbitrary combination function, for example, $f(b) = f(a)g(e)$

(4)   Given a goal $p \in X$, by the model we have $f(p) = d$, then p holds with confidence d.

Especially, when $d = 1$, p holds. Otherwise, if $d = 0$, p does not hold.

Meantime, another two problems must be solved in order that reasoning can be made in a multi-granular world. First, given an uncertain reasoning model on X and its quotient space $[X]$, how to construct a corresponding reasoning model in $[X]$? This is a projection problem. How to obtain some useful information on X from the reasoning that we draw on $[X]$, this is the problem about the relation between two reasoning models. Second, given two reasoning models on quotient sets X_1 and X_2, how to get a whole understanding about X? This is the synthesis problem of different evidences. We first discuss the projection problem.

4.3.1 Projection

An uncertain reasoning model is represented by

$$((X, D), (f, g), T, F, (A, p))$$

Where X is a domain or a set of nodes of graph G. D is a set of edges in G. A is a subset of premises, p is a goal, $f : A \rightarrow [0, 1], g : D \rightarrow [0, 1]$ is a reasoning function defined on A. T is a semi-order structure. $F: A \times D \rightarrow [0, 1]$ is a function called a reasoning rule.

In essence, so-called reasoning is to answer whether p can be inferred from A, or to what degree of confidence p does hold, when given domain structure T and reasoning rule F.

Projection problem is that given reasoning model with respect to X and its quotient set X_1, find the corresponding reasoning model on X_1.

Since X_1 is a quotient set of X, Edges D_1 on X_1 is the corresponding quotient set of D. First, we define

$$(a, b) = \{e | e = (x, y), x \in a, y \in b, (x, y) \in D\}$$

Let D_1' be a set of all equivalence classes (a, b) defined above. At present D_1' is not a partition of D. Let E_0 be a set of edges of D not belonging to any equivalence class in D_1'. Adding E_0 into D_1', we have D_1. D_1 is a quotient set of D. g_1 is undefined in E_0.

A_1 is a quotient set with respect to A. p_1 is the equivalence class corresponding to p, and $p_1 \in X_1$.

R is an equivalence relation with respect to X_1. T_1 on X_1 is an induced quotient quasi-semi order from R. If R and T are compatible, then T_1 is a quotient semi-order on X_1.

Again, the methods for constructing f_1 and g_1 are given below. For example, by using 'combination principle', we define

$$f_1(a) = G_1(f(x), x \in a \cap A), \forall a \in A_1$$
$$\forall E \in D_1, g_1(E) = G_2(g(e)), e \in E), \forall E \in D_1$$

where, G_1 and G_2 are arbitrary combination functions of their arguments. The range of g_1 is $[0, 1]$.

Taking the same F as the reasoning rule, we have a reasoning model of X_1 as

$$((X_1, D_1), (f_1, g_1), T_1, F_1, (A_1, p_1))$$

Example 4.2

Assume that

$$F(x, y) = xy \tag{4.1}$$

$$\forall a \in A_1, f_1(a) = \max_{x \in a \cap A} f(x) \, , \, \forall a \in A_1$$

$$g_1(E) = \max_{e \in E} g(e) \tag{4.2}$$

We have the following proposition.

Proposition 4.1

$((X, D), (f, g), T, F, (A, p))$ is known. After reasoning, we have $f(p) = d$. Let $((X_1, D_1), (f_1, g_1), T_1, F_1, (A_1, p_1))$ be the corresponding reasoning model on X_1, where X_1 is a quotient set of X. F, f_1 and g_1 are defined by Formulas (4.1) and (4.2). Then from the reasoning model on X_1, we have $f_1(p_1) \geq f(p) = d$.

Proof:

Assume that in X from $x_1 \in A$ and via $x_1 \to x_2 \to \ldots \to x_m = p$, we infer p and $f(p) = d$.

According to the reasoning steps, by induction, when $n = 1$, the conclusion obviously holds. Now assuming that for $n < m$, the conclusion holds, we show that for $n = m$ the conclusion still holds.

Assume that $x_{m-1} \in a_i \in X_1$. From the assumption, we have $f_1(a_i) \geq f(x_{m-1})$.

(1) If $x_m \in a_i$, since $g(x_{m-1}, x_m) \leq 1$, we have

$$f(x_m) = f(x_{m-1}).g(x_{m-1}, x_m) \leq f(x_{m-1}) \leq f_1(a_i)$$

Since $p = x_m \in a_i$, we have $a_i = p_1$. Namely

$$f_1(p_1) \geq f(x_m) = f(p) = d$$

(2) If $x_m \notin a_i$, assuming that $x_m \in a_{i+1} = p_1$, since $e = (x_{m-1}, x_m) \in D$, we have $(a_i, a_{i+1}) \in D_1$. From the above definition, we have

$$g((a_i, a_{i+1})) = \max_{e \in (a_t, a_{t+1})} g(e) \geq g((x_{m-1}, x_m))$$

Again,

$$f_1(p_1) = f_1(a_{i+1}) = f_1(a_i)g((a_i, a_{i+1}))$$
$$\geq f(x_{m-1}).g((x_{m-1}, x_m)) = f(x_m) = f(p) = d$$

The proposition indicates that the projection defined above satisfies the 'homomorphism principle'. That is, if in the high (coarse) abstraction level, we infer that p_1 holds with confidence $<d$, then in the low (fine) level, the corresponding p holds with confidence $<d$ as well.

Simply speaking, if there is no solution in some regions of high abstraction level, i.e., p_1 holds with low confidence, then, there isn't any solution in the corresponding regions of any lower level. This means that based on the result that we infer from high abstraction levels, the possible solution regions in low levels are narrowed. This is the key for reducing computational complexity by hierarchical problem-solving strategy, as discussed in Chapter 2.

When equivalence relation R corresponding to X_1 is incompatible with the semi-order structure T of X, we must revise R such that it is compatible with T, as we have discussed in Chapter 1.

4.3.2 Synthesis

In our reasoning model, uncertain information is represented at different grain-size worlds. The information observed from different perspectives and aspects will have different forms of uncertainty. We will consider how to synthesize the information with different uncertainties.

Assume that X_1 and X_2 are two quotient sets of X. Two reasoning models $((X_1, D_1), (f_1, g_1), T_1, F, (A_1, p_1))$ and $((X_2, D_2), (f_2, g_2), T_2, F, (A_2, p_2))$ on X_1 and X_2 are given. The synthesis of reasoning is to find a new reasoning model $((X_3, D_3), (f_3, g_3), T_3, F, (A_3, p_3))$ in the synthetic space X_3 of X_1 and X_2.

According to the approach indicated in Chapter 3, we have

(1) X_3: the least upper bound of spaces X_1 and X_2
(2) D_3: the least upper bound of spaces D_1 and D_2
(3) T_3: the least upper bound of semi-order structures T_1 and T_2.

In fact, when X_3 and T_3 are fixed, D_3 is uniquely defined. Therefore, X_3 is defined first, then T_3 and finally D_3 is obtained from T_3.

After the projection operation of attribute functions on X has been decided, the synthetic functions f_3 and g_3 are known based on the synthetic method shown in Section 3.6. Let

$$A_3 = \{x | x \in A_1 \cup A_2, x \in X_3\}$$
$$p_3 = \{x | x \in p_1 \cap p_2, x \in X_3\}$$

If the same reasoning rule F is used, we have a reasoning model in the synthetic space X_3 as follows.

$$((X_3, D_3), (f_3, g_3), T_3, F, (A_3, p_3))$$

We next use our synthetic approach to analyze Dempster-Shafer combination rule (or D-S combination rule) in Belief Theory.

Example 4.3

First, we introduce briefly some basic concepts in Belief Theory (Shafer, 1976).

Assume that X is a finite domain, $P(X)$ is a power set of X. Define a function $m : P(X) \to [0, 1]$ such that

(1) $m(\varnothing) = 0$
(2) $\sum_{A \in P(X)} m(A) = 1$

m is called a basic probability assignment on X. Let $Bel(A) = \sum_{B \in A} m(B)$. $Bel(A)$ is said to be a belief function.

Since belief function (Bel) is defined on $P(X)$, when $P(X)$ is regarded as a new set X_1, then Bel is just a function on X_1. Therefore, Bel is an attribute function on $P(X)$.

Assume that m_1 and m_2 are two given attribute functions on X_1 and X_2, respectively. We have two problem spaces (X_1, T_1, m_1) and (X_2, T_2, m_2), where T_i is a topology on X_i, $i = 1, 2$.

The synthesis of the two spaces is as follows.

Let X_3 be the least upper bound of spaces X_1 and X_2, T_3 be the least upper bound of topologies T_1 and T_2.

Define a projection operation of attribute functions as follows.

Assume that m_3 is an attribute function on X_3.

Letting $p_i : (X_3, T_3, m_3) \to (X_i, T_i, m_i)$ be a nature projection, we have $p_i m_3 = m_i, i = 1, 2$. That is,

$$m_i(a) = \sum_{x \in a} m_3(x), a \in X_i, i = 1, 2 \tag{4.3}$$

As mentioned in Section 3.6, the synthesis of quotient spaces (X_1, T_1, m_1) and (X_2, T_2, m_2) is equivalent to that m_3 satisfies Formula (4.3). But the solution of m_3 is not unique. Some optimal criterion must be introduced.

It's known that the attribute function in the coarse level, except itself, cannot provide more information to the attribute function in the fine level. In other words, besides that m_3 satisfies (4.3), it must preserve a maximal uncertainty, or in terms of information theory, 'a maximal entropy'.

When X is a finite set, the entropy of $f : X \rightarrow [0, 1]$ can be defined as

$$I(f) = -\sum_{x \in X} f(x) \ln f(x) \tag{4.4}$$

The maximal criterion is

$$I(m_3) = \max_m I(m) \tag{4.5}$$

where the range m is all basic probability assignments which satisfy (4.3).

When X is a finite set, the two quotient spaces of X are

$$X_1 = \{A_1, A_2, ..., A_n\}, X_2 = \{B_1, B_2, ..., B_m\}$$

The least upper bound space X_3 of X_1 and X_2 is

$$X_3 = \{D_{ij} | D_{ij} = A_i \cap B_j, A_i \in X_1, B_j \in X_2\}$$

We first assume that all $D_{ij} \neq \varnothing$. Let

$$m_1(A_i) = a_i, m_2(B_j) = b_j, m_3(D_{ij}) = d_{ij}$$

From (4.3), we have

$$\begin{cases} a_i = \sum_{j=1}^{m} d_{ij}, j = 1, 2, ..., n \\ b_j = \sum_{i=1}^{n} d_{ij}, i = 1, 2, ..., m \end{cases} \tag{4.6}$$

From (4.4), we can write

$$I(m_3) = -\sum_{ij} d_{ij} \ln d_{ij} \tag{4.7}$$

Under the constraint (4.6), we next find the maximum of Formula (4.7).

Using Lagrange multiplier, we have

$$I_1(m) = \sum_{i,j} d_{ij} \ln d_{ij} + \sum_{i=1}^{n} \lambda_i \left(a_i - \sum_j d_{ij} \right) + \sum_{j=1}^{m} u_j \left(b_j - \sum_i d_{ij} \right)$$

Finding the partial derivative of the formula above with respect to each d_{ij}, and letting its result be zero, we have a set of equations

$$\ln d_{ij} + 1 - \lambda_i - u_i = 0, \quad i = 1, 2, ..., n; \; j = 1, 2, ..., m \tag{4.8}$$

Letting $\beta_i = \lambda_i - \frac{1}{2}$ and $\gamma_i = u_j - \frac{1}{2}$, substituting into (4.8), we have

$$\ln d_{ij} = \beta_i + \gamma_j, \quad i = 1, 2, ..., n; \; j = 1, 2, ..., m \tag{4.9}$$

Again from (4.6), we can write

$$\begin{cases} a_i = \sum_{j=1}^{m} e^{\beta_i} e^{\gamma_j} = e^{\beta_i} \sum_{j=1}^{m} e^{\gamma_j} \\ b_j = \sum_{i=1}^{n} e^{\beta_j} e^{\gamma_j} = e^{\gamma_j} \sum_{i=1}^{n} e^{\beta_i} \end{cases} \tag{4.10}$$

Since m_1 and m_2 are basic probability assignments in X_1 and X_2, we have

$$\sum_{i=1}^{n} a_i = 1, \sum_{j=1}^{m} b_j = 1$$

Letting $\sum_{j=1}^{m} e^{\gamma_j} = t, \sum_{i=1}^{n} e^{\beta_i} = s$, we obtain $a_i = te^{\beta_i}$, $b_j = se^{\gamma_j}$ and $t-s=0$.

Letting $t=s=1$, we have

$$a_i = e^{\beta_i}, b_j = e^{\gamma_j}, i = 1, 2, ..., n; \; j = 1, 2, ..., m$$

Finally, $d_{ij} = a_i b_j, i = 1, 2, ..., n; \; j = 1, 2, ..., m$.

This is just the *D-S* combination rule, where $D_{ij} \neq \varnothing$, m_1 and m_2 are basic probability assignments. The combination rule that we obtained is from the maximal entropy principle.

In case of some of D_{ij} being empty, we will discuss this next.

Example 4.4

$X = \{a, b, c, d\}$ is a domain. $X_1 = \{\{a, b\}, \{d, c\}\}$ and $X_2 = \{\{a, b, c\}, \{d\}\}$ are two quotient sets of X. Let

$$A_1 = \{a, b\}, A_2 = \{c, d\}, B_1 = \{a, b, c\}, B_2 = \{d\}$$
$$m_1(A_1) = \frac{1}{3}, m_1(A_2) = \frac{2}{3}, m_2(B_1) = \frac{1}{4}, m_2(B_2) = \frac{3}{4}$$

Since $D_{11} = A_1 \cap B_1 = A_1$, $D_{12} = A_1 \cap B_1 = \varnothing$, $D_{21} = \{c\}$ and $D_{22} = \{d\}$, we have

$$m_3(D_{12}) = m_3(\varnothing) = 0$$

If m_3 satisfying Formula (4.6) exists, from $A_1 \subset B_1$, we have

$$m_3(A_1) \leq m_3(B_1)$$

Since $B_1 = A_1 \cup D_{21} = D_{11} \cup D_{21}$, $m_2(B_1) = m_3(D_{11}) + m_3(D_{12}) = \frac{1}{4}$.

That is, $m_3(D_{11}) = \frac{1}{4}$. But from $m_3(D_{11}) + m_3(D_{12}) = m_1(A_1) = \frac{1}{3}$, we have $m_3(D_{11}) = \frac{1}{3}$. This is a contradiction. Therefore, there does not exist such a m_3 that satisfies Formula (4.6).

As discussed in Section 3.6, when the m_3 satisfying Formula (4.6) does not exist, similar to the least-squares, a criterion can be introduced. Combining with the given criterion, an optimal solution can be obtained.

When some of D_{ij} are empty, m_3 is defined as follows.

Let

$$I = \{(i,j) | i = 1, 2, ..., n; j = 1, 2, ..., m\}$$
$$I_1 = \{(i,j) | D_{ij} = \varnothing, (i,j) \in I\}$$
$$I_2 = I/I_1$$

Formula (4.6) becomes

$$\begin{cases} a_i - \sum_j d_{ij} = 0, i = 1, 2, ..., n \\ b_j - \sum_i d_{ij} = 0, j = 1, 2, ..., m \\ d_{ij} = 0, (i,j) \in I_2 \end{cases} \tag{4.11}$$

Formula (4.11) may not have a solution, so a weighted least-squares function is used as shown below.

$$Q_1(m, m_1, m_2) = \sum_{i=1}^{n} p_i \left(a_i - \sum_j d_{ij} \right)^2 + \sum_{i=1}^{m} q_i \left(b_{ji} - \sum_i d_{ij} \right)^2$$

where p_i and q_j are weights (constants).

As an optimal criterion, 'the maximal entropy principle' is still used. That is,

$$Q_2(m) = \sum_{(i,j) \in I_2} d_{ij} \ln d_{ij}$$

Let

$$Q_1(m, m_1, m_2) = Q_2(m) + \frac{1}{2} Q_1(m, m_1, m_2) \tag{4.12}$$

Find a m_3 such that the right hand side of Formula (4.12) is minimum.

Let $m_3(D_{ij}) = d_{ij}$ and subject to the constraint

$$\sum_{(i,j)} d_{ij} = 1, d_{ij} \geq 0 \tag{4.13}$$

By using the Lagrange multiplier, we have

$$Q_3(m, m_1, m_2) = Q(m, m_1, m_2) + \lambda \left(\sum d_{ij} - 1 \right) \tag{4.14}$$

Finding the partial derivative of Formula (4.14) with respect to each $d_{ij}(i,j) \in I_2$ and letting the result be zero, we have a set of equations.

$$\ln d_{ij} + p_i \left(a_i - \sum_j {}' d_{ij} \right) + q_i \left(b_j - \sum_i {}' d_{ij} \right) + \lambda = 0, (i,j) \in I_2 \tag{4.15}$$

Where, the first sum $\sum'$ is only over all j in $(i,j) \in I_2$, the second sum $\sum'$ is only over all i in $(i,j) \in I_2$.

For d_{ij} in $(i,j) \in I_2$, letting $d_{ij} = a_i b_j$ and substituting into Formula (4.15), we have

$$\ln d + \ln a_i + \ln b_j + p_i \left(a_i - \sum_j {}' d a_i b_j \right) + q_i \left(b_j - \sum_j {}' d a_i b_j \right) + \lambda = 0$$

Or

$$\ln d + \ln a_i + \ln b_j + p_i a_i \left(1 - \sum_j {}' d b_j \right) + q_i b_j \left(1 - \sum_j {}' d a_i \right) + \lambda = 0 \tag{4.16}$$

Let

$$p_i = -\frac{\ln a_i}{a_i \left(1 - \sum_j {}' d b_j \right)} \quad \text{and} \quad q_j = -\frac{\ln b_j}{a_{bj} \left(1 - \sum_i {}' d a_i \right)} \tag{4.17}$$

Formula (4.16) changes as $\ln d + \lambda = 0, (i,j) \in I_2$. We have $\lambda = -\ln d$.

Since $\sum_{I_2} d_{ij} = 1$, we have $d\sum' a_i b_j = 1$, i.e., $d = 1/(\sum' a_i b_j)$.

Finally, we have

$$d_j = \begin{cases} \dfrac{a_i b_j}{\sum' a_i b_j}, & (i,j) \in I_2 \\ 0, & (i,j) \in I_1 \end{cases} \tag{4.18}$$

Where, the sum $\sum'$ is over all $(i,j) \in I_2$.

Formula (4.18) is just the *D-S* combination rule.

We therefore conclude that, the *D-S* combination rule can be inferred from the synthetic method of quotient spaces by using 'maximal entropy principle'. It is noted that *D-S* rule is simple and is easy to be used, but weights p_i and q_j shown in Formula (4.17) are artificial. It means that we might choose some other optimal criteria such that different combination rules would be obtained to aim at different issues.

Domain structural knowledge, the relationships among elements, for example, the age order among people, the Euclidean metric relations in a two-dimensional image, etc., is not considered either in membership function or in belief function. But it is quite important in multi-granular computing. In our model, taking all factors, including domain, structure and attribute, into consideration and when being transformed from one grained world to the others, their structures are required to satisfy the homomorphism principle. By the principle, it's known that if a proposition is rejected in a coarse-grained world, it must be false in the fine-grained world. Therefore, due to the principle we can benefit from multi-granular computing.

4.3.3 Experimental Results

In this section, we will show the advantage of multi-level graph search (or reasoning) based on quotient space theory by data validation (He, 2011).

The experimental setting is searching the shortest path on three different kinds of networks, i.e., random, small-world and scale-free networks that randomly generated from data. The numbers of their nodes are 100, 200, 300, 400 and 500, respectively. The experiments are implemented on a Pentium 4 computer (main frequency 3.00 GHz, memory capacity 2 GB) using Windows XP SP3. Our method is multi-level (generally, 5–6 levels) search based on quotient space theory. Dijkstra and Floyd algorithms are well-known search algorithms (see Dijkstra, 1959; Floyd, 1962, for more details).

From the results (Tables 4.2–4.4), it's shown that two orders of magnitudes of CPU time can be saved by multi-level search when the scale of networks becomes larger. But the performances slightly reduce, i.e., the ratio between the optimal path found and the real shortest path is 85% in the multi-level search.

Table 4.2: Total CPU Time (in seconds) in Random Networks

Number of Nodes	100	200	300	400	500
Our method	0.939	1.356	3.112	6.634	12.171
Dijkstra	1.719	9.797	91.141	565.391	1002.125
Floyd	0.940	4.220	118.630	212.030	511.560

Table 4.3: Total CPU Time (in seconds) in Small-World Networks

Number of Nodes	100	200	300	400	500
Our method	0.640	2.403	6.659	14.330	22.262
Dijkstra	2.758	10.546	87.239	700.540	1100.200
Floyd	0.790	4.783	132.743	230.412	498.317

Table 4.4: Total CPU Time (in seconds) in Scale-Free Networks

Number of Nodes	100	200	300	400	500
Our method	0.437	1.734	4.297	8,187	15.562
Dijkstra	2.045	8.236	86.431	668.400	998.354
Floyd	0.780	4.060	108.598	206.580	466.250

4.4 Reasoning Networks (2)

In the preceding section, we discussed an uncertain reasoning model in OR-graph. An uncertain reasoning model in AND/OR graph is now discussed. Let's, first, consider the following example.

Example 4.5

In two players, perfect-information games, such as chess, checkers and GO, there are two adversary players who alternate in making moves. At each turn, each player makes one move according to the rules of the game which define both what moves are legal and what effect each possible move will have. Each player has complete information about his opponent's position and all available choices, viewing the opponent's failure as his own success. The game begins from a specified initial state and ends in a position that can be defined as a win for one player and a loss for the other, or possibly as a draw based on the same criterion.

An AND/OR tree, or game tree, is a representation of whole possible plays of the game. The root node denotes the initial position of the game, its successors are the positions that the first player can reach in one move, and their successors are the second player's replies, and so on. Terminal or leaf nodes are labeled as WIN (1), LOSS (−1) or DRAW (0). Each path from the root to a leaf node represents a different complete play of the game, as shown in Fig. 4.2.

The moves available to one player from a given position can be represented by OR links, whereas the moves available to his opponent are AND links, since each of them must be considered in response.

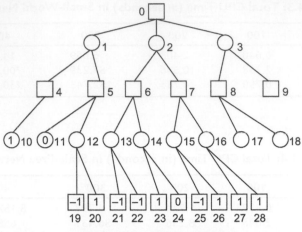

Figure 4.2: A Game Tree

We call the first player MAX and his opponent MIN. Correspondingly, the game positions where it is MAX's or MIN's turn to move are named as MAX and MIN positions, respectively. We distinguish between MAX and MIN positions using a different node shape: the former is represented by squares and the latter by circles. The leaf nodes are labeled as WIN, LOSS or DRAW, depending on whether they represent a win, loss or draw position from MAX's viewpoint.

At the root node, player MAX has three choices. If MAX chooses $0 \rightarrow 1$, MIN $1 \rightarrow 4$, and MAX only $4 \rightarrow 10$, terminal node 10 marked '1', MAX win. If after MAX chooses $0 \rightarrow 1$, MIN chooses $1 \rightarrow 5$ rather than $1 \rightarrow 4$, then MAX has 2 choices: either $5 \rightarrow 11$ or $15 \rightarrow 12$, if the former, MAX reaches terminal node 11 marked '0'-draw, otherwise, MAX reaches node 11,...

Once the leaf nodes are assigned their WIN−LOSS−DRAW status, each node in the game tree can be labeled as WIN, LOSS, or DRAW by a bottom-up labeling procedure. The labeling procedure is the following.

As shown in Fig. 4.3, let's walk through the analysis of the game tree from left to right and from bottom to top. Terminal node 10 is assigned as '1', then node 4 is assigned as '1' as well, since MAX only has one choice at node 4. Terminal nodes 19 and 20 are assigned as '−1' and '1', respectively. At node 12, MIN has two choices, $12 \rightarrow 19$ and $12 \rightarrow 20$, and has assignments '−1' and '1', respectively. MIN chooses the minimal one '−1', i.e., $12 \rightarrow 19$. Then, the assignment of node 12 is '−1'. At node 5, MAX has two choices, $5 \rightarrow 11$ and $5 \rightarrow 12$, and has assignment '0' and '−1', respectively. MAX chooses the maximal one '0', i.e., $5 \rightarrow 11$. Then, the assignment of node 5 is '0'. Finally, we have the overall assignments as shown in Fig. 4.3. The root node is assigned as '0'. This means that MAX has a strategy such that he does not lose the game no matter what

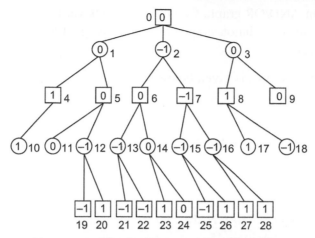

Figure 4.3: The Assignment of a Game Tree

strategy MIN used. Similarly, MIN has a strategy such that he does not lose the game no matter what strategy MAX used.

A strategy for MAX is to explore a sub-graph T^* (or sub-tree) of graph T which is rooted at s and contains one successor of every non-terminal MAX node in T^* and all successors of every non-terminal MIN node in T^*. The sub-graph T^* is called a solution graph.

As mentioned in Chapter 1, many reasoning processes can be explicitly represented by AND/OR graphs (or trees). AND/OR graphs and OR graphs differ only in the relations between nodes and their successors. The former has two kinds of nodes. The MAX positions are OR nodes which are identical to the nodes in OR graphs. The MIN's positions are AND nodes which are unique to AND/OR graph since a response must be contemplated to each of them. If T^* is a solution sub-graph, all its leaf nodes have been assigned. The assignment of a non-terminal OR node is the minimal one among assignments of all its successors. The assignment of a non-terminal AND node is the maximal one among assignments of all its successors. The assignment process going through from bottom to up, finally, we have the assignment of root node. It is called the assignment of solution graph T^*.

Solution graph T^* having the maximal assignment at root node is called the optimal solution graph or the optimal strategy for player MAX. Therefore, the optimal strategy of a finite game can be transformed into solving the optimal solution graph of a corresponding AND/OR graph.

In a rule-based first-order logic deductive system, if axioms and reasoning rules are given, the verification of a goal formula can be transformed into whether the formula belongs to a solution graph of an AND/OR graph. Certainly, the backward reasoning can be used as well, i.e., whether there is a solution graph with the given goal formula as its root and given facts as its leaves.

A backward reasoning example is given below.

Example 4.6

From known facts and reasoning rules, infer whether TEACHER (zhang) has retired or not.

Known Facts:

> PROFESSION (zhang) = TEACHER
> EDUCATION-AGE (zhang) = 45
> SEX (zhang) = MALE,...

Reasoning Rules

> R_1: TEACHER (x) $\wedge$ AGE $(x) \geq 60 \wedge$ SEX $(x) =$ MALE $\rightarrow$ RETIRE
> R_2: TEACHER (x) $\rightarrow$ UNDERGRADUATE (x)
> R_3: UNDERGRADUATE (x) $\rightarrow$ AGE $(x) \geq 20$
> R_4: EDUCATION-AGE (x) $\rightarrow$ AGE $(x) \geq y + 20$,...

The known facts are assigned as '1' as shown in Fig. 4.4. If b is an AND node and has successors $a_1, a_2, ..., a_n$, the assignment $f(b)$ of b is $\min_i(f(a_i)), i = 1, 2, ..., n$, where $f(a_i)$ is an assignment of a_i. If b is an OR node and has successors $a_1, a_2, ..., a_n$, the assignment $f(b)$ of b is $\max_i(f(a_i))$. Finally, the assignment of root node is '1', i.e., the confirmation of RETIRE (zhang).

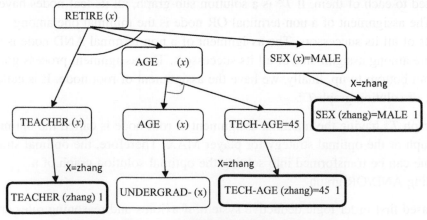

Figure 4.4: Backward Reasoning

The above discussion is confined to deterministic cases, i.e., both facts and reasoning rules are certainty. The problem is that when both known facts and reasoning rules are uncertain, how can a reasoning model be established? As discussed in Section 4.3, uncertain information can be represented at different grain-size worlds. And a reasoning function defined on a set of edges D depicts the uncertainty of causal relations.

In the next section, our discussion will focus on the projection and synthesis problems of AND/OR reasoning model.

4.4.1 Modeling

X is a domain. Given a premise A, A is a subset of X. f is an attribute function defined on A. f depicts the uncertainty of A. Therefore, a premise can be represented by (A, f).

Reasoning Rules

If all events $a_1, a_2, \ldots, a_n$ hold, it implies b. We define $a_1, a_2, \ldots, a_n$ as AND sub-nodes of b. If any of events $a_1, a_2, \ldots, a_n$ holds, it implies b. We define $a_1, a_2, \ldots, a_n$ as OR sub-nodes of b.

If b has either OR sub-nodes or AND sub-nodes, these sub-nodes may be represented by a disjunctive normal form. For example,

$$b = (a_{11} \wedge a_{12} \wedge \ldots \wedge a_{1n}) \vee (a_{21} \wedge a_{22} \wedge \ldots) \vee \ldots \vee (a_{n1} \wedge a_{n2} \wedge \ldots)$$

Let $a_i = (a_{n1} \wedge a_{n2} \wedge \ldots)$. We decompose these sub-nodes into two levels, $a_1, a_2, \ldots, a_n$ are OR sub-nodes of b, and $a_{i1}, a_{i2}, \ldots, a_{in}$ are AND sub-nodes of a_i. The causal relations among events of X are represented by an AND/OR graph. The graph's structure is denoted by T.

Reasoning Function

D is a set of edges in X. Define $g : D \rightarrow [0, 1], g(e) = g((a, b))$, where (a, b) is an edge. Therefore, function g is an uncertainty measurement of causal relation between events a and b, and is called reasoning function.

Reasoning Rule

(1) If b is an AND node and $a_1, a_2, \ldots, a_n$ are its AND sub-nodes, we define

$$f(b) = F_1(f(a_i), g(e_i), e_i = (a_i, b), i = 1, 2, \ldots, n) \tag{4.19}$$

where, F_1 is a combination function of its arguments.

(2) If b is an OR node and $a_1, a_2, \ldots, a_n$ are its OR sub-nodes, we define

$$f(b) = F_2(f(a_i), g(e_i), e_i = (a_i, b), i = 1, 2, \ldots, n) \tag{4.20}$$

where, F_2 is a combination function of its arguments.

Given a goal event $p, p \in X$, the process of finding p from a given premise A is represented by a reasoning model

$$((X, D), (f, g), T, F_1, F_2, (A, p))$$

where, A is a premise, f is an attribute function on A representing the uncertainty of A. p is a goal, D is a set of edges, g is a reasoning function defined in D, F_1 and F_2 are reasoning rules representing AND nodes and OR nodes, respectively, T is the structure of AND/OR graph.

Similar to Section 4.3, the transformation of the model among different grain-size worlds should be discussed, namely, the projection and synthesis problems.

Assume that reasoning rules are unchanged during the transformation. The projection and synthesis approaches of X, D, A, p, f and g are the same as that presented in Section 4.3. We now focus our attention on the projection and synthesis of AND/OR relations, i.e., structure T.

4.4.2 The Projection of AND/OR Relations

$((X, D), (f, g), T, F_1, F_2, (A, p))$ is a reasoning model. X_1 is a quotient space of X. We'll construct a corresponding reasoning model in X_1.

According to the method presented in Section 4.3.1, a model $((X_1, D_1), (f_1, g_1), F_1, F_2, (A_1, p_1))$ can be constructed.

Now, we define the projection T_1 of structure T.

Regarding all nodes in T as OR nodes, we have a structure T'. Assume that R_1 is an equivalence relation with respect to X_1. Viewing T' as a semi-order, R_1 is assumed to be compatible with T'. Based on the method shown in Section 4.3.1, a quotient semi-order T'_1 of T' can be constructed. Namely, T'_1 is a projection of T' on X_1.

Assume that $b \in (X_1, T'_1)$, $(a_1, a_2, ..., a_n)$ are all sub-nodes on X_1 of b and is called a set of sub-nodes of b.

Definition 4.1

$(a_1, a_2, ..., a_n)$ is a set of AND sub-nodes of b. Equivalently, $\forall y \in b$, there exist $x_i \in a_i, i = 1, 2, ..., n$, $x_i \in X$ and y such that $(x_1, x_2, ..., x_n)$ is a set of AND sub-nodes of y. Otherwise, b is said to be an OR node. Then, we have a structure T_1 of X_1 and a reasoning model on X_1 as

$$((X_1, D_1), (f_1, g_1), T_1, F_1, F_2, (A_1, p_1))$$

Example 4.7

Given an AND/OR graph (X, D, T) as shown in Fig. 4.5(a). Let

$$X_1 = \{a_1 = \{1\}, a_2 = \{2,3\}, a_3 = \{4\}, a_4 = \{5\}, a_5 = \{6,8,9\}, a_6 = \{7\}\}$$

Find a corresponding AND/OR graph (X_1, D_1, T_1) on X_1.

Solution:

We first transform the AND/OR graph (X, D, T) into a semi-order set. It is known that the semi-order is compatible with the equivalence relation corresponding to X_1. Graph (X_1, T_1) can be constructed as shown in Fig. 4.5(b).

According to the definition of the projection of AND relations, we have an AND/OR graph as shown in Fig. 4.5(c).

We next show that the projection defined in Definition 4.1 satisfies the homomorphism principle under a certain condition.

$((X, D), (f, g), T, F_1, F_2, (A, p))$ is a reasoning model. X_1 is a quotient apace of X. R_1 is an equivalence relation with respect to X_1. Assume that R_1 and T are compatible. Let $P: X \rightarrow X_1$ be a projection.

Assume that $\forall a \in A_1, A_1 = p(A)$. We define $f_1(a) = \max_{x \in a \cap A} f(x)$.

$\forall E \in D_1, D_1 = p(D)$, we define $g_1(E) = \max_{e \in E} g(e)$.

Let $F_1(y) = \min_x f(x)g((x, y))$.

where, x is an AND sub-node of y and (x, y) is an edge.

Let $F_2(y) = \max_x f(x)g((x, y))$.

where, x is an OR sub-node of y.

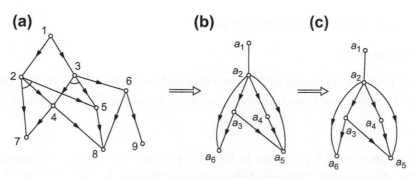

Figure 4.5: Quotient Set and AND/OR Graph

Let the projection of the given model be

$$((X_1, D_1), (f_1, g_1), T_1, F_1, F_2, (A_1, p_1))$$

Theorem 4.1

Under the definition above, if $f(p) = d$ is the consequence inferred on X, and $f_1(p_1) = d_1$ is the consequence inferred on X_1, then $d_1 \geq d$, namely, the homomorphism principle is satisfied.

Lemma 4.1

For $x_1, x_2, \ldots, x_n, y \in X$, $(x_1, x_2, \ldots, x_n)$ is a set of sub-nodes of y. The value of $f(x_i)$ is known. $a_i = p(x_i)$, where $p : X \to X_1$ is a projection. Assume that $f_1(a_i) \geq f(x_i)$. If $f(y) = d$ is inferred from $f(x_i)$ and $f_1(p(y)) = d_1$ is inferred from $f_1(a_i)$ according to the reasoning rule, then $d_1 \geq d$.

Proof:

For simplicity, assume that $g(e) = 1$

First, assume that y is an AND node, namely, $f(y) = \min\limits_{x_i} f(x_i)$.

If $\exists i, p(y) = b = a_i, f_1(p(y)) = f_1(a_i) \geq f(x_i) \geq f(y) = d$. If $\forall i, b \neq a_i$, from the definition of T_1, a_i is a sub-node of b on (X_1, T_1). If b is an OR node, then

$$f_1(b) \geq f_1(a_i) \geq f_1(x_i) \geq f_1(y)$$

If b is an AND node, then b has no more sub-node except $a_i, i = 1, 2, \ldots, n$. Otherwise, assuming that c is an another sub-nodes of b, namely, for $\forall i, c \neq a_i$, from Definition 4.1, there exists a sub-node x_{n+1} of y. Since $c \neq a_i$ we have $x_{n+1} \neq x_i, i \leq n$. This is a contradiction. Thus, $\{a_1, a_2, \ldots, a_n\}$ are the whole AND sub-nodes of b. Therefore,

$$f_1(b) = \min\limits_i f_1(a_i) = f_1(a_{i0}) \geq f(x_{i0}) \geq f(y) = d$$

Similarly, when y is an OR node, the same is true.

The Proof of Theorem 4.1

Assume that T is a solution graph in X rooted at p and the value of T is d. The theorem can be proved by induction from leaf nodes to the root node of T and Lemma 4.1.

Example 4.8

Given an AND/OR graph (X, F) shown in Fig. 4.6(a), a set $A = \{2, 4, 5\}$ of premises and a goal $p = \{13\}$. Assume that $f(2) = 4, f(4) = 5$ and $f(5) = 6$. $X_1 = \{1, 2, 3, 4, \{5, 9\}, 6,$

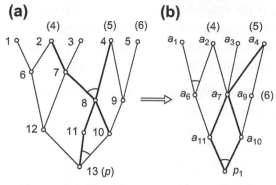

Figure 4.6: The Homomorphism Principle

$\{7,8\}, 10, \{11,12\}, 13$. F_1, F_2, f_1, g_1 are defined as shown in Theorem 4.1. p_1 is the corresponding goal in X_1 and the projection of p. Find $f(p)$ and $f(p_1)$.

Solution:

From graph (X, T) shown in Fig. 4.6(a), we construct a corresponding graph (X_1, T_1) (see Fig. 4.6(b)). In Fig. 4.6(a), sub-graph T shown as a bold line is a solution graph with respect to p. From T, we have the result $f(p) = 4$. In Fig. 4.6(b), sun-graph T_1 shown in bold is a solution graph corresponding to p_1. From T_1, we have the result $f_1(p_1) = 5 \geq f(p) = 4$.

Note that the reasoning model constructed by using the projection of AND/OR relations T defined in Definition 4.1 does not guarantee the satisfaction of the homomorphism principle. It not only depends on the definition of the projection but also the forms of f, g, F_1, F_2 and whether R_1 is compatible with T or not.

In general, it is unlikely to present a uniform definition of projection of T such that in any reasoning model the homomorphism principle is satisfied. Theorem 4.1 shows that the existence of such a projection only under a certain condition.

4.4.3 The Synthesis of AND/OR Relations

In this section we discuss the synthesis of AND/OR relations of two quotient spaces.

In two quotient spaces with AND/OR structures, we have their reasoning models below

$$((X_1, D_1), (f_1, g_1), T_1, F_1, F_2, (A_1, p_1))$$
$$((X_2, D_2), (f_2, g_2), T_2, F_1, F_2, (A_2, p_2))$$

where X_1 and X_2 are quotient spaces of X.

The synthetic procedure is the following. First, having transformed given AND/OR graphs into their corresponding OR graphs, we then find the synthesis of the transformed OR graphs. The synthetic OR graph is transformed into a corresponding AND/OR graph. The latter is regarded as the synthesis of given AND/OR graphs.

Assume that (X_1, T_1) is an AND/OR graph. If all its nodes are regarded as OR nodes, we have an OR graph denoted as $(X_1, \hat{T}_1)$. Given

$$((X_1, D_1), (f_1, g_1), T_1, F_1, F_2, (A_1, p_1))$$
$$((X_2, D_2), (f_2, g_2), T_2, F_1, F_2, (A_2, p_2))$$

The synthetic rules are shown below.

X_3 is the least upper bound of spaces X_1 and X_2.

A_3 is the image of $A_1 \cup A_2$ on X_3, simply denoted by $A_3 = A_1 \cup A_2$.

$p_3 = p_1 \cap p_2$ or $p_3 = p_1 \cup p_2$.

ζ_3 is the synthetic semi-order structure of ζ_1 and ζ_2, where ζ_1 and ζ_2 are the corresponding OR graph structures of T_1 and T_2, respectively.

f_3 is the synthesis of f_1 and f_2 on A_3

D_3 is the synthesis of g_1 and g_2 on D_3.

g_3 is the synthesis of g_1 and g_2 on D_3

We have $((X_3, D_3), (f_3, g_3), \zeta_1, F_1, F_2, (A_3, p_3))$.

Note that taking the image of $p_1 \cap p_2$ on X_3 as p_3, it implies that p_1 and p_2 are two solutions of the same goal from different perspectives. If $p_1 \cap p_2 = \emptyset$, it means that there exists a contradiction between the solutions inferred from different perspectives, or p_1 and p_2 are actually two independent problems being mistaken as two perspectives on the same problem.

While taking the image of $p_1 \cup p_2$ on X_3 as p_3, it implies that we solve p_1 and p_2 together in the hope of that premises A_1 and A_2 might be favorable for solving p_2 and p_1, respectively. Therefore, the definition of p_3 depends on actual demand.

Now, we transform ζ_3 into the corresponding AND/OR structure T_3.

Suppose that $(x_1, x_2, ..., x_n)$ is a set of sub-nodes of y in structure ζ_3. Let

$$y = b_1 \cap b_2 \text{ and } x_i = a_{1i} \cap a_{2i}, i = 1, 2, ..., n$$

where, $b_1, a_{1i} \in X_1$ and $b_2, a_{2i} \in X_2$.

$(x_1, x_2, \ldots, x_n)$ is called a set (T_3) of AND sub-nodes of y, if and only if $(a_{11}, a_{12}, \ldots, a_{1n})$ is a set (T_1) of AND sub-nodes of b_1 and $(a_{21}, a_{22}, \ldots, a_{2n})$ is a set (T_2) of AND sub-nodes of b_2.

Otherwise, $(x_1, x_2, \ldots, x_n)$ is called a set (T_3) of OR sub-nodes of y.

Therefore, we have a reasoning model with AND/OR structure.

$$((X_3, D_3), (f_3, g_3), T_3, F_1, F_2, (A_3, p_3))$$

It is called the synthesis of the reasoning models in X_1 and X_2.

Note that the transformation from ζ_3 to T_3 is not unique. For example, we can define as follows.

$(x_1, x_2, \ldots, x_n)$ is called a set (T_3) of AND sub-nodes of y, if and only if $(a_{11}, a_{12}, \ldots, a_{1n})$ is a set (T_1) of AND sub-nodes of b_1 or $(a_{21}, a_{22}, \ldots, a_{2n})$ is a set (T_2) of AND sub-nodes of b_2.

Otherwise, $(x_1, x_2, \ldots, x_n)$ is called a set (T_3) of OR sub-nodes of y.

So far we have provided a theoretical framework for the synthesis of different reasoning models. To illustrate its applications, we give an example below.

Example 4.9

There are 100 pupils in a class. In the first semester they took examinations in Chinese and Mathematics. Fifteen out of 100 pupils did not pass the Chinese test. Twenty pupils did not pass the Mathematics test. After make-up examinations only half of them passed these examinations. According to administration regulations, those who did not pass two course tests will fail to go up to the next grade, while those who did not pass one of them will remain in the class.

In the second semester, the pupils took one examine in Physics. Twenty pupils did not pass the test. After make-up examination only half of them passed the test. Those who have accumulatively two courses below pass level will fail to go up to the next grade based on the regulations. Determine how many pupils fail to go up to the next grade and how many pupils have one course below pass level in two semesters.

Since we don't know the details of each pupil's scores, we can only make estimates.

First, by using the synthetic approach, we make the estimation under 'maximal entropy principle'. Assume that A_1 represents a set of pupils who pass the Chinese test. The others are represented by A_2.

Similarly, B_1 represents a set of pupils who pass the Mathematics test. The others represented by B_2.

Therefore, $A_2 \cap B_2$ represents those who do not pass these two examinations. While $A_1 \cap B_1$ represents those who pass these two examinations. $A_1 \cap B_2$ and $A_2 \cap B_1$ represent those who only pass one of the examinations.

Thus, $\{A_1 \cap B_1, A_1 \cap B_2, A_2 \cap B_1, A_2 \cap B_2\} = X$.

X_3 can be regarded as a synthetic space of $X_1 = (A_1, A_2)$ and $X_2 = (B_1, B_2)$. We have

$$f_1(A_1) = 85, f_1(A_2) = 15$$
$$f_2(B_1) = 80, f_2(B_2) = 20$$

Using the 'maximal entropy principle', namely, no matter whether pupils pass Chinese examination, the probability that they pass the Mathematics examination is assumed to be the same. We have a synthetic function $f_3(.)$ of f_1 and f_2 below.

$$f_3(A_1 \cap B_1) = 68, f_3(A_1 \cap B_2) = 17$$
$$f_3(A_2 \cap B_1) = 12, f_3(A_2 \cap B_2) = 3$$

The reasoning network is shown in Fig. 4.7. The network has four levels, from top to down, the first level — the first semester examination, the second level — the first semester make-up examination, the third level — the second semester examination, and the fourth level — the second semester make-up examination. Where nodes without marks indicate those who pass these two tests, nodes marked '1' indicate those who only pass one of the tests, nodes marked '2' indicate those who do not pass any test before make-up examination, nodes marked 'x' indicate those who fail to go up to the next grade.

We number each node as shown in Fig. 4.7. The numbers close to each edge are the values of $g(e)$. The numbers within brackets are the values of $f_3(.)$.

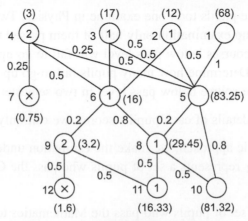

Figure 4.7: A Reasoning Network

The 'maximal entropy principle' is also used for analyzing the physics examination. Therefore, $g((5, 10)) = 0.8$, $g((5, 8)) = 0.2$, etc. as shown in Fig. 4.7.

Reasoning rule is $f(y) \sum_x f(x)g((x, y))$, where the sum $\sum$ is over all sub-nodes of y. The final results are $0.75 + 1.6 = 2.35(\%)$ of pupils who fail to go up to the next grade after two semesters, and $16.33(\%)$ of pupils who still do not pass one course's test after make-up examinations.

"Maximal entropy principle' means that no additional information is added in the synthetic process. If an additional knowledge is added, the conclusion will be different. For example, assume that 'if a pupil does badly in his studies, generally, the score of each course is low'. This means that the probability that a pupil passes the Mathematics test will depend on whether he passes the Chinese test or not. In one extreme, those pupils who do not pass the Chinese test must not pass the Mathematics test, then we have $f_3(4) = 15, f_3(3) = 5, f_3(2) = 0, f_3(1) = 80$.

To estimate the result of the Physics test we, however, still use the 'maximal entropy principle'. From Fig. 4.7, we have 4.75% pupils who fail to go up to the next grade after two semesters, and 13.63% pupils who still have one course below pass level after the make-up examination.

If another extreme is adopted, namely, the pupils who do not pass the Chinese test must pass the Mathematics test, then we have

$$f_3(4) = 0, \quad f_3(3) = 20, \quad f_3(2) = 15, \quad f_3(1) = 65$$

The 'maximal entropy principle' is still used for analyzing the Physics examination. We have 1.75% pupils who fail to go up to the next grade and 17% pupils who do not pass one of the examinations.

Three estimation results are listed in Table 4.5.

It is noted that the maximal entropy estimation is somewhere between the two extreme cases, the most pessimistic and the most optimistic estimations.

Table 4.5: The Comparison of Three Different Estimations

Type of estimations	Fail to go up to the next grade (%)	Do not pass one of the examinations (%)	Others (%)
The most pessimistic	4.75	13.63	81.62
The maximal entropy	2.35	16.33	81.32
The most optimistic	1.75	17.00	81.2

4.4.4 Conclusion

In this section, the uncertain reasoning model on an AND/OR graph (OR graph) is defined. The projection structure from space X to its quotient space is discussed and how to synthesize a spatial structure from structures of two different quotient sets is also involved. We prove that only under a specific definition of projection and a certain reasoning rule, the homomorphism of quotient structures holds. As mentioned in the section, the homomorphism principle is very important in quotient structure analysis. The efficiency of multi-granular computing depends on the satisfaction degree of the homomorphism principle to a great extent. The aim of analyzing coarse grained spaces strives for denying the existence of 'the solution' in some regions of the spaces. The larger the region the more efficient the multi-granular computing is.

4.5 Operations and Quotient Structures

There is a variety of operations defined on a domain. In fact, an operation implicitly defines an interrelationship among elements of the domain. Under different grain-size worlds, the following issues should be answered. The induction of a corresponding operation on a quotient space from an operation defined on its original space, and the synthesis of two operations defined on different grain-size spaces becomes a new operation on their synthetic space, i.e. a finer space.

Let us consider two simple examples.

Example 4.10

$X = \{0, 1, 2, \ldots, n, \ldots\}$ is a set of non-negative integers, X_1 is a quotient set of X denoted by $X_1 = \{a_0, a_1, \ldots, a_{q-1}\}$, where $a_i = \{n | n = i + mq, m = 0, 1, 2, \ldots\}, 0 \le i < q$.

Let '+' be a common addition operation on X. Define an operation on X_1 as follows.

$$a_k = a_i \oplus a_j \Leftrightarrow k \equiv (i+j)(\mathrm{mod}\ q)$$

Let $p : X \rightarrow X_1$ be a natural projection.

Obviously, for $\forall x, y \in X$, we have $p(x + y) = p(x) \oplus p(y)$.

It implies that the projection of the sum '+' of any two elements x and y on X is identical to the sum '$\oplus$' of the projections of these two elements on X_1. Projection p with the preceding property is called a 'homomorphism transform' from $(X, +) \rightarrow (X_1, \oplus)$. Operation '$\oplus$' can be regarded as an induced addition operation on X_1 from the addition operation '+' on X.

Unfortunately, there is not such an induced operation for many operations in general.

Example 4.11

$X = (-\infty, +\infty) = E^1$ is a one-dimensional Euclidean space, $X_1 = \{a, b, c\}$ is a quotient space of X, where $a = (-\infty, 0), b = [0], c = (0, +\infty)$.

Now we discuss operation '$+$' on X. We show there does not have any induced operation '$\oplus$' on X_1 such that projection $p : X \rightarrow X_1$ is homomorphic.

Proof:

By reduction to absurdity, otherwise assume there is an induced operation $\oplus$ on X_1.

By taking $x = -1 \in a$ and $y = 2 \in c$, from the homomorphism property of p we have

$$a \oplus c = p(x) \oplus p(y) = p(x + y) = p(1) = c$$

If taking $x = -2 \in a$ and $y = 1 \in c$, then we have

$$a \oplus c = p(x) \oplus p(y) = p(x + y) = p(-1) = a$$

This is a contradiction, and hence there does not have to be any induced operation such that p is homomorphic.

However, in what conditions does a homomorphic-induced operation exist? In modem algebra, for some structures such as groups there are some related results. A result is given below as an example.

Example 4.12

X is a group, X_1 is a normal sub-group of X. Let $X_2 = X/X_1$ be a quotient group of X with respect to X_1. An induced operation is defined on X_2 as follows.

$$(xX_1)(yX_1) = (xy)X_1$$

If p is a $X \rightarrow X_2$ projection, then p is a homomorphism transformation.

From the example, it is known that only under certain conditions can an operation with homomorphism property on a quotient space be induced.

Assume that N is an operation on X and X_1 is a quotient space of X. If there exists an operation N_1 on X_1 such that $p : (X, N) \rightarrow (X_1, N_1)$ is a homomorphism projection, then N_1 is said to be a quotient operation on X_1 with respect to N, or simply a quotient operation.

As mentioned before, generally, there is not a quotient operation on a quotient space. Similar to semi-order discussed in Chapter 1, we can adjust the quotient space by merging and refining approaches such that a corresponding quotient operation exists.

4.5.1 The Existence of Quotient Operations

X is a domain. X_0 is the coarsest quotient space of X, namely, a quotient space regarding all elements of X as an equivalence class.

Assume that N is a binary-operation on X, namely

$$N : X \times X \to X$$

Given a quotient space X_1 of X, obviously, we have $X_0 < X_1 < X$.

It is obvious that N has a corresponding quotient operation N_0 on X_0 as long as we define $N_0(a, a) = a, a \in X_0$.

If there is not a quotient operation N_1 on X_1, the problem is whether the finest quotient space $\underline{X}$ exists such that

$$(1)\ \underline{X} < X_1 \text{ and } (2)\ \underline{X} \text{ has a quotient operation } \underline{N}$$

Or whether the coarsest quotient space $\overline{X}$ exists such that

$$(1)\ X_1 < \overline{X} \text{ and } (2)\ \overline{X} \text{ has a quotient operation } \overline{N}$$

If such quotient operations exists, $\underline{X}$ and $\overline{X}$ are operational lower and upper bound spaces of X_1 with respect to operation N, respectively, $\underline{N}$ and $\overline{N}$ are lower and upper quotient operations of N corresponding to X_1, respectively, or simply lower and upper quotient operations of X_1.

Obviously, if $\underline{X} = X_1$, then $N_1 = \underline{N}$ is a quotient operation on X_1.

We next discuss the existence of upper and lower quotient operations.

Proposition 4.2

X is domain. N is a binary-operation on X. X_1 is a quotient space of X. There exist upper and lower quotient operations of N corresponding to X_1.

Proof:

Let

$$A = \{X_a | X_a < X_1,\ there\ exists\ a\ quotient\ operation\ on\ X_a\}$$
$$B = \{X_a | X_a > X_1,\ there\ exists\ a\ quotient\ operation\ on\ X_a\}$$

Since $X_0 \in A$ and $X \in B$, i.e., A and B are non-empty, from Proposition 1.2 in Chapter 1, we know that all quotient spaces of X constitute a complete semi-order lattice according to the quotient inclusion relation. Therefore, there exist both the least upper bound space $\underline{X}$ on A and the greatest lower bound space $\overline{X}$ on B.

We only need to show there exist quotient operations on $\underline{X}$ and $\overline{X}$, respectively.

From the definition of the least upper bound space, we can see that for $\forall a \in \underline{X}$, there exists $a_\alpha \in X_\alpha$ such that $p_\alpha(a) = a_\alpha$, where p_α is the projection from $\underline{X} \rightarrow X_\alpha$. Regarding a and a_α as sub-sets of X and $a \subset a_\alpha$, we have $a = \bigcap_\alpha a_\alpha$. As stated above, it is known that X_α has a quotient operation N_α.

For $\forall a, b \in \underline{X}$, let $a = \bigcap_\alpha a_\alpha$ and $b = \bigcap_\alpha b_\alpha$, where $a_\alpha, b_\alpha \in X_\alpha$. From $N_\alpha(a_\alpha, b_\alpha) = c_\alpha \in X_\alpha$, letting $c = \bigcap_\alpha c_\alpha$, since $c_\alpha \in X_\alpha$, we have $c = \bigcap_\alpha c_\alpha \in \underline{X}$.

Define $\underline{N} = \underline{N}(a, b) = c$. Since $X_\alpha < \underline{X}$, then given $a \in \underline{X}$ letting $p_\alpha(a) = a_\alpha \in X_\alpha$ and $p_\alpha(b) = b_\alpha \in X_\alpha$, a_α and b_α are unique. Therefore, c defined above is unique, namely, $\underline{N}$ is uniquely defined.

We next only need to prove that $\underline{p} : (X, N) \rightarrow (\underline{X}, \underline{N})$ is homomorphic.

Let $\underline{p} : X \rightarrow \underline{X}$ and $p_\alpha : X \rightarrow X_\alpha$.

Since $\underline{X}$ is the least upper bound space of $\{X_\alpha\}$, we have that for $\forall x \in X, \underline{p}(x) = \bigcap_\alpha p_\alpha(x)$ holds.

Given $x, y \in X$, let $\underline{p}(x) = a, \underline{p}(y) = b$ and $p_a(x) = a_a, p_a(y) = b_a$.

Assume $N(x, y) = z$. Let $c_a = p_a(z)$ and $c = \bigcap c_a$. Since N_α is a quotient operation, we have $\forall \alpha, p_\alpha(N(x, y)) = N_\alpha(p_\alpha(x), p_\alpha(y)) = N_\alpha(a_\alpha, b_\alpha) = c_\alpha$.

By intersection operation, we have

$$\underline{p}(N(x, y)) = \bigcap_\alpha p_\alpha(N(x, y)) = \bigcap_\alpha c_\alpha = c$$

From the definition of $\underline{N}$, we have $\underline{N}(\underline{p}(x), \underline{p}(y)) = \underline{N}(a, b) = c$.

Finally, we can write

$$\underline{p}(N(x, y)) = \underline{N}(\underline{p}(x), \underline{p}(y))$$

Namely, $\underline{N}$ is a quotient operation on $\underline{X}$. In other words, $\underline{N}$ is a lower quotient operation of X_1.

We now prove there is an upper quotient operation of X_1.

Let $\overline{X}$ be the infimum of B. For $\forall a, b \in \overline{X}$, let

$$d = \bigcup_{\substack{x \in a \\ y \in b}} N(x, y), x, y \in X$$

We now show that any two elements in d are $\overline{R}$-equivalent, where $\overline{R}$ is an equivalence relation corresponding to $\overline{X}$.

$\forall \alpha$, R_α is assumed to be an equivalence relation corresponding to X_α. p_α is a projection from $X \rightarrow X_\alpha$. N_α is a quotient operation on X_α.

Given $x_1, x_2 \in a$ and $y \in b$, let $z_1 = N(x_1, y)$ and $z_2 = N(x_2, y)$. Since $x_1, x_2 \in a$ and $\overline{X}$ is the infimum of B, there exist $x_1, x_3, x_4, \ldots, x_n = x_2$ such that

$$x_1 \sim x_3 (R_{a1}), x_i \sim x_{i+1} (R_{ai}), i = 3, 4, \ldots, n-1$$

There is no lost generality in assuming that $x_1 \sim x_2 (R_a)$, we have

$$N_a(p_a(x_1), p_a(y)) = p_a(N(x_1, y)) = p_a(z_1) \text{ and}$$
$$N_a(p_a(x_2), p_a(y)) = p_a(N(x_2, y)) = p_a(z_2)$$

Since $x_1 \sim x_2 (R_a)$, we have $p_\alpha(x_1) = p_\alpha(x_2)$.

Thus, $p_a(z_1) = N_a(p_a(x_1), p_a(y)) = N_a(p_a(x_2), p_a(y)) = p_a(z_2)$.

As $\overline{X}$ is the infimum of B, from the definition of infimum we obtain $z_1 \sim z_2 (\overline{R})$.

Similarly, for $\forall x_1, x_2 \in a, y_1, y_2 \in b$, $N(x_1, y_1)$ and $N(x_2, y_2)$ are $\overline{R}$-equivalent.

We conclude that any two of elements in d are $\overline{R}$-equivalent.

Let c be an equivalence class on $\overline{X}$ containing d. Define $\overline{N}(a, b) = c$.

From the result above, c is uniquely defined and satisfies

$$\forall x, y \in X, \; \overline{p}(N(x, y)) = \overline{N}(\overline{p}(x), \overline{p}(y))$$

Where, $\overline{p}$ is a projection from $(X, N) \rightarrow (X_1, \overline{N})$.

It follows that $\overline{N}$ is an upper quotient operation of N with respect to X_1

4.5.2 The Construction of Quotient Operations

We have proved that for any quotient space there exist unique upper and lower quotient operations. Now we discuss the construction of them, namely, $\underline{N}$ and $\overline{N}$, when X, N and X_1 are given, especially, if X is a finite set. In this section, X is assumed to be a finite set.

Lower Quotient Operation

N is a binary-operation on X. X_1 is a quotient space of X. R_1 is an equivalence relation corresponding to X_1.

Define relation R_i recursively as follows.

$$\forall z_1, z_2 \in X, z_1 \sim z_2 (R_2) \Leftrightarrow \exists x_1 \sim x_2 (R_1), y_1 \sim y_2 (R_1), \text{ and}$$
$$z_1 = N(x_1, y_1), z_2 = N(x_2, y_2) \text{ or } z_1 \sim z_2 (R_1)$$

Let $R_2 = L(R_1)$. Generally, define $R_i = L(R_{i-1})$, $i > 1$.

Since X is a finite set, there exists a minimal integer n such that $R_n = R_{n+1}$.

Let $\underline{R}$ be an equivalence relation with R_n as its base. Namely,

$$x \sim y\left(\underline{R}\right) \Leftrightarrow \exists x_1, x_2, \ldots, x_m, x = x_1, x_m = y \text{ and}$$

$$x_i \sim x_{i+1}(R_n), i = 1, 2, \ldots, m-1, \text{ or simply } \underline{R} \sim R_n$$

Let X be a quotient space with respect to $\underline{R}$. For $\forall a, b \in \underline{X}$, let

$$d = \bigcup_{\substack{x \in a \\ y \in b}} N(x, y), x, y \in X$$

We next show that any two of elements in d are $\underline{R}$-equivalent.

For $\forall z_1, z_2 \in d$, there exist $x_1 \sim x_2(\underline{R})$ and $y_1 \sim y_2(\underline{R})$ such that $z_1 = N(x_1, y_1)$ and $z_2 = N(x_2, y_2)$.

From the definition of $\underline{R}$, there exist $x_1 = u_1, u_2, \ldots, u_m = x_2$ and $y_1 = v_1, v_2, \ldots, v_m = y_2$ such that $u_i \sim u_{i+1}(R_n)$ and $v_i \sim v_{i+1}(R_n)$.

Letting $w_i = N(u_i, v_i)$ then $w_i \sim w_{i+1}(R_{n+1})$. Since $R_{n+1} = R_n$, have $w_i \sim w_{i+1}(\underline{R}), i = 1, 2, \ldots, m-1$.

Especially, $w_i \sim w_m(\underline{R})$, hence $z_1 = w_1 \sim w_m = z_2(\underline{R})$.

Namely, any two of elements in d are $\underline{R}$ equivalent.

Let c be an equivalence class in X containing d. Hence c is an element of $\underline{X}$.

Define $\underline{N}(a, b) = c$, from the definition, $\underline{N}$ is uniquely defined. Similar to Proposition 4.2, it can be proved that $\underline{N}$ is a quotient operation on $\underline{X}$.

Finally, it only needs to show that $\underline{X}$ is the upper bound of a family of quotient spaces A defined in Section 4.5.1.

Suppose there exists a quotient operation N' on space $X' : X' < X_1$ and R' is an equivalence relation corresponding to X'.

Since $X' < X_1$, $R' < R_1$. Namely, from $x_1 \sim y(R_1)$, we have $x \sim y(R')$.

By induction, when $i=1$, $x \sim y(R_1) \Rightarrow x \sim y(R')$ holds. Assuming that for $i < k$ $x \sim y(R_i) \Rightarrow x \sim y(R')$ holds, we next show that for $i = k$ the conclusion holds as well.

From $x \sim y(R_k)$ and based on the definition of relation R_i, we have two cases.

One is $x \sim y(R_{k-1})$, and then we have $x \sim y(R')$. Or there exist $x_1 \sim x_2(R_{k-1})$ and $y_1 \sim y_2(R_{k-1})$ such that $x = N(x_1, y_1)$ and $y = N(x_2, y_2)$. Then $x_1 \sim x_2(R')$ and $y_1 \sim y_2(R')$.

Since N' is a quotient operation, we can write

$$p'(x) = p'(N(x_1, y_1)) = N'(p'(x_1), p'(y_1))$$
$$= N'(p'(x_2), p'(y_2)) = p'(N(x_2, y_2)) = p'(y)$$

That is, $x \sim y(R')$ holds.

By induction, for any $x \sim y(R_n)$, we have $x \sim y(R')$. Since $\underline{R}$ is an equivalence relation with R_n as its base, we have $R' < \underline{R}$.

Therefore, X is the upper space of A. And $\underline{N}$ is the lower quotient operation of N with respect to X_1.

The above result is stated by the proposition below.

Proposition 4.3

X is a finite set. X_1 is a quotient space of X. N is a binary-operation on X. The operation $\underline{N}$ defined as before is the lower quotient operation of X_1, and X is the operational lower bound space of X_1 with respect to N.

Example 4.13

Assume that $X = \{a_0, a_1, a_2, ..., a_9\}$. Operation '+' on X is defined as

$$a_i + a_j = a_k \Leftrightarrow k \equiv (i + j) \pmod{10}$$

Let $X_1 = \{b_0, b_2, ..., b_9\}$, where $b_0 = \{a_0, a_1\}, b_i = a_i, i \neq 0, 2$. Find the lower quotient operation and the lower bound space on X_1 with respect to operation '+'.

Solution:

Let R_1 be an equivalence relation with respect to X_1. Now we find R_2.

Since $a_{2i} + a_0 = a_{2i}, a_{2i} + a_2 = a_{2i+2}, i < 4$, we have $a_{2i} \sim a_{2i+2}, i < 4$.

Similarly, $a_{2i-1} \sim a_{2i+2}(R_2), 1 \leq i < 5$.

It is easy to know that $R_2 = R_3$. Namely,

$$\underline{X} = X_2 = \{\{a_0, a_2, ..., a_8\}, \{a_1, a_3, ..., a_9\}\} = \{d_0, d_1\}$$

Operation $\oplus$ defined on X_1 is as follows

$\oplus$	d_0	d_1
d_0	d_0	d_1
d_1	d_1	d_0

Upper Quotient Operation

X is a domain. N is a binary-operation on X. X_1 is a quotient space of X. R_1 is an equivalence relation corresponding to X_1.

Define R^i recursively as follows.

$\forall x, y \in X, x \sim y(R^2) \Leftrightarrow x \sim y(R_1)$ and for $\forall z_1 \sim z_2(R_1)$, $N(x, z_1) \sim N(y, z_2)(R_1)$ and $N(z_1, x) \sim N(z_2, y)(R_1)$ hold.

Let $R^2 = H(R_1)$

It is easy to show by induction that R^i is an equivalence relation.

Generally, define $R^i = H(R^{i-1}), i \geq 3$. Since X is finite, there exists a minimal integer n such that $R^n = R^{n+1}$.

Let $\overline{R} = R^n$. $\overline{X}$ is a quotient space corresponding to $\overline{R}$. Now we define an operation $\overline{N}$ on $\overline{X}$ as follows.

$$\forall a, b \in \overline{X}, \ d = \bigcup_{\substack{x \in a \\ y \in b}} N(x, y), x, y \in X$$

We first show that any two of elements in d are $\overline{R}$-equivalent.

For $\forall z_1, z_2 \in d$, assume that $z_1 = N(x_1, y_1)$ and $z_2 = N(x_2, y_2)$, where $x_1, x_2 \in a$ and $y_1, y_2 \in b$, namely, $x_1 \sim x_2(\overline{R})$ and $y_1 \sim y_2(\overline{R})$.

Since $\overline{R} = R^n$ we can write $x_1 \sim x_2(R^n)$ and $y_1 \sim y_2(R^n)$.

From the definition of R^n, it follows that $N(x_1, y_1) \sim N(x_2, y_2)(R^{n+1} = R^n = \overline{R})$.

Namely, $z_1 \sim z_2(\overline{R})$ holds.

By letting c be an element of $\overline{X}$ containing d, obviously c is uniquely defined by a and b.

Define $\overline{N}(a, b) = c$. We next show that $\overline{N}$ is a quotient operation on $\overline{X}$.

For $\forall x, y \in X$, letting $\overline{p} : X \rightarrow \overline{X}$ and $a = \overline{p}(x), b = \overline{p}(y)$, then $\overline{p}(N(x, y)) \subset \overline{p}(d) = c$.

Moreover, $\overline{N}(\overline{p}(x), \overline{p}(y)) = \overline{N}(a, b) = c$.

Since c is an element of $\overline{X}$ and $\overline{p}(N(x, y)) \neq \emptyset$, then $\overline{p}(N(x, y)) = c$.

Thus, $\overline{p}(N(x, y)) = \overline{N}(\overline{p}(x), \overline{p}(y))$.

Finally, we show that quotient space $\overline{X}$ is the infimum of a family of quotient spaces B defined in Section 4.5.1.

Given $X' \in B$, R' is its corresponding equivalence relation. Since $X_1 < X'R_1 < R'$, namely, for $\forall x, y \in X$, if $x \sim y(R')$ then $x \sim y(R_1)$ holds.

By induction on i, assuming that for $i<k$, if $x \sim y(R')$ then $x \sim y(R^i)$. We show next that the conclusion still holds for $i=k$.

Assume that $x_1 \sim x_2(R')$ and $y_1 \sim y_2(R')$. From the induction assumption, for $\forall i < k$, $x_1 \sim x_2(R^i)$ and $y_1 \sim y_2(R^i)$ hold.

Since $X' \in B$, there exists a quotient operation N' such that

$$p'(N(x_1, y_1)) = N'(p'(x_1), p'(y_1)) = N'(p'(x_2), p'(y_2))$$
$$= p'(N(x_2, y_2))$$

where p' is a projection from $X \to X'$.

We have $N(x_1, y_1) \sim N(x_2, y_2)(R')$.

Similarly, $N(y_1, x_1) \sim N(y_2, x_2)(R')$.

From the induction assumption, it is known that for k-1

$$N(x_1, y_1) \sim N(x_2, y_2)(R^{k-1}) \text{ and } N(y_1, x_1) \sim N(y_2, x_2)(R^{k-1})$$

From the definition of R^k, obtain $x_1 \sim x_2(R^k)$.

By induction, for $\forall x, y \in X$, $x \sim y(R') \Rightarrow x \sim y(R^n)$ holds. Namely, $x \sim y(\overline{R})$ holds or $\overline{R} < R'$.

There is a quotient operation on $\overline{X}$ and $\overline{X}$ is the infimum of B. In other words, $\overline{N}$ is the upper quotient operation on X_1.

We have the following proposition.

Proposition 4.4

X is a finite set. X_1 is a quotient set of X. N is a binary-operation on X. $\overline{N}$ defined above, i.e., $\overline{N}(a, b) = c$, is the upper quotient operation on X_1 and $\overline{X}$ is the operational upper bound space of X_1 with respect to N.

The approach for constructing $\overline{N}$ and $\overline{X}$ shown in Proposition 4.4 can be improved so that it is easy to be computed.

(X, N) is given, where X is a finite set. X_1 is a quotient space of X. R_1 is an equivalence relation corresponding to X_1.

Let $R(1) = R_1$. Define a relation $R(2)$ as follows.

$\forall x, y \in X, x \sim y(R(2)) \Leftrightarrow x \sim y(R_1)$ while for $\forall z \in X$, have $N(x, z) \sim N(y, z)$ and $N(x, z) \sim N(y, z)(R_1)$.

Let $R(2) = K(R(1))$. Generally, define $R(i) = K(R(i-1)), i > 2$.

It is easy to prove that $R(i)$ is an equivalence relation.

Since X is a finite set, there exists a minimal integer n such that $R(n) = R(n+1)$.

Let $R' = R(n)$ and X' be a quotient space corresponding to R'.

$\forall a, b \in X'$, define

$$d = \bigcup_{\substack{x \in a \\ y \in b}} N(x, y), x, y \in X$$

Let c be an equivalence class on X' containing d

Define $N'(a, b) = c$.

We have a proposition below.

Proposition 4.5

Under the definition and notations above, X' is an operational upper bounded space of X_1, and N' is an upper quotient operation of X_1 with respect to N.

Proof:

The proposition can be proved in much the same way as that in Proposition 4.4.

Note that definition $R(i) = K(R(i-1))$ differs from definition $R^i = H(R^{i-1})$ (see Section 4.5.2). The former is that for all $z \in X$, $N(x, z) \sim N(y, z)(R(i-1))$ and $N(z, x) \sim N(z, y)(R(i-1))$ hold. However, the latter is that for all $\forall z_1 \sim z_2 (R^{i-1})$, $N(x, z_1) \sim N(y, z_2)(R^{i-1})$ and $N(z_1, x) \sim N(z_2, y)(R^{i-1})$ hold. Obviously, the former is a specific case of the latter. Therefore, finding $\bar{R}$ from $R(i)$ is much easier than from R^i.

Note that instead of definition $R(i) = K(R(i-1))$, we may use definition $R'(i)$: $\forall x, y \in X, x \sim y(R(i)) \Leftrightarrow x \sim y(R(i-1))$ and for $\forall z \in X$, $N(x, z) \sim N(y, z)(R_1)$ and $N(z, x) \sim N(z, y)(R_1)$ hold.

Assume that n is a minimal integer such that $R'(n) = R'(n+1)$.

Let $R'' = R'(n)$ and X'' be a quotient space corresponding to R''. We have the following property.

Property 4.1

For $\forall a, b \in X''$, letting $d = \bigcup_{\substack{x \in a \\ y \in b}} N(x, y)$, we can see that $p_1(d)$ is an element of X_1, where p_1 is a projection from X to X_1.

This property indicates that the result obtained from operation N on X'' is uniquely defined on X_1. Sometimes, for example in qualitative reasoning, it's only needed that the quotient space rather than its quotient operation corresponding to N has such a property. Generally, $X'' < \overline{X}$, sometimes it's only needed to find X'' instead of $\overline{X}$ so that the computational complexity will be reduced.

To illustrate the procedure of finding $(\overline{X}, \overline{N})$, we give an example below.

Example 4.14

Assume that $X = \{a_0, a_1, ..., a_9\}$. Define an operation $\oplus$ on X as

$$a_i \oplus a_j = a_k \Leftrightarrow k = (i + j) \ (\text{mod}10)$$

Let quotient space $X_1 = \{\{a_0, a_2, a_5, a_7\}, \{a_1, a_6\}, \{a_3, a_4, a_8, a_9\}\}$. Find the upper quotient operation $\overline{\oplus}$ on X_1 with respect to $\oplus$.

Solution:

Let R_1 be an equivalence relation corresponding to X_1. Find $R^2 = H(R_1)$.

Let $b_1 = \{a_0, a_2, a_5, a_7\}$, $b_2 = \{a_1, a_6\}$ and $b_3 = \{a_3, a_4, a_8, a_9\}$.

Since $a_0 \oplus a_1 = a_1, a_1 \in b_2$ and $a_2 \oplus a_1 = a_3, a_3 \in b_3$, a_0 and a_2 are not equivalent with respect to R^2.

Similarly, a_0 and a_7, a_2 and a_5 are not R^2-equivalent. However, $a_0 \sim a_5(R^2)$ and $a_2 \sim a_7(R^2)$. Therefore, b_1 is decomposed into $\{a_0, a_5\}$ and $\{a_2, a_7\}$.

Similarly, it can be proved that $a_1 \sim a_6(R^2)$, $a_3 \sim a_8(R^2)$ and $a_4 \sim a_9(R^2)$.

Finally, we have $R^2 : \{a_0, a_5\}, \{a_1, a_6\}, \{a_2, a_7\}\{a_3, a_8\}, \{a_4, a_9\}$.

We observe that $R^3 = H(R^2) = R^2$. Namely, $\overline{R} = R^2$.

Let $C_0 = \{a_0, a_5\}, C_1 = \{a_1, a_6\}, C_2 = \{a_2, a_7\}, C_3 = \{a_3, a_8\}, C_4 = \{a_4, a_9\}$.

We have a quotient operation $\overline{\oplus}$ on $\overline{X}$ as follows.

$\overline{\oplus}$	C_0	C_1	C_2	C_3	C_4
C_0	C_0	C_1	C_2	C_3	C_4
C_1	C_1	C_2	C_3	C_4	C_0
C_2	C_2	C_3	C_4	C_0	C_1
C_3	C_3	C_4	C_0	C_1	C_2
C_4	C_4	C_0	C_1	C_2	C_3

Note that since operation $\overline{\oplus}$ is commutative, the table above is symmetric.

The above approach is only available when X is finite. When X is an infinite set, finding the upper (lower) quotient operation is more complicated. We next show some specific cases, i.e., X is a real set.

Quotient Operations on Real Quotient Spaces

X is a one-dimensional Euclidean space, i.e., real axis. Let quotient space $X_1 = \{(-\infty, 0), [0], (0, +\infty)\}$ or simply $X_1 = \{-, 0, +\}$. This kind of quotient space is used in qualitative reasoning with numbers extensively (Murthy, 1988; William, 1988). We will discuss the structure of upper (lower) quotient operation of common 'addition' and 'multiplication' with respect to X_1 below.

Common 'addition' on X is denoted by N. We find the upper (or lower) quotient operation of N with respect to X_1.

It's obvious that the quotient space corresponding to the lower quotient operation $\underline{N}$ of N with respect to X_1 is $\underline{X} = X_0$, i.e., the coarsest quotient space.

We now show that the quotient space corresponding to the upper quotient operation $\overline{N}$ on X_1 is $\overline{X} = X$.

Assume that $a \in \overline{X}$. If a contains more than one element of X, then assume that $x_1, x_2 \in a, x_1 - x_2 = d \neq 0$. Since $\overline{N}$ is a quotient operation, letting $x_3 = -x_2$ we have

$$\overline{p}(N(x_2, x_3)) = \overline{p}(0)$$

$$\overline{p}(N(x_1, x_3)) = \overline{N}(\overline{p}(x_1), \overline{p}(x_3)) = \overline{N}(\overline{p}(x_2), \overline{p}(x_3))$$

$$= \overline{p}(N(x_1, x_2)) = \overline{p}(d) = \overline{p}(0)$$

Namely, $\overline{p}(d) = \overline{p}(0)$ or $d \sim 0(\overline{R})$, where $\overline{p} : X \to \overline{X}$ is a projection.

Since $R_1 < \overline{R}$, we have $d \sim 0(R_1)$. But $d \neq 0$, this is a contradiction. Therefore, any element of $\overline{X}$ can only contain one element of X at most, i.e., $\overline{X} = X$.

From the discussion above, unfortunately, the upper (lower) bound space with respect to X_1 is the finest (coarsest) space. This is worthless. We will find a new way to solve the problem in the subsequent section.

Now we discuss the quotient operation of common 'multiplication'.

The common multiplication on X is denoted by N_1. We find the upper (lower) quotient operation of N_1 with respect to X_1.

Define an operation $\otimes$ on X_1 as follows.

$$
\begin{array}{c|ccc}
\otimes & - & 0 & + \\
\hline
- & + & 0 & - \\
0 & 0 & 0 & 0 \\
+ & 0 & + & -
\end{array}
$$

For simplicity, let $a_1 = +$, $a_0 = 0$ and $a_2 = -$.

It is obvious that $\otimes$ is a quotient operation on X_1 and satisfies:

(1) $a \in X_1$, $a \otimes a_1 = a$ thus a_1 is an identity element on $(X_1, \otimes)$.

(2) $\otimes$ is commutative and associative, so an integral power of an element on X_1 can be defined as follows.

   $\forall a \in X_1$, define $a^n = a \otimes a \otimes \ldots \otimes a$, where n is an integer. Thus, $\forall a \in X_1$, $a^{2i} = a_1$. When $a \neq a_0$, for any a, $a^{2i+1} = a$ holds

4.5.3 The Approximation of Quotient Operations

In the preceding section, we have shown that in the quotient space $X_1 = \{-, 0, +\}$ of real space X, the upper and lower space corresponding to 'addition' operation are the finest and coarsest ones, respectively. So the upper and lower quotient operations obtained are valueless in reality. But in qualitative reasoning with numbers, space X_1 is widely used. We need to find a way to extricate ourselves from this predicament.

First let us see an example.

Example 4.15

A bathtub is shown in Fig. 4.8. F_1 is the variation of input flow. F_1 is the variation of output flow. H is the variation of gage height. We have

$$
H = C(F_1 - F_2) = C(F_1 + (-F_2))
$$

Let $F_3 = -F_2$, we obtain $H = C(F_1 + F_3)$.

From the preceding formula, it is known that the sign of H can't be determined exactly by the signs of F_1 and F_3. Namely, we can't judge the value of H exactly on quotient space $X_1 = \{-, 0, +\}$.

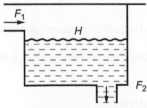

Figure 4.8: Turn on the Water in Bathtub

If F_1 is fixed, for example, $F_1 = a$, then refining X_1 we have X_2 as follows

$$X_2 : (-\infty, -a), [a], (-a, 0), [0], (0, +\infty)$$

The elements of X_2 are denoted by b_1, b_2, b_3, b_4 and b_5, respectively.

Hence, we have

$$F_1 + b_1 = [-], F_1 + b_2 = [0], F_1 + b_3 = [+], F_1 + b_4 = [+], F_1 + b_5 = [+]$$

In other words, if $F_1 = a$ then the sign of H can be decided exactly by the variation of F_2 on X_2. Or the value of H on X_1 can be determined by the value of F_2 on X_2 uniquely.

The example shows that under some given initial conditions, when we analyze a system at X_1 space, it is not necessary to find the upper (lower) quotient operation on X_1 with respect to N. As long as X_1 is properly refined, it can still meet the demand of a certain qualitative analysis.

Two refinement approaches are given below.

Successive Refinement Method

N is a binary-operation on X denoted by (X, N). X_1 is a quotient space of X. $p_1 : X \rightarrow X_1$ is a projection.

Define an operation on X_1 as follows. It is called a pseudo-quotient operation corresponding to N.

$$\forall a, b \in X_1, \text{ define } N_1(a, b) = p_1 \left(\bigcup_{\substack{x \in a \\ y \in b}} N(x, y) \right)$$

If in the right hand side of the formula, for $\forall a, b \in X_1$, $N_1(a, b)$ is an element of X_1, then N_1 is a quotient operation on X_1, otherwise N_1 is a pseudo-quotient operation. Now transforming the problem represented at space (X, N) to space (X_1, N_1), if we find some results obtained from operation N_1 are not unique on X_1, for example, $N_1(a_1, b_1)$ is not single value on X_1, then a_1 and b_1 are refined. After refinement, if some results of operation N_1 we are interested in are still not single-valued, the refining process continues until all results we needed are single-valued.

If a problem represented at space (X, N) is deterministic, the refining process can go on until a proper space is obtained. If a problem represented at (X, N) is not completely certain, the proper space may not be found.

Let us see Example 4.15 again.

From $H = C(F_1 + F_3)$, when $F_1 > 0$ and $F_3 < 0$, we can see that the value of $N_1(F_1, F_3) = C(F_1 + F_3)$ on space $X_1 = \{-, 0, +\}$ is not single-valued. The equivalence classes $(-\infty, 0)$ and $(0, +\infty)$ that F_1 and F_3 belong to must further be refined.

Generally, for the sum of $a + b$, if $a \in (-\infty, 0)$ and $b \in (0, +\infty)$, then letting $e > 0$ be an integer, intervals $(-\infty, 0)$ and $(0, +\infty)$ are divided into $a_1 = (-\infty, -e), a_2 = [-e], a_3 = (-e, 0)$ and $b_1 \in (0, e), b_2 = [e], b_3 \in (e, +\infty)$, respectively. Thus, the sum of $a_i + b_i$ can be listed as follows.

$$
\begin{array}{c|ccc}
+ & a_1 & a_2 & a_3 \\
\hline
b_1 & - & ? & ? \\
b_2 & - & 0 & + \\
b_3 & ? & + & + \\
\end{array}
$$

After refinement, only two out of nine combinations are uncertain. If the values that we are interested in are not contained in these two uncertain classes, we will have a proper space X_2 and in the space the sum '+' can be uniquely defined. Otherwise, space X_2 will further be decomposed.

The deficiency of the method is that we don't have a clear and definite criterion for judging what the proper refinement is needed.

Next, we give a successive approximation of the refinement method similar to the approach for finding $\overline{X}$, when X is finite (see Propositions 4.4 and 4.5).

Successive Approximation

Given (X, N). X_1 is a quotient space of X corresponding to R_1. Let $\{x_1, x_2, x_3, \ldots, x_n, \ldots\}$ be a sequence of elements on X

Define a relation $R(x_i)$ as follows

$$\forall x, y \in X, x \sim y(R(x_1)) \Leftrightarrow x \sim y(R_1)$$

And we have

$$N(x, x_1) \sim N(y, x_1)(R_1) \text{ and } N(x_1, x) \sim N(x_1, y)(R_1)$$

Generally, define

$$R(x_i) = I(R(x_{i-1}), R_1, x_i)$$

$$\forall x, y \in X, x \sim y(R(x_i)) \Leftrightarrow x \sim y(R(x_{i-1}))$$

$$\text{And } N(x, x_i) \sim N(y, x_i)(R_1), \ N(x_i, x) \sim N(x_i, y)(R_1)$$

We show that $R(x_i)$ is an equivalence relation below.

From induction on n, when $n=1$, for $x \sim y, y \sim z(R(x_1)) \Leftrightarrow x \sim y, y \sim z(R_1)$ and $N(x, x_1) \sim N(y, x_1) \sim N(z, x_1)(R_1)$, $N(x_1, x) \sim N(x_1, y) \sim N(x_1, z)(R_1)$.

Since R_1 is an equivalence relation, we have that $x \sim z(R_1)$ and $N(x, x_1) \sim N(z, x_1)(R_1)$, $N(x_1, x) \sim N(x_1, z)(R_1)$. Hence, $x \sim z(R(x_1))$ holds.

Namely, $R(x_1)$ is an equivalence relation.

Assuming that for $n < k$, $R(x_n)$ is an equivalence relation, we show that $R(x_k)$ is also an equivalence relation.

We only need to show that the transitivity of the relation holds.

Assume that $x \sim y, y \sim z(R(x_k))$. From the definition of $R(x_k)$, we know that $x \sim y, y \sim z(R(x_{k-1}))$. Since $R(x_{k-1})$ is an equivalence relation, $x \sim z(R(x_{k-1}))$. Again from $N(x, x_k) \sim N(y, x_k)(R_1)$ and $N(y, x_k) \sim N(z, x_k)(R_1)$, we have $N(y, x_k) \sim N(z, x_k)(R_1)$.

Similarly, $N(x_k, x) \sim N(x_k, z)(R_1)$.

Therefore, $x \sim z(R(x_k))$.

We obtain that $R(x_k)$ is an equivalence relation.

By induction, we conclude that $R(x_i)$ is an equivalence relation.

Let $X(i)$ be a quotient space corresponding to $R(x_i)$. Hence, the results obtained from operation N on any element in $X(i)$ and one of elements $x_1, x_2, \ldots, x_{i-1}$ are unique. Namely, for $\forall a \in X(i)$, by letting $d_1 = \bigcup_{x \in a} N(x, x_j)(d_2 = \bigcup_{x \in a} N(x_j, x)), j < i$, $p_1(d_1)$ or $p_1(d_2)$ is an element of X_1, where $p_1 X \to X_1$ is a projection.

To a certain degree $X(i)$ can be regarded as an approximation of $\overline{X}$. Here, a sequence of elements $\{x_1, x_2, \ldots, x_n, \ldots\}$ is selected in accordance with specific conditions, for example, the initial values. The deficiency of the method is that $\forall a, b \in X(i)$, $d = \bigcup_{\substack{x \in a \\ y \in b}} N(x, y)$ may not be ensured to be single-valued on X_1.

Since $X_1 < X(1) < X(2) < \ldots < X(n) < \ldots < \overline{X}$ the successive approximation method is regarded as a refinement one as well.

To show the refining process, we give a simple example.

Example 4.16

X is a real set. N is a common addition. $X_1 = \{(-\infty, 0), [0], (0, +\infty)\}$. Taking a sequence $\{-3, 2, 10, -8, \ldots\}$ of elements on X, find the successive approximation of N with respect to X_1.

Solution:

R_1 is an equivalence relation corresponding to X_1. From R_1 and $x_1 = -3$, we have $R(x_1)$:
$(-\infty, 0), [0], (0, 3), [3], (3, +\infty)$.

From $R(x_1)$ and $x_2 = 2$, we have

$$R(x_2) : \ (-\infty, -2), [-2], (-2, 0), [0], (0, 3), [3], (3, +\infty)$$

Similarly,

$$R(x_3 = 10) : (-\infty, -10), [-10], [-10, -2], [-2], (-2, 0)[0], (0, 3), [3], (3, +\infty), \dots$$

A sequence $\{x_1, x_2, \dots, x_n\}$ of elements on X is given. With $-x_1, -x_2, \dots, -x_n$ and zero as
points of division, divide interval $(-\infty, \infty)$ into $(n+2)$ open sets. It's easy to know that
$X(x_n)$ is just a quotient space composed by the corresponding $(n+2)$ open sets and $(n+1)$
points of division.

We summarize the methods for finding $\underline{R}$, $\overline{R}$ and the approximation of $\overline{R}$ in Table 4.6,
where X is a domain, N is a binary-operation on X, X_1 is a quotient space of X, and R_1 is
its corresponding equivalence relation.

4.5.4 Constraints and Quotient Constraints

In many reasoning processes, we are confronted with a variety of constraints. Therefore, in
a hierarchical reasoning process, the constraint propagation across different grain-size
worlds must be considered.

The Definition of Constraints

Table 4.6: The formulas for finding $\underline{R}, \overline{R}$ and the approximation of $\overline{R}$

X is a finite set	Find $(\underline{X}, \underline{R})$	$R_i = L(R_{i-1}), i > 2$ $R_1 > R_2 > \dots > R_n = R_{n+1} = \underline{R}$
	Find $(\overline{X}, \overline{R})$	$R^i = H(R^{i-1}), i > 2, R^1 = R_1$ $R_1 = R^1 < R < \dots < R^n = R^{n+1} = \overline{R}$
		$R(i) = K(R(i-1)), i > 2, R(1) = R_1$ $R_1 = R(1) < R(2) < \dots < R(n) = R(n+1) = \overline{R}$
X is an infinite set	Given a set $\{x_1, x_2, \dots, x_n, \dots\}$. Find the approximation of $\overline{R}$	$R(x_i) = I(R(x_{i-1}), R_1, x_i), i > 2, R(x_0) = R_1$ $R = R(x_0) < R(x_1) < \dots < R(x_n) < \dots$

Definition 4.2

If C is a subset of a product space $X \times Y$, then C is said to be a constraint on X and Y. When $X=Y$, C is simply called a constraint on X.

From the definition, it is known that a constraint C on X and Y is a relation on X and Y.

For $\forall x \in X$, let $C(x) = \{y|(x,y) \in C\}$.

$C(x)$ is said to be a section of C at $x \in X$.

Similarly, a section $C_1(y)$ of C at $y \in Y$ can be defined.

For example, $f : X \rightarrow Y, f(x) = y$ is a function.

Letting $C = \{(x,y)|y = f(x)\} \subset X \times Y$, then C is a constraint corresponding to function $y = f(x)$.

Again, given inequality $x + y \geq 0$, by letting $C = \{(x,y)|x+y \geq 0\} \subset X \times Y$, then C is a constraint corresponding to $x + y \geq 0$.

If N is a binary-operation on X, letting

$$C = \{(x_1, x_2, y)|y = N(x_1, x_{2,})\} \subset (X \times X) \times X$$

then C is a constraint on $(X \times X)$ and X. In other words, an operation can be regarded as a constraint.

We next discuss the representations of constraints at different grain-size worlds.

Quotient Constraints

First, we consider the quotient space representation of a product space.

$Z = X \times Y$ is a product space, X_1 and Y_1 are quotient spaces of X and Y, respectively. Their corresponding equivalence relations are R_1 and R_2, respectively. Define an equivalence relation $R = R_1 \times R_2$ on Z as

$$\forall a_1 = (x_1, y_1), a_2 = (x_2, y_2) \in Z, a_1 \sim a_2(R) \Leftrightarrow x_1 \sim x_2(R_1) \text{ and } y_1 \sim y_2(R_2)$$

$[Z] = [X \times Y]$ is a quotient space of Z corresponding to equivalence relation R. On the other hand, the product space $X_1 \times Y_1$ of X_1 and Y_1 can be proved to be equivalent to $[Z] = [X \times Y]$, when viewing $X_1 \times Y_1$ as a quotient space of Z. Therefore, in the following discussion we will use $X_1 \times Y_1$ to represent the quotient space corresponding to R, and R is the equivalence relation of $X_1 \times Y_1$.

Definition 4.3

C is a constraint on X and Y. X_1 and Y_1 are quotient spaces of X and Y, respectively. Their corresponding equivalence relations are R_1 and R_2, respectively. Define

$$\overline{C} = \left\{ (a,b) \mid \exists x \in a, y \in b, (x,y) \in C, (a,b) \in X_1 \times Y_1 \right\}$$

$$\underline{C} = \left\{ (a,b) \mid \forall x \in a, y \in b, (x,y) \in C, (a,b) \in X_1 \times Y_1 \right\}$$

$\overline{C}$ and $\underline{C}$ are said to be outer and inner quotient constraints on X_1 and Y_1. If $\overline{C} = \underline{C}$, $\overline{C}$ is said to be a quotient constraint on X_1 and Y_1.

Example 4.17

X_1 and Y_1 both are intervals $[0,d]$ of real numbers. $X_1 = \{a_1, a_2, a_3, a_4\}$, where $a_1 = [0, x_1)$, $a_2 = [x_1, x_2)$, $a_3 = [x_2, x_3)$, $a_4 = [x_3, d]$, and $Y_1 = \{b_1, b_2, b_3, b_4, b_5\}$, where $b_1 = [0, y_1)$, $b_i = [y_{i-1}, y_i)$, $i = 2, 3, 4$, $b_5 = [y_4, d]$, X_1 and Y_1 are quotient spaces of X and Y, respectively. C, $\overline{C}$ and $\underline{C}$ are shown in Fig. 4.9.

When using $\overline{C}$ as a quotient constraint on quotient spaces X_1 and Y_1, the strong point is that the homomorphism principle is satisfied. Namely, if a problem on X has a solution satisfying constraint C, then the same problem on X_1 must have a solution satisfying constraint $\overline{C}$. If set $\overline{C}$ is much larger than C, under the weak constraint $\overline{C}$ the solution on $X_1 \times Y_1$ may not provide a useful cue for solving the same problem on X. Therefore, some stronger constraint $C^* : \underline{C} \subset C^* \subset \overline{C}$ may be used to narrow the problem-solving space on X but it doesn't guarantee the satisfaction of the homomorphism principle.

Example 4.18

In qualitative reasoning with numbers, Kuipers (1988) presented a concept of 'envelope constraints'. We next show the relationship between his notion of 'constraint' and ours.

Assume that $f_1 : X \to R^1$ and $f_2 : X \to R^1$, where $\forall x \in X, f_1(x) \leq f_2(x)$, and R^1 is a real set.

If $y = C(x)$ is a set-valued mapping from X to R^1 and satisfies

$$f_1(x) \leq C(x) \leq f_2(x)$$

then $C(x)$ is just the envelope constraint of x and y defined by Kuipers. $f_1(x)$ and $f_2(x)$ are called upper and lower envelopes, respectively and denoted by $C(f_1, f_2)$.

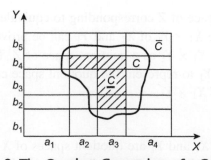

Figure 4.9: The Quotient Constraints of a Constraint

Let

$$C = \left\{ (x,y) \middle| f_1(x) \le y \le f_2(x), (x,y) \in X \times R^1 \right\}$$

From our definition, C is a constraint on X and R^1, and it's just the envelope constraint $C(f_1, f_2)$. It is obvious that the envelope constraint is a specific case of the constraint defined in this section.

Kuipers also presented an envelope constraint propagation approach. We cite it here.

The upper and lower envelopes $f_2(x)$ and $f_1(x)$ of the constraint between x and y are given as shown in Fig. 4.10. Let $r(y)$ and $I = [a_1, a_2]$ be the variation range of y and x, respectively. Now, we find the new variation range of x, when range $r(y)$ propagates across $C(f_1, f_2)$.

According to the envelope constraint propagation method, projecting the lower endpoint of $r(y)$ across envelope $f_2(x)$, we have a point b_2 on X. Similarly, when projecting the upper endpoint of $r(y)$ across envelope $f_1(x)$, we have b_1. Finally, we obtain an interval $II = [b_2, b_1]$ on X. Letting $III = I \cap II = [b_2, a_2]$, we have III. This is a new variation range of X.

From our viewpoint, a quotient space of $Y(= R^1)$ is defined as

$$Y_1 = \{a = r(y)\} \cup \{y | y \notin r(y)\}, \quad X_1 = X$$

Let

$$C = \left\{ (x,y) \middle| f_1(x) \le y \le f_2(x), (x,y) \in X \times R^1 \right.$$

Finding the projection $\overline{C}$ of C on $X_1 \times Y_1$ and the section $\overline{C}_1(a)$ of $\overline{C}$ at $a \in Y_1$, we have $\overline{C}_1(a) = \{x | \exists y \in r(y), (x,y) \in C\}$. Namely, $\overline{C}_1(a) = [b_2, b_1]$.

The section $\overline{C}_1(a) = [b_2, b_1]$ indicates the variation range of x under the constraint C when $y \in r(y)$. By intersecting $[b_2, b_1]$ with $[a_1, a_2]$, we have an interval $[b_2, a_2]$. This is the same as the variation range of x obtained by the Kuipers method. Therefore, the envelope

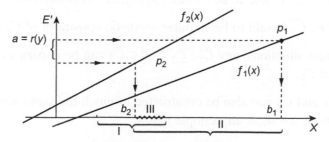

Figure 4.10: The Propagation of Envelope Constraints

constraint propagation presented by Kuipers is a specific example of the quotient constraint construction methods.

The Relationship of Constraints

Projection of Constraints C is a constraint on X and Y. X_1 and Y_1 are quotient spaces of X and Y, respectively. Now, we find a constraint on X_1 and Y_1 corresponding to C.

We have defined the equivalence relation corresponding to quotient space $X_1 \times Y_1$ of $X \times Y$. However, C is a subset of $X \times Y$. The constraint on X_1 and Y_1 should be a subset of $X_1 \times Y_1$. Naturally, the induced constraint of C on X_1 and Y_1 is defined as $p(C)$, where p is a projection from $X \times Y \rightarrow X_1 \times Y_1$.

It is easy to know that $p(C) = \overline{C}$, where $\overline{C}$ is the outer quotient constraint of C.

The combination of Constraints C_1 and C_2 are two constraints on X and Y. If the combination C_3 of constraints C_1 and C_2 has to satisfy both constraints C_1 and C_2, then it's denoted by

$$C_3 = C_1 \cap C_2$$

If the combination constraint C_3 is only expected to satisfy either C_1 or C_2, then it's denoted by

$$C_3 = C_1 \cup C_2$$

The Synthesis of Constraints X_1 and X_2 are quotient spaces of X. Y_1 and Y_2 are quotient spaces of Y. C_1 (or C_2) is a constraint on X_1 and Y_1 (or X_2 and Y_2). We now find the synthesis of constraints C_1 and C_2.

The synthesis of constraints C_1 and C_2 is defined as follows.

Let X_3 be the supremum of X_1 and X_2, Y_3 be the supremum of Y_1 and Y_2, p_1 and p_2 be the projections from $X_3 \times Y_3$ to $X_1 \times Y_1$ and $X_2 \times Y_2$, respectively.

Let $D_1 = p_1^{-1}(C_1)$ and $D_2 = p_2^{-1}(C_2)$.

Define $\underline{C_3} = D_1 \cap D_2$, $\underline{C_3}$ is said to be an inner synthetic constraint of C_1 and C_2.

Define $\overline{C_3} = D_1 \cup D_2$, $\overline{C_3}$ is said to be an outer synthetic constraint of C_1 and C_2.

According to different situations, any $C_3^* : \underline{C_3} \subset C_3^* \subset \overline{C_3}$ can be chosen as synthetic constraint of C_1 and C_2.

The synthesis of C_1 and C_2 can also be constructed in much the same way as that stated in Chapter 3. To illustrate we show an example below.

Example 4.19

X and Y are real sets. Lebesgue measures μ^x and μ^y are defined on X and Y, respectively.

Let X_i and Y_i be quotient spaces of X and Y, respectively. Assume that each element of X_i and Y_i, $i=1,2$, is measurable on X and Y, respectively.

C_i is a measurable set on $X_i \times Y_i$, $i=1,2$. A measure μ on product space $X_i \times Y_i$ is defined as a product measure of μ^x and μ^y.

Let X_3 be the supremum space of X_1 and X_2. Y_3 be the supremum space of Y_1 and Y_2. Since all elements on X_i and Y_i are measurable on X and Y, respectively, the elements of X_3 and Y_3 are measurable as well.

Let p_i, $i=1,2$, be a projection from $X_3 \times Y_3 \to X_i \times Y_i$.

Assume that C_3 is a measurable set on $X_3 \times Y_3$ and satisfies

$$\mu(C_3 \Theta p_1(C_1)) + \mu(C_3 \Theta p^{-1}(C_2)) = \inf_{C \subset X_3 \times Y_3} \{\mu(C \Theta p_1 n^{-1}(C_1)) + \mu)C \Theta p_2^{-1}(C_2))\}$$

Where $A \Theta B$ indicates the symmetric difference between A and B and is defined as

$$A \Theta B = \{x | (x \in A \ and \ x \notin B) \ or \ (x \in B \ and \ x \notin A)\}$$

$\mu(A)$ indicates the measure of A on $X_3 \times Y_3$.

Namely, the synthetic constraint of C_1 and C_2 is defined as a set C_3 on $X_3 \times Y_3$ such that the sum of the measures of its symmetric differences with $p_1^{-1}(C_1)$ and $p_2^{-1}(C_2)$ is minimum.

4.6 Qualitative Reasoning

An exactly quantitative description of the world being analyzed is not always available. For example, in the early stage of engineering design of a device, one may not know the exact value of all parameters of the device. In this case the incomplete knowledge can be used by representing the device in a qualitative form. By using the qualitative description we can get a better understanding of the device at the desired level. A reasoning based on the qualitative description of the world is called qualitative reasoning. The device's behaviors can be predicted and the decisions can be made using the reasoning. Therefore, qualitative reasoning is to provide a broad picture of the functioning of the world by taking a step back from the detail. There is a great deal of interest in developing such techniques both by engineers and AI researchers.

In this section, the representation of qualitative reasoning in our multi-granular world model and its reasoning procedure are discussed.

4.6.1 Qualitative Reasoning Models

In common sense, if we say, 'Someone is 185 cm tall', it is regarded as a quantitative representation by describing an attribute with numbers. If we just say, 'Someone is tall', this is just a qualitative representation. In professional fields, for example, for a differential equation, if an analytical or a numerical solution is required, it needs a quantitative analysis. Meanwhile, only the existence and the properties of the solution are desired, it only needs a qualitative analysis. Qualitative analysis is widespread not only in common sense but also in professional fields.

In AI, researchers have been paying close attention to qualitative description and reasoning recently. They proposed several new fields such as qualitative physics, mechanics, etc. In these fields, people do not seek the precise solution of the problems but only the qualitative variation or variation trend of physical quantities is concerned.

In fact, 'Tall' is an uncertain description of '185 cm' height of a person. A qualitative description of a variable is just a coarse-grained description of the variable with real number. Therefore, qualitative reasoning can be represented by a multi-granular world model. However, reasoning on some quotient space may be regarded as 'quantitative'. But it may also be considered as 'qualitative' when the more precise analysis is required and vice versa. Therefore, quantitative and qualitative are relative.

Qualitative reasoning is the reasoning with qualitative representation. From the above observations, it is known that the projection and synthetic approaches of quotient spaces presented in the previous chapters can be applied to qualitative reasoning.

4.6.2 Examples

Example 4.20

Williams (1988) presented a so-called qualitative algebraic reasoning that mixes qualitative with quantitative information. His approach is briefly introduced below.

Let $(R, +, \times)$ be real with operators '+' and '×'. Let $S' = \{-, 0, +, ?\}$ be a qualitative algebra with operators $\oplus$ and $\otimes$ shown below.

$\oplus$	-	0	+	?
-	-	-	?	?
0	-	0	+	?
+	?	+	+	?
?	?	?	?	?

$\otimes$	-	0	+	?
-	+	0	-	?
0	0	0	0	0
+	-	0	+	?
?	?	?	?	?

A unary operator $\ominus$ is defined as

$\ominus$	
$-$	$+$
0	0
$+$	$-$
$?$	$?$

Define a projection $[x] : R \to S'$ as

$$[x] = \begin{cases} +, & x > 0 \\ 0, & x = 0 \\ -, & x < 0 \end{cases}$$

Element '?' corresponds to the entire real axis $(-\infty, \infty)$.

Qualitative algebra $(S', \oplus, \otimes)$ has the following properties.

Associative Law:

$$(s \oplus t) \oplus u = s \oplus (t \oplus u)$$
$$(s \otimes t) \otimes u = s \otimes (t \otimes u)$$

Identity Element:

$$s \oplus 0 = s$$
$$s \otimes [+] = s$$

Commutative Law:

$$s \oplus t = t \oplus s$$
$$s \otimes t = t \otimes s$$

Distributive Law:

$$s \otimes (t \oplus u) = s \otimes t \oplus s \otimes u$$

An integral power of element s is defined as $s^n = s \otimes s \otimes \ldots \otimes s$, where n is an integer.

Williams constructed a qualitative reasoning system with numbers based on hybrid algebra $(R \cup S', +, \times, \oplus, \otimes, [])$. Its reasoning procedure is the following.

(1) An equation with real number is simplified based on space $(R, +, \times)$.
(2) The simplified equation is projected on space $(S', \oplus, \otimes)$.
(3) Then, the projected equation is operated using qualitative operators on space $(S', \oplus, \otimes)$.

The advantage of the above qualitative reasoning procedure is the following. If the sign of some quantities is known rather than the precise value, the quantities cannot be operated on real space R using standard real operators. But they can be operated on S' using qualitative operators. Moreover, since on $(S', \oplus, \otimes)$ for any element t, $t^{2i+1} = t$, any polynomial can be transformed into a quadratic polynomial. This is a specific property that does not occur in real space R. But the weakness of operation on $(S', \oplus, \otimes)$ is that the projection of $(R, +)$ on $(S', +)$ is not homomorphism. In our terms, it means that operator $\oplus$ is not a quotient operation of S', i.e., the operation $\oplus$ on space $S = \{-, 0, +\}$ does not necessarily have a unique result. For example, $[+] \oplus [-]$ does not have a unique result on S.

Now, we analyze Williams's hybrid algebra from the multi-granular computing viewpoint (Zhang and Zhang, 1989c, 1990b).

Let $p((-\infty, 0)) = -, p(0) = 0$ and $p((0, +\infty)) = +$. Therefore, $S = \{-, 0, +\}$ is a quotient space of $R = (-\infty, \infty)$. p is a projection from R to S. Operators $\oplus$ and $\otimes$ of S are the projections of operators $+$ and $\times$ of R, respectively.

It is easy to know that operator $\otimes$ is a quotient operation of S but $\oplus$ is not. As stated before, the upper bound space of S with respect to operator $\oplus$ is R itself.

Thus, in our terms, Williams's qualitative reasoning with numbers is a reasoning on quotient space S with respect to the projections of operators $+$ and $\times$. Since $\oplus$ is not a quotient operator on S, in order to get a unique result from the operation, the approximate approach for finding upper bound space as shown in the above section can be used for solving the problem.

Example 4.21

Murthy (1988) presented a qualitative reasoning at multiple resolutions. We briefly introduce this as follows.

(1) Q_1 space denoted by $(\pm)(0, nonzero)$ is identical to $S = \{-, 0, +\}$.
     The relationships $>, =, <$ between quantities on Q_1 can be expressed as follows.
     If $[a - b] = +$, then $a > b$. If $[a - b] = 0$, then $a = b$. If $[a - b] = -$, then $a < b$.
     Where $[a]$ denotes the sign of a.
     It is noted that if $[a] \neq [b]$ and a and b have different signs, then $[a + b]$ is uncertain. This ambiguity can be solved by moving to the next Q_2 space.

(2) Q_2 space is denoted by $(\pm)$ $(0, infinitesimality, large)$.
     Refining Q_1 space, first interval $(-\infty, 0)$ is divided into $(-\infty, -e)$ and $(-e, 0)$, then interval $(0, +\infty)$ is divided into $(0, e)$ and $(e, +\infty)$. Interval $a \in (-e, 0)$ or $a \in (0, e)$ is called 'infinimality'. Interval $a \in (-\infty, -e)$ or $a \in (e, \infty)$ is said to be 'large'. Therefore, on Q_2 space in addition to relations $>, =$ and $<$, the other two relations $\gg, \sim$ can be introduced as follows.
     Relation $a \gg b$, if a is large and b is infinitesimality.

Relation $a \sim b$, if both a and b are infinitesimality or large.

On Q_1 space, operations $[a] \neq [b]$ and $[a + b]$ are ambiguity. But on Q_2 space, if a is large and b is infinitesimality, then $[a + b] = [a]$, i.e., the signs of $a + b$ and a are the same. But if both a and b are infinitesimality or large, the sign of $[a + b]$ is still uncertain. These ambiguities can be solved by introducing Q_3 space.

(3) Q_3 space is denoted by $(\pm)(0, y^z)$, where y is the base (e.g., 2 or 10) and z is an integer.

The real number is divided by the logarithmic distance between two numbers, i.e., if $|a| = y^z$, then $\log(a) = z$. Therefore, when $\log a > \log b$, then $[a + b] = [a]$, in other words, when the order of magnitude of a is bigger than b, the orders of magnitude of $a+b$ and a are the same. If $[a] = [b]$ and $\log a = \log b$, then $[a + b] = [a]$.

While $[a] \neq [b]$ and $\log a = \log b$, the sign of $[a + b]$ is uncertain. To resolve the ambiguity a finer resolution is needed. The Q_4 space is introduced.

(4) Q_4 -space is denoted by $(\pm)(x * y^z)$, where y and z as shown in (3) and x is a number with n significant digits. As n increases the accuracy of the description increases, while $n \to \infty$ the Q-space approaches the real space R.

In order to solve the uncertainty of the sign of $[a + b]$, Murthy gradually refines the Q-space so that the uncertainty of computational results reduces.

From the viewpoint presented in this book, Murthy's Q-spaces of multiple resolutions are quotient spaces of real number at different granularities. The successive refinement approach presented by Murthy is just an approximation method for constructing an operational space of $S = \{-, 0, +\}$ with respect to real addition. The approximation method for constructing operational space we presented can be used for general quotient space and any binary-operator. So the method can be applied to Murthy's qualitative reasoning as well.

Example 4.22

Kuipers (1988) proposed a qualitative reasoning with incomplete quantitative measures. His basic idea is the following.

Assume that a system has several parameters and the relations among parameters are represented by algebra formulas, differential equations, or functions. Now, only partial knowledge of the parameters is known, for example, the variation range of the parameters, and the variation range can be represented by intervals. The problem is how to narrow the variation ranges via the known variation ranges of parameters and relations among them. Kuipers called it the propagation of incomplete quantitative knowledge and divides it into four categories.

(1) Propagation via arithmetic constraints $(+, \times, -)$,
(2) Propagation via monotonic function constraints,

(3)   Propagation via number spaces,

(4)   Propagation via temporal points D/D_t, where D/D_t indicates the differential operation on t.

For example, $z = x - y$ is known. And the variation ranges of x and y are known to be $[1, 1.01]$ and $[0.864, 0.948]$, respectively. It's easy to find the variation range of z via the arithmetic constraint $z = x - y$. It's $[0.052, 0.146]$.

Again, constraint $\frac{dy}{dt} = x$ is known. The variation range of x in temporal interval $[t_0, t_1]$ is $[0.051, 1.01]$. Assume that $y(t_0)$ at t_0 ($t_0 = 0$). Now find the variation range of $y(t_1)$. From the mean value theorem, there exists $x^* \in [t_0, t_1]$ such that $x(t^*) = \frac{y(t_1) - y(t_0)}{t_1 - t_0} = y(t_1)/t_1$. If the variation range of t_1 is $[2, 3]$, then the variation range of $y(t_1)$ is $[0.051, 1.01] \times [2, 3] = [0.102, 3.03]$.

We next use the quotient space model to explain the above examples.

First, assume that x, y and z are three parameters and $z = x - y$ is a constraint. I_1 and I_2 are variation ranges of x and y, respectively. Find the variation range of z.

Let X, Y and Z (real sets) be spaces that x, y and z are located, respectively. Let $X_1 = \{I_1 \text{ and } x | x \notin I_1, x \in X\}$ and $Y_1 = \{I_2 \text{ and } y | y \notin I_2, y \in Y\}$ be quotient spaces of X and Y, respectively. $z = x - y$ is regarded as a constraint on space $X \times Y$ and Z, i.e., $C = \{(x, y, z) | z = x - y\} \subset (X \times Y) \times Z$. $I_1 \times I_2$ is an element of $X_1 \times Y_1$.

Second, find the section $C(I_1 \times I_2)$ of C on $I_1 \times I_2$.

$$C(I_1 \times I_2) = \{z | z = x - y, x \in I_1, y \in I_2\}$$

$C(I_1 \times I_2)$ is the variation range of z and an interval in Z denoted by I_3. Let Z_1 be a quotient space of Z.

$Z_1 = \{I_3, z | x \notin I_3, z \in Z\}$. I_3 is just an element of Z_1.

Therefore, the propagation of incomplete quantitative knowledge under different constraints is equivalent to finding the quotient constraint of a given quotient space.

4.6.3 The Procedure of Qualitative Reasoning

As viewed from different granularities, a qualitative reasoning is reasoning on some quotient space of the original space. The procedure of qualitative reasoning is summarized as follows.

(1)   The variables, parameters and the constraints among these variables and parameters in the original problem space are analyzed and then simplified.

(2)   All certain and uncertain information is represented in its proper quotient space.

(3) According to the analytical requirement, a proper qualitative space is constructed. The space is also a quotient space of the original one.
(4) All constraints and operators are projected on the qualitative space.
(5) The reasoning is made in that space.

The concepts of quotient operation, quotient constraint, the projection and synthetic method, and the approximation of upper space presented in the preceding sections can be used for making reasoning on quotient space.

4.7 Fuzzy Reasoning Based on Quotient Space Structures

In this section, we present a framework of fuzzy reasoning based on quotient space structures. They are: (1) introduce quotient structure into fuzzy set theory, i.e., establish fuzzy set representations and their relations in multi-granular spaces, (2) introduce the concept of fuzzy set into quotient space theory, i.e., fuzzy equivalence relation and its reasoning, (3) the transformation of three different granular computing methods, (4) the methods for transforming statistical reasoning models into quotient space structures. The combination of the two (fuzzy set and quotient space) methodologies is intended to embody the language-processing capacity of fuzzy set method and multi-granular computing capacity of quotient space method (Zhang and Zhang, 2003a, 2003b, 2003d).

There are three basic methods for granular computing, fuzzy set (Zadeh, 1979, 1997, 1999), rough set (Pawlak, 1982, 1991, 1998) and quotient space theory (Zhang and Zhang, 2003c). In fuzzy set theory, concepts are represented by natural language. So the theory is a well-known language-formalized model and one of granular computing favorable tools. We believe that a concept can be represented by a subset. Different concepts reflect different grain-size subsets. A family of concepts composes a partition of whole space. Thus, different families of concepts constitute different quotient spaces (knowledge bases). The aim of granular computing is to investigate the relation and translation among subsets under a given knowledge base. The same problem can be studied in different quotient spaces (knowledge bases). Then the results from different quotient spaces are synthesized together to further understand the problem. We intend to combine the two methods and apply to fuzzy reasoning.

4.7.1 Fuzzy Set Based on Quotient Space Model

Fuzzy Sets Represented in Quotient Space

Assume a fuzzy set on X and its membership function is $\mu_A(x) : X \to [0, 1]$. $[X]$ is a quotient space of X.

Definition 4.4

A is a fuzzy set on quotient space $[X]$. Define its membership function as $[\mu]_A([x]) : [X] \to [0, 1]$, where $[\mu]_A([x]) = f(\mu_A(x), x \in [x])$. f is a given function.

When the membership function of $\underline{A}$ is regarded as attribute function f on X, the fuzzy processing on quotient spaces is equivalent to the projection, synthesis and decomposition of attribute function f under the quotient space framework. Let us see an example.

A reasoning rule: 'if u is a, then u is b'. When a and b are fuzzy concepts, the rule becomes a fuzzy reasoning rule $(a) \to (b)$.

Assume that a and b are described by fuzzy sets $\underline{A}$ on X and $\underline{B}$ on Y, respectively. Then rule $(a) \to (b)$ can be represented by a fuzzy relation from X to Y, or a fuzzy subset on $X \times Y$ denoted by $\underline{A} \to \underline{B}$. We have

$$(\underline{A} \to \underline{B})(x, y) = (\underline{A}(x) \wedge \underline{B}(y)) \vee (1 - \underline{A}(x))$$

Using the above rule, if input $\underline{A}'$ then we have $\underline{B}'$ as follows

$$B'(y) = \bigvee_{x \in X} \left[A'(x) \wedge (A \to B)(x, y) \right] \tag{4.21}$$

Assume that $[X]$ is a quotient space of X. If regarding $\underline{A}$ and $\underline{B}$ as fuzzy sets on $[X]$, two questions have to be answered, i.e., what is the result obtained when regarding Formula (4.21) as a reasoning rule? What is the relation between the above result and the reasoning result obtained from space X?

$\underline{A}$ is a fuzzy set on X. $[A]$ is an induced fuzzy set on $[X]$ and defined as follows.

$$\mu_{[A]}([x]) = \max\{\mu_A(x) | x \in [x]\}, \text{ where } [x] \in [X] \tag{4.22}$$

$$\mu_{[A]}([x]) = \min\{\mu_A(x) | x \in [x]\}, \text{ where } [x] \in [X] \tag{4.23}$$

The quotient membership functions defined by Formulas (4.22) and (4.23) are quotient fuzzy subsets defined by the maximal and minimal principles.

For notational simplicity, in the following discussion, the underline below the signs of fuzzy sets is omitted.

Theorem 4.2 (Weakly Falsity- or Truth-Preserving Principle)

A, A' and B are fuzzy subsets on X and Y, respectively. $[X]$ is a quotient space of X. $[A], [A']$ and $[B]$ are fuzzy subsets on $[X]$ and $[Y]$ induced from A, A' and B, according to the maximal and minimal principles. B' is inferred from A' based on rule $A \to B$. $[B']$ is inferred from $[A']$ based on rule $[A] \to [B]$. We have

$$[B'] ([y]) \geq \max \{B'(y) | y \in [y]\} \tag{4.24}$$

$$[B'] ([y]) \leq \min \{B'(y) | y \in [y]\} \tag{4.25}$$

Formulas (4.24) and (4.25) show the falsity- and truth-preserving principles of fuzzy reasoning on quotient spaces in some sense. For example, if a fuzzy concept having degree of membership $\geq a_0$ is regarded as 'truth', otherwise as 'falsity', Formula (4.24) embodies the falsity-preserving principle of fuzzy reasoning. If $[B']([y]) < a_0$, then $B'(y) < a_0$. Namely, if the degree of membership of a conclusion (y) on a quotient space is $< a_0$ then degree of membership of the corresponding conclusion (y) on the original space must be $< a_0$. Similarly, Formula (4.25) embodies the truth-preserving principle of fuzzy reasoning, where $[B']([y]) > a_0$, then $B'(y) > a_0$.

The definition of membership functions on quotient spaces can be defined in different ways. Then, the relation of fuzzy reasoning between quotient spaces is different. However, the fuzzy reasoning can always benefit by the truth- and falsity-preserving principle and the like.

4.7.2 Fuzzified Quotient Space Theory

Fuzzy concepts can be introduced to quotient space theory in different ways, for example, introduce fuzzy concepts to domain X, fuzzy structures to topologic structure T, etc. In the section, fuzzy equivalence relations are introduced to fuzzy reasoning.

From Section 2.4, the following theorem holds.

Basic Theorem

The following three statements are equivalent:

(1) A fuzzy equivalence relation on X
(2) A normalized isosceles distance on some quotient space of X
(3) A hierarchical structure on X.

From the theorem, it's known that a fuzzy equivalence relation is equivalent to a deterministic distance so that a fuzzy problem can be handled under the deterministic framework. Second, in quotient space (X, f, T), T is an inherent topologic structure of X and independent of distance d introduced from fuzzy equivalence relation. Third, quotient space $[X]$ is composed by $\{[x] = \{y | R(x, y) = 1\} | x \in X\}$. If we define a quotient space as $X(\lambda) = \{[x] = \{y | R(x, y) \geq \lambda\} | x \in X\}$, then define a distance function on $X(\lambda)$ as $d_\lambda([x], [y]) = 1 - R'_\lambda(x, y)$, where $x \in [x], y \in [y]$ and

$$R'_\lambda(x, y) = \begin{cases} 1, & R(x, y) \geq \lambda \\ R(x, y)/\lambda \ other \end{cases} \tag{4.26}$$

It can be proved that the definition by Formula (4.26) is unique for $[x]$ and $[y]$. d_λ is a distance function on $X(\lambda)$. $\{(X(\lambda), d_\lambda)|0 \le \lambda \le 1\}$ is a sequence of nested quotient spaces (metric spaces). If $\lambda_1 < \lambda_2$, then $X(\lambda_1)$ is a quotient space of $X(\lambda_2)$. Space $X(0)$ consists of one point.

(X, T) is a topologic space. Now a quotient topology T_λ is introduced to each quotient space $X(\lambda)$ of (X, T). Then, $X(\lambda)$ has two structures (d_λ, T_λ), i.e., a multi-structure space, one induced from topology, one induced from fuzzy concept. Actually, for example, the interpersonal relationship is a multi-structure space, where the relationship of their place of residence amounts to T and their blood relationship amounts to d_λ.

Fixed x, regarding $R(x, y)$ as a membership function of a fuzzy subset, we have a space $(X(\lambda), d_\lambda)$ composed by fuzzy subsets on $[X]$. If the reasoning on $(X(\lambda), d_\lambda)$ is the same mode as in common quotient spaces, then d_λ represents the precision of its conclusions, i.e., the nearer the distance d_λ the more accurate the conclusions.

4.7.3 The Transformation of Three Different Granular Computing Methods

Fuzzy set, rough set and quotient space-based granular computing have different perspectives and goals. But they have a close relationship.

In rough set, a problem is represented by $(U, A, \{I_a, a \in A\}, \{V_a, a \in A\})$, where U is a domain, A is a set of attributes, I_a is an attribute function, and V_a is the range of a. When V_a is discrete, domain U is generally partitioned by I_a. By combining different I_a then we have different partitions of U. When V_a is continuous, I_a is discretized. Then, U is partitioned as the same as the discrete case.

In other words, normalizing the attribute function, i.e., $0 \le I(x) \le 1$, it can be regarded as a fuzzy set on U. If given a data table, it can be transformed to a set of fuzzy sets on U. Then, mining a data table is equivalent to studying a set of fuzzy sets.

On the other hand, given a set $\{A_i\}$ of fuzzy sets on X, for each fuzzy set $A : \mu_A(x)$, letting $\{A(\lambda) = \{x|\mu_A(x) > \lambda\}, 0 \le \lambda \le 1\}$ be a family of open sets, then from $\{A_i\}$ we have a family of open sets. Using the open sets, a topologic structure T on U can be uniquely defined. We have a topologic space (U, T). Then, the study of a family $\{A_i\}$ of fuzzy sets can be transformed to that of topologic space (U, T). The study of space (U, T) may use the quotient space method. Thus, the quotient space method is introduced to the study of fuzzy sets. The concept of granularity represented by fuzzy set is transformed to a deterministic topologic structure. So the quotient space method provides a new way of granular computing.

Conversely, given a topologic space (X, T), $\forall x \in X$, letting $U(x) = \{$all open sets containing $x\}$, $U(x)$ is called a neighborhood system of x. According to (Yao and

Zhong, 1999), neighborhood system $U(x)$ can be regarded as a qualitative fuzzy set. So a topology space (X, T) can be regarded as a family of fuzzy sets. A neighborhood system description of a fuzzy set is presented in Lin (1996, 1997) and Yao and Chen (1997).

The three granular computing methods can be converted to each other. The integration of these methods is a subject worthy of further study.

4.7.4 The Transformation of Probabilistic Reasoning Models

In the section, we will discuss how to transform a probabilistic description to a deterministic model.

We have given reasoning model $((C, D), (f, g), F, H, (A, p))$ based on quotient space theory (Sections 4.1–4.4). A function $g(a, b)$ defined on edge $e(a \to b)$ is regarded as a probability, i.e., the conditional probability of b given a. Let $d(a, b) = |\ln (g(a, b))|$, i.e., $d(a, b)$ is regarded as a distance from a to b (a topologic structure T). The finding of a solution from A to goal p with maximal probability is equivalent to that of the shortest path from A to p under distance d. Assume that if $A \to a_1 \to a_2 \to \cdots \to p$ is the solution with maximal probability, then its probability is $g(A, a_1) \times g(a_1, a_2) \times \cdots \times g(a_n, p)$, from $d(a, b) = |\ln (g(a, b))|$, we have $d(A, a_1) + d(a_1, a_2) + \cdots + d(a_n, p)$. So the maximal probability solution (the former) is equivalent to the shortest path finding (the latter).

Reasoning on a probabilistic model can be transformed to a deterministic shortest path-finding problem, i.e., non-deterministic concepts such as fuzzy and probability are transformed to deterministic structures. Therefore, deterministic and non-deterministic problems can be studied under the same framework. Especially, in multi-granular computing, under quotient space structures, the falsity- and truth-preserving principles, projection, and synthetic methods that we have discussed in the previous sections can be used in either deterministic or non-deterministic case.

4.7.5 Conclusions

In the section, the falsity- and truth-preserving principles of reasoning are proposed. The principles show that introducing structure into the quotient space model is very important, that is, domain structure is an important concept in granular computing. We also show that the combination of quotient space method and other methods will provide a new way for granular computing.

Automatic Spatial Planning

Chapter Outline

To illustrate the applications of our theory, some topics of automatic spatial planning, i.e., automatic robot planning will be discussed in this chapter. We will pay attention to how the theory is applied to these problems, and how multi-granular computing can reduce the computational complexity.

The ability to reason about actions and their effects is a prerequisite for intelligent behavior. AI planning is to construct plans by reasoning about how available actions can be applied to achieve given goals. In robotic assembly, there are two kinds of planning. One is the derivation of an ordered sequence of actions that can be used to perform the assembly task. It is usually called task planning. For a robot to execute a sequence of actions, it must be provided with motion commands that will affect these actions. In general, motion planning deals with determining a path in free space, along with an object that can be moved from its initial position to a desired destination. This is the second kind of robot planning known as motion planning.

Quotient Space Based Problem Solving. http://dx.doi.org/10.1016/B978-0-12-410387-0.00005-6

In this chapter, only the above two specific topics of robot planning rather than the whole field are addressed.

5.1 Automatic Generation of Assembly Sequences
5.1.1 Introduction

As industrial robots come into wider use in assembly applications, interest in automatic robot program generation for assembly tasks is growing. The choice of the sequence in which parts or subassemblies are put together in the mechanical assembly of a product can be stated as follows.

Given a product W consisting of N parts, to find an assembly sequence automatically such that all assembly requirements such as geometrical, technological constraints, etc. are satisfied.

An assembly planning problem begins with each part in separation. The goal is to move them all into a given final configuration. For a product with N parts, the total number of all possible permutations of N parts is $N!$. Since different kinds of subassemblies can be used in the assembly process so that the total number of all possible combination of N parts will be $(2N-3)!!$ For example, as shown in Fig. 5.1, product W consists of parts 1, 2, 3 and 4. There is no such assembly sequence that only one part is moved at a time in the plane. If subassemblies are used, then we may have assembly sequences. For example, parts 1 and 4 are combined into a subassembly (1,4), and parts 2 and 3 into a subassembly (2,3) first. Putting subassemblies (1,4) and (2,3) together, then we have the final product. Therefore, the derivation of assembly planning is hard.

Assembly plans can be classified into several kinds. In sequential plans the assembly motion can be divided into a finite sequence of steps such that at any moment all moving parts are moving along the same trajectory. However, some plans cannot be built this way, since it requires that at least two parts be moved simultaneously in different directions. A monotonic plan is a sequential plan in which parts are always moved directly to their final positions. A linear plan is a sequential plan in which there is only one part moving at a time.

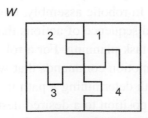

Figure 5.1: Assembly Sequences

Since general assembly planning is very complicated, so far much work having been done is limited to some specific kind of plans. Moreover, most planning systems consider only rigid motions, in which the parts are not deformed, and assume that each disassembly task of a product is the inverse of a feasible assembly task of the same product.

Mello and Sanderson (1989a, 1989b) presented a monotonic sequential assembly planning algorithm. The algorithm is complete and its computational complexity is $O(3^N)$, where N is the number of parts composing the product. Wolter (1989) presented a linear monotonic assembly planning algorithm called XAP/1. Its complexity is $O(2^N)$. These algorithms confront with exponential explosion in their computational complexity.

In this section, based on the principle of the hierarchical quotient space model presented in Chapter 1, we give a monotonic assembly planning algorithm. Under some conditions, the algorithm has a polynomial complexity $O(sN^2)$, where s is all possible assembly directions and $s \leq O(N)$ generally. Therefore, the complexity is $\leq O(N^3)$ (Zhang and Zhang, 1990c).

5.1.2 Algorithms

In the following discussion, we assume that the disassembly task of a product is the inverse of a feasible assembly task of the same product. So the problem of generating assembly sequences can be transformed into that of generating disassembly sequences for the same product. And rigid motions are also assumed here.

Directed Graph $G(p, d)$

Assume that a product W consists of N parts. We call the relative positions and interconnections among the parts of product W its structure. Assume that c is a subset of W. If the structure of any part in c is the same as its structure in W, c is said to be a component. Suppose that each component has two parts at least.

Let a set of possible disassembly trajectories of all parts in W be $D = \{d(0), d(1), ..., d(s-1)\}$. Given a component p and a possible disassembly trajectory d, a directed graph $G(p, d)$ can be constructed as follows.

Each part of p corresponds to a node. We obtain a set of nodes.

Given a disassembly direction d and a part e, when e moves along direction d from its initial position in W, the sweep volume of e is said to be a trajectory of e along d.

Definition 5.1

Given a direction d and parts a and b, if b intersects with the trajectory of a along direction d, b is said to be in front of a along direction d. It is denoted by $a < b(d)$. If b is moving along the opposite direction to d, it does not collide any part of component p, b is

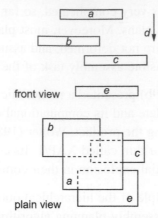

Figure 5.2: Two Views of a Component p

said to be an element immediately in front of a along direction d, or simply the front element of a.

For each element a of p and its front element b, a directed edge (a, b) is constructed. We obtain a directed graph called a disassembly directed graph along the direction d. It is denoted by $G(p, d)$.

For example, a component p consists of four parts: a, b, c and e. Its front and plain views are shown in Fig. 5.2, where e is the front element of a, and c is the front element of b. $G(p, d)$ is shown in Fig. 5.3. Since from $a \rightarrow b \rightarrow c$ we have $a \rightarrow c$, sometimes, the directed edge $a \rightarrow c$ can be omitted, as shown in Fig. 5.3.

Compressed Decomposition

Assume that $G(p, d)$ is a disassembly directed graph of p corresponding to the direction d. If each directed loop in $G(p, d)$ is shrunk to a point, we have a compressed graph denoted as $E(G(p, d))$ or simply $E(p, d)$. Obviously, $E(p, d)$ is a directed tree, or a directed acyclic graph.

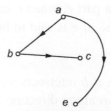

Figure 5.3: A Directed Graph

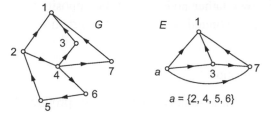

Figure 5.4: The Compressed Decomposition

There are two kinds of nodes in $E(p,d)$. $U(E(p,d))$ is a set of nodes which only contain one of $G(p,d)$'s nodes. $V(E(p,d))$ is a set of nodes which contain more than one of $G(p,d)$'s nodes; namely, a set of components in $E(p,d)$.

The process of decomposing $G(p,d)$ into $U(E(p,d))$ and $V(E(p,d))$ is called a compressed decomposition of $G(p,d)$. While $U(E(p,d))$ and $V(E(p,d))$ compose a compressed decomposition graph of $G(p,d)$.

For example, $G(p,d)$ is decomposed into $U(E) = \{1,3,7\}$ and $V(E) = \{a\}$, where $a = \{2,4,5,6\}$ shown in Fig. 5.4.

Assume that $E(p,d)$ is a compressed graph of $G(p,d)$. From our theory, $E(p,d)$ is a quotient space of $G(p,d)$, where a node in $E(p,d)$ is a subset of nodes in $G(p,d)$. If a node in $E(p,d)$ contains more than one of $G(p,d)$'s nodes, it is said to be a component. Therefore, the compressed decomposition of $G(p,d)$ is a process of constructing its quotient spaces.

Since $E(p,d)$ is a directed tree, there exist linear assembly plans. Due to the compressed decomposition, the problem of planning assembly sequences of $G(p,d)$ is transformed into a set of sub-problems, the planning assembly sequences of components in $E(p,d)$. By successively using the compressed decomposition, we will finally have an assembly plan of the overall product.

Assume that $E(p,d)$ is a compressed graph of $G(p,d)$, or it is simply denoted by E. E is a direct acyclic graph. For all $\forall a \in E$, we define the fan-in $r(a)$ of a as the number of directed edges of E which terminate in a.

Since E is a directed acyclic graph, there exists $a \in E$ such that $r(a) = 0$. If $r(a) = 0$, a is said to be a 1-class node. Generally, for $r(a) = 0$, if the highest class of a's father nodes is k, then a is a $(k+1)$-class node.

Thus, the assembly procedure of E is the following. Taking out all 1-class nodes, then all 2-class nodes are merged to their own father nodes along the opposite direction of d, respectively. Generally, If 1- to k-class nodes have been merged, then all $(k+1)$-class nodes are merged to their own father nodes along the opposite directions of d, respectively. The process is continued, we finally have graph E. The process is called E-assembly.

Cyclic Compressed Decomposition

Assume that a set of possible disassembly trajectories of produce W is $D = \{d(0), d(1), ..., d(s-1)\}$.

Component c and disassembly direction $d \in D$ are given. After the compressed decomposition of $G(c, d)$ along d, if we have a set $V(E(c, d)) = \{c\}$ of components, then c is said to be undecomposable corresponding to d.

Cyclic Compressed Decomposition Algorithm — Algorithm I

Product W and a set $D = \{d(0), d(1), ..., d(s-1)\}$ of possible disassembly directions are given. We compose a new infinitely cyclic sequence $D = \{d(i), i = 0, 1, 2, ...\}$, where $d(i) = d(i(\bmod s))$ when $i \geq s$.

Loop

Given an index i and a set $B(i)$ of components, for $\forall c \in B(i)$, define a label $\beta(c)$.

Initially, $i = 0$, $B(0) = \{W\}$, $\beta(W) = 0$, $d(i) = d(0) \in D$.

If $B(i) = \varnothing$, success.

Otherwise, for $\forall c \in B(i)$, to find the compressed decomposition of c along direction $d(i) \in D$.

If c is undecomposable

If $\beta(c) = s - 1$, failure

Otherwise, let $\beta(c) \leftarrow \beta(c) + 1$, c is included in set $B(i+1)$.

Otherwise, c is decomposed into some new components, and they are included in set $B(i+1)$.

By letting $\beta(\cdot) = 0$ and $i \leftarrow i + 1$, go to Loop.

Note that when c is decomposed, $G(c, d)$ is decomposed into $V(E(c, d))$ and $U(E(c, d))$, where the nodes of $V(E(c, d))$ are said to be new components of c.

Assembly Planning Algorithm — Algorithm II

Assume that algorithm I succeeds. We have a set

$$H = \{E(c_1, d_1), E(c_2, d_2), ..., E(c_n, d_n)\} \text{ of compressed graphs}$$

If nodes in some compressed graph $E(c_i, d_i)$ are parts, then c_i is called a 1-class component. Generally, 1-k class components have been defined. Then, when the level of nodes in compressed graph $E(c_i, d_i)$ of c_i is less than or equal to k-class, and at less one node is k-class, then c_i is called a $(k+1)$-class component.

The assembly procedure is the following.

Each 1-class component in H is assembled, according to its compressed graph. Assume that 1-k class components have been assembled. Then, $k+1$ class components are assembled, until the overall product W is assembled.

Obviously, if Algorithm I succeeds, it means that the compressed decomposition has been done along all directions $D = \{d(0), d(1), ..., d(s-1)\}$. If there is a component which has continuously been decomposed for s times, and is still undecomposable, then its label is $(s-1)$, i.e., algorithm I fails. Since algorithm I succeeds, it shows that the labels of all components are less than $(s-1)$. Therefore, all components in W have been decomposed into the union of parts.

On the other hand, since product W only has N parts, W must be demounted into single parts in N-1 time decompositions at most.

When each component of a directed tree $E(c, d)$ has been decomposed, we have a directed graph $F(c, d)$. Obviously, $E(c, d)$ is a quotient space of $F(c, d)$. Moreover, graph $F(c, d)$ can be reconstructed, by replacing each component of $E(c, d)$ with its corresponding compressed decomposition graph along some direction.

By repeatedly using the compressed decomposition, a sequence of quotient spaces can be obtained. The upper level graph is a quotient space of its lower level one. And the lower level graph is gained by replacing some nodes of its high level graph with their corresponding directed trees.

5.1.3 Examples

Example 5.1

Product W consisting of six parts is shown in Fig. 5.5, to find its assembly sequences.

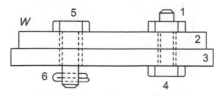

Figure 5.5: Product W

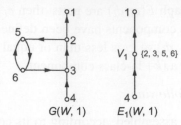

G(W, 1)   E₁(W, 1)

Figure 5.6: Graphs $G(W, 1)$ and $E_1(W, 1)$

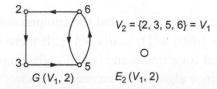

G (V₁, 2)   E₂(V₁, 2)

Figure 5.7: Graphs $G(v_1, 2)$ and $E_2(v_1, 2)$

From empirical knowledge of product W, we know that there are four possible disassembly trajectories. Namely, $d(1):(\uparrow)$, $d(2):(\downarrow)$, $d(3):(\leftarrow)$ and $d(4):(\rightarrow)$.

First, from the geometric knowledge, we construct a directed graph $G(W, 1)$ of W along direction $d(1)$. By the compressed decomposition of $G(W, 1)$, $E_1(W, 1)$ is obtained, where $v_1 = \{2, 3, 5, 6\}$ and $\beta(\cdot) = 1$ (see Fig. 5.6).

The directed graph $G(v_1, 2)$ of v_1 along $d(2)$ is constructed shown in Fig. 5.7. By the compressed decomposition of $G(v_1, 2)$, we have $E_2(v_1, 2)$, where $v_2 = \{2, 3, 5, 6\} = v_1$ and $\beta(v_2) = 1$.

The directed graph $G(v_2, 3)$ of v_3 along $d(3)$ is constructed, and is shown in Fig. 5.8. By the compressed decomposition of $G(v_2, 3)$, we have $E_3(v_2, 3)$, where $v_3 = \{2, 3, 5\}$ and $\beta(v_3) = 0$ (see Fig. 5.8).

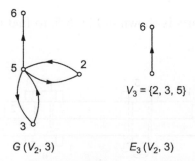

G (V₂, 3)   E₃ (V₂, 3)

Figure 5.8: Graphs $G(v_2, 3)$ and $E_3(v_2, 3)$

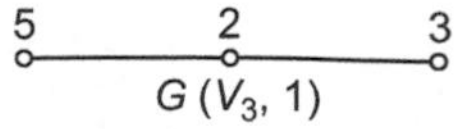

$$5 \quad\quad 2 \quad\quad 3$$
$$\circ\!\!-\!\!-\!\!-\!\!-\!\!-\!\!-\!\!-\!\!\circ\!\!-\!\!-\!\!-\!\!-\!\!-\!\!-\!\!-\!\!\circ$$
$$G\,(V_3,\,1)$$

Figure 5.9: Graph $G(v_3, 1)$

The directed graph $G(v_3,1)$ of v_3 along $d(1)$ is constructed, and is shown in Fig. 5.9. This is a directed tree. The compressed decomposition process terminates.

Now, the assembly process goes on in the opposite directions. First, since $G(v_3,1)$ is a directed tree, simply by putting part 2 on part 3, fitting part 5 onto parts 2 and 3 along the opposite direction of $d(1)$, we obtain subassembly $v_3 = \{2,3,5\}$.

Second, by inserting part 6 into part 5 from left to right, the opposite direction of $d(3)$ in $E_3(v_2,3)$, we have subassembly $v_2 = \{2,3,5,6\}$, where $v_2 = v_1$.

Finally, based on $E_1(W,1)$, by fitting v_1 onto part 4, and screwing part 1 on part 4, we have product W.

From a technological point of view, it is awkward to fit v_1 onto part 4. To prohibit the awkward assembly trajectory, the right one is moving part 4 upward to v_1.

In order to overcome the above defect, it only needs to revise the construction process of directed graph $G(p,d)$ as follows.

(a,b) is a directed edge of $G(p,d)$. If the disassembly of b along direction d is not allowable, then edge (a,b) is represented by a double-headed arrow $(a \leftrightarrow b)$. It means that parts a and b can be assembled in two different directions. We can choose one of them depending on the technological requirement. The revised directed graph is denoted by $\overline{G}(p,d)$. Graph $\overline{G}(p,d)$ is compressed to tree $\overline{E}(p,d)$. The rest of the compressed decomposition procedure remains unchanged. The revised algorithm I may satisfy the technological requirement as well.

Example 5.2

Product W is as shown in Fig. 5.5. The procedure of inserting part 2 or/and part 3 into part 4 is not allowable.

Some directed graphs and compressed directed graphs $\overline{G}(W,1)$, $\overline{E}_1(W,1)$, $\overline{G}(v_1,2)$ and $\overline{E}_2(v_1,2)$ are shown in Fig. 5.10. The rest is the same as Example 5.1.

The final assembly procedure is the following. Since $\overline{E}_3(v_2,3)$ and $\overline{E}_4(v_3,1)$ are the same as $E_3(v_2,3)$ and $E_4(v_3,1)$, respectively, the first two assembly steps are the same as before. Then, we have the subassembly $v_2 = \{2,3,5,6\}$. From $\overline{E}_2(v_1,2)$ we insert part 4 into v_2. From $\overline{E}_1(W,1)$ screwing part 1 into v_1, we have the overall product W.

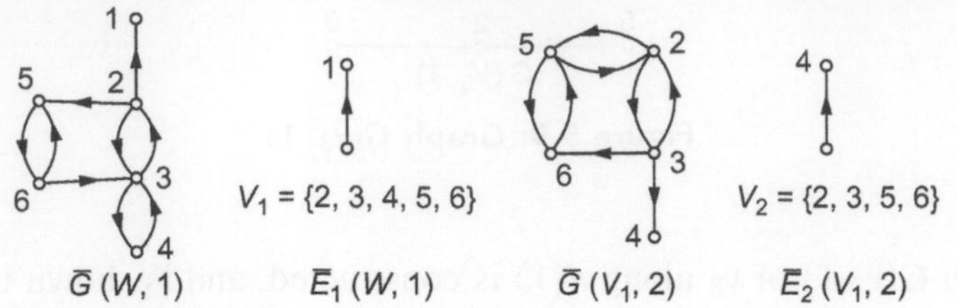

Figure 5.10: Graphs $\overline{G}(W, 1)$, $\overline{E}_1(W, 1)$, $\overline{G}(v_1, 2)$ and $\overline{E}_2(v_1, 2)$

5.1.4 Computational Complexity

The Completeness of Algorithms

First we show the completeness of the above algorithms.

If the successively compressed decomposition, i.e., algorithm I succeeds, from algorithm II, it is known that there exists an assembly plan.

If algorithm I fails, there exists a component c such that $\beta(c) = s - 1$. We will next show there does not exist a monotonic assembly plan of product W along the given assembly (disassembly) trajectories $D = \{d(0), d(1), ..., d(s-1)\}$.

Proof:

Assume there is an assembly plan F. Given a component c such that $\beta(c) = s - 1$, where c is a component of product W, letting F^{-1} be the disassembly plan corresponding to F, then there must exist some stage of F^{-1} such that c is disassembled along some direction d. Therefore, c is decomposable. This is in contradiction with $\beta(c) = s - 1$.

Proposition 5.1

Assume that product W has N parts. The computational complexity of algorithm I is $\leq 2sN(N-1)$, where s is the total number of the possible disassembly trajectories of W.

Proof:

Assume that $c_1, c_2, ..., c_n$ is a set of mutually disjoint components of W. Each component c_i has a_i parts.

The computational complexity for constructing each directed graph $G(c_i, d)$ of c_i along some direction $d \in D$, where $D = \{d(0), d(1), ..., d(s-1)\}$ is a set of possible disassembly trajectories of W, is less than or equal to $a_i(a_i - 1)$. This can be simply shown as follows.

Assume that a component b has m parts, i.e., $b_1, b_2, ..., b_m$. Given a direction d, we construct a $m \times m$ matrix C as follows.

When

$$i \neq j, \quad c_{ij} = \begin{cases} 1, & \text{if } b_i < b_j(d) \\ 0, & \text{otherwise} \end{cases}$$

$$c_{ii} = 0, \quad i = 1, 2, ..., m$$

Now, a directed graph $G(b, d)$ is constructed as follows.

If $c_{ij} = 1$ then a directed edge (b_i, b_j) in $G(b, d)$ is constructed. Since the number of the entities in C, except $c_{ii} = 0$, is $m(m-1)$, the computational complexity for constructing $G(b, d)$ is $m(m-1)$ at most.

Therefore, the total computational complexity for constructing directed graph $G(c_1, d), G(c_2, d), .., G(c_n, d)$ along some direction d is

$$\leq a_1(a_1 - 1) + a_2(a_2 - 1) + ... + a_n(a_n - 1) \leq N(N-1)$$

For s possible disassembly trajectories, the total complexity for constructing directed graph $G(W, d)$ is

$$\leq sN(N-1)$$

Now, we consider the complexity for obtaining the compressed graph $E(c, d)$ from $G(c, d)$, where component c has a parts. Given a node $b_1 \in G(c, d)$, starting from b_1, we find a directed path $b_1 \rightarrow b_2 \rightarrow ... \rightarrow ....$ If in some step, we have a node $b_m \in E(c, d)$, which is a leaf of $G(c, d)$, then b_m belongs to $E(c, d)$. This means that $E(c, d)$ has two nodes at least, namely, c is decomposed into the union of b_m and c/b_m at least. Or in some step, we find a directed loop l, shrinking l into a point, from point l a directed path is explored. The process continues. After a steps, either c is decomposed into two parts at least, or c is undecomposable along d direction.

For each $G(c, d(i))$ along directions $d(i), i = 0, 1, 2, ..., s - 1$ making compressed decomposition, after s time decompositions either c is decomposed or $c \in B(s - 1)$, i.e., algorithm I fails. The computational complexity $\leq sa$, where a is the number of parts in c.

Now, for each of the directed graphs $G(c_1, d), G(c_2, d), .., G(c_n, d)$ along directions $d(i), i = 0, 1, 2, ..., s - 1$ repeatedly making decomposition, respectively, its complexity is $\leq s(a_1 + a_2 + ... + a_n) \leq sN$, where a_i is the number of parts in component c_i.

In other words, after less than or equal to sN decompositions, either at least one of the components in W is decomposed or W is undecomposable, i.e., algorithm I fails.

On the other hand, so long as product W has been decomposed for N-1 times at most, it must be decomposed into single parts.

The total complexity of the successively compressed decomposition is $\leq sN(N-1)$.

By adding the complexities for constructing the directed graph and making compressed decomposition together, we obtain the total complexity $\leq sN(N-1)$.

Corollary 5.1

If $s \sim O(N)$, the complexity of algorithm I is $\sim O(N^3)$.

Proposition 5.2

If the complexity of assembling two parts (or components) is regarded as 1, then the complexity of algorithm II is $\leq (N-1)$.

5.1.5 Conclusions

A product W consists of N parts. If all possible permutations of the parts are considered, the number of possible assembly sequences would be $N!$. This implies that it is not the right way to find the assembly sequences by considering all possible combinations. The essence of multi-granular computing is to break the problem into manageable ones. In our assembly sequences generation, by the cyclic compressed decompositions the product W is decomposed into different kinds of subassemblies hierarchically. Let's consider Example 5.1 again. By the compressed decomposition along the direction $d(1)$, we break the product W into subassembly v_1, parts 1 and 4. And from the compressed decomposition along the direction $d(2)$, it shows that the subassembly V_1 is undecomposable, and is denoted by v_2. Then, by the compressed decomposition along the direction $d(3)$, the subassembly v_2 is split into sub-subassembly v_3 and part 6. Finally, v_3 is decomposed into single parts 2, 3 and 5. We finally have a tree structure as shown in Fig. 5.11. The upper level node is a quotient space of its lower level nodes. The assembly of product W simply goes on from bottom to top along the tree. Therefore, the computational complexity is reduced.

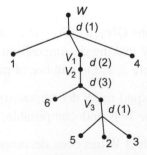

Figure 5.11: The Disassembly Tree

5.2 The Geometrical Methods of Motion Planning

The problem addressed here is a specific motion planning problem, known as the findpath problem in robotics. The problem is stated as follows: Given the descriptions of an object and a collection of obstacles in a 2- or 3-dimensional space, given also the initial and desired final configurations for the object, to find a collision-free path that moves the object to its goal, or determine that no possible path exists.

The common theme in motion planning work is the idea of representing the problem in such a way that the object to be moved is a point, and the point is moved through a configuration space that may not necessarily be equal to the 2-or 3-dimensional space of the physical problem. It is called configuration space representation, or C_{space} for short (Lozano-Perez, 1973; Lozano-Perez and Wesley, 1979; Brooks and Lozano-Perez, 1982; Brooks, 1983).

5.2.1 Configuration Space Representation

A Planar Moving Object Without Rotation

As shown in Fig. 5.12, A is a convex polygonal moving object and B is a convex polygonal obstacle. Assume that A is a rigid object moving among obstacles without rotation.

We associate a local coordinate frame with A. The configuration of A can be specified by the x, y position of the origin a of the local coordinate frame, and a θ value indicating the rotation of the local frame relative to the global one. The space of all possible configurations of A is its configuration space. A point in the space represents a particular position of a, the reference point of A, and an orientation of A.

Due to the presence of obstacles some regions of the configuration space are not reachable. These regions are called configuration obstacles, illegal or forbidden regions. Therefore, the moving object is shrunk to a point in the configuration space, and the

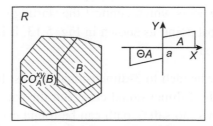

Figure 5.12: Configuration Obstacle of A

obstacles are expanded to form configuration obstacles (see Fig. 5.12 shaded area). The formal definition of configuration obstacle is given below.

Definition 5.2

The configuration space of moving object A is denoted by $Cspace_A$. Symbol $CO_A(B)$ represents the configuration obstacle of B in $Cspace$. We have

$$CO_A(B) = \{x \in Cspace_A | (A)_X \cap B \neq \varnothing\} \tag{5.1}$$

where $(A)_X$ indicates the moving object A with configuration x.

Obviously, if $\forall x \in CO_A(B)$ then $(A)_X$ collides with B. Otherwise, $\forall x \notin CO_A(B)$, $(A)_X$ does not intersect B.

Definition 5.3

Let $CI_A(B)$ be the interior points of B in $Cspace_A$. Thus,

$$CI_A(B) = \{x \in Cspace_A | (A)_X \subseteq B\} \tag{5.2}$$

Obviously, $CI_A(B) \subseteq CO_A(B)$.

Therefore, 'findpath' problem can be stated as to find a sequence of configurations of A such that they are inside of $CI_A(R)$ but outside of $CO_A(B_i)$, where $B_i, i = 1, 2, \ldots, n$ are obstacles and R is the whole physical space (see Fig. 5.12).

The key issue of path planning is to construct configuration obstacles.

5.2.2 Finding Collision-Free Paths

Once configuration obstacles or their approximations have been constructed, there are several strategies for finding a path outside the configuration obstacles for a moving point that represents object A.

Visibility Graph

If all obstacles B_i are polygons and A is also a polygon with a fixed orientation, then $CO_A^{xy}(B_j)$ obstacles with parameter (x, y) are polygons as well. The shortest safety path of A consists of a set of line segments which connect the starting point, some vertices of polygon $CO_A^{xy}(B_j)$ and the goal point, as shown in Fig. 5.13. It is called the visibility graph method or V_{graph} method.

The V_{graph} algorithm can be extended to 3-dimensional spaces. If $CO_A^{xyz}(B_i)$ is known, the safety path can be found as the 2-dimensional case. But the path being found is not necessarily optimal. Sometimes, no safety path can be found even if it does have a collision-free path.

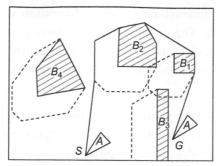

Figure 5.13: Visibility Graph Method

When A is a 3-dimensional object with rotation, $CO_A(B)$ is a complex curved object in a 6-dimensional space, the V_{graph} method cannot be used directly. Some approximations may be adopted such as the slice projection approach, etc.

Subdivision Algorithm

The fundamental process of the subdivision algorithm (Brooks and Lozano-Perez, 1982) is that configuration space is first decomposed into rectangles with edges parallel to the axes of the space, then each rectangle is labeled as E (empty) if the interior of the rectangle nowhere intersects *Cspace* obstacles, F (full) if the interior of the rectangle everywhere intersects *Cspace* obstacles, or M (mixed) if there are interior points inside and outside of *Cspace* obstacles. A free path is found by finding a connected set of empty rectangles that include the initial and goal configurations. If such an empty cell path cannot be found in the initial subdivision of *Cspace*, then a path that includes mixed cells in found. Mixed cells on the path are subdivided, by cutting them with a single plane normal to a coordinate axis, and each resulting cell is appropriately labeled as empty, full, or mixed. A new round of searching for an empty-cell path is initiated, and so on iteratively until success is achieved. If at any time no path can be found through non-full cells of greater than some preset minimal size, then the problem is regarded as insoluble.

Other Methods

There are several known geometric approaches for finding collision-free paths such as the generalized cone method (Brooks, 1983), the generalized Voronoi graph method, etc. We will not discuss the details here.

5.3 The Topological Model of Motion Planning

The idea of representing the motion planning problem in configuration space is to transform the moving object into a point and have the point move through that space. Generally, this is simpler than to consider the original object moving through the physical space, although the dimensions of the configuration space are usually higher than those of the physical one. The drawback of the above geometric approaches is in need of considering all geometric details throughout the entire planning process. When the environment is rather complicated, the computational complexity will increase rapidly.

From the multi-granular computing strategy, the problem can be solved in such a way that the problem is treated in some coarse-grained space by ignoring the geometric details first, after that we go deeply into the details of the physical space in some regions that contain the potential solutions. Since the less-promising regions have been pruned off in the first step, the computational complexity can be reduced by the strategy.

If the motion planning problem can be represented by a topological model, and under certain conditions the geometric details can be omitted, then we may deal with the problem in the simplified topologic space. Thus, we discuss the topological model first (Zhang and Zhang, 1982a, 1982b, 1988a, 1988b, 1988c, 1988d, 1988e, 1990c; Schwatz and Shatic, 1983a, 1983b; Chien et al., 1984; Toussaint, 1985).

5.3.1 The Mathematical Model of Topology-Based Problem Solving

Some problem solving can be stated as follows. From a given starting state, by a finite number of operations, then the final goal is reached. This is similar to the concept of arcwise connectivity in topology.

Arcwise Connected Set

E^n is an n-dimensional Euclidian space. For $\forall x, y \in A$, $A \subset E^n$, if there exists a finite set $x = x_1, x_2, x_3, \ldots, x_n = y$ of points such that point x connects to y by a set $\overline{x_1 \ x_2}, \overline{x_2 \ x_3}, \ldots, \overline{x_{n-1} \ x_n}$ of broken lines in A, then A is called arcwise connected. That is, any two points in A can be interconnected by a finite set of broken lines in A. If x is a starting state, y is a goal state, and a broken line connected x_i with x_{i+1} regarded as an operator, then the problem of judging whether x and y belong to the same arcwise connected set is equivalent to finding out whether there is a finite number of operations such that the given starting state can be transformed into the given goal state.

The Topologic Model of Problem Solving

X is a domain. Introducing a topology T into X, then we have a topologic space (X, T). Assume that $P = \{p_\alpha\}$ is a set of mappings. If $\forall p \in P, p : X \to X$ is a mapping, p is called an operator on X. Assume that P satisfies the following conditions.

$\forall p^1, p^2 \in P$, letting $p^3 = p^1 \circ p^2$, i.e., p^3 is the composition of p^1 and p^2 then $p^3 \in P$. Namely, P is closed with respect to the composition operation.

Definition 5.4

Assume that P is a set of operations on X. If for $\forall p \in P$ and $\forall x \in X$, x and $p(x)$ belong to the same arcwise connected component on (X, T), P and T are called consistent. If x and y belong to the same arcwise connected set, there exists $p \in P, p(x) = y$, then P is called complete.

In a general topologic space, the arcwise connectivity can be defined as follows.

(X, T) is a topologic space and $A \subset X$. If for $\forall x, y \in A$ there is a continuous transformation $r : [0, 1] \rightarrow (X, T)$ and $r(0) = x, r(1) = y$, where $[0, 1]$ is a closed interval in real axis, then A is called an arcwise connected set, and $r : [0, 1] \rightarrow (X, T)$, $r(0) = x, r(1) = y$, is called a path that connects points x and y.

Since the combination of an operation is still an operation, the implement of a finite number of operations is equivalent to that of one operation. So the problem solving can be restated as follows.

Starting state x_0, goal state x_1 and a set P of operations are given. The aim of problem solving is to find if there is an operation $p \in P$ such that $p(x_0) = x_1$. If such an operation exists, it's said that the corresponding problem has a solution; otherwise, there is no solution. If the solution exists, the goal is to find the corresponding operator p.

Proposition 5.3

Assume that a set P of operations and topology T on (X, T) are consistent and complete. x_0 and x_1 are starting and goal states, respectively. The corresponding problem has a solution $\Leftrightarrow x_0$ and x_1 belong to the same arcwise connected component on X.

Proof:

$\Rightarrow$: If the problem has a solution, there exists $p \in P, p(x_0) = x_1$. Since P is consistent, x_0 and $p(x_0) = x_1$ belong to the same arcwise connected set.

$\Leftarrow$: If x_0 and x_1 belong to the same arcwise connected set, from the completeness of P, there exists $p \in P, p(x_0) = x_1$.

The proposition shows that a problem solving can be transformed into the arcwise connectivity judgment problem in a topologic space.

We introduce some properties of connectivity below.

Primary Properties of Connectivity

Definition 5.5

(X, T) is a topologic space. If X cannot be represented by the union of two non-empty and mutually disjoint open sets, then X is called connected.

$A \subset X$, if A is regarded as a topologic sub-space (A, T_A) and connected, then A is a connected set on X, where T_A is an induced topology on A from T.

Property 5.1

If A is arcwise connected, then A is connected.

Property 5.2

Assume that $f : (X, T_1) \rightarrow (Y, T_2)$ is a continuous mapping. (X, T_1) and (Y, T_2) are topologic spaces. If X is connected, then $f(X)$ is connected on Y.

Property 5.2 shows that the continuous image of a connected set is still connected.

Property 5.3

$A, B \subset (X, Y)$, if A and B are connected and $A \cap B \neq \emptyset$, then $A \cup B$ is connected.

Property 5.4

If A is connected and $A \subset B \subset \overline{A}$, then B is connected, where $\overline{A}$ is the closure of A.

Definition 5.6

(X, T) is a topologic space. If $\forall x \in X$, for any neighborhood u of x, there exists a (arcwise) connected neighborhood $v(x)$, $x \in v(x) \subset u$, of x, X is called locally (arcwise) connected.

Property 5.5

If (X, T) is connected and locally arcwise connected, then X is arcwise connected.

Property 5.6

$A \subset E^n$ is an open connected set, then A is arcwise connected, where E^n is an n-dimensional Euclidian space.

Properties 5.5 and 5.6 show that in a certain condition, arcwise connectivity can be replaced by connectivity; the judgment of the latter is easier than the former.

5.3.2 The Topologic Model of Collision-Free Paths Planning

In this section, the topologic model of problem solving above will be applied to collision-free paths planning (Chien et al., 1984; Zhang and Zhang, 1988a, 1988b, 1988c, 1988d, 1988e).

Problems

Assume that A is a rigid body. The judgment of whether there is any collision-free path of body A, moving from the initial position to the goal position among obstacles, is a collision-free paths detection problem. When the paths exist, the finding of the paths is the collision-free paths planning problem.

For simplicity, assume that A is a polyhedron and obstacles $B_1, B_2, ..., B_n$ are convex polyhedrons.

First, we discuss domain X and its topology.

Assume that O is any specified point of A. D is the range of activity of point O. S is a unit sphere. C is a unit circle.

O is a point taken from A arbitrarily. Via point O any direction on A is taken and denoted by OT. The position of A is represented by the coordinate $a = (a_1, a_2, a_3), a \in D$ of point O, direction OT is represented by angles $(\varphi_1, \varphi_2), (\varphi_1, \varphi_2) \in S$, and the rotation of A around OT is represented by angle $(\varphi_3), \varphi_3 \in C$.

$D \times S \times C$ is the product topologic space of D, S and C, where D is a three-dimensional Euclidian topology, S is a sphere Euclidian topology and C is a circle Euclidian topology. For any $x \in D \times S \times C$, A_0. If A at x does not meet with any obstacle, x is called a state of A.

Definition 5.7

$X = \{x | x \text{ is a state of } A\}$ is a set of all states of A. If X is regarded as a subspace of $D \times S \times C$, there is a topology on X denoted by (X, T). (X, T) is a state space corresponding to A.

P is a set of operations. The operations over A mean all possible movements of A, including translation, rotation, and their combination. If object A moves from state x_0 to x_1 without collision by operation p then $p(x_0) = x_1$; otherwise, i.e., with collision then $p(x_0) = \varnothing$. The latter means that operation p is impracticable for state x_0.

From the definition, it's known that P and topology T on (X, T) are consistent and complete.

From Proposition 5.3, we have the following proposition.

Proposition 5.4

Starting state x_0 and goal state x_1 are given. Object A moves from x_0 to x_1 without collision $\Leftrightarrow$ x_0 and x_1 belong to the same arcwise connected component on (X, T).

When A and obstacles A_i are polyhedrons (X, T) is locally arcwise connected.

From Property 5.5, we have

Proposition 5.5

Starting state x_0 and goal state x_1 are given. Object A moves from x_0 to x_1 without collision $\Leftrightarrow$ x_0 and x_1 belong to the same connected component on (X, T).

Rotation Mapping Graph (RMG)

From Propositions 5.4 and 5.5, it's known that a collision-free paths planning problem can be transformed into that of judging if two points belong to the same connected component in a topologic space. For a three-dimensional rigid object, its domain X on (X, T) (collision-free paths planning) has six parameters, i.e., X is six-dimensional. It's hard to jude the connectivity of any set in a six-dimensional space. Thus, we introduce the concept of rotation mapping graph (RMG) and its corresponding algorithms.

Definition 5.8

$A \subset X_1 \times X_2$ is a subset of a product space $X_1 \times X_2$. Construct a mapping $F : X_1 \to X_2$ as $\forall x \in X_1, F(x) = \{y | (x, y) \in A\}$, then F is a mapping corresponding to A, where each $F(x) \subset X_2$ is a subset on X_2.

Conversely, assume that $F : X_1 \to X_2$, $F(x)$ is a subset on X_2. Construct a set $G(F) = \{(x, y) | x \in X_1, y \in F(x) \subset X_1 \times X_2$. $G(F)$ is called a map corresponding to F. Now, we use the map to depict the domain X of (X, T).

Assume that X is a state space $(X \subset D \times S \times C)$, $\forall a \in D$ corresponding to A. Let $f(a) = \{\varphi = (\varphi_1, \varphi_2, \varphi_3) | (a, \varphi_1, \varphi_2, \varphi_3) \in X\}$. Obviously, we have $f(a) \subset S \times C$. Thus, $f : D \to S \times C$ is a map corresponding to X, f is called a rotation mapping of A.

Definition 5.9

Assume that f is a rotation mapping of A. Let $G(f) = \{(a, f(a)) | a \in D\}$ be a map corresponding to f. $G(f)$ is called a rotation mapping graph of A.

From the definition, we have $G(f) = (X, T)$. By the rotation mapping graph, a six-dimensional space is changed to a set mapping graph from three-dimensional domain to three-dimensional range. Therefore, the connectivity problem of a high dimensional space is changed to that of the connectivity on several low dimensional spaces.

Now, we show the relation between a rotation mapping graph and its corresponding mapping by the following example.

Example 5.3

As shown in Fig. 5.14, E is a two-dimensional set, to find its corresponding mapping, where a product space is represented by a rectangular coordinate system.

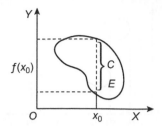

Figure 5.14: The Relation Between a RMG and a Mapping

For $x_0 \in X$, letting $f(x_0) = \{y|(x_0, y) \in E\}$, we have $f : X \rightarrow Y$. As shown in Fig. 5.14, via point x_0 construct a line perpendicular to X and the intersection of the line and E is set C. Projecting C on Y, we have $f(x_0)$.

Obviously, $G(f) = \{(x, f(x))|x \in X\} = E$. When f is single valued, $G(f)$ is a graph corresponding to $f(x)$ and can be regarded as the extension of a general graph.

Characteristic Networks

Definition 5.10

Assume that $G(D, f)$ is the RMG of A. $D_1 \subset D$ satisfies:

(1) D_1 and its closure $\overline{D}_1$ are arcwise connected sets on D
(2) Let $G(D_1) = \{(a, f(a))|a \in D_1\}$. Assume that $G(D_1)$ has m arcwise connected components on $G(D, f)$ denoted by $G_1(D_1), G_2(D_1), ..., G_m(D_1)$.
(3) For $\forall a \in D_1$, letting $G(a) = (a, f(a))$, then $G(a)$ has just m arcwise connected components on $G(D, f)$ denoted by $G_1(a), G_2(a), ..., G_m(a)$ and
$\forall i, G_i(a) \subset G_i(D_1), i = 1, 2, ..., m$.

Then, set D_1 is called a homotopically equivalent class of D.

Example 5.4

A graph $E \subset X \times Y$ is shown in Fig. 5.15, to find the homotopically equivalent classes of X.

Solution:

Let $D_1 = [a_0, a_1]$, $D_2 = [a_1, a_2]$, $D_3 = [a_2, a_3]$ and $D_4 = [a_3, a_4]$. From the above definition, D_1, D_2, D_3 and D_4 are homotopically equivalent classes of X, respectively, or D_1, D_2, D_3 and D_4 compose a set of homotopically equivalent classes of X.

If $D = [a_1, a_4]$, then D is not a homotopically equivalent class of X. Since $G(D)$ is simply connected in RMG, $a_1 \in D$, $G(a_1)$ is not connected, i.e., it has two components, D is not a homotopically equivalent class.

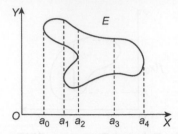

Figure 5.15: The Homotopically Equivalent Classes

If $D_4 = [a_2, a_3]$ and $D_5 = [a_3, a_4]$, obviously D_4 and D_5 are homotopically equivalent classes of X, respectively.

If $D_1 = [a_0, a_1]$, $D_2 = [a_1, a_2]$ and $D_3 = [a_2, a_4]$, then D_1, D_2 and D_3 compose a maximal set of homotopically equivalent classes of X. Namely, if E composes a maximal set of homotopically equivalent classes of X, when adding arbitrary element e of X to E and $e \notin E$, then $E \cup \{e\}$ is no longer a set of homotopically equivalent classes of X.

We now construct a characteristic network as follows.

Assume that $f : R \rightarrow Y$ and $G(f)$ is a graph of f.

(1) R is decomposed into the union of n mutually disjoint regions, and $R = R_1 \cup R_2 \cup \ldots \cup R_n$ is a set of homotopically equivalent classes.

(2) Each $G(R_i)$ has m_i components denoted by $<i, 1>, <i, 2>, \ldots <i, m_i>$, $i = 1, 2, \ldots, n$

(3) A set V of nodes composed by $<i, j>$, $i = 1, 2, \ldots n$, $j = 1, 2, \ldots, m_i$.

(4) Nodes $<i_1, j_1>, <i_2, j_2> \in V$ are called neighboring if and only if the components corresponding to $<i_1, j_1>$ and $<i_2, j_2>$ have common boundaries on $G(f)$, where $G(i, j)$ is the component corresponding to $<i, j>$.
     If $\overline{G(i_1, j_1)} \cap \overline{G(i_2, j_2)} \neq \varnothing$ then we say that the two components $G(i_1, j_1)$ and $G(i_2, j_2)$ have a common boundary, where $\overline{G(i, j)}$ is the closure of $G(i, j)$ on $G(f)$.

(5) Linking each pair of neighboring nodes of V by an edge, we have a network $N(G(f))$. It is called a characteristic network of $G(f)$.

For a state $x \in X = G(f)$, x must belong to some component $G(i, j)$ of $G(f)$, i.e., some node v of V. Namely, v is called a node corresponding to the state x. It is denoted by $x \in v$. We have the following theorem.

Theorem 5.1

An initial state x_0 and a goal state x_1 are given. Assume that x_0 and x_1 correspond to nodes v_0 and v_1, respectively. Then, a rigid body A moves from x_0 to x_1 without collision if and only if there is a connected path from v_0 to v_1 on $N(G(f))$.

Proof:

$\Rightarrow$: If there exists a collision-free path from x_0 to x_1. From Proposition 5.4, it is known that x_0 and x_1 belong to the same arcwise connected set of $G(f)$. From the definition of the arcwise connected, there exists a continuous mapping $r: [0,1] \rightarrow X(= G(f))$ such that $r(0) = x_0$ and $r(1) = x_1$. Obviously, the map $r([0,1])$ passes through a set $G(i,j)$ of components on $G(f)$ which correspond to a set of nodes along a path from v_0 to v_1 on $N(G(f))$. This means there exists a connected path from v_0 to v_1 on $N(G(f))$.

$\Leftarrow$: Assume there exists a connected path $v_0, v_2, v_3, ..., v_n = v_1$ from v_0 to v_1. For $\forall x_i \in v_i$, $i = 1, 2, ..., n$, letting $y_i \in \overline{v_i} \cap \overline{v_{i+1}}$, where $\overline{v_i}$ is the closure of the component corresponding to v_i, and y_i is a point at the common boundary of $\overline{v_i}\,\overline{v_{i+1}}$.

Therefore, we have a finite sequence of points on $G(f)$, namely,

$$x_0, y_0, x_2, y_2, ...x_i, y_i...x_n = x_1 \tag{5.3}$$

Obviously, both x_i and y_i belong to $\overline{v_i}$, and both y_i and x_{i+1} belong to $\overline{v_{i+1}}$. From the definition of the homotopically equivalent class, $\overline{v_i}, i = 0, 2, ..., n$ is arcwise connected. Hence, x_0 and x_1 belong to the same arcwise connected component. From Proposition 5.4, there exists a collision-free path from x_0 to x_1.

To illustrate the construction of the characteristic network, a simple example is given below.

Example 5.5

A graph E is shown in Fig. 5.16. We now find its corresponding characteristic network.

Solution:

X is divided into the union of three regions and they compose a set of homotopically equivalent classes of X.

$$D_1 = [a_0, a_1], \quad D_2 = [a_1, a_2], \quad D_3 = [a_2, a_4]$$

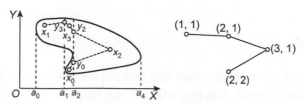

Figure 5.16: Characteristic Networks

To find the components of each $G(D_i)$, we have

> $G(D_1)$ has only one component denoted by $G(1,1)$
> $G(D_2)$ has two components denoted by $G(2,1)$ and $G(2,2)$
> $G(D_3)$ has only one component denoted by $G(3,1)$

Each node corresponding to $G(i,j)$ is denoted by $<i,j>$. Then, we have a network $N(G(f))$ as shown in Fig. 5.16. It is a characteristic network of E.

Given $x_0 \in G(2,2)$ and $x_1 \in G(1,1)$, we now find a collision-free path from x_0 to x_1. From Fig. 5.16, x_0 and x_1 belong to nodes $<2,2>$ and $<1,1>$ respectively. From the characteristic network, we have a connected path:

$$<2,2> \rightarrow <3,1> \rightarrow <2,1> \rightarrow <1,1>$$

Letting $y_0 \in \overline{G(2,2)} \cap \overline{G(3,1)}$, $y_2 \in \overline{G(3,1)} \cap \overline{G(2,1)}$, $y_3 \in \overline{G(2,1)} \cap \overline{G(1,1)}$ and $x_2 \in G(3,1)$, $x_3 \in G(2,1)$. we have a path: $x_0, y_0, x_2, y_2, x_3, y_3, x_1$ as shown in Fig. 5.16.

From the example, we can see that by the topologic model, the problem of finding a collision-free path in an infinite set $G(f)$ is transformed into that of finding a connected path in a finite network $N(G(f))$ so that the computational complexity is reduced.

5.4 Dimension Reduction Method

The RMG of moving object A among obstacles is usually high-dimensional. The judgment of the connectivity of $D(f)$ is rather difficult when the environment of A is cluttered up with obstacles. Based on the multi-granular computing strategy, we may observe the connectivity of the high-dimensional graph from its quotient space, if the connectivity is preserved in that space. Since the quotient space is simpler than the original one generally, this will make the complexity reduced.

Based on the basic idea above, we present a dimension reduction method for investigating the connectivity of high-dimensional graph. Roughly speaking, if E is a subset in a high-dimensional space $X(X = X_1 \times X_2)$ there exists a unique mapping $f : X_1 \rightarrow X_2$ such that $G(f) = E$. If f satisfies certain conditions, the connectivity of E can be inferred from the connectivity of the domain $D(f)$ of f and $f(x)$. This is called a dimension reduction method.

5.4.1 Basic Principle

We now use some topologic terminologies and techniques to show the basic theorems of the dimension reduction method. Readers who are not familiar with the contents are referred to Eisenberg (1974) and Sims (1976).

The mappings discussed in point set topology are usually single-valued. But the mappings concerned here are multi-valued. It is necessary to extend some concepts of topology to the multi-valued mappings.

For simplicity, the spaces addressed here are assumed to be metric spaces.

Definition 5.11

X_1 and X_2 are two metric spaces, F is a mapping from the points in X_1 to the subsets in X_2, i.e., $\forall x \in X_1$, $F(x)$ is a subset of X_2. F is said to be a multi-valued mapping from $X_1 \rightarrow X_2$, or F is a mapping from X_1 to X_2 for short, and is denoted by $F : X_1 \rightarrow X_2$.

Definition 5.12

$F : X_1 \rightarrow X_2$ is a mapping. A neighborhood $B(F(x_0))$ of $F(x_0)$ is given. If there exists a δ such that for $x \in B(x_0, \delta)$ have $F(x) \subset B(F(x_0))$, then F is said to be semi-continuous at x_0, where $B(F(x_0))$ is an open set containing $F(x_0)$, and $B(x_0, \delta)$ is a δ-sphere of x_0, i.e., $B(x_0, \delta) = \{y | d(x_0, y) < \delta\}$, where $d(x, y)$ is a metric function on X_1.

If $F(x)$ is semi-continuous at any point of X_1, then $F(x)$ is semi-continuous on X_1.

Definition 5.13

F_1 and F_2 are two mappings from $X_1 \rightarrow X_2$. For $\forall x \in X_1$, by letting

$F(x) = F_1(x) \cap F_2(x)$, $D = \{x | F(x) \neq \varnothing\}$, F is a mapping from $D \rightarrow X_2$ and is called an intersection mapping of F_1 and F_2.

Definition 5.14

F_1 and F_2 are two mappings from $X_1 \rightarrow X_2$. Letting $F(x) = F_1(x) \cup F_2(x)$,

F is a mapping from $X_1 \rightarrow X_2$ and is called a union mapping of F_1 and F_2.

Theorem 5.2

$F : X_1 \rightarrow X_2$ is a semi-continuous mapping. If X_1 is connected and for $\forall x \in X_1$, $F(x)$ is connected, then $F(X_1)$ is connected on X_2.

Proof:

Assuming that $F(X_1)$ is not connected, then $F(X_1) = A_1 \cup A_2$, where A_1 and A_2 are mutually disjoint non-empty open sets. Let

$$A_i^{-1} = \{x | F(x) \cap A_i \neq \varnothing\} \ i = 1, 2$$

Since $\forall x \in X_1$, $F(x)$ is connected and sets A_1 and A_2 are separated, then either $F(x) \subset A_1$ or $F(x) \subset A_2$ holds. We assume that $F(x) \subset A_1$.

For any $x_1 \in A_1^{-1}$, there exists $y_1 \in F(x_1) \subset A_1$. Let $u(F(x_1)) = A_1$. Since A_1 is open, $u(F(x_1)) = A_1$ is a neighborhood of $F(x_1)$.

From the semi-continuity of F, for $u(F(x_1))$ there exists a $B(x_1, \delta)$ such that when $x \in B(x_1, \delta)$, $F(x) \subset u(F(x_1)) = A_1$ holds. Namely, $x \in A_1^{-1}$. We have $B(x_1, \delta) \subset A_1^{-1}$. Thus, A_1^{-1} is open.

Similarly, A_2^{-1} is also open.

Finally, we show that $A_1^{-1} \cap A_2^{-1} = \varnothing$ must hold. Otherwise, there exists $x \in A_1^{-1} \cap A_2^{-1}$, that is, $x \in A_1^{-1} \cap A_2^{-1}$ and $F(x) \cap A_2 \neq \varnothing$. Since $F(x)$ is connected and sets A_1 and A_2 are separated, we have $F(x) \subset A_1$ and $F(x) \subset A_2$. This is in contradiction to $A_1 \cap A_2 = \varnothing$.

Therefore, $X_1 = A_1^{-1} \cup A_2^{-1}$, i.e., X_1 can be represented by the union of two mutually disjoint non-empty open sets. This is in contradiction to that X_1 is connected.

The theorem is proved.

Theorem 5.3

$F : X_1 \rightarrow X_2$ is a semi-continuous mapping. $\forall x \in X_1$, $F(x)$ is compact. X_1 is connected and for $\forall x \in X_1, F(x)$ is also connected. Then, the image $G(X_1, F) = \{(x, y) | x \in X_1, y \in F(x)\}$ of F is a connected set in the product space $X_1 \times X_2$.

Proof:

Let mapping $G : X_1 \rightarrow X_1 \times X_2$ be $G(x) = \{(x, y) | y \in F(x)\} = (x, F(x))$.

From the definition of the product topology, it is known that given $x_1 \in X_1$ and a neighborhood $B(G(x_1))$ of $G(x_1)$, for $\forall z \in G(x_1)$, there exists a neighborhood of z such that $B(z) = B(x_1, \delta(z)) \times B(y)$, where $z = (x_1, y)$ and $B(z) \subset B(G(x_1))$.

Since $F(x_1)$ is compact $G(x_1)$ is also compact in $X_1 \times X_2$. Besides, $B = \{B(z) | z \in G(x_1)\}$ is an open covering of $G(x_1)$, then there exists a finite number of sub-coverings $B(z_1), B(z_2), ..., B(z_m)$.

Let $\delta = \min_{1 \leq i \leq m} \delta(z_i)$, $B(F(x_1)) = \cap_{i=1}^{m} B(y_i)$, where $z_i = (x_i, y_i)$.

Therefore, we have $B(x_1, \delta) \times B(F(x_1)) \subset B(G(x_1))$.

Finally, from the semi-continuity of F, for $B(F(x_1))$, there exists a neighborhood $B(x_1, \delta_1)$ of x_1 such that $F(B(x_1, \delta_1)) \subset B(F(x_1))$.

Letting $\delta_2 = \min(\delta, \delta_1)$, for $x \in B(x_1, \delta_2)$ we have

$$F(x) \subset F(B(x_1, \delta_1)) \subset B(F(x_1))$$

Thus, for $x \in B(x_1, \delta_2)$ we have

$$(x, F(x)) = G(x) \subset B(x_1, \delta_2) \times B(F(x_1))$$

$$\subset B(x_1, \delta) \times B(F(x_1)) \subset B(G(x_1))$$

Namely, G is semi-continuous at x_1. Since x_1 is an arbitrary point in X_1, G is semi-continuous on X_1.

On the other hand, since $F(x)$ is connected, we have that $G(x) = (x, F(x))$ is also connected.

From Theorem 5.2, we conclude that $G(X_1)$ is a connected set in $X_1 \times X_2$.

Theorem 5.4

For $E \subset X_1 \times X_2$, E is compact. $F : X_1 \to X_2$ is a mapping corresponding to E, i.e., $G(X_1, F) = E$. Then, F is a semi-continuous mapping from $X_1 \to X_2$.

Proof:

Since $G(X_1, F) = E$ is compact, if F is not semi-continuous, there exist $x_0 \in X_1$ and $u(F(x_0))$ such that for any n, there has $x_n \in X_1, d(x_n, x_0) < \frac{1}{n}$ such that $F(x_n) \not\subset u(F(x_0))$, where $d(x, y)$ is a metric function on X_1. Namely, $y_n \in F(x_n)$ and $y_n \notin u(F(x_0))$ exist.

Let $z_n = (x_n, y_n) \in E$. Since E is compact, there exists a sub-sequence (still denoted by z_n) such that $z_n \to z_0 = (x_0, y_0) \in E$, i.e., $y_0 \in F(x_0)$.

Since $u(F(x_0))$ is open and $y_0 \in F(x_0)$, there exists a positive number δ such that $B(y_0, \delta) \subset u(F(x_0))$. Thus, there exists n_0 when $n > n_0$ have $y_n \in B(y_0, \delta) \subset u(F(x_0))$. This is in contradiction with $y_n \notin u(F(x_0))$.

Therefore, F is semi-continuous.

Corollary 5.2

If moving object A is a polyhedron and the obstacles consist of a finite number of convex polyhedrons $B_1, B_2, ..., B_n$, then the rotation mapping $D \to S \times C$ of A among the obstacles is a semi-continuous mapping, where D is the activity range of A, S is a unit sphere and C is a unit circle.

Proof:

From Theorem 5.4, it's only needed to prove that the RMG corresponding to A is compact.

Assume that G is a RMG corresponding to A. Since $G \subset D \times S \times C$ and sets D, S and C are bounded subsets in three-dimensional Euclidian space, from topology, it's known that in n-dimensional Euclidian space, the necessary and sufficient condition of a compact set is that it's a bounded closed set. Thus, in order to show the compactness of set G, it's only needed to show that set G is closed.

First we made the following agreement. When object A only touches obstacles, its state is still regarded as a point in G. When object A overlaps with obstacles, i.e., they have common inner points, its state is regarded as not belonging to G.

In order to show that G is closed, it's only needed to show that the complement G^c of G is open.

For any $z_0 = (x_0, \varphi_0) \in G^c (x_0 \in D, \varphi_0 \in S \times C)$, from the above agreement, it's known that when A and obstacle B_i (may as well assume that B_1) have common inner points, i.e., there exists $x_1 \in A° \cap B_i°$, where $A°$ is an inner kernel of A. Thus, there exists a neighborhood $B(x_1) \subset A \cap B_i$ of x_1.

Assume that x_1 is a fixed point O. Some direction via point x_1 is denoted by OT_0. Then $z_0 = (x_0, \varphi_0)$ can be represented by $z_0 = (x_1, \varphi_1)$. In fact, $z_0 = (x_0, \varphi_0)$ and $z_0 = (x_1, \varphi_1)$ correspond the same position of A. The different representations of the same position in A due to the different options of its fixed point and direction.

Let $B(z_0) = B(x_1) \times S \times C$. Obviously, $B(z_0)$ is a neighborhood of z_0. Since $B(x_1) \subset B_1$ no matter A locates at arbitrary position of $B(z_0)$, A and B_1 always have common inner points. In other words, any point in $B(z_0)$ always belong to G^c. Thus, G^c is open, i.e., G is closed.

G is a bounded closed set and compact, from Theorem 5.4, mapping F is semi-continuous.

Theorem 5.5

F_1 and F_2 are the mappings from X_1 to X_2 and satisfy: X_1 is connected, and $\forall x \in X_1$, $F_1(x)$ and $F_2(x)$ are connected and compact sets. Let F be the union mapping of F_1 and F_2. If there exists a $x_0 \in X_1$ such that $F_1(x_0) \cap F_2(x_0) \neq \varnothing$ then the image of F, i.e., $G(X_1, F) = \{(x, F(x) | x \in X_1\}$, is a connected set in the product space $X_1 \times X_2$.

Proof:

From Theorem 5.3, we have that $G(X_1, F_1)$ and $G(X_1, F_2)$ are connected. Since there exists a $x_0 \in X_1$ such that $F_1(x_0) \cap F_2(x_0) \neq \varnothing$ then $G(X_1, F_1) \cap G(X_1, F_2) \neq \varnothing$. From Property 5.3 in Section 5.3, we know that $G(X_1, F_1) \cup G(X_1, F_2) = G(X_1, F)$ is a connected set.

Theorems 5.2–5.5 underlie the basic principle of the dimension reduction method that related to the connectivity structure of a set in a product space. Namely, the connectivity problem of a set $E \subset X_1 \times X_2$, or an image $R = G(X_1, F)$ in the product space $X_1 \times X_2$, under certain conditions can be transformed to that of considering the connectivity of domain X_1 and $F(x)$, respectively. Since $F(x) \subset X_2$ obviously the dimensions of both X_1 and X_2 are lower than that of $X_1 \times X_2$. So the dimension is reduced.

Furthermore, if X_1 or X_2 is also a product space, then a set on X_1 or X_2 can be regarded as an image of a mapping in an even lower space. By repeatedly using the same principle, a high-dimensional problem can be decomposed into a set of one-or two-dimensional problems.

In the collision-free paths planning, its state space can be regarded as an image of mapping $D \to S \times C$. From Theorem 5.2, the state space can also be regarded as an image of mapping $D \times C \to S$, $D \times S \to C$ or $S \times C \to D$. Therefore, according to the concrete issue, we can choose state space representations based on different mappings which will bring considerable convenience to path planning.

In fact, the dimension reduction method is one of the specific applications of the truth and falsity preserving principles in quotient space theory.

5.4.2 Characteristic Network

In Section 5.3, we presented a general principle for constructing a characteristic network which represents the connected structure of a set. In this section, we will use the dimension reduction method for constructing the characteristic network.

The Connected Decomposition of a Mapping

$F: X_1 \to X_2$ is a mapping. $\forall x \in X_1$, $F(x)$ may not be connected. To use the theorems above, $F(x)$ must be connected. Therefore, X_1 is decomposed into the union of several sets first. Furthermore, for each set of X_1, F is decomposed into the union of several mappings $F_i, i = 1, 2, ..., n$ such that each $F_i(x)$ is connected. Then, Theorem 5.2 is applied to each $F_i, i = 1, 2, ..., n$, then integrate them together.

In Section 5.3, the concept of the homotopically equivalent class is introduced. We now extend the concept to sets in general product spaces.

Definition 5.15

$F: X_1 \to X_2$ is a mapping, where X and Y are topologic spaces. Let the image of F be $G = G(X, F)$. If $D \subset X$ satisfies

(1) D and $\overline{D}$ are arcwise connected on X
(2) Assume that $G(D, F)$, the image of F on D, has m connected components
     $G(1), G(2), ..., G(m)$, then $\forall x \in D$, $G(x, F) = (x, F(x))$ has just m connected components.

(3) If G has m components $G(1), G(2), ..., G(m)$ then $P(G_i) = D, i = 1, 2, \cdots, m$, where $P : G \rightarrow X$ is a projection. Then, D is said to be a homotopically equivalent class of G with respect to X, or D is a homotopically equivalent class for short.

If $G(D, F)$ has m connected components, denoted by $G(1), G(2), ..., G(m)$, letting $F(i)$ be a mapping corresponding to $G(i)$, then $F(i)$ is called the connected decomposition of F with respect to D.

Let's see an example.

Example 5.6

As shown in Fig. 5.17, G is a set on plane XOY. Assume $G = G(X, F)$, where F is a mapping corresponding to G.

Now, $X = [a, c]$ is decomposed into two homotopically equivalent classes $D(1) = [a, b]$ and $D(2) = [b, c]$.

Graph $G(D(1), F)$ has two connected components G_1 and G_2. Their corresponding mappings are $F(1, 1)$ and $F(1, 2)$, respectively.

Graph $G(D(2), F)$ has one component G_3. Its corresponding mapping is $F(2, 1)$.

Thus, $F(i, j)$ is the connected decomposition of F. $F(i, j)$ is called a connected component of F on $D(i)$.

The Construction of Characteristic Networks

$F : X_1 \rightarrow X_2$ is a semi-continuous mapping. X_1 is decomposed into the union of several mutually disjoint and homotopically equivalent classes, and is denoted by $X_1 = \bigcup_{i=1}^{n} D(i)$.

The connected decompositions of F on $D(i)$ are $F(i, 1), F(i, 2), ...$ Let

$$G(i, j) = G(D(i), F(i, j)), i = 1, 2, ...$$

The construction of a characteristic network is as follows.

(1) For each $G(i, j)$, constructing a node $v(i, j)$, we have a set $V = \{v(i, j), i = 1, 2, ..., n, j = 1, 2, ...\}$ of nodes.

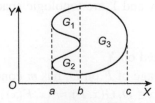

Figure 5.17: Connected Decomposition

(2) For $v(i_1, j_1)$ and $v(i_2, j_2) \in V$, if their corresponding components $G(i_1, j_1)$ and $G(i_2, j_2)$ are neighboring in $X_1 \times X_2$, i.e., the intersection of their closures is non-empty, then $v(i_1, j_1)$ and $v(i_2, j_2)$ is said to be neighboring.

(3) Linking each pair of neighboring nodes in V with an edge, we have a network $N(G(X_1, F))$. It is called a characteristic network corresponding to $G(X_1, F)$, or a characteristic network corresponding to F.

Proposition 5.6

$x_1, x_2 \in G(X_1, F)$ are connected, i.e., x_1 and x_2 belong to the same connected component of $G(X_1, F)$, if and only if there exists a connected path from v_1 to v_2, where v_1 and v_2 are nodes on $N(G(X_1, F))$ corresponding to x_1 and x_2, respectively.

Note that a $x \in G(X_1, F)$ corresponds to a node $v \in N(G(X_1, F))$ that means $x \in G(v)$, where $G(v)$ is a set of $G(X_1, F)$ corresponding to node v.

Example 5.7

A set G as shown in Fig. 5.17 is given. G is decomposed into sets G_1, G_2 and G_3 as shown in Fig. 5.17. Its characteristic network is shown in Fig. 5.18.

Note that to judge the neighboring relationship between G_1 and G_2, their closures $\overline{G_1}$ and $\overline{G_2}$ are constructed only on $G(D(1), F)$. Since the intersection between their closures is empty, G_1 and G_2 are not neighboring. However, to judge the neighboring relationship between G_1 and G_3, their closures are constructed on $G(D(i), F(i, j))$.

Generally, to judge the neighboring relationship between two sets $G(D(i), F(i, j))$ and $G(D(t), F(t, k))$, their closures are constructed on $G(D(i) \cup D(t), F)$.

Certainly, X_1 can also be decomposed into three homotopically equivalent classes $D(1) = [a, b], D(2) = [b]$ and $D(3) = [b, c]$. And we have a characteristic network as shown in Fig. 5.19.

Where

$$G_1 = G(D(1), F(1, 1)), \quad G_2 = G(D(1), F(1, 2)), \quad G_3 = G(D(2), F) \quad \text{and} \quad G_4 = G(D(3), F)$$

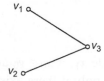

Figure 5.18: A Characteristic Network

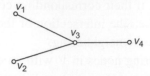

Figure 5.19: Characteristic Network

Obviously, if X_1 is decomposed into the union of maximal sets of homotopically equivalent classes, the number of nodes in the corresponding characteristic network will be minimal.

Finally, we analyze the dimension reduction method from quotient space based granular computing view point.

$G(D(1), F)$ is a mapping graph of F and is regarded as a subset in a Euclidian space. It's a finest space.

Now X_1 is decomposed into the union $X_1 = \cup_i D_i$ of homotopically equivalent classes. For $\forall x \in D_i, i = 1, 2, ..., m$, $(x, F_{ij}), j = 1, 2, ..., k$, is regarded as a quotient space composed by equivalence classes and is denoted by (G^2, T^2). Each element on (G^2, T^2) is a connected set on G. The problem solving in space G can be transformed into the corresponding problem solving on (G^2, T^2) since these two spaces have the truth preserving property.

If regarding (D_i, F_{ij}) as an equivalence class, we have a quotient space (G^3, T^3). It still has the truth preserving property; so the original problem can also be transformed into a corresponding problem in (G^3, T^3) space. Moreover, the problem in (G^3, T^3) can be further transformed into a corresponding problem in a characteristic network. Thus, the characteristic network method of path planning is an application of quotient space theory.

Collision-Free Paths Planning

Assume that a moving object A is a polyhedron with a finite number of vertices and the obstacles $B_1, B_2, \cdots, B_n$ are convex polyhedrons with a finite number of vertices.

Let $f_i : D \to S \times C$ be the rotation mapping of A with respect to obstacle $B_i, i = 1, 2, ...n$, i.e., $F : D \to S \times C$ is an intersection mapping of f_i.

Let $F_i : D \to S \times C, F = \cup_i F_i$ be the connected decompositions of F.

According to the preceding procedure, we may have a characteristic network $N(A)$ and the following proposition.

Proposition 5.7

Given an initial state x_0 and a goal state x_1, if $x_0 \in v_0$ and $x_1 \in v_1$ then object A can move from x_0 to x_1 without collision, if and only if there exists a connected path from v_0 to v_1 on $N(A)$.

An Example

Assume that the moving object A is a tetrahedron (Fig. 5.20). The initial coordinates of its four vertices are $O(0,0,0)$, $H(1,0,0)$, $K(0,1,0)$ and $J(0,0,1)$. Plane T_1OT_2 is an obstacle.

We next analyze the topologic structure of the RMG of the tetrahedron A due to obstacle T_1OT_2.

The state of a rigid object A can be defined by the coordinates of any non-colinear three points on A, e.g., O, H and K. The coordinate of the point O is (a_1, a_2, a_3). Its range is the upper half space, i.e., $a_3 \geq 0$ and is denoted by D. If point O is fixed, the range of H is a unit sphere S with O as its center and $OH = 1$ as its radius, i.e., $S((\alpha, \beta) \in S)$. If points O and H are fixed, the range of K is a unit circle C with O as its center. And the circle is on the plane perpendicular to line OH via K, i.e., $\gamma \in C$. Generally, D, S and C are represented by rectangular, sphere and polar coordinate systems, respectively.

The RMG of the moving object A is a subset of space $D \times S \times C$ (six-dimensional), i.e., the state space of A.

From Section 5.3, we know that the RMG of A can be regarded as an image of mapping $g : D \times S \to C$. Since the obstacle is a plane, the state space of A remains unchanged for coordinates a_1, a_2 and horizontal angle β on S; so it's only related to three parameters, i.e., a_3, α and γ.

Now, we discuss its characteristic network.

(1) Fix a_3 and α, to find $g(\cdot)$.
     As shown in Fig. 5.21, through K we compose a plane P perpendicular to line OH. l is an intersecting line between planes P and T_1OT_2. Through line OH we compose a plane perpendicular to T_1OT_2. OE is an intersecting line between the composed plane and P.

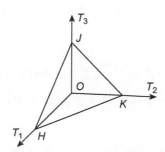

Figure 5.20: Tetrahedron A

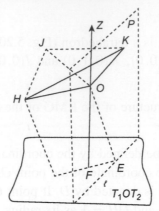

Figure 5.21: The Relation Between $g(\cdot)$ and OE

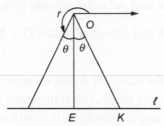

Figure 5.22: Plane P

As shown in Fig. 5.22, in plane P, the line through point O and parallel to l is used as a reference axis. The position of point K can be represented by the angle $0 \le \gamma \le 2\pi$ related to the axis.

Obviously, if $OE \ge 1$, the range of point K is the entire unit circle and is denoted by $g(\cdot)^1 = C$.

Similarly, the range of point J is also the same circle when it is transformed to a constraint of point K, i.e., $g(\cdot)^2 = C$.

Thus, $g(\cdot) = g(\cdot)^1 \cap g(\cdot)^2 = C$, i.e., $g(\cdot)$ has only one component.

When $0 \le OE \le 1$, $g(\cdot)^1 = (-\pi/2 + \varphi, 3\pi/2 - \varphi)$ and $g(\cdot)^2 = (\varphi, 2\pi - \varphi)$, where $\cos \varphi = OE$.

Thus,

$$g(\cdot) = g(\cdot)^1 \cap g(\cdot)^2 = (-\pi/2 + \varphi, 3\pi/2 - \varphi) \cap (\varphi, 2\pi - \varphi)$$
$$= (\varphi, 3\pi/2 - \varphi) \cup (3\pi/2 + \varphi, 2\pi - \varphi)$$

$g(\cdot)$ has two components:

$$g_1(\cdot) = (\varphi, 3\pi/2 - \varphi) \quad \text{and} \quad g_2(\cdot) = (3\pi/2 + \varphi, 2\pi - \varphi)$$

The second component will disappear when $3\pi/2 + \varphi = 2\pi - \varphi$, i.e., $\varphi = \pi/4$. Therefore, when $OE = \sqrt{2}/2$, the mapping has two components. When $0 \le OE \le \sqrt{2}/2$, it has only one component.

(2) The relationship between $g(\cdot)$ and OH

In (1) we discuss the relation between $g(\cdot)$ and OE. Actually, the length of OE depends on the position of OH, i.e., coordinate a_3 and α.

Assume that the coordinate of the point O is (a_1, a_2, a_3). The coordinate a_3 is divided into four intervals: (i) $a_3 \ge 1$, (ii) $1/\sqrt{2} \le a_3 < 1$, (iii) $1/\sqrt{3} \le a_3 \le 1/\sqrt{2}$, (iv) $0 \le a_3 < 1/\sqrt{3}$. Each interval of a_3 is further divided into several sub-intervals based on the value of α.

The partition of a_3 and α is shown below (Fig. 5.23), where $D(i,j) = \{$the i-th interval of a_3, the j-th interval of $\alpha\}$.

To show the procedure of calculating $g(\cdot)$, we take interval $1/\sqrt{3} \le a_3 \le 1/\sqrt{2}$ as an example.

Fixing point O, through O we compose a line OT_3' parallel to T_3-axis (Fig. 5.24). The position of OH is defined by angle α. Then, angle α is divided into four intervals.

(i) $0 \le \alpha \le \pi/2 - \theta$, (ii) $\pi/2 - \theta < \alpha \le \pi/2 - \theta_1$, (iii) $\pi/2 - \theta_1 < \alpha$
$\le \pi/2 + \theta_1$, (iv) $\pi/2 + \theta_1 < \alpha \le \pi - \theta$

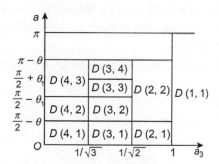

Figure 5.23: The Partition of (a_3, α)

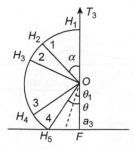

Figure 5.24: The Relation Between $g(\cdot)$ and OH

where, $OF = a_3, OH_i = 1$. When $1/\sqrt{3} \le a_3 \le 1/\sqrt{2}$, the range of point H on S is $0 \le \alpha \le \pi - \theta$, where $\cos\theta = a_3, \cos\theta_1 = \sqrt{2}a_3$ and $OE = a_3/\sin\alpha$.

We can write that

When $0 \le \alpha \le (\pi/2) - \theta$, $g(\cdot) = C$ since $OE \ge 1$.

When $\pi/2 - \theta < \alpha \le \pi/2 - \theta_1$ $g(\cdot)$ has two components since $1/\sqrt{2} \le OE < 1$.

When $\pi/2 - \theta_1 < \alpha \le \pi/2 + \theta_1$, $g(\cdot)$ has one component since $1/\sqrt{3} \le OE \le 1/\sqrt{2}$.

When $\pi/2 + \theta_1 < \alpha \le \pi - \theta$, $g(\cdot)$ has two components since $1/\sqrt{2} \le OE < 1$.

Let $1/\sqrt{2} \le OE < 1$ be the k-th component of $g(\cdot)$ on $D(i,j)$. If $g(\cdot)$ is connected, then it is denoted by $g_1(i,j)$.

Let $G_k(i,j) = G(D(i,j), g_k(i,j))$, i.e., $G_k(i,j)$ is the image of $g_k(i,j)$.

Similarly, we have the following results.

When $a_3 \ge 1$, $g(\cdot)$ has one component, i.e., $g(1,1) = C, 0 \le \alpha \le \pi$.

When $1/\sqrt{2} \le a_3 < 1$,

$0 \le \alpha \le \pi/2 - \theta$, $g(\cdot)$ has one component, i.e., $g_1(2,1) = C$.

$\pi/2 - \theta < \alpha \le \pi - \theta$, $g(\cdot)$ has two components, i.e., $g_1(2,2)$ and $g_2(2,2)$.

When $0 \le a_3 < 1/\sqrt{3}$

$0 \le \alpha \le \pi/2 - \theta$, $g(\cdot)$ has one component, i.e., $g_1(4,1)$.

$\pi/2 - \theta < \alpha \le \pi/2 - \theta_1$, $g(\cdot)$ has two components, i.e., $g_1(4,2)$ and $g_2(4,2)$ $\pi/2 - \theta_1 < \alpha \le \pi - \theta$, $g(\cdot)$ has one component, i.e., $g_1(4,3)$.

(3)   Characteristic network

Each $G_k(i,j)$ corresponds to a node $v_k(i,j)$. We have a set V of nodes.

Nodes v_1 and v_2 of V are neighboring if their corresponding $G_k(i,j)$, $k = 1, 2$, are neighboring in the state space.

Linking any pair of neighboring nodes by an edge, we obtain a characteristic network $N(A)$ (Fig. 5.25).

(4)   Find collision-free paths

Given an initial state $x^0 = (a_1^0, a_2^0, a_3^0, \alpha^0, \beta^0, \gamma^0)$, where

$$\frac{1}{\sqrt{3}} \le a_1^0 < \frac{1}{\sqrt{2}},$$

$$\frac{\pi}{2} + \theta_1 < \alpha^0 \le \pi - \theta,$$

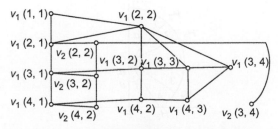

Figure 5.25: Characteristic Networks

$$\frac{3\pi}{2} + \theta_0 \le \gamma^0 < 2n - \theta_0$$

$$\cos\theta = a_s^0, \ \cos\theta_1 = a_s^0\sqrt{2} \quad \text{and} \quad \cos\theta_0 = OE$$

And given a goal state $x^1 = (a_1^1, a_2^1, a_3^1, \alpha^1, \beta^1, \gamma^1)$, where

$$0 \le a_3^1 < \frac{1}{\sqrt{3}},$$

$$\theta_0^1 \le \gamma^1 < \frac{3\pi}{2} - \theta_0^1,$$

$$\frac{\pi}{2} - \theta_1^1 < \alpha^1 \le \pi - \theta_1^1,$$

$$\cos\theta^1 = a_1^1, \ \cos\theta_1^1 = a_3^1\sqrt{2} \quad \text{and} \quad \cos\theta_0^1 = OE^1$$

Then,

$$x^0 \in v_2(3,4), \ x^1 \in v_1(4,3)$$

From the characteristic network $N(A)$, we have a collision-free path of A.

$$x^0 \in v_2(3,4) \to x^2 \in v_2(2,2)\left(1/\sqrt{2} \le a_3^2 < 1\right) \to$$
$$x^3 \in v_1(2,1)(0 \le \alpha \le (\pi/2 - \theta)) \to x^4 \in v_1(2,2)\left(\theta_0^1 \le \gamma^4 < 3\pi/2 - \theta_0^1\right) \to$$
$$x^5 \in v_1(1,1)\left(\pi/2 - \theta_1^1 < \alpha^5 \le \pi - \theta^1\right) \to x^6 \in v_1(3,3)\left(1/\sqrt{3} \le a_2^6 < 1/\sqrt{2}\right) \to$$
$$x^1 \in v_1(4,3)\left(0 \le a_3^1 < 1/\sqrt{3}\right).$$

Note that only one parameter changes in each step. For example, from state $x^0 \to x^2$, only the coordinate a_3 changes from $a_3^0 \to a_3^2$. The range of each parameter is indicated in the brackets.

The moving process of A is shown in Fig. 5.26.

(5) Conclusions

The configuration space representation and the like are usually used in both geometric and topologic approaches to motion planning. The main difference is that in the geometric model the geometric structure of C_{space} is investigated, while in the topologic model only the topologic structure is concerned.

Taking the 'piano-mover' problem as an example, by the subdivision algorithm presented in Brooks and Lozano-Perez (1982), the real C_{space} is divided. Even though the connectivity network constructed consists of 2138 arcs linking 1063 nodes, it is still an approximation of the real C_{space}. But in the topologic algorithm (see Section 5.5 for the details), the characteristic network constructed only consists of 23 nodes linked by 32 arcs, however, it is homotopically equivalent to the real C_{space}. Therefore, from the connectivity point of view, the topologic model is precise (Zhang et al., 1990a).

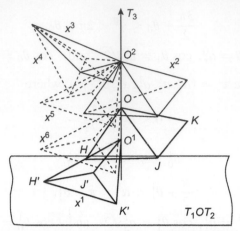

Figure 5.26: The Movement of Tetrahedron A

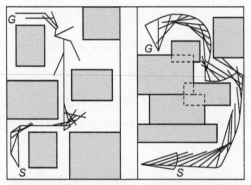

Figure 5.27: Path Planning of a 2D Rod

Since in topologic model, the motion proceeds in the coarse-grained world the computational complexity may be reduced under certain conditions. In 1980s we implemented the 'piano-mover' problem by topologic method on PDP 11/23 machine. The program is written by FORTRAN 4 and takes about dozens of seconds CPU time for implementation. More results will be given in Section 5.5. We also implemented dozens of experiments on ALR-386/II machine for a 2D rod moving among obstacles using programing language PASCAL and take less than 15 seconds time for implementation. One of the examples is shown in Fig. 5.27.

5.5 Applications

In this section, the theory and technique presented in the preceding sections will be applied to two motion planning problems. One is the planning for a planar rod moving among obstacles. The other is the planning for a multi-joint arm (Zhang and Zhang, 1982a, 1982b, 1988b, 1990a).

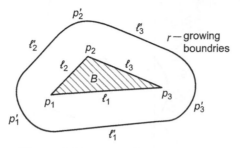

Figure 5.28: *r*-Growing Boundaries

The main point for using the theory to a real motion planning problem is how to decompose the domain into homotopically equivalent classes. There are three kinds of boundaries which are used for the decomposition. Namely, the original boundaries of the obstacles, the r-growing boundaries of the obstacles, and some specific curves called the disappearance curves arising in the regions cluttered up with the obstacles.

5.5.1 The Collision-Free Paths Planning for a Planar Rod

Assume that the length of rod A is r. The obstacles are assumed to be composed of a finite number of convex polygons. One of the end points of rod A is regarded as a fixed point O. The activity range of point O is a region in a two-dimensional plane. The rod itself is regarded as a reference axis OT. The activity range of OT-axis is its orientation angle.

The state space of A is X. We regard X as an image of mapping $F: D \rightarrow C$, where D is the activity range of point O and C is a unit circle.

The Homotopically Equivalent Decomposition of Domain D

Definition 5.16

Assume that the length of rod A is r. We define the r-growing boundaries of obstacles as follows.

As shown in Fig. 5.28, B is an obstacle. We construct new lines parallel to and at a distance r from each edge of B, and draw arcs with each vertex of B as its center and r as its radius which are tangent to the new lines. The boundary composed of these new lines and arcs is called the r-growing boundary of obstacle B (Fig. 5.28).

Definition 5.17

B_1 and B_2 are two obstacles (Fig. 5.29). $l'_1 p l'_2$ is a segment of r-growing boundary of B_2. $G(A)$ is an edge of B_1. If $G(A)$ is inside of $l'_1 p l'_2$ in part then we said that l_1 and l_3 compose a 'lane'.

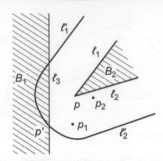

Figure 5.29: A 'Lane'

As shown in Fig. 5.29, at point p_1 there exist the feasible orientations of OT along the direction of the lane, but at point p_2 there does not have any feasible orientation since it is blocked by obstacle B_1. Under the edge l_2, there is an area where rod A does not have any feasible orientation along the direction of the lane. It is called a shaded area. The boundary of the shaded area can be computed as follows.

As shown in Fig. 5.30, we regard the boundary l_3 as X_2-axis, the line perpendicular to l_3 through point p as X_1-axis and the angle θ formed by OT and X_2-axis as a parameter. The equations of the boundary S of the shaded area are shown below.

$$\begin{cases} x_1 = r\sin\theta, \\ x_2 = r\cos\theta - actg\theta, \end{cases} \quad \theta_0 \le \theta \le \frac{\pi}{2}$$

$$x_1 = r, \quad \frac{\pi}{2} \le \theta \le \theta_1$$

where, (x_1, x_2) is the coordinate of the points on S, $\theta_0 = \sin^{-1}\frac{a}{r}$, θ_1 is the angle formed by l_2 and X_2-axis, and a is the distance between point p and boundary l_3.

The boundary S is called a disappearance curve, since some orientation components will disappear when the rod going across the boundary.

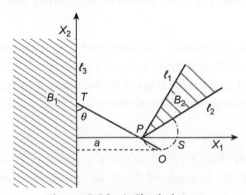

Figure 5.30: A Shaded Area

The Decomposition of the Homotopically Equivalent Classes

The original boundaries and r-growing boundaries of obstacles and the disappearance curves will divide domain D into several connected regions denoted by $D(1), D(2), ..., D(m)$.

We will show that $D^0(i)$ is a homotopically equivalent class, where set D^0 is the inner kernel of D.

Let $F : D \to C$ be the rotation mapping of A. Given $x \in D$, it is easy to find $F(x)$ or each component of $F(x)$.

Given $x \in D$, using x as center and r as radius, we draw a circle C counter clockwise. C is divided into several arcs by the central projections of obstacles from x on C. Then each arc corresponds to a component of $F(x)$.

As shown in Fig. 5.31(a), $F(x)$ is decomposed into three components $F_1(x), F_2(x)$ and $F_3(x)$. As shown in Fig. 5.31(b), each arc $\overset{\frown}{ab}$ corresponds to a component $F_i(x)$. $c(d)$ is the point of intersection between obstacle B_1 (B_2) and radius $ax(bx)$. Points c and d are called intersection points of component $F_i(x)$ on obstacles or simply the intersection points of $F_i(x)$. As shown in Fig. 5.31(a), component $F_1(x)$ can be represented by (1,2) or (8,2), where numbers 1, 2 and 8 indicate the numbers of edges l_1, l_2 and l_8 of obstacles, respectively. And the intersection points of $F_1(x)$ locate in edges l_1, l_2 and l_8. Similarly, $F_2(x)$ is denoted by (3,4), (7,4) or (9,4), etc. By this notation a component may have different representations but they should be regarded as being the same component.

Definition 5.18

A mapping $F : (X, d_1) \to (Y, d_2)$, where X and Y are metric spaces. If $x_1 \in X$, for $\forall \varepsilon > 0$, $\exists \delta > 0$ such that when $x \in B_1(x_1, \delta)$, we have

$$F(x) \subset B_2(F(x_1), \varepsilon), F(x_1) \subset B_2(F(x), \varepsilon)$$

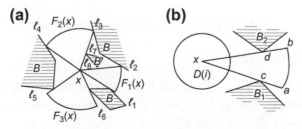

Figure 5.31: The Connected Decomposition of F

where

$$B_1(x_1, \delta) = \{y | d_1(x, y) < \delta\}$$

$$B_2(A, \varepsilon) = \{y | \exists x \in A, d_2(x, y) < \varepsilon\}$$

Then F is said to be continuous at x_1. If $\forall x \in X$, F is continuous, then F is said to be continuous on X.

Proposition 5.8

The $D^0(i)$ defined above is a homotopically equivalent class with respect to the rotation mapping F of rod OT, i.e., F is continuous on $D^0(i)$.

Proof:

$\forall x \in D^0(i)$ $F_1(x)$ is a connected component of $F(x)$. As shown in Fig. 5.31(b), there is no obstacle inside the sector (abx). But there is at least an intersecting point between edge $ax(bx)$ and the obstacles. There doesn't lose generality in assuming that only one such point exists at each edge, i.e., $c(d)$, where $c \in B_1 (d \in B_2)$, B_1 and B_2 are obstacles.

If arc $\overset{\frown}{ab}$ is degraded into a point, then x is a point at the boundary of some shaded area or a is a concave vertex of some obstacle. This is a contradiction.

If $c(d)$ is a vertex of some obstacle, then $c \neq a(d \neq b)$. Otherwise, x belongs to a vertex of some r-growing boundary. This is a contradiction, too.

Thus, the length of $\overset{\frown}{ab}$ is assumed to be positive, a and b are not vertices of obstacles and sector (abx) is at a positive distance from the rest of obstacles except B_1 and B_2. Therefore, given $\varepsilon > 0, \exists \delta$ for $\forall y \in B(x, \delta)$, we construct every rounds with y as its center and r (the length of the rod) as its radius. The sectors, parts of the rounds that locate between obstacles B_1 and B_2, are non-empty. And the sector is at a distance from the rest of obstacles except B_1 and B_2. Thus, the arc corresponding to the sector is a connected component of $F(y)$ denoted by $F_1(y)$ satisfying

$$F_1(y) \subset B(F_1(x), \varepsilon), F_1(x) \subset B(F_1(y), \varepsilon)$$

Namely, $F_1(x)$ is continuous at x.

For each component $F_1(x), F(x), ..., F_m(x)$ of $F(x)$, we conduct the same analysis and obtain that when x changes from x_1 to x_2 in $D^0(i)$ continuously, each component $F_1(x), F(x), ..., F_m(x)$ will change from $F_1(x_1), F_2(x_1), ..., F_m(x_1)$ to $F_1(x_2), F_2(x_2), ..., F_m(x_2)$ continuously, respectively. Thus, $D^0(i)$ is a homotopically equivalent class.

The Construction of Characteristic Network

(1) Domain D is divided into several connected regions by the original boundaries, r-growing boundaries of obstacles, and the boundaries of the shaded areas. The connected regions are denoted by $D(1), D(2), ..., D(m)$.

(2) To find the components of $F(x)$ on each region $D(i)$, it only needs to find the components of $F(x_i)$ for any $x_i \in D(i)$. Then, we have a set $G(i) : G(i) = \{G(i, t, s), G(i, t_2, s_2), ...\}$. $i = 1, 2, ..., m$ of components.

  Where, $G(i, t, s)$ denotes the image of component $\{t, s\}$ of $F(x)$ on $D(i)$, and component $\{t, s\}$ represents the component lied between edges l_t and l_s.

(3) Node $v(i, t, s)$ is constructed with respect to each $G(i, t, s)$. We have a set V of nodes. Assume that $D(i)$ and $D(j)$ are neighboring. According to different forms of their common edge, there are four different linking rules.

  (a) l'_r is their common edge, where l'_r is the r-growing boundary of edge l_r. Assume that $D(j)$ is on the inside of l'_r, i.e., $D(j)$ is located between l'_r and l_r. Then $G(j, t, r)$ and $G(j, r, s)$ in $G(j)$ are linked with $G(i, t, s)$ in $G(i)$.

  (b) p' is their common edge, where p' is a r-growing boundary of vertex p. $D(j)$ is on the inside of p'. Then $G(j, t, r)$ and $G(j, q, s)$ in $G(j)$ are linked with $G(i, t, s)$ in $G(i)$.

  If p is a concave vertex, i.e., the angle corresponding to vertex p is greater than 180, then $G(i, q, s)$ in $G(i)$ is not linked with any $G(j, t, s)$ in $G(j)$.

  (c) If s is their common edge, where s is the boundary of the shaded area corresponding to lane (l_r, l_q) and $D(i)$ is on the inside of s, then $G(j, r, q)$ in $G(j)$ is not linked with any $G(i, t, s)$ in $G(i)$.

  (d) $G(i, t, s)$ in $G(i)$ is linked with $G(j, t, s)$ in $G(j)$, i.e., the components with the same name in $G(i)$ and $G(j)$.

Based on the preceding rules, linking the nodes in the set V, we have a network $N(A)$. $N(A)$ is the characteristic network corresponding to the rod A.

Examples

Example 5.8

The obstacles are shown in Fig. 5.32. Find the characteristic network of rod OT.

Solution:

D is divided into 13 regions shown in Fig. 5.32. Taking the number of each region $D(i)$ as the horizontal ordinate, and the number (double index) of each component as the vertical ordinate, if $G(i, t, r)$ exists, and then we draw a node $v(i, t, r)$ in the point where the horizontal ordinate is i and the vertical ordinate is (t, r). Then, we have the characteristic network as shown in Fig. 5.33.

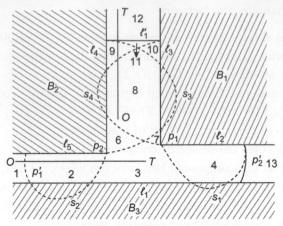

Figure 5.32: One-Dimensional Rod

number\component	node\region	1	2	3	4	5	6	7	8	9	10	11	12	13
1	(5, 1)													
2	(1, 4)													
3	(1, 2)													
4	(3, 4)													
5	(5, 2)													
6	(3, 1)													

Figure 5.33: Characteristic Network

If s_2, the boundary of shaded area, is the common edge of $D(2)$ and $D(3)$, then $G(3,3,4)$ is not linked with any point in $G(2)$, according to the rule.

If p_1 is the common edge of $G(1)$ and $G(2)$, where the two included sides of p_1 are l_3 and l_2, then $G(2,1,2)$ and $G(2,3,4)$ are linked with $G(1,1,4)$, according to the rule. But $D(2)$ is on the inside of s_2, component $G(2,3,4)$ disappears. Finally, $G(2,1,2)$ is connected to $G(1,1,4)$. Moreover, $G(2,5,1)$ is connected to $G(1,5,1)$ with the same name.

The same rules are applied to other components. Finally, the characteristic network we obtained is shown in Fig. 5.33.

From Fig. 5.33, we can see that the characteristic network consists of three disconnected sub-networks. This implies that rod OT can't move from a state to an arbitrary state, e.g., from state $v(1,1,4)$ rod OT can't move to state $v(8,3,4)$, since there is no connected path from node $v(1,1,4)$ to node $v(8,3,4)$ in the network (Fig. 5.33).

Example 5.9

The 'Piano Mover' problem is that given a 'piano' A and the obstacles as shown in Fig. 5.34, find a path from the initial position S to the goal position G.

For simplicity, piano A is shrunk to a broken-line while the boundaries of obstacles B_1 and B_2 are enlarged by the size $1/2\ d$, where d is the width of the piano A.

Domain D, the XOY plane, is divided into 10 regions as shown in Fig. 5.35.

Its characteristic network is shown in Fig. 5.36.

The final result implemented by computers is shown in Fig. 5.37.

5.5.2 Motion Planning for a Multi-Joint Arm

Multi-Joint Arm

A multi-joint arm R consists of A_0A_1 axis and m arms $A_iA_{i+1}, i = 0, 1, ..., m - 1$, as shown in Fig. 5.38.

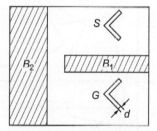

Figure 5.34: Piano Mover

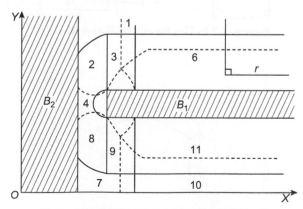

Figure 5.35: The Partition of Domain D

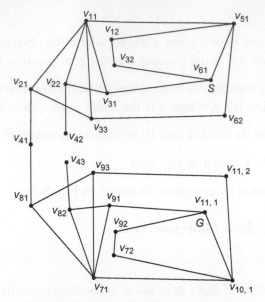

Figure 5.36: Characteristic Network

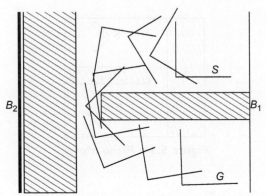

Figure 5.37: The Result of Piano Mover

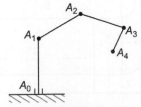

Figure 5.38: A Multi-Joint Arm

The rotation angle about A_0A_1 is denoted by θ_0. The rotation angle of each arm $L = A_{i-1}A_i$ around A_{i-1} is represented by θ_i. The length of arm L_i is r_i. The obstacles are assumed to be composed by a finite number of convex polyhedrons.

The problem is to find a collision-free path for the arm from the initial position to the goal position.

Rotation Mapping

Assume that $X \subset D \times Y$ is the state space of a moving object and $F : D \to Y$ is its rotation mapping. X is assumed to be compact. In fact, when D and Y are the subsets of Euclidean space, so long as X is bounded and closed X is compact. $D_1, D_2, \cdots, D_l$ are the homotopically equivalent classes of D. $F_1, F_2, \cdots, F_k$ are the connected decompositions of F.

Let $G(i,j) = G(D_i, F_j)$ be the image of component F_j on D_i.

D_i and D_j are neighboring if and only if $\overline{D_i} \cap \overline{D_j} \neq \varnothing$, where $\overline{D}$ is the closure of D.

Some properties of the image of the rotation mapping are given below.

Proposition 5.9

F is a mapping from $D \to Y$. $G(D, F)$ is the image of F. Assume that $G(D, F)$ is compact and $\forall x \in D$, $F(x)$ has a finite number of connected components. Let $D_1 \subset D$ be a homotopically equivalent class of F. F_1 is a connected component of F on D_1. Then we have that $F_1 : D_1 \to Y$ is semi-continuous.

Proof:

Let $G_1 = G(D_1, F_1)$ and $\overline{G_1}$ be the closure of G_1. Let $\overline{F_1}$ be a mapping corresponding to $\overline{G_1}$. Since $G_1 \subset G(D, F)$, $\overline{G_1} \subset \overline{G(D, F)} = G(D, F)$. $\overline{G_1}$ is a closed subset of the compact set $G(D, F)$. $\overline{G_1}$ is also compact. From Theorem 5.4, we have that $\overline{F_1} : D_1 \to Y$ is semi-continuous.

Again, F_1 is a connected component of F on D_1. So G_1 is a closed set on $D_1 \times Y$, i.e., $\overline{G_1} \cap (D_1 \times Y) \subset G_1$. We have $\overline{G_1} \cap (D_1 \times Y) = G_1$.

Namely, $\forall x \in D_1$, have $\overline{F_1}(x) = F_1(x)$. We conclude that $F_1 : D_1 \to Y$ is semi-continuous.

Definition 5.19

$G(D, F)$ is compact, D_1 and D_2, $D_1, D_2 \subset D$, are two homotopically equivalent classes. Let G_i be a connected component of $G(D_i, F)$. $F_i(\overline{F_i})$ is a mapping corresponding to $G_i(\overline{G_i})$, $i = 1, 2$. If D_1 and D_2 are neighboring and $\forall x \in \overline{D_1} \cap \overline{D_2}$, we have $\overline{F_1}(x) \cap \overline{F}(x) \neq \varnothing$, then

G_1 and G_2 are called regular neighboring, where $\overline{D}$ is the closure of D. $G(D, F)$ is the image of F on D.

Corollary 5.3

If $G_1 = G(D_1, F_1)$ and $G_2 = G(D_2, F_2)$ are regular neighboring, by letting F_{12} be the union mapping of F_1 and F_2, then $F_{12} : D_1 \cup D_2 \to Y$ is semi-continuous.

Proposition 5.10

Under the same assumption of Corollary 5.3, by letting $\overline{F_{12}}$ be a mapping corresponding to $(\overline{G_1 \cup G_2})$, and $A \subset D_1 \cup D_2$ be a connected subset, then $G(A) = \{(x, \overline{F_{12}}(x)) | x \in A\}$ is a connected set.

Proof:

From Corollary 5.3 and dimension reduction principle, it now only needs to prove that $\forall x \in (\overline{D_1 \cup D_2})$, $\overline{F_{12}}(x)$ is connected.

From the definition of the homotopically equivalent class, it easy to show that $\forall x \in D_1(D_2)$, $F_1(x)(F_2(x))$ is connected. We now show that $\forall x \in \overline{D_1}(\overline{D_2})$, $\overline{F_1}(x)(\overline{F_2}(x))$ is connected.

By reduction to absurdity, assume that for $\forall x \in \overline{D_1}$, $\overline{F_1}(x)$ is not connected. Since $\overline{F_1}(x)$ is compact, there exists $\varepsilon > 0$ such that $\overline{F_1}(x) = A_1 \cup A_2$, where A_1 and A_2 are non-empty, $B(A_1, \varepsilon) \cap B(A_2, \varepsilon) = \varnothing$, and $B(A_1, \varepsilon) = \{y | \exists x \in A, d(y, x) < \varepsilon\}$.

Since $\overline{F_1}(x)$ is semi-continuous, there exists δ, $\forall y \in B(x, \delta)$ such that

$$\overline{F_1}(y) \subset B\left(\overline{F_1}(x), \varepsilon/2\right) = B(A_1, \varepsilon/2) \cup B(A_2, \varepsilon/2)$$

We obtain

$$\left[(B(x, \delta) \times Y) \cap \overline{G_i}\right] \subset B(x, \delta) \times [B(A_1, \varepsilon/2) \cup B(A_2, \varepsilon/2)]$$

However, $B(x, \delta) \times B(A_1, \varepsilon/2)$ and $B(x, \delta) \times B(A_2, \varepsilon/2)$ are separated sets. Again, it is known that $B(x, \delta) \cap D_1$ is connected. $\forall x \in D_1$, $F_1(x)$ is connected and $F_1 : D_1 \to Y$ is semi-continuous. Thus, $(B(x, \delta) \times Y) \cap G_1$ is a connected set, so it can only belong to either $B(x, \delta) \times B\left(A_1, \frac{\varepsilon}{2}\right)$ or $B(x, \delta) \times B(A_2, \varepsilon/2)$.

Assume $(B(x, \delta)) \times Y) \cap B(x, \delta) \times B\left(A_1, \frac{\varepsilon}{2}\right) \subset B\left(x, \delta\right) \times B\left(A_1, \frac{\varepsilon}{2}\right)$, i.e., $\forall y \in B(x, \delta)$, we have $F_1(y) \subset B\left(A_1, \frac{\varepsilon}{2}\right)$. Hence, $B\left(A_2, \frac{\varepsilon}{2}\right) = \varnothing$. This is in contradiction with the assumption. We have that $\overline{F_1}(x)$ is connected.

Similarly, $\exists x \in \overline{D_2}$, $\overline{F_2}(x)$ is connected.

$\forall x \in \overline{D_1}/\overline{D_2}$, we have $\overline{F_{12}}(x) = \overline{F_1}(x)$. Therefore, $\overline{F_{12}}(x)$ is connected.

Similarly, $\forall x \in \overline{D_2}/\overline{D_1}$, we have $\overline{F_{12}}(x) = \overline{F_2}(x)$. Therefore, $\overline{F_{12}}(x)$ is connected as well.

When $x \in \overline{D_1} \cap \overline{D_2}$, since $\overline{F_{12}}(x) = \overline{F_1}(x) \cup \overline{F_2}(x)$ and $\overline{F_1}(x) \cap \overline{F_2}(x) \neq \varnothing$, we have that $\overline{F_{12}}(x)$ is connected.

Finally, since $\overline{F_{12}} : (\overline{D_1} \cap \overline{D_2}) \to Y$ is semi-continuous and A is a connected set, from the dimension reduction theorem, we conclude that $G(A)$ is connected.

From the proposition, we can see that if two images G_1 and G_2 are regular neighboring, then the problem of considering the connectivity of $\overline{G_1} \cup \overline{G_2}$ can be transformed into that of the connectivity of $\overline{D_1} \cup \overline{D_2}$. If D_1 and D_2 are regular neighboring, then the connectivity of $\overline{D_1} \cup \overline{D_2}$ can also be transformed into that of still lower dimensional space. This is just the principle of dimension reduction.

Characteristic Network

(1) A_i is the end point of a robot arm. All possible positions of A_i among obstacles are called the domain of A_i denoted by $D(i)$.

(2) $F_i : D(i-1) \to D(i)$ is a mapping, $\forall x \in D(i-1)$, $F_i(x)$ denotes all possible positions of the end point A_i of arm $L_i = A_{i-1}A_i$ among obstacles, when the other end point A_{i-1} is located at x.

In fact, $F_i(x)$ is the rotation mapping of x. The only difference is that $F_i(x)$ is represented by the positions of A_i rather that the rotation angle θ_i. F_i is the rotation mapping of the robot arm on $D(i-1)$.

$D(i)$ can be defined by F_i recursively.

Let $D(0) = \{A_0\}$. i.e., $D(0)$ is a point A_0.

If $D(1), \cdots, D(i)$ have been defined, then we define $D(i)$ as follows.

$$D(i) = \bigcup_{x \in D(i-1)} F_i(x).$$

(3) The connected decomposition mapping F_i.

$D(i-1)$ is divided into several homotopically equivalent and connected regions $D(i-1,1), D(i-1,2), \cdots, D(i-1,j), \cdots$.

Assume that the connected decomposition sub-mapping F_i on $D(i-1,j)$ is $F(i,j,1), F(i,j,2), F(i,j,k), \cdots$.

The image of $F(i,j,k)$ on $D(i-1,j)$ is $G(D(i-1,j), F(i,j,k))$ denoted by $G(i,j,k)$. Moreover, let each pair $G(i,j,k)$ of neighboring images be regular neighboring. When the moving object is a polyhedron and the obstacles consist of a finite number of polyhedrons, the homotopically equivalent set decomposition of D and the connected decomposition of F will make the neighboring images $G(i,j)$ become regular neighboring.

(4) Characteristic network of arm L_i

Using the same method presented in Section 5.4.2, we have the characteristic network of L_i denoted by $N(i)$.

The Construction of Characteristic Network

Assume that $N(1), N(2), \cdots, N(m)$ are characteristic networks corresponding to L_i, $i = 1, 2, \ldots, m$, respectively.

We compose a product set $S = N(1) \times N(2) \times \cdots \times N(m)$.

Let $v = (v_1, v_2, \ldots, v_m) \in S$ and $E_0(v) = \{A_0\}$.

Assuming that $E_0(v), E_1(v), \cdots, E_{i-1}(v)$ have been obtained, we define

$$E_i(v) = [F(v_i)(E_{i-1}(v))] \cap D(v_i), \quad i = 1, 2, \ldots, m - 1$$

$$E_m(v) = F(v_m)(E_{m-1}(v))$$

where, $F(v_i)$ is a connected component with respect to point v_i, $D(v_i)$ is a domain corresponding to v_i.

Definition 5.20

Given $v = (v_1, v_2, \ldots, v_m) \in S$, if $E_m(v) \neq \varnothing$ then v is a node of characteristic network $N(R)$, i.e., we have a set V of nodes, $V = \{v | E_m(v) \neq \varnothing, v \in S\}$.

Definition 5.21

Given $v^1 = (v_1^1, v_2^1, \ldots, v_m^1)$ and $v^2 = (v_1^2, v_2^2, \ldots, v_m^2)$, where $v^1, v^2 \in V$. v^1 and v^2 are called neighboring if and only if $\forall i$, v_i^1 and v_i^2 are neighboring in $N(i)$.

Linking each pair of neighboring nodes in V with a line, we have a network $N(R)$, or N for short. It is called a characteristic network of a multi-joint arm R.

Next, an example of motion planning for a 3D manipulator is shown below.

Example 5.10

A manipulator and its environment are shown in Fig. 5.39. The initial and final configurations are shown in Fig. 5.39(a) and Fig. 5.39(b), respectively. Based on the dimension reduction principle, we have developed a path planning program for a three-joint arm among the obstacles composed by a finite number of polyhedrons and spheres, using C language. The program has been implemented on SUN 3/260 workstation. One of the results is shown in Fig. 5.39. The CPU time for solving the problem is 5−15 seconds in average.

5.5.3 *The Applications of Multi-Granular Computing*

In motion planning for a multi-joint arm, the concept of multi-granular computing has been used for solving several problems.

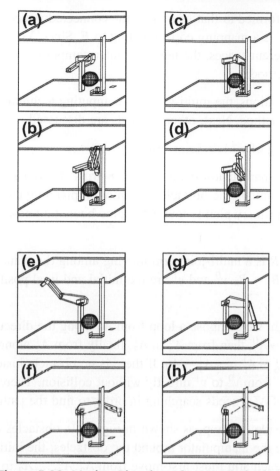

Figure 5.39: Motion Planning of a 3D Manipulator

In the construction of characteristic network $N(R)$, we regard $N(R)$ as a subset of the product set $N(1) \times N(2) \times \cdots \times N(m)$. To find a connected path from the initial state v^0 to the final state v^1 in $N(R)$, a connected path from v_1^0 to v_1^1 in $N(1)$ is found first, then a connected path from v_2^0 to v_2^1 in $N(2)$ is found such that the path merged from these two is a connected path from (v_1^0, v_2^0) to (v_1^1, v_2^1) in the product space $N(1) \times N(2)$. The process continues until a connected path from v^0 to v^1 is found, or the existence of collision-free paths is disproved.

This is a typical application based on multi-granular computing. Since $N(i)$ is the projection of $N(R)$, however, 'projection' is one of the multi-granular computing approaches as mentioned in the above chapters.

The dimension reduction method itself is an application based on the multi-granular computing technique as well. The original problem of finding the connected structure of a set $E \subset X_1 \times X_2$ is transformed to that of finding the connected structure of X_1 and $\forall x \in X_1$, $F(x)$, where F is a mapping corresponding to E. Since X_1 and $F(x)$ both are the projections of E on different spaces, the multi-granular computing technique underlies the dimension reduction method.

In the proceeding applications, the multi-granular computing technique is used mainly through the projection method. Next, other methods are discussed.

The Hierarchical Planning of a Multi-Joint Arm

R is a multi-joint planar manipulator composed of m arms. To find a collision-free path from state v^0 to state v^1 among the obstacles, the motion planning can be made in the following way. First, a primary plan is found by some heuristic knowledge. Then, the plan is refined.

As shown in Fig. 5.40, R is a multi-joint arm moving among the planar environment consisting of obstacles $B_1 - B_4$. v^0 and v^1 are the initial and final positions of R, respectively.

To plan the primary path, we compose a loop from A_0 along the direction v^0. i.e., $A_0 \rightarrow A_1^0 \rightarrow A_2^0 \rightarrow ... \rightarrow A_7^0$, then from A_7^0 to A_7^1, finally from A_7^1 along the direction v^1 back to A_0. i.e., $A_7^1 \rightarrow A_6^1 \rightarrow A_5^1 ... \rightarrow A_1^1 \rightarrow A_0$. If there is no obstacle inside the loop, then the manipulator can 'move' from v^0 to v^1 directly without collision. Therefore, in this case only a limited portion of $N(r)$ needs searching in order to find the path.

If there are obstacles inside the loop, as shown in Fig. 5.40, obstacles B_1 and B_2 are inside the loop. Then, to move the manipulator around the obstacles, the initial positions of end points $A_3, A_4, ..., A_7$ of each arm must first move from $A_3^0, A_4^0, ..., A_7^0$ to the left of obstacle B_1. In other words, from a high abstraction level, we first estimate the primary moving path of R by ignoring the interconnection between arms. Namely, the end point A_7 of arm 7 first moves along the direction v^0 from A_7^0 to the left of obstacle B_1, i.e., point A_2^0, then moves to A_1^2, finally moves to A_7^1 along the direction v^1.

End points $A_6, A_5, ..., A_2$ move in a similar way.

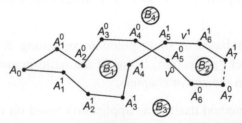

Figure 5.40: Motion Planning of a Multi-Joint Arm

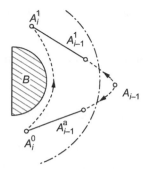

Figure 5.41: A Rod Moves Around an Obstacle

If the end point A_i of arm A_iA_{i-1} needs to move from one side of obstacle B to the other (Fig. 5.41), then the end point A_{i-1} must move from the inside of the r-growing boundary to the outside of the boundary and then back to the inside of B. Namely, the moving trajectory of point A_{i-1} is constrained by the trajectory of point A_i.

By using these kinds of heuristic information, the primary moving path of R can be worked out. Then under the guidance of the primary path, a final path can be found.

In three-dimensional case, some proper sections can be used. The two-dimensional characteristic networks can be constructed on these sections. By using the neighboring relationship between the nodes on the neighboring two-dimensional characteristic networks, the characteristic network of the three-dimensional case can be constructed.

As shown in Fig. 5.42(a), we construct the sections $P_1, P_2, ..., P_n$. Let N^i be the two-dimensional characteristic network on section P_i.

If N^i on P_i is a connected network, P_i is said to be a connected section. Therefore, when net N^i is a connected one, section P_i does not intersect with any obstacle.

Assume that P_{i-1} and P_{i+1} are two neighboring sections of P_i. If one of P_{i-1} and P_{i+1} is a connected section, then when finding a connected path from state v_i^0 to v_i^1 on P_i, we first

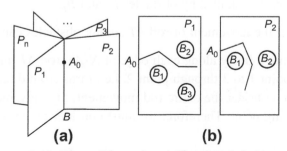

Figure 5.42: Three-Dimensional Characteristic Network

transform the state v_i^0 to a state v_{i-1}^0 on P_{i-1}, then on P_{i-1} move state v_{i-1}^0 to state v_{i-1}^1. Finally, v_{i-1}^1 is transformed to state v_i^1 on P_i.

Thus, the three-dimensional case can be handled in the similar way as in the two-dimensional case.

5.5.4 The Estimation of the Computational Complexity

Schwartz and Shatic (1983a) presented a topologic algorithm for two-dimensional path planning. Its computational complexity is $O(n^5)$, where n is the number of edges of polygonal obstacles. Schwartz and Shatic (1983b) also presented a topologic algorithm for solving 'piano-mover'. Its computational complexity is $n^{2^{O(d)}}$, where n is the number of obstacles and d is the degree of freedom of moving object.

Reif (1979) and Reif and Sharir (1985) presented a revised algorithm. Its complexity is e^d, and proved that the general 'piano-mover' is a PSPACE-hard problem, i.e., NP-hard problem at least.

In a word, the complexity of collision-free paths planning increases with d exponentially even though by using topologic approaches.

Next, we estimate the complexity of the dimension reduction method by taking motion planning for a planar rod as an example.

Fig. 5.42(a) shows a rod AT and its environment. When the end point A of rod AT moves from the initial state $A(s)$, there are three possible moving directions, i.e.,(B_8, B_4), (B_4, B_7) and (B_7, B_8), or (8, 4), (4, 7) and (7, 8) for short, as shown in Fig. 5.42(b). There is no path along the direction (7, 8). Along the direction (8, 4), from point 1 there are two possible moving direction (8, 1) and (1, 4). Along direction (1, 4), from point 2 there also exist two possible moving directions (1, 2) and (2, 4). But direction (2, 4) is a blind alley, etc. We finally have a network shown in Fig. 5.42 (c). It is called a characteristic network of point A denoted by $N(A)$.

Network $N(A)$ represents the connected structure of the domain of point A. Each edge (B_i, B_j) represents an area surrounded by obstacles B_i and B_j.

Based on network $N(A)$, the movement of rod AT among obstacles can be planned.

Although point A can move freely along each edge of $N(A)$, rod AT may not. For example, when AT moves from point 1 to 3 through point 2, i.e., turns from direction (B_1, B_4) to direction (B_1, B_2), if we consider the entire rod movement, the movement may not be possible at the intersecting point. Therefore, we must consider the movement at each intersecting point.

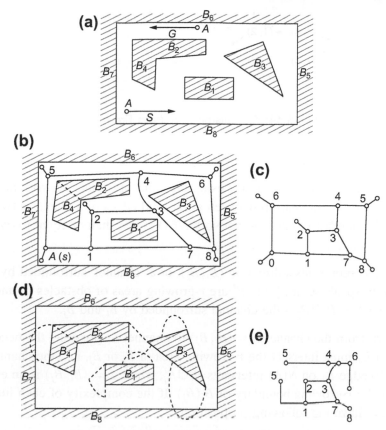

Figure 5.43: Path Planning of a Planar Rod

Whether rod AT can turn from one direction to the other may be judged by finding the boundary of the shaded area, presented in the above sections. In the example, the boundaries of each shaded area are shown in Fig. 5.43(d) by the dotted lines.

From Fig. 5.43(d), we can see that turning from direction $(4, 7)$ to $(2, 6)$, from $(8, 3)$ to $(5, 3)$, or from $(3, 2)$ to $(6, 2)$ is impossible. The others are possible. The characteristic network is shown in Fig. 5.43(e).

Given the initial state corresponding to direction $(8,4)$ and goal state corresponding to direction $(6,2)$, we now plan a collision-free path. From $(8,4)$ we search the collision-free paths as shown below.

Finally, we have a collision-free path from S to G (Fig. 5.44):

$$S = (8, 4) \to (1, 4) \to (1, 2) \to (1, 3) \to (2, 3) \to (6, 3) \to (6, 2) = G$$

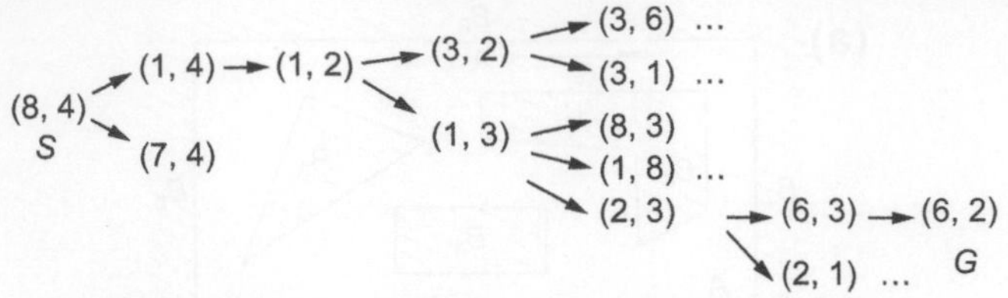

Figure 5.44: A Collision-Free Path From S to G

Next, we estimate its computational complexity.

Assume there are n convex polygons. By using the concept of dual network and the Euler formula concerning the relationship between points and edges of a planar network, it can be proved that the number of edges in network $N(A)$ is less than or equal to cn, where c is a constant.

Each edge in $N(A)$ represents a direction (B_i, B_j), or a 'channel' surrounded by obstacles B_i and B_j. Strictly speaking, if B_i' and B_j' are r-growing areas of obstacles B_i and B_j, respectively, then $L = B_i' \cap B_j'$ is the channel surrounded by B_i and B_j.

To make the turn from the channel $L = (B_i, B_j)$ to channel L_1 possible, the necessary condition is that L_1 must intersect the r-growing area of B_i or B_j, i.e., the channel corresponding to edge L_1 on $N(A)$ intersects $B_i' \cup B_j'$, where $L = (B_i, B_j)$ is an edge of $N(A)$, $B_i'(B_j')$ is the r-growing boundary of $B_i(B_j)$. If the complexity of each judgment is regarded as 1, we have the following proposition.

Proposition 5.12

If the environment consists of n convex polygons, the computational complexity for planning the motion of two-dimensional moving rod is $\leq O(n^2)$, if using the above hierarchical planning method.

Certainly, this is just a rough estimation. It is shown that the multi-granular computing strategy has a potential in reducing the computational complexity.

CHAPTER 6

Statistical Heuristic Search

Chapter Outline

In computer problem solving, we know that many types of real problems are conveniently described as a task of finding some properties of graphs. Recall that a graph consists of a set of nodes, which represent encodings of sub-problems. Every graph has a unique node s called the root node, representing the initial problem in hand. Certain pairs of nodes are connected by directed arcs, which represent operators available to the problem solver. If an arc is directed from node n to node p, node p is said to be a successor of n and node n is said to be a father of p. The number of successors emanating from a given node is called the branching factor (or branching degree) of that node, and is denoted by m. A sequence $n_1, n_2, ..., n_k$ of nodes, where each n_i is a successor of n_{i-1}, is called a path from node n_1 to node n_k with length k. The cost of a path is normally understood to be the sum of the costs of all the arcs along the path.

Quotient Space Based Problem Solving. http://dx.doi.org/10.1016/B978-0-12-410387-0.00006-8

A tree is a graph in which each node (except one root node) has only one father. A uniform m-ary tree is a tree in which every node has the same branching factor m.

Now, we consider a problem in hand that is incomplete knowledge or highly uncertain. In order to solve the problem, the search means is generally adopted, i.e., to search the solution in a problem solving space or a search graph. Thus, search is one of the main fields in artificial intelligence. If the size of the space is small, the exhaustive and blind search strategy can be adopted. But if the space becomes larger some sort of heuristic information should be used in order to enhance the search efficiency.

Heuristic search is a graph search procedure which uses heuristic information from sources outside the graph. Some heuristic search algorithms, for example A^*, have been investigated for the past thirty years. In those algorithms, taking BF (Best-First) for example, the promise of a node in a search graph is estimated numerically by a heuristic node evaluation function $f(\cdot)$, which depends on the knowledge about the problem domain. The node selected for expansion is the one that has the lowest (best) $f(\cdot)$ among all open nodes.

But for many known algorithms, the computational complexity depends on the precision of the heuristic estimates, and for lack of global view in the search process the exponential explosion will be encountered when the node evaluation function estimated is not very precise. For example, Pearl (1984a, 1984b) made a thorough study about the relations between the precision of the heuristic estimates and the average complexity of A^*, and it is confirmed that a necessary and sufficient condition for maintaining a polynomial search complexity is that A^* be guided by heuristics with logarithmic precision. In reality, such heuristics are difficult to obtain.

Based on the similarity between the statistical inference and heuristic search, we consider a heuristic search as a random sampling process, and treat evaluation functions as random variables. Once a searching direction is chosen, it's regarded as if making a statistical inference. By transferring the statistical inference techniques to the heuristic search, a new search method called statistical heuristic search algorithm, SA for short, is obtained. Some recent results of SA search are presented in this chapter (Zhang and Zhang, 1984, 1985, 1987, 1989a, 1989b).

In Section 6.1, the principle of SA is discussed. The procedure of SA is divided into two steps hierarchically. First it identifies quickly the most promising subpart (sub-tree) of a search graph by using some statistical inference method. The sub-trees which contain the goal with lower probability are rejected (pruned). The most promising one is selected. Second, it expands nodes within the selected sub-tree using some common heuristic search algorithm. These two steps are used alternately.

In Section 6.2 the computational complexity of *SA* is discussed. Since a global judgment is added in the search, and the judgment is just based on the difference rather than the precision of the statistics extracted from different parts of a search graph, the exponential explosion encountered in some known search algorithms can be avoided in *SA*. It's shown that under Hypothesis I, *SA* may maintain a polynomial mean complexity.

In Section 6.3, in order to implement a global judgment on sub-trees, the subparts of a search graph, information which represents their global property should be extracted from the sub-trees. The extraction of global information is discussed. Moreover, both global information extraction and statistic heuristic search process will be explained by the quotient space theory.

In Section 6.4, Hypothesis I is compared with the conditions which induce a polynomial mean complexity of A^*. It indicates that, in general, Hypothesis I which yields a polynomial mean complexity of *SA* is weaker than the latter.

In Section 6.5, from the hierarchical problem solving viewpoint, the statistical heuristic search strategy is shown to be an instantiation of the multi-granular computing strategy.

6.1 Statistical Heuristic Search

6.1.1 Heuristic Search Methods

1 BF Algorithm

Assume that G is a finite graph, s_0 is a node and s_g is a goal node in G. Our aim is to find a path in G from s_0 to s_g. We regarded the distance between two nodes as available information and define its distance function g^* as

$$g^*(n) = k(s_0, n), \forall n \in G,$$

where $k(s_0, n)$ is the shortest path from s_0 to n

Define h^* as

$$h^*(n) = k(n, s_g), \forall n \in G,$$

where $k(n, s_g)$ is the shortest path from n to s_g

Let $f^*(n) = g^*(n) + h^*(n), \forall n \in G. f(n)$ is the evaluation function of $f^*(n)$, denoted by $f(n) = g(n) + h(n), \forall n \in G$, where $g(n)$ and $h(n)$ are evaluation functions of $g^*(n)$ and $h^*(n)$, respectively.

Several best-first strategies in heuristic search differ in the type of evaluation functions they employ. The most popular algorithm in use is A^* search which uses an additive evaluation function $f(n) = g(n) + h(n)$ and $\forall n \in G \; h(n) \leq h^*(n)$. Algorithm A^* has the following properties.

Property 6.1

If there exists a path from s_0 to s_g and algorithm A^* can find the shortest path from s_0 to s_g, then A^* is called admissible.

If $h(n)$ has the following constraint, i.e., $\forall n_1, n_2, \; h(n_1) \leq h(n_2) + c(n_1, n_2)$, where $c(n_1, n_2)$ is the path from n_1 to n_2, $h(n)$ is called monotonic.

Property 6.2

If $h(\cdot)$ is monotonic, when A^* expands any node n, we always have $g(n) = g^*(n)$.

Property 6.3

If $h(n)$ is monotonic then the values of $f(n)$ corresponding to the sequence of nodes that expanded by A^* are non-decreasing.

Obviously, if the values of $f(n)$ are strictly increasing, then the nodes expanded by A^* are mutually non-repeated.

2 The Probabilistic Model of Heuristic Search

Nilsson (1980) presented A^* algorithm and discussed its properties. Pearl (1984a, 1984b) from probabilistic viewpoint, analyzed the relation between the precision of the heuristic estimates and the average complexity of A^* comprehensively.

Pearl assumes that a uniform m-ary tree G has a unique goal node s_N at depth N at an unknown location. A^* algorithm searches the goal using evaluation function $f(n)$, $f(n) = g(n) + h(n)$, where $g(n)$ is the depth of node n, $h(n)$ is the estimation of $h^*(n)$, and $h^*(n)$ is the distance from n to s_N. Assume that $h(n)$ is a random variable ranging over $[0, h^*(n)]$ and its distribution function is $F_{h(n)}(x) = P[h(n) \leq x]$. $E(Z)$ is the average number of nodes that expanded by A^*, until the goal s_N is found, and is called the average complexity of A^*.

One of his results is the following.

For any node in a uniform m-ary tree, there exist two fixed positive numbers ε, λ and a normalizing function $\phi(\cdot)$ such that

$$P\left[\left|\frac{h(n) - h^*(n)}{\phi(h^*(n))}\right| \geq \varepsilon\right] \geq \frac{\alpha}{m}, \alpha > 1 \quad \text{and} \tag{6.1}$$

$$P\left[\left|\frac{h(n) - h^*(n)}{\phi(h^*(n))}\right| \geq \lambda\right] \leq \frac{\beta}{m}, \beta < 1 \tag{6.2}$$

$h(n)$ is called an evaluation function having a typical error of order $\phi(N)$, where N is the depth of the search.

Property 6.4

If $h(n)$ has a typical error of order $\phi(N)$ and $\lim\limits_{n \to \infty} \frac{\phi(N)}{N} < \infty$, then the mean complexity of the corresponding A^* search is $E(Z) = \exp\{c\phi(N)[1 + O(1)]\}$, where c is a positive constant.

From Property 6.4, it's known that if $h(n)$ is estimation with a typical error of order $\phi(N) = \sqrt{N}$, then the mean complexity of A^* is greater than N^k, where k is a given positive integer. This means that the mean complexity of A^* is not polynomial.

Corollary 6.1

If $h(n)$ is an estimation function with a typical error of order $\phi(N)$, then the necessary and sufficient condition that A^* has a polynomial mean complexity is that $\phi(N)$ is a function with logarithmic order.

A specific case: if there exist $\varepsilon > 0$ and $\alpha > 1$ such that

$$P\left[\left|\frac{h(n) - h^*(n)}{h^*(n)}\right| \geq \varepsilon\right] \geq \frac{\alpha}{m}, \varepsilon > 0, \alpha > 1, \tag{6.3}$$

then $E(Z) \sim O(c^{cN}), c > 0$

Formula (6.3) shows that so long as the probability that the relative error of $h(n)$ is greater than any positive number is greater than $\frac{1}{m}$, the complexity of A^* is exponential. So the exponential explosion of A^* search cannot be avoided generally, since it is already difficult to make the function estimation less than very small positive number moreover less than any small positive number.

It is difficult to avoid the exponential explosion for A^* search. The reason is that the global information is not to be fully used in the search. The complexity of A^* search depends on the accuracy of the evaluation function estimation; the accuracy requirement is too harsh. Actually, the information needed in search is only the distinction of evaluation functions between two types of paths containing and not containing goal node, while not necessarily needing the precise values. So the 'distinction' is much more important than the 'precision' of evaluation function estimation. We will show next how the statistical inference methods are used to judging the 'distinction' among search paths effectively, i.e., to decide which path is promising than the others based on the global information.

6.1.2 Statistical Inference

Statistical inference is an inference technique for testing some statistical hypothesis - an assertion about distribution of one or more random variables based on their observed samples. It is one major area in mathematical statistics (Zacks, 1971; Hogg et al., 1977).

1 *SPRT* Method

The Wald Sequential Probability Ratio Test or *SPRT* method is follows.

Assume that $x_1, x_2, \ldots, x_n, \ldots$ is a sequence of identically independent distribution (*i.i.d.*) random variables. $f(x, u)$ is its distributed density function. There are two simple hypotheses $H_0 : \mu = \mu_0$ and $H_1 : \mu = \mu_1, \mu_1 \neq \mu_0$. Given n observed values, we have a sum:

$$s_n = \sum_1^n \ln \frac{f(x_i; \mu_1)}{f(x_i; \mu_0)}, \ n \geq 1$$

According to the stopping rule, when $-b < s_n < a$ the sampling continues, if $s_R < -b$, hypothesis H_0 is accepted and the sampling stop at the R-th observation; if $s_R \geq a$, hypothesis H_1 is accepted, where a and b are two given constants and $0 < a < b < \infty$.

The *SPRT* has the following properties.

Property 6.5

If hypotheses H_0 and H_1 are true, then the probability that the stopping variable R is a finite number is one.

Property 6.6

If $P_\mu(|Z| > 0) > 0$, then $P_\mu(R > n) \leq e^{-cn}, c > 0$, where R is a stopping random variable of the *SPRT*, where $Z \underline{\Delta} \ln \frac{f(x,\mu_1)}{f(x,\mu_0)}$.

Property 6.7

Given a significance level(α, β), letting $A = \frac{1-\beta}{\alpha}$, $B = \frac{\beta}{1-\alpha}$, $Z_i \underline{\Delta} \ln \frac{f(x_i,\mu_1)}{f(x_i,\mu_0)}$ and $Z \underline{\Delta} \ln \frac{f(x,\mu_1)}{f(x,\mu_0)}$. If $E_{\mu_i}(|Z|) < \infty, E_{\mu_i}(Z) \neq 0 \ (i = 0, 1)$, then the mean of stopping variable, the average sample size, of *SPRT* is

$$E_{\mu_i}(R) \approx \frac{\alpha \ln \frac{1-\beta}{\alpha} + (1 - \alpha)\ln \frac{\beta}{1-\alpha}}{E_{\mu_i}(Z)} \tag{6.4}$$

$$\text{If } (x; \mu) = \frac{1}{\sigma\sqrt{2\pi}}\exp\left[-\frac{1}{2}\left(\frac{x - \mu}{\sigma}\right)^2\right],$$

then

$$Z \triangleq \ln \frac{f(x; \mu_1)}{f(x; \mu_0)} = \frac{1}{2\sigma^2} \left[2x(\mu_1 - \mu_0) + \left(\mu_0{}^2 - \mu_1{}^2 \right) \right]$$

$$s_n \triangleq \sum_{i=1}^{n} Z_i = \frac{1}{2\sigma^2} \left[2(\mu_1 - \mu_0) \sum_{1}^{n} x_i + n\left(\mu_0{}^2 - \mu_1{}^2 \right) \right]$$

If the distribution of the random variable is normal, then the stopping rule of *SPRT* is as follows.

$$\begin{cases} \text{If } \sum_{1}^{n} x_i \geq \dfrac{\sigma^2 g_1}{\mu_1 - \mu_0} + \dfrac{n}{2} (\mu_1 + \mu_0), & \text{hypothesis } H_0 \text{ rejected} \\[3mm] \text{If } \sum_{1}^{n} x_i \leq \dfrac{\sigma^2 g_2}{\mu_1 - \mu_0} + \dfrac{n}{2} (\mu_1 + \mu_0), & \text{hypothesis } H_0 \text{ accepted} \\[3mm] \text{Otherwise, } \text{the observation } x_{n+1} \text{ continues} \end{cases} \qquad (6.5)$$

where $g_1 = \ln \frac{1-\beta}{\alpha}$ and $g_2 = \ln \frac{\beta}{1-\alpha}$. The Type I error is $P_1 \leq \alpha$. The Type II error is $P_2 \leq \beta$. Type I error means rejecting H_0 when it is true. Type II error means that when H_1 is true but we fail to reject H_0.

2 ASM Method

Asymptotically Efficient Sequential Fixed-width Confidence Estimation of the Mean, or *ASM*, is the following.

Assume that $x_1, x_2, \ldots, x_n, \ldots$ is a sequence of identically independent distribution (*i.i.d.*) random variables and its joint distributed density function is F, $F \in \Re$, where $\Re$ is a set of distribution functions with finite fourth moments. Given $\delta > 0$ and $\gamma (0 < \gamma < 1)$, we use the following formula to define stopping variable $R(\delta)$, i.e., $R(\delta)$ is the minimal integer that satisfies the following formula

$$R \geq \frac{\alpha^2}{\delta^2} \left\{ \frac{1}{R} \left(1 + \sum_{1}^{R} (x_i - \bar{x}_R)^2 \right) \right\} \qquad (6.6)$$

where $\bar{x}_R = \frac{1}{R} \sum_{1}^{R} x_i$, $\phi(x) = \frac{1}{\sqrt{2\pi}} \int_{-\infty}^{x} e^{-t^2/2} dt$ and $\alpha = \phi^{-1} \left(\frac{1+\gamma}{2} \right)$

Let μ be the mean of $\{x_i\}$. The following theorem holds.

Theorem 6.1

Under the above definition, we have

Property 6.8

$\forall F \in \mathfrak{R}$, the probability of $\mu \in (\overline{x}_{R(\delta)} - \delta, \overline{x}_{R(\delta)} + \delta)$ is greater than γ, where, $(\overline{x}_{R(\delta)} - \delta, \overline{x}_{R(\delta)} + \delta)$ is a fixed-width confidence interval and is denoted by $(\overline{x}_{R(\delta)}, \delta)$ in the following discussion, and μ is the mean of $\{x_k\}$.

Property 6.9

If $\delta_1 < \delta_2$, then we have $R(\delta_2) < R(\delta_1)$ *a.s.* and $\lim_{\delta \to 0} R(\delta) = \infty$ *a.s.*, where *a.s.* indicates almost surely, or almost everywhere.

Property 6.10

$\forall F \in \mathfrak{R}$, we have

$$\lim_{\delta \to 0} \frac{\delta^2 E(R(\delta))}{a^2 \sigma^2(F)} = 1, \tag{6.7}$$

where, $\sigma^2(F)$ is the variance of F and $E(R(\delta))$ is the mean of $R(\delta)$.

Property 6.11

$P(R(\delta) > n) \sim O(\exp(-cn^2))$, $c > 0$ constant. Let $\alpha = 1 - \gamma$. From $a^2 \sim O(|\ln(1 - \gamma)|)$ and Property 6.3, we have:

$$E(R(\delta)) \sim O\left(\frac{|\ln \alpha|}{\delta^2}\right) \tag{6.8}$$

Both Formulas (6.4) and (6.8) provide the order of the mean of stopping variable, i.e., the order of the average sample size. In Pearl's probabilistic model, the average complexity of a search algorithm is the average number of nodes expanded by the algorithm. If we regard a heuristic search as a random sampling process, the average number of expanded nodes is just the average sample size. Therefore, Formulas (6.4) and (6.8) provide useful expressions for estimating the mean computational complexity of search algorithms.

In the above discussion, for simplicity, we assume that the sequence $\{x_i\}$ of random variables is identically independent distribution either in algorithm *SPRT* or *ASM*. In Section 6.3, we will further show that when weakening the *i.i.d.* constraint Formulas (6.4) and (6.8) still hold.

6.1.3 Statistical Heuristic Search

1 The Model of Search Tree

Search tree G is a uniform m-ary tree. There are root node s_0 and unique goal node s_N at depth N. For each node p at depth N, define a value $(\nu(p))$ such that

$v(s_N) \leq \sum\limits_{p \in \text{the } N-\text{th level}} v(p)$, where s_N are goal nodes. Obviously, if $v(s_N) < \sum\limits_{p \in \text{the } N-\text{th level}} v(p)$, then s_N is a unique goal node.

For any node n in G, $T(n)$ represents a sub-tree of G rooted at node n. If n locates at the i-th level, $T(n)$ is called the $i-$ subtree (Fig. 6.1).

When search proceeds to a certain stage, the subtree G' composed by all expanded nodes is called expanded tree. $T(n) \cap G'$ is the expanded subtree in $T(n)$.

Heuristic information: For $n \in G$, $f(n)$ is a given function value. Assume that $f(n)$ is the estimation of $\left\{ \min\limits_{p \in T(n), p \in \text{the } n-\text{th level}} (v(p)) \right\}$. Therefore, the procedure of A^* (or BF) algorithm is to expand the nodes that have the minimal value of $f(n)$ among all open nodes first.

2 Statistic$^{(an)}$

In order to apply the statistical inference methods, the key is to extract a proper statistic from $f(n)$. There are several approaches to deal with the problem. We introduce one feasible method as follows.

Fixed $n \in G$, let $T_k(n)$ be an expanded tree of $T(n)$ and k is the number of nodes in $T_k(n)$. Let

$$a_k(n) = F(f(p), p \in T_k(n)), \tag{6.9}$$

where, F is a composition function of $f(p)$.

When a node of $T(n)$ is expanded, we have a statistic $a_k(n)$. When we said that the observation of a subtree in $T(n)$ is continued, it means that the expansion of nodes in $T(n)$ is continued, and a new statistic $a_k(n)$ is calculated based on Formula (6.9). $a_k(n)$ is called a new observed value.

In order to use Formulas (6.4) and (6.8), for $\{a_k(n)\}$ we make the following assumption.

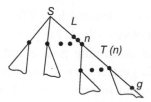

Figure 6.1: A Search Tree

Assumption I

For any $n \in G$, $\{a_k(n) - \mu(n)\}$ is assumed to be a set of identically independent random variables. Let L be a shortest path from $s_0 \rightarrow s_N$. If $n \in L$, then $\mu(n) = \mu_0$; while $n \notin L$, then $\mu(n) = \mu_1 > \mu_0$, where $\mu(n)$ is the mean of $\{a_k(n)\}$.

In the following discussion, if we say 'to implement a statistical inference on subtree T', it means 'to implement a statistical inference on statistic $\{a_k(n)\}$ corresponding to T'. $\{a_k(n)\}$ is called a statistic of a subtree, or a global statistic.

3 SA Algorithm Routine

Given a hypothesis testing method S, introducing the method to a heuristic search algorithm A, then we have a statistical heuristic search algorithm SA. Its routine is the following.

Step 1: expand the root node s_0, we have m successors, i.e., 0-subtrees. The subtrees obtained compose a set U.

Step 2: Implement statistical inference S on U.

(1) If U is empty, algorithm SA fails. It means that the solution path is deleted mistakenly.

(2) For each $i-$ subtree in U, expand node n that has the minimal value of $a_k(n)$ among all expanded nodes. If there are several such nodes, then choose one that has the maximal depth. If there are still several nodes at the maximal depth, then choose any one of them. The newly expanded nodes are put into U as the successors of each subtree. Then implement a statistical inference on each subtree in U.

   (a) When a node at depth N is encountered, if it's a goal node then succeed; otherwise fail.

   (b) If the hypothesis is accepted in some i-subtree T, then all nodes of subtrees are removed from U except T. the subtree index $i \leftarrow i + 1$ and go to Step 2.

   (c) If the hypothesis is rejected in some i-subtree T, then all nodes in T are removed from U and go to Step 2.

   (d) Otherwise, go to Step 2.

In fact, the SA algorithm is the combination of statistical inference method S and heuristic search BF. Assume that a node is expanded into m sub-nodes $n_1, n_2, \cdots, n_m$. A subtree rooted at n_j in the i-th level is denoted by i-$T(n_j)$, i.e., i-subtree. Implementing the statistical inference S over i-subtrees $T(n_1), T(n_2), \cdots, T(n_m)$, prune away the i-subtrees with low probability that containing goal g and retain the i-subtrees with high probability, i.e., their probability is greater than a given positive number. The BF search continues on the nodes of the reserved sub-tree, e.g., i-$T(n_1)$. That is, the search continues on the $(i+1)$-subtrees under i-$T(n_1)$. The process goes on hierarchically until goal g is found.

Obviously, as long as the statistical decision in each level can be made in a polynomial time, through N levels (N is the depth at which the goal is located), the goal can be found in a polynomial time. Fortunately, under certain conditions *SPRT* and many other statistical inference methods can satisfy such a requirement. This is just the benefit which *SA* search gets from statistical inference.

6.2 The Computational Complexity

6.2.1 SPA Algorithms

Definition 6.1

Assume that in *SA* search *SPRT* is used as statistical inference method S, and for judging $m\ i-$ subtrees the significance level $(\alpha/(i+1)^2, \alpha/(m-1)(i+1)^2)$, $i = 1, 2, \cdots$, is chosen. Under the above conditions, the *SA* search is called *SPA*1 with significant level $\left(\alpha, \frac{\alpha}{m-1}\right)$, or simply *SPA*1 algorithm.

Variable $\{a_k(n)\}$ obeys the $N(\mu, \sigma^2)$ distribution. Construct a simple hypothesis:

$$H_0 : \mu = \mu_0; H_1 : \mu = \mu_1, \mu_1 > \mu_0$$

In Formulas (6.4) and (6.5), $\frac{\alpha}{(i+1)^2}$, $\frac{\alpha}{(m-1)(i+1)^2}$ and $N(\mu; \sigma^2)$ replacing α, β and $f(x; \mu)$, respectively, then we have the following lemma.

Lemma 6.1

For judging $m\ i-$ subtrees, the asymptotically mean complexity of *SPA1* is

$$\sim mb[|\ln \alpha| + 2|\ln(i + 1)|] \sim b_2 \ln(i + 1),$$

where $b = 2\sigma^2/(\mu_1 - \mu_0)^2$

Proof:

From Formula (6.5), when $f(x; \mu)$ is $N(\mu; \sigma^2)$, the mean of stopping variable R can be represented by the following expression approximately.

$$E_{\mu_0}(R) \approx \frac{\left(\alpha \ln \frac{1-\beta}{\alpha} + (1 - \alpha)\ln \frac{\beta}{1-\alpha}\right)\sigma^2}{-\frac{1}{2}(\mu_1 - \mu_0)^2} \sim \frac{2\sigma^2}{(\mu_1 - \mu_0)^2}|\ln \alpha|$$

$$E_{\mu_1}(R) \approx \frac{\left((1 - \beta)\ln \frac{1-\beta}{\alpha} + \beta\ln \frac{\beta}{1-\alpha}\right)\sigma^2}{-\frac{1}{2}(\mu_1 - \mu_0)^2} \sim \frac{2\sigma^2}{(\mu_1 - \mu_0)^2}|\ln \alpha|$$

Therefore, in order to judge $m\ i-$ subtrees with significant level $(\alpha/(i+1)^2, \alpha/(m-1)(i+1)^2)$, the asymptotically mean complexity is

$$\sim mb_1[|\ln \alpha| + 2|\ln(i + 1)|] \sim b_2 \ln(i + 1),$$

where $b_1 = 2\sigma^2/(\mu_1 - \mu_0)^2$.

Theorem 6.2

α_0 and β_0 are given. Let $\alpha = \min(\alpha_0/A, \beta_0/A), A = \sum_1^\infty (1/i)^2$. $\{a(n)\}$ has a normal distribution $N(\mu; \sigma^2)$. Using $SPA1$ algorithm under level $(\alpha, \alpha/(m-1))$, the mean complexity of finding a solution path in G is $O(N \ln N)$ with probability $(1 - b)$. b is the error probability, where $b = \alpha_0 + \beta_0$, the Type I error $P_1 \leq \alpha_0$ and Type II error $P_2 \leq \beta_0$.

Proof:

From Lemma 6.1, the mean complexity for judging m i-subtrees is $\sim b_2 \ln(i + 1)$. Thus, using $SPA1$ algorithm, the mean complexity of finding a goal is:

$$\sim \sum_1^{N-1} b_2 \cdot \ln(i+1) = b_2 \cdot \ln(N!)$$

From the Sterling formula $N! = \sqrt{2\pi N}(N/e)^N \cdot \exp[(\theta/12)N]$, we obtain:

$$b_2 \cdot \ln(N!) \sim O(N \ln N)$$

For judging m 1-subtrees, $P_1 \leq \alpha$. In general, for judging m i-subtrees, $P_1 \leq \alpha/(i+1)^2$. The total error probability of Type I is:

$$P_1 \leq \sum_{i=0}^N \frac{\alpha}{(i+1)^2} \leq \alpha \sum_1^\infty \left(\frac{1}{i}\right)^2 = \alpha A \leq \alpha_0$$

Similarly, $P_2 < \beta_0$.

It is noted that we use the minimum of mean statistics among all i-subtrees to estimate μ_0, and the average of mean statistics of the rest (except the minimal one) of i-subtrees to estimate μ_1. This will produce new errors. We will construct new SA algorithms to overcome the defect.

Corollary 6.2

Assume that $\{a_k(\cdot)\}$ has a distribution function $f(x; \mu)$. Let

$$Z \triangleq \frac{f(x; \mu_1)}{f(x; \mu_0)}, E\widehat{\mu}_i(|Z|) < \infty, E\widehat{\mu}_i Z \neq 0, i = 0, 1$$

The mean complexity of $SPA1$ algorithm is $O(N \ln N)$.

The theorem and corollary show that $SPA1$ algorithm can overcome the exponential explosion of complexity only in average sense. This means that in some cases, the statistical inference will still encounter a huge computational complexity. In order to overcome the shortage, we will discuss the revised version $SPA2$ of $SPA1$.

Definition 6.2

In *SA*, *SPRT* is performed over m i-subtrees using a level $(\alpha_i = \alpha/(i+1)^2, \beta_i = \alpha/(m-1)$ $(i+1)^2)$ and a given threshold d_i, $d_i = 2b_2 \ln(i+1) \cdot \ln((i+1)/\alpha), i = 0, 1, 2, \cdots$, where $b_2 = 4m\sigma^2/(\mu_1 - \mu_2)^2$. If the sample size exceeds d_i then the hypothesis H_0 is rejected. We define the *SA* as *SPA2* under level $(\alpha, \alpha/(m-1))$, and denoted by *SPA2* for short.

It's noted that parameters μ_1, μ_0 and σ^2 are generally unknown. We may use the following formula to estimate σ^2.

$$s_n = (1/(n-1)) \sum_1^n (x_i - \bar{x})^2,$$

where $\bar{x} = (1/n) \sum_1^n x_i$.

Theorem 6.3

α_0 and β_0 are given. Let $\alpha = \min(\alpha_0/A, \beta_0/A), A = 2\sum_1^\infty (1/i)^2$. $\{a_k(\bullet)\}$ has a normal distribution. Using *SPA2* under level $(\alpha, \alpha/(m-1))$, the upper bound of the complexity of finding a solution path in G is $\leq O(N \ln^2 N)$ with probability $(1-b)$. b is the error probability, where $b = \alpha_0 + \beta_0$, the Type I error $P_1 \leq \alpha_0$ and Type II error $P_2 \leq \beta_0$.

Proof:

In i-subtrees, the threshold is $d_i = 2b^2 \ln(i+1)\ln\frac{i+1}{\alpha} \sim O(\ln^2 N)$. So the upper bound of the total complexity is $\sum_1^N c \ln^2(i+1) \sim O(N \ln^2 N)$.

Thus, the upper bound of complexity of *SPA2* $\leq O(N \ln^2 N)$.

Now, we consider the error probability.

If in the searching process the sample size has never surpassed the threshold, from Formulas (6.5) and (6.6), it is noted that judging m i-subtrees, the error probability of Type I $\leq \alpha/(i+1)^2$. So the total error probability is:

$$P_1 \leq \sum_{i=0}^N \frac{\alpha}{(i+1)^2} \leq \alpha \sum_1^\infty \left(\frac{1}{i}\right)^2 = \frac{\alpha A}{2} < \frac{\alpha_0}{2}$$

In some searching stage, if the sample size surpasses the threshold and H_0 is rejected, the error probability does not change if the subtrees being deleted do not contain the goal, and the error probability will increase if the subtrees being deleted contain the goal. We estimate the incremental error probability as follows.

From Property 6.6 in Section 6.1.2, the distribution of the stopping variable R of *SPRT* is

$$P(R > n) \leq e^{-cn} = \int_n^\infty ce^{-cx}dx \qquad (6.10)$$

Assume $P(R > n) = e^{-cn}$. In i-subtrees their level is $(\alpha/(i+1)^2, \alpha/(m-1)(i+1)^2)$ and the mean of R is $b_2 \ln(i+1)$, where $b_2 = 4m\sigma^2/(\mu_1 - \mu_0)^2$. From Formula (6.10), we have $E(R) = \int_0^\infty cx \cdot e^{-cx} dx = \frac{1}{c}$.

Thus, $c_i = 1/(b_2 \ln(i+1))$, c_i is the value of c corresponding to i-subtrees.

The probability that the sample size surpasses the threshold d_i is

$$P(R > d_i) = \exp(-c_i d_i) = \alpha^2/(i+1)^2 < \alpha/(i+1)^2$$

Namely, when the sample size surpasses the threshold, the rejection of H_0 will cause the new error probability $\leq \alpha/(i+1)^2$. The totally incremental error probability of Type I is

$$\leq \sum_0^N \frac{\alpha}{(i+1)^2} < \frac{\alpha_0}{2}$$

Finally, the total error probability of Type I is $P_1 \leq \frac{\alpha_0}{2} + \frac{\alpha_0}{2} = \alpha_0$.

Similarly, Type II error $P_2 \leq \beta_0$.

Certainly, when the sample size surpasses the threshold, the rejection of H_0 does not change the error probability of Type II.

Corollary 6.3

Assume that $\{a_k(\cdot)\}$ has a distribution function $f(x; \mu)$ and satisfies

$$Z = f(x; \mu_1)/f(x; \mu_0), E_{\widehat{\mu_i}}(|Z|) < \infty, \quad E_{\widehat{\mu_i}}(Z) \neq 0, i = 0, 1$$

The upper bound of the complexity of *SPA2* is $\leq O(N \ln^2 N)$.

SPA algorithms constructed have the following shortcoming. The distribution function $f(x; \mu)$ should be known beforehand. Generally this is unpractical so it has to be assumed as a normal distribution $N(\mu; \sigma^2)$ sometime. Even so, its parameters μ_1, μ_2 and σ^2 are still unknown generally. Although their values can be estimated from some data it will cause new errors certainly. We will use *ASM* statistical inference method to overcome the shortcoming.

6.2.2 SAA Algorithms

(α_0, β_0) is given. Let $\alpha = \min(\alpha_0, \beta_0)$ and $\gamma = 1 - \alpha$. Assume that $c = \mu_1 - \mu_0 > 0$. For any node $n \in G$, there are m successors $p_1, p_2, \cdots, p_m$. $T(p_i)$ is a subtree rooted at p_i. For any subtree $T(p_i)$, let $\gamma = 1 - \alpha$, $\delta = c/4$. Apply *ASM* statistical inference to *SA* search, we have confidence intervals $I(p_i, \delta)$, $i = 1, 2, \cdots, m$.

Assume that $I(p_1, \delta)$ is the leftmost interval among m confidence intervals along a number line. If $I(p_1, \delta)$ and $I(p_i, \delta)$, $i = 2, \cdots, m$ are disjoint, $T(p_1)$ is accepted; otherwise all subtrees are rejected and the algorithm fails.

In fact, *ASM* is a sequential testing method. First, letting $R=1$ and using Formula (6.6) as hypothesis testing, if the formula is satisfied, then we have the corresponding interval $I(p_i, \delta)$, otherwise the sampling continues.

Definition 6.3

In *SA* search, if the *ASM* is used as statistical inference method S, and when testing i-subtrees $\gamma_i = 1 - \alpha/(i+1)^2, \delta < c/4$, then the *SA* search is called *SAA* algorithm with level α, or simply *SAA* algorithm.

Theorem 6.4

Assume that $\{a_k(\cdot)\}$ satisfies Hypothesis I and has a finite forth moment. Given (α_0, β_0), letting $\alpha = \min(\alpha_0/A, \beta_0/A)$, $A = m\sum_1^\infty \left(\frac{1}{i}\right)^2$, then *SAA* algorithm with level α can find the goal with probability $\geq 1 - b(b \leq \alpha_0 + \beta_0)$, and the order of its mean complexity is $O(N \ln N)$.

Proof:

Since for i-subtrees $\gamma_i = 1 - \alpha/(i+1)^2, \delta > 0$, from Formula (6.8) we have that the order of mean complexity of *ASM* for testing i-subtrees is

$$O\left(\left|\ln\left(\alpha/(i+1)^2\right)\right|\right) \sim O(\ln i)$$

Thus, the order of total mean complexity is

$$\sum_1^{N-1} O(\ln i) \sim O(N \ln N)$$

For judging i-subtrees, the error probability of Type I is $\leq \alpha/(i+1)^2$ and Type II is $\leq (m-1)\alpha/(i+1)^2$. The total error probability for judging i-subtrees is $\leq m\alpha/(i+1)^2$.

Thus, the total error probability of *SAA* algorithm is

$$\leq \sum\left(\frac{\alpha m}{(i+1)^2}\right) < \alpha m \sum \left(\frac{1}{i}\right)^2 = \alpha A = \min(\alpha_0, \beta_0) \leq \alpha_0 + \beta_0$$

SAA is superior to *SPA* in that it's no need to know what distribution function $f(x; \mu)$ is in advance, and the calculation of statistics is quite simple.

In general, $c = \mu_1 - \mu_0$ is unknown. So it's difficulty to choose a proper width of confidence interval in *SAA* based on $\delta < \frac{c}{4}$. In practice, approximate δ can be chosen as a rule of thumb. Sometime, *SAA* may work in the following way. Given an arbitrary constant δ_1, if $I(p_1, \delta_1)$ intersects with other intervals $I(p_i, \delta_1), i \neq 1$, new constant $\delta_2 < \delta_1$ is tried, until a proper value of δ is got.

The revised *SAA* is as follows.

Let $\delta_1, \delta_2, \cdots, \delta_i, \cdots$ be a sequence of strictly and monotonically decreasing positive numbers, e.g., $\delta_i = \frac{\delta}{i}, i = 1, 2, \cdots$. In the i-th turn search, let the width of confidence interval be δ_i. Since $\delta_i \to 0$ so long as $\mu_1 - \mu_0 = c > 0$, c is a constant, there always exists i_0 such that if $i \geq i_0$ then $\delta_i < \frac{c}{4}$. So we can overcome the difficulty brought about by the unknown c; certainly the computational complexity of *SAA* will increase N^2 times, i.e., the order of complexity becomes $O(N^3 \ln^2 N)$.

If we choose a lower bound $\delta_0 > 0$ of δ_i, when $\delta_i < \delta_0$ δ_i no longer decreases, i.e., let $\delta_i = \delta_0$. Then, the order of mean complexity of *SAA* will not increase.

Under the same significance level, the mean $E(R)$ of stopping variable of *SPRT* is minimal, i.e., the mean complexity of *SA* constructed by *SPRT* is minimal. But the distribution function $f(x; \mu)$ should be known beforehand in the *SPA* search, i.e., under a more rigor condition.

6.2.3 Different Kinds of SA

In Section 6.2.1 and 6.2.2 we construct *SA* by using *SPRT* and *ASM* as statistical inference methods. Since the two methods are sequential and fully similar to search, it's easy to understand that the introducing the methods to the benefit of search. If there is any other kind of statistical inference method, e.g., non-sequential, can this get the same effect? We'll discuss below.

Assume that $\{x_k\}$ and $\{y_k\}$ are two *i.i.d.* random variables having finite fourth moments. Their distribution functions are $f(x; \mu_0)$ are $f(x; \mu_1), \mu_0 < \mu_1$, respectively. Let simple hypotheses be $H_0 : \mu_0 = \mu_1, H_1 : \mu_0 < \mu_1$. From statistics, it's known that if a statistical inference method S satisfies the following properties, the statistical decision can be made in a polynomial time.

The properties are

(1) Given significance level α, the mean of the stopping variable R satisfies
     $E(R) \sim O(\delta^{-2}|\ln \alpha|)$, where $E(R)$ is the mean of R and $\delta = |\bar{x} - \bar{y}|$.
(2) $P(R < \infty) = 1$, S terminates with probability one.
(3) When $n > 0$, $P(R > n) \leq e^{-cn}, c > 0$, where $c > 0$ is a constant.

As we know, both *SPRT* and *ASM* satisfy the above properties. $E(R)$ is proportional to $|\ln\alpha|$ which underlies the complexity reduction of the *SA* search algorithms by using *SPRT* and *ASM* as statistical inference methods. If the variances σ_1 and σ_2 of $\{x_k\}$ and $\{y_k\}$ are known, μ−test and t-test may be adopted. For example, using μ−test to determine the validity of $\mu_0 = \mu_1$, that is, whether the mean of random variable X is equal to that of Y, we may use the following composite statistic.

$$\mu = (\overline{X} - \overline{Y})/\sqrt{\sigma^2{}_1/l + \sigma^2{}_2/n}$$

where $\overline{X}$ and $\overline{Y}$ are the means of $\{x_k\}$ and $\{y_k\}$, respectively, l and n are the sample sizes of $\{x_k\}$ and $\{y_k\}$, respectively.

When search reaches node p it has m sub-nodes $p_1, p_2, \cdots, p_m$. Let $T(p_i)$ be a sub-tree rooted at p_i. The means of statistics x_i of sub-trees $T(p_1), \cdots, T(p_m)$ are assumed to be $\bar{x}_1 \leq \bar{x}_2 \leq \cdots \leq \bar{x}_m$, respectively.

Now, we use μ−testing method to judge whether the means of $T(p_1)$ and $T(p_2)$ are equal. Significance level (α, β) and sample size (l, n) are given, where l and n are the numbers of expanded nodes of $T(p_1)$ and $T(p_2)$, respectively. In the testing process, sample size $l + n$ is gradually increased, for example, $l + n = 1, 2, \cdots$.

From $\phi(k_\alpha) = 1 \quad \alpha$, we have k_α, where $\phi(\cdot)$ is a standard normal distribution function.

If $|\mu| \rangle k_\alpha$ then $T(p_2), T(p_3), \cdots, T(p_m)$ are deleted.

If $|\mu| \leq k_\alpha$ then the total sample size $(l + n)$ is increased by 2, i.e., sub-trees $T(p_1)$ and $T(p_2)$ are expanded by search algorithm A. μ−test continues.

It's noted that in the μ−test, when calculating the composite statistic μ we replace $\overline{X}$ by $\bar{x}_1$ and $\overline{Y}$ by $\bar{x}_2$.

In order to terminate the search in time, we choose a threshold $d(i) \sim O(\ln^2 i)$ for the i-th level nodes. If the sample size $\geq d(i)$, then sub-tree $T(p_1)$ is accepted.

It can be proved that the above algorithm has the same order of mean complexity as that of *SPA* algorithm.

If the variances of $\{x_k\}$ and $\{y_k\}$ are finite but unknown, the sequential t-test constructed from Cox theorem can be used.

By combining different kinds of statistical inference methods and heuristic searches and successively using these searches, a variety of *SA* algorithms can be obtained.

If the global statistics extracted from each subtree in G satisfy Hypothesis I, then the *SA* search constructed from S has the following properties which are our main conclusions about *SA*.

(1) The mean complexity of the *SA* is $O(N \ln N)$, *N* is the depth at which the goal is located.

(2) Given $\alpha(\alpha < 1)$, using the *SA* search for the first time the goal can be found with probability α.

(3) Based on the property $P(R > n) \leq O(\exp(-cn))$, given a proper threshold, then the upper bound of the complexity of each time *SA* search is $O(N \ln^2 N)$.

(4) In some *SA* search stage, a wrong search direction might be chosen but the search can terminate in a polynomial mean time, due to the polynomial judgment time of the statistical inference. Consequently, by applying the *SA* search successively, the goal can also be found with polynomial mean complexity.

6.2.4 The Successive Algorithms

In a word, under a given significance level (α, β), the *SPA* (*SPA*1 or *SPA*2) search can avoid the exponential explosion and results in the polynomial complexity $O(N \ln N)$ (or $O(N \ln^2 N)$). Unfortunately, the solution path may mistakenly be pruned off or a wrong path may be accepted, i.e., the error probability is $b = \alpha + \beta$. In other words, in light of the *SPA* search, a real goal can only be found with probability (1-*b*).

The mean of stopping variable *R* of the statistical inference is $E(R) \sim O(\delta^{-2}|\ln \alpha|)$. No matter the *i*-subtree containing goal can be found or not, the search stops with mean computation $\sim O(\delta^{-2}|\ln \alpha_i|)$ certainly. Thus, the search stops with mean complexity $O(N \ln N)$ in the first round search. Imagine that if the goal node cannot be found in the first round search, *SA* search is applied to the remaining part of *G* once again. Thus, the probability of finding a real goal is increased by $b(1 - b)$, or error probability is decreased to $b \cdot b = b^2,...$, the repeated usage of *SA* continues until the goal is found. We call this procedure successive *SA*, or *SA* for short. How about its computational complexity? Does it still remain the polynomial time?

Using the *SA* search, in the first time the probability of finding the goal is $(1 - b)$. Its complexity is $c(N \cdot \ln N)$. Thus, the equivalent complexity is

$$t_1 = (1 - b)c(N \cdot \ln N)$$

In general, the probability that the goal is found by *SA* search just in the *i*-th time is $b^{i-1}(1 - b)$, and the complexity is $ci(N \cdot \ln N)$. The equivalent complexity is

$$t_i = b^{i-1}(1 - b)ic(N \cdot \ln N)$$

The total mean complexity of *SA* is

$$T = \sum_{i=1}^{\infty} t_i = \sum_{i=1}^{\infty} b^{i-1}(1 - b)icN \cdot \ln N$$

Since $|b| < 1$, we have

$$T = \frac{c}{1-b} N \cdot \ln N \sim O(N \cdot \ln N)$$

We have the following theorem.

Theorem 6.5

In a uniform m-ary tree, using the successive *SA* search, a goal can be found with probability one, and the order of its mean complexity remains $O(N \cdot \ln N)$.

6.3 The Discussion of Statistical Heuristic Search

6.3.1 Statistical Heuristic Search and Quotient Space Theory

The heuristic search generally implements on a tree. A tree is a specific case of a sequence of quotient spaces. If in a sequence of hierarchical quotient spaces, the number of elements in each level is finite, then it's a tree. Assume that *SA* implements its search on a uniform m-tree. Let $\{p_1^1, p_2^1, ..., p_m^1\}$ be the sub-nodes in the first level. From quotient space point of view, it is equivalent to the partition $X_0 = \{T_1^1, T_2^1, ..., T_m^1\}$ of domain X, where T_k^1 is a set of leaf nodes of the subtree rooted at p_k^1. Thus, set X_0 is a quotient set of the set of the overall leaf nodes. The statistic $a(n)$ of p_k^1 is extracted from set T_k^1.

A heuristic search on a tree or graph can be restated as follows. A statistical heuristic search is sampling on some level (quotient space) of a search space, extracting statistics and making statistical inference on the level. So we can transfer the statistical heuristic search from a tree (graph) to a sequence of quotient spaces.

1 The Quotient Space Model of Heuristic Search

$f : X \rightarrow R$ is a function defined on X. To find $x^* : f(x^*) = \max_{x \in X} f(x)$, there are several ways. In heuristic search, an estimation function $g(x)$ of $f(x)$ and a tree structure of X are introduced, then using $g(x)$ as a guidance to find the optimal solution x^* on the tree. The same problem can be solved by the quotient space method. First, we transform the problem of finding the optimal solution on space (X, f) into a set of its quotient spaces $([X], [f])$. Then, by letting the grain-size of the quotient space [X] approaching to zero, then the optimal solution on [X] will approach to the optimal solution on X. If an estimation function of $[f]$ on $([X], [f])$ is introduced, then we may solve the problem on the quotient spaces. From the above statement we can see the connection between heuristic search and quotient space problem solving methods.

On the other hand, in statistical inference some statistic is used to estimate function $f(x)$. Thus, the statistical inference method can be used to judging which the solution is.

These mean that we can integrate heuristic search, quotient space method and statistical inference to form a new statistical heuristic search model — a quotient space model of statistical heuristic search.

Assume that X is a set of random variables in a basic probability space $(\Omega, \mathcal{F}, P)$, $X_0 < X_1 < X_3 ... < ... < X$ is a sequence of hierarchical quotient spaces of X, and $R_0, R_1, R_2 ....$ are their corresponding equivalence relations, where $X_1 < X_2$ denotes that X_1 is a quotient space of X_2, and X_i is a finite set.

$X_i = \{A_1^i, A_2^i, ..., A_k^i\}$, let $a(n)$ be a statistic of A_n^i, $1 \le n \le k$. Based on $a(n)$ implementing a statistical inference S, if A_n^i is accepted and $i = N$, then A_n^i is a goal and success; otherwise fail.

If $n < N$, then A_n^i is partitioned into $A_n^i = \{A_1^{i+1}, A_2^{i+1}, ..., A_s^{i+1}\}$ by equivalence relation R_{i+1}. From A_n^{i+1}, $1 \le n \le s$ extracting statistic $a(n)$ implement statistic inference S based on $a(n)$,.... Where, statistic $a(n)$ is extracted from a subset of X, so it represents the global information of the subset.

This is a quotient space model of statistical heuristic search.

6.3.2 Hypothesis I

All conclusions about SA we made are under Hypothesis I. We have a further discussion on the hypothesis.

Hypothesis I

Assume that G is a uniform m-ary tree. $\forall n \in G$ let $T(n)$ be a subtree rooted at n. Statistic $\{a(n)\}$ extracted from $T(n)$ (called global statistic) satisfies

(1) $\forall n \in G$, $\{a(n) - \mu(n)\}$ is an i.i.d. random variable having a finite fourth moment, $\mu(n)$ is the mean of $a(n)$.
(2) $\forall n \in L$ (L is a solution path), $E(a(n)) = \mu_0$; $\forall n \notin L$, $E(a(n)) = \mu_1, \mu_1 > \mu_0$.

In essence, this means that the statistics extracted from $T(n), n \in L$ should be different from that extracted from $T(n), n \notin L$ statistically. In order to apply the statistical inference, in a sense the hypothesis is necessary. But the constraint given in Hypothesis I (2) may be relaxed. Let us examine some relaxed cases.

1 Inconsistent cases

(1) In Hypothesis I, for each $n \in L$, $E(a(n)) = \mu_0$ and $n \notin L$, $E(a(n)) = \mu_1$, i.e., the above equalities hold consistently. We now may relax the constraints as follows. There exist constants μ_0 and $c > 0$ such that for each $\forall n \in L$, $E(a(n)) \le \mu_0$; $n \notin L$, $E(a(n)) \ge \mu_0 + c$; and $\forall n \in G, E(a(n))$ is finite.

Since $E(R) \sim O(\delta^{-2}|\ln \alpha|)$, i.e., $E(R)$ is inverse proportion to δ^2 or proportion to $|\ln\alpha|$, where $\delta = \mu_1 - \mu_0$, $E(R)$ only depends on the difference between μ_1 and μ_0. Therefore, as long as $\mu_1 - \mu_0 > c > 0$, even μ_1 and μ_0 are changing, the order of the mean complexity of *SA* does not change any more.

(2) In some cases, although $E(a(n))(n \in L)$ is less than $E(a(n))(n \notin L)$, there does not exist a constant c independent of N such that the former is different from the latter.

We now discuss these kinds of relaxed conditions.

Assume that n_0 and n_1 are nodes at the k-th level, where $n_0 \in L, n_1 \notin L$. If there exists constant $a > 0$ such that $(\mu_1(n_1) - \mu_0(n_0)) > k^{-a}$, then for k-subtrees implementing statistical inference S, the order of the complexity is

$$E(R) \sim O\big(k^{-a}\big)^{-2}|\ln\alpha| \sim O\big(k^{2a}|\ln \alpha|\big) \leq O\big(N^{2a}|\ln \alpha|\big)$$

Thus, the order of the total complexity of *SA* is

$$\sum_1^N O\big(i^{2a}|\ln \alpha_i|\big) \sim O\big(N^{2a+1}|\ln \alpha|\big)$$

where $\alpha_i = \alpha/(i+1)^2$.

The order of mean complexity of *SA* still remains polynomial. We have the following theorem.

Theorem 6.6

G is a tree. $\forall n_0, n_1 \in G$, n_0 and n_1 are nodes at the k-th level, where $n_0 \in L$, $n_1 \notin L$. If there exist constants $a > 0$ and $c > 0$, such that $(\mu_1(n_1) - \mu_0(n_0)) > k^{-a}$ $((\mu_1(n_1) - \mu_0(n_0)) > c \ln k)$. Then, the order of total complexity of *SA* algorithm is

$$\sim O\big(N^{2a+1}|\ln \alpha|\big) \sim O(N \ln N|\ln \alpha|)$$

2 Mixed Cases

'False Goals': If there are $A(N)$ nodes not belonging to L such that $E(a(n)) \geq \mu_0 + c$ does not hold, i.e., the global statistics extracted from the subtrees rooted at such nodes do not satisfy $E(a(n)) \geq \mu_0 + c(c > 0)$, then in searching process those nodes statistically are not much different from the nodes belonging to L. There seems to be $A(N)$ 'false goals' in G. The complexity of *SA* will increase by $A(N)$ times at most. As long as $A(N)$ is a polynomial of N which is the depth the goal is located at, *SA* can also avoid the exponential explosion.

3 $\{x_k\}$ is not *i.i.d*

In hypothesis I, it's assumed that statistic $\{a(n) - \mu(n)\}$ is *i.i.d.* and has finite fourth moment. Now, we relax the constraints and only assume that $a(n)$ is independent and has variance $\sigma_n > \sigma > 0$, i.e., give up the requirement of the identical distribution

In the proof of the polynomial complexity of *SA*, we use formulas $E(R) \sim O(\delta^{-2}|\ln\alpha|)$ and $P(R > n) \le c_1 e^{-cn}$. The above two formulas are based on central limit theorem and Chow-Robbins lemma. However, the precondition of central limit theorem is the *i.i.d.* assumption of $\{x_k\}$. But the *i.i.d.* assumption is only the sufficient condition but not necessary. In Gnedenko (1956), the central limit theorem is based on the relaxed conditions as shown in Lemma 6.2.

Lemma 6.2

$x_1, x_2, \cdots, x_n, \cdots$ are mutually independent random variables. Let $Dx_i = b_i, B_n^2 = \sum_1^n b_i^2, E(x_i) = a_i$, where Dx_i is the variance of x_i. If there exists $\delta > 0$ such that when $n \to \infty$,

$$\frac{1}{B_n^{2+\delta}} \sum_{k=1}^{n} M|x_k - a_k|^{2+\delta} \to 0 \tag{6.11}$$

Thus, $n \to \infty$, we uniformly have

$$P\left\{\frac{1}{B_n} \sum_{k=1}^{n}(x_k - a_k) < x\right\} \to \frac{1}{\sqrt{2\pi}} \int_{-\infty}^{x} e^{-\frac{t^2}{2}} dt \tag{6.12}$$

The above lemma does not require the identical distribution of $\{x_k\}$. Then we have the following corollary.

Corollary 6.4

Assume that $\{x_k\}$ are mutually independent and have finite fourth moments. Their variances $b_k \ge \sigma > 0$. Formula (6.12) uniformly holds for x (see Formula 6.12).

Proof:

Since $\forall i,\ b_i \ge \sigma > 0, B_n^2 \ge n\sigma^2$. Let $\delta = 2 > 0$. Since x_k has finite fourth moment, $\forall k,\ M|x_k - a_k|^4 \le A < \infty$.

Substituting the above formula into the left-hand side of Formula (6.11), we have:

$$n \to \infty,\ \frac{1}{B_n^{2+\delta}} \sum_{1}^{n} M|x_k - a_k|^{2+\delta} \le \frac{1}{(n\sigma^2)^2} \cdot nA = \frac{1}{n}\left(\frac{A}{\sigma^4}\right) \to 0$$

Namely, Formula (6.11) holds. From Lemma 6.2, Formula (6.11) uniformly holds for x.

We replace the *i.i.d.* condition of $\{x_k\}$ by the following conditions, i.e. $\{x_k\}$ are mutually independent, and have variances $b_k \geq \sigma > 0$ and finite fourth moments. Similarly, we can revise Chow-Robbins lemma under the same relaxed condition. Since many statistical inference methods are based on the central limit theorem, we have the following theorem.

Theorem 6.7

$\forall n \in G$, $\{a(n)\}$ is the global statistic of nodes and satisfies

(1)   Random variables $\{a(n)\}$ are mutually independent and have variances $\sigma_n > \sigma > 0$ and finite fourth moments.
(2) $\forall n_0 \in L$ and $\forall n_1 \notin L$, $E(a(n_1)) - E(a(n_0)) > c > 0$, constant $c > 0$, where n_0 and n_1 are brother nodes.

Then, the corresponding *SA* can find the goal with probability one, and the mean complexity $\sim O(N \cdot \ln N)$.

In the following discussion, when we said that $\{x_k\}$ satisfies Hypothesis I, it always means that $\{x_k\}$ satisfies the above relaxed conditions.

6.3.3 The Extraction of Global Statistics

When a statistical heuristic search algorithm is used to solve an optimization problem, by means of finding the minimum (or maximum) of its objective function, the 'mean' of the statistics is used generally. However, the optimal solution having the minimal (or maximal) objective function does not necessarily fall on the subset with the minimal (or maximal) mean objective function. Therefore, the solution obtained by the method is not necessarily a real optimal solution.

In order to overcome the defect, we will introduce one of the better ways below, the *MAX* statistic.

1 The Sequential Statistic

We introduce a new sequential statistic and its properties as follows (Kolmogorov, 1950).

Assume that $X_1, X_2, ..., X_n$ is a sub-sample with n elements from a population, and their values are $(x_1, x_2, ..., x_n)$. Based on ascending order by size, we have $x_1^*, x_2^*, ..., x_n^*$. If $X_1, X_2, ..., X_n$ have values $(x_1, x_2, ..., x_n)$ then define $X_k^{(n)}$ as x_k^*. $(X_1^{(n)}, X_2^{(n)}, ..., X_n^{(n)})$ is called a set of sequential statistics of $(X_1, X_2, ..., X_n)$.

Lemma 6.3

Assume that population X has distributed density $f(x)$. If $(X_1, X_2, ..., X_n)$ is a simple random sample of X and $(X_1^{(n)}, X_2^{(n)}, ..., X_n^{(n)})$ is its sequential statistic, then its joint distributed density function is

$$g(x_1^*, x_2^*, ..., x_n^*) = \begin{cases} n! \prod_{i=1}^{n} f(x_i^*), x_1^* \leq x_2^* \leq \cdots \leq x_n^* \\ 0, \text{ otherwise} \end{cases}$$

Let X be the maximal statistic of the sub-sample with size n. X has a distributed density function below

$$g(x) = n(F(x))^{n-1}f(x)$$

where $F(x) = \int_{-\infty}^{x} f(t)dt$. From Lemma 6.3, we have

$$P\left(X_n^{(n)} \leq y\right) = \int_{0}^{y} n(F(y))^{n-1}f(y)dy = F(y)^n$$

Definition 6.4

Under the above notions, let:

$$F_n^*(x) = \begin{cases} 0, & x \leq x_1^* \\ k/n, x_k^* & < x \leq x_{k+1}^* \\ 1, & x > x_n^* \end{cases}$$

$F_n^*(x)$ is called the empirically distributed function of $F(x)$.

Lemma 6.4

Assume that $X_1, X_2, ..., X_n$ is a simple random sub-sample from a population that has distributed function $F(x)$. $F_n^*(x)$ is its empirically distributed function. Then for a fixed x, $\infty < x < \infty$, we have

$$P\left\{ \lim_{n \to \infty} F_n^*(x) = F(x) \right\} = 1$$

When $n \to \infty$, the distributed function $\frac{\sqrt{n}(F_n^*(x) - F(x))}{\sqrt{F(x)[1-F(x)]}}$ approaches to $N(0,1)$.

2 *MAX* Statistical Test

Definition 6.5

The *MAX*1 test with parameter (ε, δ) is defined as follows.

Give $0 < \varepsilon$ and $\delta < 1$, X and Y are two random variables. Their observations have upper bounds. Let n be sample size. $X_n^{(n)}$ and $Y_n^{(n)}$ are their maximal statistics respectively, when using sequential test.

The orders of observations of X and Y are $x_1^* \leq x_2^* \leq \ldots \leq x_n^*$ and $y_1^* \leq y_2^* \leq \ldots \leq y_n^*$, respectively. Assuming that $x_n^* > y_n^*$, then $x_k^* < y_n^* \leq x_{k+1}^*$. Let $d = k/n$.

$$N_1 = \frac{|\ln \varepsilon/2|}{2\left(\frac{1-d}{2}\right)^2} \tag{6.13}$$

$N' > \frac{|\ln \varepsilon/2|}{2\delta^2}$ and it has the same order of N_1.

If $n \geq N'$, stop and the algorithm fails.

Otherwise,

$$\text{if } n > \max\left\{N_1, \frac{k}{1 - 2\delta}\right\} \tag{6.14}$$

we may conclude that the maximum of X is greater than the maximum of Y.

If $n < N'$, the observation continues.

Definition 6.6

The *MAX2* test with parameter (ε, δ) is defined as follows.

In the definition of *MAX1* test, the statement 'If $n \geq N'$, stop and the algorithm fails' is replaced by 'If $n \geq N'$, when $x_n^* > y_n^* (y_n^* < x_n^*)$ we may conclude that the maximum of $X(Y)$ is greater than the maximum of $Y(X)$', then we have *MAX2* test.

Definition 6.7

If in the i-level search of *SA*, the *MAX1* (or *MAX2*) with parameter (ε_i, δ) is used as statistical inference method, then the corresponding *SA* search is called *SA(MAX1)* (or *SA(MAX2)*) search with significant level α ($\alpha = \Sigma \varepsilon_i$) and precision δ.

3 The Precision and Complexity of MAX Algorithms

Lemma 6.5 (Kolmogorov Theorem)

$F(X)$ is a continuous distributed function. Let $D_n^+ = \sup_{-\infty < x < \infty} (F_n^*(x) - F(x))$. Then we have $\lim_{n \to \infty} \{\sqrt{n} D_n^+ \leq \alpha\} = 1 - e^{-2\alpha^2}$.

Lemma 6.6

Assume that $F_n^*(X)$ is the empirically distributed function of $F(X)$ and $F(X)$ is continuous. Given $0 < \alpha, \beta < 1$, then when $N > \frac{|\ln \beta|}{2\alpha^2}$, we have

$$P\{F_n^*(x) - F(x) > \alpha\} \leq \beta$$

Proof:

In Lemma 6.5, we use limit distribution to approximate distribution function D_n^+. Thus, we have

$$P\{D_n^+ \leq \alpha\} = P\{\sqrt{n}D_n^+ \leq \sqrt{n}\alpha\} \sim 1 - e^{-2n\alpha^2}$$

When $n > \frac{|\ln \beta|}{2\alpha^2}$, we have $e^{-2n\alpha^2} < \beta$, i.e. $P\{F_n^*(x) - F(x) > \alpha\} \leq \beta$.

Proposition 6.1

X and Y are two bounded random variables and their continuously distributed functions are $F(x)$ and $G(x)$, respectively. Their maximums are x^0 and y^0 respectively, where $x_n^0 > y_n^0$. Let $F(y^0) = d^0$. Assume that $d^0 = 1 - 2\delta$. Given $\varepsilon > 0$, let

$$N_1 = \frac{|\ln \varepsilon/2|}{2\left((1 - d^0)/2)^2\right)} = \frac{|\ln \varepsilon/2|}{2\delta^2}$$

Thus, if $n > N$ and $x_n^0 > y_n^0 (x_n^0 < y_n^0)$, then we can judge that the maximum of $X(Y)$ is greater than the maximum of $Y(X)$ with probability $(1 - \varepsilon)$.

Proof:

Since $F(X)$ is continuous and $F(y^0) = d^0 < 1$. Assume that the corresponding orders of observations of X and Y are $x_1^* \leq x_2^* \leq \dots \leq x_n^*$ and $y_1^* \leq y_2^* \leq \dots \leq y_n^*$, where $x_n^* > y_n^*$, then we have $x_k^* < y_n^* \leq x_{k+1}^*$. Let $d = \frac{k}{n}$ and $N_2 = \frac{|\ln \varepsilon/2|}{|\ln(1-\delta)|}$.

When $n > N_2$, we have

$$\left(d^0 + \delta\right)^n = (1 - \delta)^n < \varepsilon/2 \tag{6.15}$$

When δ is small enough, we have $N_1 > N_2$. Thus, when $n > N_1$ by letting $\beta = \delta$ and $\alpha = \varepsilon/2$, from Lemma 6.6, we have

$$P\{F(x) - F_n^*(x) > \delta\} \leq \varepsilon/2 \tag{6.16}$$

When $P\{F(x) - F_n^*(x) \leq \delta\}$ holds, from Lemma 6.2 and Formula (6.15), we have

$$P\{X_n^* \leq y^0\} = F(y^0)^n \leq (F(y^0) + \delta)^n < \varepsilon/2 \tag{6.17}$$

Thus, when $n > N_1$ from Formulas (6.16) and (6.17), the correct rate of the judgment is $(1 - \varepsilon)$, and the computational complexity is $O(\delta^{-2}|\ln \varepsilon|)$.

In fact, the value of d^0 is not known in advance, so in *MAX*1 test we replace d^0 by d. This will produce some error. In order to guarantee $d \leq 1 - 2\delta$, we may replace N_1 in Formula (6.13) by the following value

$$N = \max\left\{\frac{|\ln \varepsilon/2|}{2((1 - d)/2)^2}, \frac{k}{1 - 2\delta}\right\} \tag{6.18}$$

Corollary 6.5

Under the assumption of Proposition 6.1, the correct rate of judgment by *MAX*1 test is $(1 - \varepsilon)$, and its complexity is $O(\delta^{-2}|\ln \varepsilon|)$.

4 The Applications of *SA(MAX)* Algorithms

The *SA* search based on statistical inference method *MAX* is called *SA(MAX)* algorithm. In the section, we will use *SA(MAX)* to find the maximum of a function.

$f : D \rightarrow R$ is a bounded function on D, where D is a subset of an n-dimensional Euclidean space. So it's needed to transform the maximum finding problem of functions into that of *SA(MAX)* search.

Assume that $f(z) : D \rightarrow R$ is a measurable function, where D is a measurable set in an n-dimensional space. The measure of D is μ, a finite number. Assume that $\mu(D) = 1$.

Regarding (D, μ) as a measure space, define a random variable ξ from $f(x)$ as follows.

$$P\{\xi < y\} = \mu\{x|f(x) < y\}$$

When using *SA(MAX)* algorithm to find the maximum of functions, the given requirement is the following.

(1) $\mu(D_{i+1}) < c$, where c is a given positive number.
(2) When D is finite, $|D_{i+1}| < c$, generally let $c=1$.

Now, we consider the precision and complexity of *SA(MAX)* algorithm in the finding of the maximum of functions.

Theorem 6.8

$f(z) : D \rightarrow R$ is a measurable function on D and $\mu(D) = 1$. Assume that $F(y)$ $(F(y) = P\{z|f(z) < y\})$ is continuous. *SA(MAX)* algorithm is used to find the maximum of functions. Given $0 < \varepsilon$ and $\delta < 1$, the *MAX*1 is used as an inference method, and in the i-th level the parameter used is $(\frac{\varepsilon}{L}, \delta)$. When the algorithm succeeds, then the probability of $z^0 \in D*$ is greater than $(1 - \varepsilon)$, and the complexity is $O\left(\frac{L|\ln \varepsilon/L|}{\delta^2}\right)$, where z^0 is the maximum of $f(z)$, $D_L = D*$ and L is the total number of levels that *SA* reaches.

Proof:

If the algorithm succeeds, i.e. the judgment of *MAX*1 succeeds at every time, then the correct probability of judgment at every time is greater than $\left(1 - \frac{\varepsilon}{L}\right)$. The total correct probability is greater than $(1 - \varepsilon)$.

From Proposition 6.1, we have:

$$N_1 \sim O\left(\frac{|\ln \varepsilon/L|}{\delta^2}\right)$$

Thus,

$$P(MAX1) \sim O\left(\frac{|\ln \varepsilon/L|}{\delta^2}\right)$$

The algorithm is performed through L levels. The total complexity of $SA(MAX)$ is $O\left(\frac{L|\ln \varepsilon/L|}{\delta^2}\right)$.

Theorem 6.9

Under the same condition as Theorem 6.8, given $0 < \varepsilon$ and $\delta < 1$, $SA(MAX2)$ algorithm with parameter $\left(\frac{\varepsilon}{L}, \delta\right)$ at each level is used to find the maximum of function f. When algorithm terminates, we have the maximum $f(z*)$; the probability of $z* \in D_L$, or $f(z*) \in \{y|F(y) > 1 - \delta\}$, is greater than $(1 - \varepsilon)$, and the order of complexity is $O\left(\frac{L|\ln \varepsilon/L|}{\delta^2}\right)$.

Proof:

Similar to Theorem 6.8, we only need to prove the $n < \frac{k}{1-\delta}$ case. Assume that when the search reaches the i-th level $n < \frac{k}{1-\delta}$, and we find the maximum $z_n^*(i)$. From Proposition 6.1, we have that the probability of $f(z_n^*(i)) \in \{y|F(y) > 1 - \delta\}$ is greater than $(1 - \varepsilon)$. On the other hand, $f(z_n^*(i))$ is a monotonically increasing function with respect to i. Let $z_n^*(L) = z^*$. We further have that the probability of $f(z^*) \in \{y|F(y) > 1 - \delta\}$ is greater than $(1 - \varepsilon)$.

Since the complexity at each level is $O\left(\frac{|\ln \varepsilon/L|}{\delta^2}\right)$. The complexity for L levels search is $N_1 \sim O\left(\frac{L|\ln \varepsilon/L|}{\delta^2}\right)$ at most.

From Theorem 6.9, it's known that different from $SA(MAX1)$ algorithm $SA(MAX2)$ never fails, but the conclusion made by $SA(MAX2)$ is weaker than $SA(MAX1)$. Secondly, since constants ε and δ can be arbitrarily small, the maximum can be found by $SA(MAX2)$ with arbitrarily credibility and precision.

5 Examples

For comparison, $SA(MAX)$ and GA (Genetic Algorithm) algorithms are used to solve the same problem (Zhang and Zhang, 1997a, 1997b).

Example 6.1

The goal is to find the maximum of function $f_1(x) = (1.02 - (x - 1/3)^2)^{10}, 0 \le x \le 1$ (Fig. 6.2).

The relation between the results obtained by the two algorithms and N is shown in Fig. 6.3, where N is the total times of calculating function $f_1(x)$. The 'black dots' show the

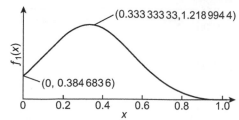

Figure 6.2: $f_1(x) = (1.02 - (x - 1/3)^2)^{10}$

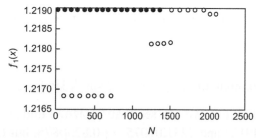

Figure 6.3: The Relation between the Maximum of $f_1(x)$ Obtained and N

results obtained by *SA(MAX)* algorithm when N=64, 128,.... We can see that the maximum of $f_1(x)$ obtained by the algorithm in each case is the real maximal value. The 'white dots' show the results obtained by *GA* algorithm when N=100, 200,.... We can see that the best result obtained by the algorithm is the value of $f_1(x)$ at x=0.3333216.

Example 6.2

The goal is to find the maximum of function $f_2(x) = |(1 - x)x^2 \times \sin(200\pi x)|, 0 \leq x \leq 1$ (Fig. 6.4).

The 'black dots' and 'white dots' in Fig. 6.5 show the results obtained by *SA(MAX)* and *GA* algorithms, respectively. The maximum obtained by *SA(MAX)* is 0.1481475 (x=0.6675003). In GA, the iteration is implemented for 20 generations and each generation has 100 individuals. The maximum obtained is 0.1479531 (x=0.6624222).

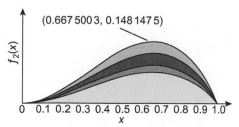

Figure 6.4: $f_2(x) = |(1 - x)x^2 \times \sin(200\pi x)|$

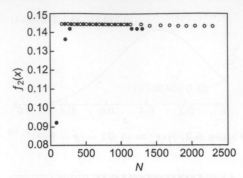

Figure 6.5: The Relation between the Maximum of $f_2(x)$ Obtained and N

Example 6.3

The goal is to find the maximum of $f_3(x) = (1 - 2\sin^{20}(3\pi x) + \sin^{20}(20\pi x))^{20}$ (Fig. 6.6).

The results are shown in Fig. 6.7. We can see that *SA(MAX)* finds two maximums of $f_3(x)$, i.e., 2231.01075, x=0.1749125 and 2231.01075, x=0.8250875, but *GA* finds only one maximum of $f_3(x)$, i.e., 2052.376 , x=0.8246953.

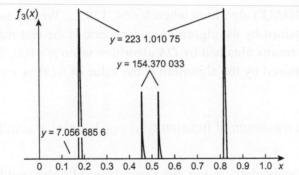

Figure 6.6: $f_3(x) = (1 - 2\sin^{20}(3\pi x) + \sin^{20}(20\pi x))^{20}$

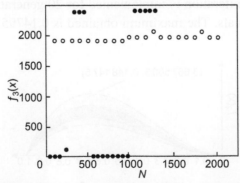

Figure 6.7: The Relation between the Maximum of $f_3(x)$ Obtained and N

From the above results, it's known that the performances of *SA(MAX)* are better than that of *GA*.

6.3.4 SA *Algorithms*

In statistical heuristic search, the statistic inference method is introduced to heuristic search as a global judgment for subsets so that the search efficiency is improved. Under a given significant level, if a search direction is accepted by *SA*, the probability $\geq 1 - a$ for finding the goal can be ensured. When a wrong direction is chosen, *SA* will terminate with the polynomial mean complexity at most. By using successively *SA* search the goal can be found with probability one and with polynomial complexity. In fact, in the new round search, a new significant level or a new statistic inference method may be used, based on the results obtained in the previous round. So a variety of *SA* algorithms can be constructed.

Now, we summarize the *SA* procedure as follows.

If a statistic inference method *S* and a heuristic search algorithm *A* are given then we have a *SA* algorithm.

(1) Set up a list OPEN of nodes. Expand root node S_0, we have m sub-nodes, i.e., m T_1-subtrees or m equivalence classes in some quotient space. Put them into m sub-lists of OPEN, each corresponds to one T_1-subtree. Set up closed list CLOSED and waiting list WAIT. Initially, they are empty. Set up a depth index i and initially $i=1$.

(2) LOOP. If OPEN is empty, go to (11).

(3) From each sub-list of OPEN choose a node and remove it from OPEN to CLOSED. And call it node n.

(4) If n is a goal, success.

(5) Expand node n, we have m sub-nodes and put them into OPEN. Establish a pointer from each sub-node to node n. Reorder nodes in sub-lists by the values of their statistics. Perform statistical inference S on each sub-list, i.e. sub-tree.

(6) If some T_i-subtree T is accepted. Remove the rest of T_i-subtrees accept T from OPEN to WAIT, go to (10) .

(7) If no T_i-subtree is rejected, go to LOOP.

(8) Remove the rejected T_i-subtrees from OPEN to WAIT.

(9) If there is more than one T_i-subtree in OPEN, go to LOOP.

(10) Index i is increased by 1 ($i = i + 1$). Repartition T_i-subtree on OPEN into its sub-subtrees and reorder the sub-aubtrees based on their statistics. Go to LOOP.

(11) If WAIT is empty, fail.

(12) Remove all nodes in WAIT to OPEN, let $i = 0$ and go to (10)

6.4 The Comparison between Statistical Heuristic Search and A^* Algorithm

6.4.1 Comparison to A^*

Are the constraints given in Hypothesis I, including relaxed cases, strict? In order to unravel the problem, we'll compare them with well-known A^* search.

Definition 6.8

Assume that $h(n)$ is an admissible estimate of $h^*(n)$, i.e. $h(n) \le h^*(n)$. If for $p_1, p_2 \in G$, we have $|h(p_1) - h(p_2)| \le d(p_1, p_2)$, where $d(p_1, p_2)$ is the distance between p_1 and p_2, then $h(\cdot)$ is called reasonable, i.e., monotonic and admissible.

Proposition 6.2

Assume that G is a uniform m-ary tree and $h(\cdot)$ is estimate with a typical error of order $\phi(\cdot)$ [Pea84]. $h(\cdot)$ is reasonable. $\{h(n)\}$ is i.i.d. and has a finite fourth moment. If A^* algorithm using $f(n) = g(n) + h(n)$ as its evaluation function has the polynomial mean complexity, then SA search using $\{h(n)\}$ as its statistic also has the polynomial mean complexity.

Proof:

Assume that $p_1 \in L$, $p_2 \notin L$ and $d(p_1, p_2) = k$. Since $h(n)$ is reasonable, we have $h(p_2) \ge h(p_1) - k$.

Since $h(\cdot)$ is an admissible estimate having a typical error of order $\phi(\cdot)$ and A^* searches g with polynomial complexity, from Property 6.1 in Section 6.1.1, we have that $\forall p \in G$, there exists $\varepsilon > 0$ (ε is independent of p) such that

$$p\left[\frac{h^*(p) - h(p)}{\ln h^*(p)} > \varepsilon\right] < \frac{\alpha}{m}, \alpha < 1$$

It does not lose generality in assuming that $\phi(n) = \ln(n)$. We now estimate the difference between $E(h(p_2))$ and $h(p_1)$.

For the part satisfying $h^*(p) - h(p) \le \varepsilon \ln h^*(p)$, we have:

$$h(p_2) \ge h^*(p_2) - \varepsilon \ln 2N$$
$$\ge h^*(p_2) - \varepsilon_1 \ln N$$
$$\ge h^*(p_1) + k - \varepsilon_1 \ln N$$

Thus, we have:

$$E(h(p_2)) \ge [h(p_1) - k]\left(\frac{\alpha}{m}\right) + \frac{m-\alpha}{m}[h^*(p_1) + k - \varepsilon_1 \ln N]$$
$$\ge h(p_1) + k(1 - 2a/m) - \varepsilon_1 \ln N$$

Let $k \geq c \ln N$, where $c(1 - 2a/m) - \varepsilon_1 = c_1 > 0$. We have:

$$E(h(p_2)) \geq h(p_1) + c_1 \ln N \qquad (6.19)$$

Letting $b(p) = h(p)$ be the local statistic of nodes, we have that when $k \geq c \ln N$, $E(b(p_2)) \geq b(p_1) + c_1 \ln N$ holds. From Formula (6.19), when $d(p_1, p_2) = k \geq c \ln N$, for subtree $T(n)$ if using the 'mean' of local statistics as its global statistic, then the global statistic from $T(n)$, $n \in L$, is $a(p) \leq b(p_1)$, and the global statistic from $T(n)$, $n \notin L$, is $a(p) \geq b(p_1) + c_1 \ln N$, i.e., the latter is larger than the former. Moreover, $k \geq c \ln N$ is equivalent to $k(N) \sim c \ln N$ that belongs to the mixed cases we have discussed in Section 6.3.2. The mean complexity of the corresponding *SA* is polynomial.

The proposition shows that if $h(n)$ is monotonic, when A^* is convergent *SA* is also convergent.

From Theorem 6.6, it's known that the proposition still holds when $h(n)$ is not monotonic.

Proposition 6.3

Assume that $h(n)$ is the lower estimation of $h^*(n)$ with a typical error of order $\phi(\cdot)$. Let

$$e(n) = \frac{h^*(n) - h(n)}{\phi(h^*(n))}$$

If $h\{(n)\}$ has a finite fourth moment, $\phi(N) \leq a \ln N, a > 0$ and $\forall n \in G, E(e(n)) \leq d$, where d is a constant, letting $h\{(n)\}$ be a local statistic of nodes, then *SA* search is convergent.

Proof:

Assume that $p_1 \in L, p_2 \notin L$ and $d(p_1, p_2) = k$. We have

$$E(e(p_i)) = \frac{h^*(p_i) - E(h(p_i))}{\Phi(h^*(p_i))}, \quad i = 1, 2$$

$$E(h(p_2)) - E(h(p_1))$$
$$\geq h^*(p_2) - E(e(p_2))\Phi(h^*(p_2)) - h^*(p_1) + E(e(p_1))\Phi(h^*(p_1))$$

Then,

$$E(h(p_2)) - E(h(p_1)) \geq k - E(e(p_2))\Phi(h^*(p_2))$$
$$\geq k - ad \ln(h^*(p_2))$$
$$\geq k - c \ln N \qquad (6.20)$$

where c is a constant.

Let $k(N) = 2c \ln N$. When $d(p_1, p_2) = h \geq k(N)$, we have:

$$E(h(p_2)) - E(h(p_1)) \geq c \ln N$$

From Theorem 6.6, the corresponding *SA* is convergent.

The proposition shows that all lower estimations $h(n)$ of $h^*(n)$ that make A^* search convergent, when using the $h(n)$ as a local statistic, we can always extract a properly global statistic from $\{h(n)\}$ such that the corresponding *SA* search is convergent.

We will show below that the inverse is not true, i.e., we can provide a large class of estimations $h(n)$ such that its corresponding *SA* is convergent but the corresponding A^* is divergent.

Proposition 6.4

Assume that $h(n)$ is a lower estimation of $h^*(n)$ and is an *i.i.d* random variable with a finite fourth moment. For $\forall n \in G$, $E(e(n)) = c < 1$, where c is a constant and $e(n) = \frac{h^*(n) - h(n)}{h^*(n)}$. If $b(n) = h(n)$ is the local statistic of node n, then the corresponding *SA* is convergent.

Proof:

From $\forall n \in G$, $E(e(n)) = c < 1$, we have $E(h^*(n)) - E(h(n)) = ch^*(n)$. Letting $p_1 \in L, p_2 \notin L$ and $d(p_1, p_2) = k$, we have

$$E(h(p_2)) - E(h(p_1)) = h^*(p_1) + k = c(h^*(p_1) + k) - h^*(p_1) + ch^*(p_1)$$
$$= (1 - c)k = c_1 k, c_1 > 0$$

From Theorem 6.6, the corresponding *SA* is convergent.

Corollary 6.6

Assume that $h(n)$ is a lower estimate of $h^*(n)$ with a typical error of order N and $\{h(n)\}$ has a finite fourth moment. For $\forall n \in G$, $E(e(n)) = c$, where c is a constant and $e(n) = \frac{h^*(n) - h(n)}{h^*(n)}$. Letting $b(n) = h(n)$ be a local statistic of nodes n, the corresponding *SA* is convergent.

Proof:

Since $h(n)$ is a lower estimate with a typical error of order N from its definition, there exists $0 < \lambda \leq 1$ such that $\forall n \in G$, $p[e(n) \geq 1] \leq \frac{\beta}{m}, \beta < 1$.

We have:

$$c = E(e(n)) = E(n|e(n) \geq \lambda) + E(n|e(n) < \lambda) < 1 \times \frac{\beta}{m} + \lambda\left(1 - \frac{\beta}{m}\right) \leq 1,$$

i.e., $E(e(n)) = c < 1$. From Proposition 6.3, we have the corollary.

According to Pearl's result, under the conditions of $h(n)$ in Corollary 6.6 the corresponding A^* is exponential, but from Corollary 6.6 *SA* is convergent. Therefore, the condition that *SA* search is convergent is weaker than that of A^* search.

Corollary 6.7

If $h(n)$ is a lower estimate, $\{h(n)\}$ has a finite four moment, for $\forall n \in G$, $E(e(n))$ are equal, and there exist $\beta < 1$ and $\alpha > 0$ such that $p[h^*(n) - h(n)/h^*(n)) < \beta] > \alpha$, then Corollary 6.6 holds.

Corollary 6.8

If $h(n)$ is the lower estimate of $h^*(n)$ with a typical error of order $\phi(\cdot)$, $\{h(n)\}$ has a finite fourth moment and $\forall n \in G$, $E(e(n)) \leq d$, where d is a constant, then the corresponding A^* is convergent. Letting $b(n) = h(n)$ be the local statistic of node n, the corresponding *SA* is also convergent.

Proof:

From Proposition 6.2 and the Pearl's result given in Property 6.4, the corollary is obtained.

From the above propositions, it's easy to see that the condition that makes *SA* convergent is weaker than that of A^*. On the other hand, the convergence of A^* is related to estimation with a typical error of order $\phi(\cdot)$ that is defined by Formulas (6.1) and (6.2). It's very difficult to confirm the two constants $\varepsilon > 0$ and $\lambda > 0$ within the two formulas. So the convergent condition of A^* is difficulty to be tested. But in *SA*, the only convergent requirement is that statistics $b(n)$ are independent and have positive variances and finite fourth moments. In general, the distribution of $b(n)$ satisfies the conditions.

6.4.2 Comparison to Other Weighted Techniques

The statistical inference methods can also be applied to weighted heuristic search. Weighted techniques in heuristic search have been investigated by several researchers (Nilson, 1980; Field et al., 1984). They introduced the concept of weighted components into evaluation function $f(n) = g(n) + h(n)$. Thus, the relative weights of $g(n)$ and $h(n)$ in the evaluation function can be controlled by:

$$f_1(n) = g(n) + \omega h(n) \text{ or}$$
$$f_2(n) = (1 - \omega)g(n) + \omega h(n) \text{ or}$$
$$f_3(n) = \omega g(n) + h(n)$$

where ω is a weight.

In statically weighted systems, a fixed weight is added to the evaluation functions of all nodes. For example, Pearl investigates a statically weighted system $f_a(n) = f(n) + ah(n)$

and showed that the optimal weight is $a_0 = \frac{1}{1+r_0}$ (the definition of r_0 and more details see Pearl (1984b)). But even the optimal weight is adopted; the exponential complexity still cannot be overcome.

For dynamic weighting, for example, the weight ω may vary with the depth of a node in the search tree, for example, $f_4(n) = g(n) + [1 + e(1 - d(n)/N)]h(n)$, where e is a constant and N is the depth that the goal is located. But the dynamic weighting fails to differentiate the nodes: which are on the solution path ($N \in L$), whereas the others ($N \notin L$) are not. Thus, neither static nor dynamic weighting can improve the search efficiency significantly.

As stated in Section 6.1.1, under certain conditions we regard heuristic search as a random sampling process. By using the statistic inference method, it can tell for sure whether a path looks more promising than others. This information can be used for guiding the weighting.

For example, the Wald sequential probability ratio test (*SPRT*) is used as a testing hypothesis in *SA* search. In some search stage if the hypothesis that some subtree T in the search tree contains solution path is rejected, or simply, subtree T is rejected, then the probability that the subtree contains the goal is low. Rather than pruning T as in *SA*, a fixed weight ω is added to the evaluation function of the nodes in T, i.e. the evaluation function is increased by ω, $f_1(n) = g(n) + \omega h(n)$. If the hypothesis that the subtree T' contains the goal is accepted, the same weight is added to evaluation functions of all nodes in the brother-subtrees of T', whose roots are the brothers of the root of T'. If no decision can be made by the statistic inference method, the searching process continues as in *SA* search. We call this new algorithm as the weighted *SA* search, or *WSA*. It is likely that the search will focus on the most promising path due to the weighting. We will show that the search efficiency can be improved by the *WSA* significantly.

For clarity and brevity, we assume that the search space is a uniform 2-ary tree, $m = 2$, in the following discussion. The *SPRT* (or *ASM*) is used as a testing hypothesis and the given significance level is (α, β), where $\alpha + \beta = b$. The complexity of an algorithm is defined as the expected number of the nodes expanded by the algorithm when a goal is found.

$f(n)$ is an arbitrary global statistic (a subtree evaluation function) constructed from heuristic information and satisfies Hypothesis I.

1 Weighting Methods

There are two cases.

$P(A) \sim O(\exp(cN))$, $c > 0$ is a known constant and $P(A)$ is the complexity of the original algorithm A (e.g., A^*) when searching the space. N is the depth at which the goal is located.

Formula $P(A) \sim O(\exp(cN))$ means there exist constants D and E such that

$$D \cdot \exp(cN) \leq P(A) \leq E \cdot \exp(cN)$$

when N is large enough. So there is no loss of generality in assuming that $P(A) = \exp(cN)$.

In the weighted SA, the weighting method is

$$f_1(n) = f(n) + s, \ s > 0 \text{ is a constant} \tag{6.21}$$
$$P(A) \sim O(N^a), \ a > 1 \text{ is a constant}$$

The weighting method is

$$f_1(n) = \lambda f(n), \ \lambda > 1 \text{ is a constant.} \tag{6.22}$$

2 Optimal Weights and the Mean Complexity

$P(A) \sim O(\exp(cN))$, $c > 0$ is a known constant

The weighted function is $f_1(n) = f(n) + s$, $s > 0$ is a constant.

Definition 6.9

A subtree is called a completely weighted, if all its subtrees have been judged to be rejected or accepted.

The subtree $T_2{}^0$ shown in Fig. 6.8 is completely weighted (where the rejected subtrees are marked with sign '×'). But subtree $T_1{}^0$ is not completely weighted.

We imagine that if a subtree is not completely weighted, the testing hypothesis is continued until it becomes a completely weighted one. Obviously, a completely weighted subtree has more expanded nodes than the incompletely weighted one. Thus, if an upper estimate of the mean complexity of the completely weighted subtree is obtained, it certainly is an upper estimate of the mean complexity in general.

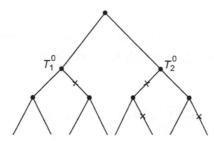

Figure 6.8: A Completely Weighted and Incompletely Weighted Subtree

We now discuss this upper estimate.

Let T be a completely weighted 2-ary tree and P_d be a set of nodes at depth d. For $n \in P_d$, from initial node s_0 to n there exists a unique path consisting of d arcs. Among these d arcs if there are i ($0 \le i \le d$) arcs marked by '×', node n is referred to as an i-type node, or i-node.

So P_d can be divided into the following subsets:

> 0-node: there is only one such node.
> 1-node: the number of such nodes is $C_d^1 = d$
>
> ....
>
> i-node: the number of such nodes is $C_d^i = d$
>
> ...
>
> d-node: the number of such nodes is $C_d^d = d$

In considering the complexity for finding a goal, we first ignore the cost of the statistic inference. Assume that the goal of the search tree belongs to 0-node so that its evaluation is $f^*(S_N) = N$, where N is the depth at which the goal is located. From algorithm A^*, it's known that every node which $f(n) < N$ must be expanded in the searching process.

If node n is an i-node, its evaluation function is $f_1(n) = f(n) + is$. All nodes whose evaluations satisfy the following inequality will be expanded.

$$f_1(n) = f(n) + is < N, \text{ i.e., } f(n) < N - is$$

From $P(A) = \exp(cN)$, it's known that the complexity corresponding to the evaluation function $f_1(n) = f(n) + is$ is $\exp(c(N - is))$. The mean complexity of each i-node (the probability that an i-node is expanded) is

$$\exp(c(N - is))/2^{N+1} = \exp(-cis)\left[\exp(cN)/2^{N+1}\right]$$

On the other hand, the mean complexity for finding a goal at depth N is at least N. Thus the mean complexity of each i-node is

$$\max\left(\exp(c(N - is)/2^{N+1}, N/2^{N+1})\right)$$
$$\le \left[(\exp(c(N - is)) + N)/2^{N+1}\right]$$

When the goal is a 0-node, the upper bound of the mean complexity for computing all d-th depth nodes is the following (ignoring the complexity for making statistic inference).

$$\frac{1}{2^{N+1}} \sum_0^d c_d^i \exp(c(N - is)) + N$$

$$= \frac{1}{2^{N+1}} \left(\sum_{0}^{d} c_d^1 (\exp(c(N - is))) + \sum_{0}^{d} c_d^i N \right)$$

$$= \frac{\exp(cN)}{2^{N+1}} (1 + \exp(-cs))^d + \frac{N}{2^{N-d+1}}$$

On the other hand, when $\alpha + \beta = b$ is a constant, from Section 6.2 it's known that the mean computational cost of *SPRT* is a constant Q for making the statistic inference of a node. When the goal is an 0-node, accounting for this cost, the mean complexity for computing all d-th depth nodes is

$$p_0(WSA) \leq Q \left[\frac{\exp(cN)}{2^{N+1}} (1 + \exp(-cs))^d + \frac{N}{2^{N-d+1}} \right]$$

Similarly, if the goal belongs to i-node, its evaluation is $f(S_N) = N + is$. Then the computational complexity of each node in the search tree is increased by a factor of $\exp(ics)$. Thus when the goal is an i-node, the mean complexity for computing all d-th nodes is

$$p_i(WSA) \leq Q \left[\exp(ics) \frac{\exp(cN)}{2^{N+1}} (1 + \exp(-cs))^d + \frac{N}{2^{N-d+1}} \right]$$

From algorithm *SA*, the probability that the goal falls into an i-node is $(1 - b)^{N-i} b^i$ if the given level is (α, β), $\alpha + \beta = b$. At depth N, there are C_N^i i-nodes, so the probability that the goal belongs to i-node is

$$C_N^i (1 - b)^{N-i} b^i, i = 1, 2, ..., N - 1$$

Accounting for all possible cases of the goal node, the mean complexity for computing all d-th depth nodes is

$$\sum_{i=0}^{N-1} c_N^i (1 - b)^{N-1} b^i p_i(WSA)$$

$$\leq \frac{Q}{2^{N+1}} \left[e^{cN} (1 + e^{-cs})^d (1 - b + be^{cs})^N \right] + \frac{QN}{2^{N-d+1}}$$

Let $F(s) = (1 + e^{-cs})(1 - b + be^{cs})$. There is an optimal weight s_0 such that $F(s_0)$ is minimal. The optimal weight $s_0 = \frac{1}{2c} \ln \left(\frac{1-b}{b} \right)$ and $F(s_0) = 1 + 2\sqrt{b(1 - b)}$.

The upper bound of mean complexity of *WSA* is

$$P(WSA) = Q \left[\frac{e^{cN}}{2^{N+1}} (1 - b + be^{sc})^N \left(\sum_{d=0}^{N} (1 + e^{-cs})^d \right) + \sum_{d=0}^{N} \frac{N}{2^{N-d+1}} \right]$$

Letting $s = s_0$, we have

$$P(WSA) = Q_1 \left[e^{cN} \left(\frac{1 + \sqrt{b(1-b)}}{2} \right)^{N+1} + N \right] \tag{6.23}$$

where, Q_1 is a constant.

Theorem 6.10

Assume $P(A) \sim O(e^{cN})$, $0 < c < \ln 2$. There exists an optimal weight $b_0 > 0$ such that

$$c < \ln \left(\frac{2}{1 + 2\sqrt{b_0(1 - b_0)}} \right)$$

The complexity of *WSA* by using the optimal weight is

$$P(WSA) \sim O(cN)$$

Proof:

Let $c = \ln f < \ln 2$, i.e., $f < 2$. From $c < \ln \left(\frac{2}{1+2\sqrt{b_0(1-b_0)}} \right)$, we have

$$\frac{f}{2} < \frac{2}{1 + 2\sqrt{b_0(1 - b_0)}}$$

We obtain

$$0 < \frac{2}{f} - 1 > 2\sqrt{b_0(1 - b_0)} \text{ since } f < 2$$

Let $h = \frac{2}{f} - 1$.

If $h > 1$, for any $0 < b_0 < 1$, we have

$$c < \ln \left(\frac{2}{1 + 2\sqrt{b_0(1 - b_0)}} \right) \tag{6.24}$$

If $h \le 1$, as long as $0 < b_0 < \frac{1-\sqrt{1-h^2}}{2}$ Formula (6.24) holds.

Substitute (6.24) into (6.22), we have

$$P(WSA) \le Q_1 \left[e^{\left(c + \ln \left(\frac{1 + 2\sqrt{b(1-b)}}{2} \right) N \right)} + N \right]$$

Thus, $P(WSA) \sim O(N)$.

From the theorem, we can see that the whole number of nodes in a 2-ary tree with N depth is $2^{N+1} = 2e^{c_0 N}$, $c_0 = \ln 2$. Therefore, when $P(A) \sim e^{cN}$ as long as $c < c_0$ then we have $P(WSA) \sim O(N)$.

Theorem 6.11

If $P(A) \sim O(N^a), a > 1$, letting $\lambda_0 = \sqrt[2a]{\frac{1-b}{b}}$ and using the weighted function $f_1(n) = \lambda_0 f(n)$, then $P(WSA) \sim O(N)$.

Proof:

Similar to Theorem 6.10, we have

$$p(WSA) \leq \frac{QN^a}{2^{N+1}}(1 - b + b\lambda^a)^N \left(\sum_{d=0}^{N} \left(1 + \lambda^{-a}\right)^d \right) + QN$$

Let $H(\lambda) = (1 - b + b\lambda^a)(1 + \lambda^{-a})$. There exists an optimum $\lambda_0 = \sqrt[2a]{\frac{1-b}{b}}$ such that $H(\lambda)$ is minimal. Substituting λ_0 into the above formula, we have

$$p\left(WSA \right) \leq Q_1 \frac{N^a}{2^{N+1}}\left(1 + 2\sqrt{b(1 - b)}\right)^{N+1} + QN$$

Letting $b < \frac{1}{2}$, we have $1 + 2\sqrt{b(1 - b)} < 2$.

Thus, when $N \to \infty$ $N^a \left(\frac{1 + 2\sqrt{b(1-b)}}{2} \right)^{N+1} \to 0$.

Finally, $P(WSA) \sim O(N)$.

3 Discussion

The estimation of c and a: Generally, whether $P(A)$ is either $O(e^{cN})$ or $O(N^a)$ is unknown generally. Even if the type of functions is known but parameters c and a are still unknown.

We propose the following method for estimating c and a

Assume that in the $2k$ level, the number of expanded nodes is $E(2k)$. Then $\frac{1}{k} \ln \frac{E(2k)}{E(k)}$ can be used to estimate c. If c does not change much with k, then $p(A)$ may be regarded as type $O(e^{cN})$, where $c \sim \frac{1}{k} \ln \frac{E(2k)}{E(k)}$.

If c approaches to zero when k increases, then we consider $\ln \frac{E(2k)}{E(k)}$. If $\ln \frac{E(2k)}{E(k)}$ is essentially unchanged, then $p(A)$ is regarded as type $O(N^a)$ and $a \sim \ln \frac{E(2k)}{E(k)}$.

Alterable significance levels: Assume that s_0 is the optimal weight for $p(A) \sim O(e^{cN}), 0 < c < \ln 2$. Value s_0 is unknown generally. We first by letting $s = s_0 + \Delta s$ then have $e^{-cs} = e^{-cs_0} \times e^{-c\Delta s}$. Letting $u = e^{-c\Delta s}$, we have

$$(1 - e^{-cs})(1 - b + be^{cs}) = \left(1 + u\sqrt{\frac{1-b}{b}}\right)\left(1 - b + \frac{1}{u}\sqrt{b(1-b)}\right)$$

$$= 1 + \left(u + \frac{1}{u}\right)\sqrt{b(1-b)}$$

Thus,

$$p(WSA) \leq Q_1 \left[\exp\left(c + \ln\frac{1 + (u + \frac{1}{u})\sqrt{b(1-b)}}{2}\right) + N\right]$$

In order to have $p(WSA) \sim O(N)$, b should be sufficiently small such that

$$c < \ln\left(\frac{2}{1 + (u + \frac{1}{u})\sqrt{b(1-b)}}\right) \qquad (6.25)$$

Since c is unknown, b still cannot be determined by Formula (6.25). In order to overcome the difficulty, we perform the statistical inference as follows. For testing i-subtrees, the significance level we used is $b_i = \alpha_i + \beta_i$, where $\{b_i\}$ is a series monotonically approaching to zero with i. Thus, when b_i is sufficiently small, Formula (6.25) will hold. For example, let $\alpha_i + \beta_i = \frac{b}{i^2}$, where b is a constant and (α_i, β_i) is a significance level for testing i-subtrees.

From Section 6.2, it's known that when using significance level $\alpha_i + \beta_i = \frac{b}{i^2}$ the mean complexity of the statistical inference is

$$c\left(\left|\ln\frac{b}{i^2}\right|\right) \sim O(\ln i)$$

where c is a constant.

Thus, replacing Q by $\ln N$ in Formula $p(WSA)$, when significance level is $b_i = \frac{b}{i^2}$ we have

$$p(WSA) \leq O(N \ln N)$$

Theorem 6.12

If $p(A) \sim O(e^{cN})$, $0 < c < \ln 2$ is a constant, letting the significance level for i-subtrees be $\alpha_i + \beta_i = \frac{b}{i^2}$, where b is a constant, then

$$p(WSA) \leq O(N \ln N)$$

Alterable weighting: When the type of the order of $P(A)$ is unknown, we uniformly adopt weight function $f_1(n) = f(n) + s$. Next, we will show that when $P(A) \sim O(N^a)$, $a > 1$, if the weight function $f_1(n) = f(n) + s$ is used what will happen to the complexity of *WSA*.

Since $f_1(n) = f(n) + s = \left(1 + \frac{s}{f(n)}\right)f(n) = \lambda_n f(n)$ the 'additive' weight s can be regarded as 'multiplicative' weight λ_n but λ_n is no long a constant. So we call it the alterable weighting.

Assume that $P(A) \sim O(N^a)$. When a node is a 0-node, $f(S_N) = N$. For any node n_1, it is assumed to be an i-node. The evaluation function of n_1 after weighting is $f_1(n_1) = \lambda_{j1}$, $\lambda_{j2}, \ldots, \lambda_{ji} f(n_1)$, where $\lambda_{j1}, \lambda_{j2}, \ldots, \lambda_{ji}$ are the weights along the path from starting node s_0 to node n_1.

According to the heuristic search rules, when $f_1(n_1) = \lambda_{j1}, \lambda_{j2}, \ldots, \lambda_{ji} f(n_1) < N$, i.e., $f(n_1) < \frac{N}{\lambda_{j_1} \ldots \lambda_{j_i}}$, node n_1 will be expanded.

It's known that the goal locates at the N level, so the evaluation $N \leq f(n) \leq 3N$, $\forall n \in G$ may be adopted.

Thus, when s fixed, $\frac{s}{f(n)}$ satisfies $1 + \frac{s}{3N} \leq 1 + \frac{s}{f(n)} = \lambda_n \leq 1 + \frac{s}{N}$.

Let $\lambda = \frac{s}{3N} + 1$ and $u = \frac{s}{N} + 1$. We have $f(n_1) < \frac{N}{\lambda_{j_1} \ldots \lambda_{j_i}} \leq \frac{N}{\lambda^i}$.

Since $P(A) \sim O(N^a)$, the mean complexity for testing each i-tree is

$$\sim \frac{1}{2^{N+1}} \left(\frac{N^a}{\lambda_i}\right)^a = \frac{N^a}{2^{N+1}} \lambda^{-ia}$$

When the goal is a t-node, $f_1(S_N) = \lambda_{j_1}, \lambda_{j_2}, \ldots, \lambda_{j_t}$, $N \leq u^t N$. The mean complexity for testing each i-node is

$$\leq \frac{1}{2^{N+1}} \left(\frac{u^t N}{\lambda^i}\right)^a = \frac{N^a}{2^{N+1}} u^{at} \lambda^{-ia}$$

Similar to Theorem 6.10, we have

$$p(WSA) \sim O\left(\left[\frac{N^a}{2^{N+1}} \left(\sum_{i=0}^{N} ((1 + \lambda^{-a})(1 - b + bu^a))^i\right) + N\right]\right) \qquad (6.26)$$

Let $\frac{s}{3N} = \varepsilon$ and

$$H(\lambda, u) = \left(1 + \lambda^{-a}\right)\left(1 - b + bu^a\right)$$
$$= \left[1 + (1 + \varepsilon)^{-a}\right]\left[1 - b + b(1 + 3\varepsilon)^a\right]$$

When $N \to \infty$, $\varepsilon \to 0$. Thus, when ε is sufficiently small, the asymptotic estimation of the above formula can be represented as

$$H(\lambda, u) \leq \left[(1 + 1 - a\varepsilon + O(\varepsilon^2)\right]\left[1 - b + b(1 + 3a\varepsilon) + O(\varepsilon^2)\right]$$
$$= (2 - a\varepsilon)(1 + 3ab\varepsilon) + O(\varepsilon^2)$$
$$= 2 + a\varepsilon(6b - 1) + O(\varepsilon^2)$$

Let $b < \frac{1}{10}$. When ε is sufficiently small, from the above formula we have $H(\lambda, u) < 2$. Substitute $H(\lambda, u) < 2$ into Formula (6.26), we have

$$p(WSA) \sim O(N^a)$$

Then, we have the following theorem.

Theorem 6.13

If $p(A) \sim O(N^a)(a > 1)$ and using the same weighted function $f_1(n) = f(n) + s$, the order of mean complexity of WSA is $O(N^a)$ at most, i.e., the same as the order of $p(A)$ at most.

The theorem shows that when the type of $p(A)$ is unknown, we may adopt $f_1(n) = f(n) + s$ as the weighted evaluation function.

6.4.3 Comparison to Other Methods

1 The Relation Among WSA, SA and Heuristic Search A

If weighted evaluation function $f_1(n) = f(n) + s$ is adopted, when $s = 0$ then WSA will be changed to common heuristic search A. If weighted evaluation function is $f_1(n) = \lambda f(n)$, when $\lambda = 1$ then WSA is changed to A as well.

In the above weighted evaluation functions, if $s = \infty$ or $\lambda = \infty$ then WSA will be changed to SA, since $s = \infty$ or $\lambda = \infty$ is equivalent to pruning the corresponding subtrees. Therefore, SA and A algorithms are two extreme cases of WSA algorithm. We also show that there exist optimal weights s_0 and λ_0 of WSA. So the performances of WSA are better than that of SA and A in general.

2 Human Problem-Solving Behavior

SA algorithms are more close to human problem-solving behavior.

Global view: In SA algorithms, the statistical inference methods are used as a global judgment tool. So the global information can be used in the search. This embodies the global view in human problem solving, but in most computer algorithms such as search, path planning only local information is used. This inspires us to use the mathematical tools for investigating global properties such as calculus of variation in the large, bifurcation theory, the fixed point principle, statistical inference, etc. to improve the computer problem solving capacity.

SA algorithms can also be regarded as the application of the statistical inference methods to quotient space theory, or a multi-granular computing strategy by using both global and local information.

Learning from experience: In successive *SA* algorithms, the 'successive operation' is similar to learning from the previous experience so that the performances can be improved. But the successive operation builds upon the following basis, i.e., the mean computation of *SA* in one pass is convergent. Different from the *SA* algorithms A^* (or *BF*) does not have such a property generally so the successive operation cannot be used in the algorithm.

Difference or precision: As we know, *SA* builds upon the difference of two statistics, one from paths containing goal, and one from paths not containing goal. Algorithm A^* builds upon the estimated precision of evaluation functions from different paths. The precise estimates of statistics no doubt can mirror the difference, but the estimates that can mirror the difference of statistics are not necessarily precise. So it's easy to see that the convergent condition of SA is weaker than that of A^*.

Judging criteria: In *SA*, the judgment is based on the difference of the means of statistics from a set of nodes. But in A^* the judgment is based on the difference among single nodes. So the judgment in *SA* is more reliable than A^*. Moreover, in A^* the unexpanded nodes should be saved in order for further comparison. This will increase the memory space.

Performances: W. Zhang (1988) uses 8-puzzle as an example to compare the performances of *WSA* and *A*. The results are shown in Table 6.1. There are totally 81 instances. The performance of *SA* is superior to *A* in 60 instances. Conversely, *A* is superior to *SA* only in 21 instances. The computational costs saved are 23.4% and 20.8%, respectively. As we know, 8-puzzle is a problem with a small size. Its longest solution path only contains 35 moves. We can expect that when the problem size becomes larger, *SA* will demonstrate more superiority.

*Where, the computational cost-the number of moves, (α, β)-significance level, ω-weight, d—when *WSA* search reaches d (depth) the statistical inference is made, and
$$\Delta p(\%) = \frac{|p(A) - p(WSA)|}{p(WSA)}.$$

---

* 8-Puzzle consists of eight numbered movable titles set in 3×3 frame. One cell of the frame is always empty thus making it possible to move an adjacent title into the empty cell. Two configurations (initial and goal) of titles are given. Find an appropriate sequence of moves for changing the initial configuration into the goal configuration. The number of moves needed to reach the goal configuration is just the computational cost.

Table 6.1: The Comparison of Performances between *WSA* and *A*

WSA Algorithm	Number of Instances	$\triangle p > 0$		$\triangle p < 0$	
		Number of Instances	Computational Cost Saved	Number of Instances	Computational Cost Increased
$\alpha = \beta = 0.01$ $\omega = 2, d = 3$	81	60 74.1%	23.4%	21 25.9%	20.8%

6.5 SA *in Graph Search*

6.5.1 *Graph Search*

Algorithm *SA* can formally be extended to graph search.

First, graph-search needs to be transferred into some sort of tree search. There are several strategies dealing with the problem. For example, the procedure presented in Nilsson (1980) is one of the strategies. It generates an explicit graph G and a subset T of graph G called the search tree.

Second, since the branching factor is not a constant, and there is not only one solution path, the depth N at which the goal is located is generally unknown, etc. There is no threshold to be given in the graph-search algorithm. One of the formal algorithm may be given as follows.

Assume that T is a search tree of G, and has m 0-subtrees $T_0^1, T_0^2, ..., T_0^m$. The evaluation function $f(n)$ (or $h(n)$) defined in A^* is chosen as the local statistic of each individual node in T. The global statistic of each 0-subtree T_0^j is defined as follows:

$$\left\{ a_1\left(T_0^j\right), a_2\left(T_0^j\right), ... \right\}, j = 1, 2, ..., m$$

Confidence probability $\gamma(0 < \gamma < 1)$ and the width $\delta(\delta > 0)$ of confidence intervals are given. Algorithm *SAA* is performed on $\{a_1(T_0^j)\}$. Then we have intervals $I(T_0^j, \delta), j = 1, 2, ..., m$.

Assume that $I(T_0^1, \delta)$ is the left most one in real axis. If $I(T_0^1, \delta)$ does not intersect with $I(T_0^j, \delta), j \neq 1$, then choose T_0^1, prune $T_0^j, j \neq 1$, and the search continues. If $I(T_0^j, \delta)$ intersects with one of $I(T_0^j, \delta), j \neq 1$, letting $\delta_2 < \delta$ and replacing the width δ of confidence intervals by δ_2, restart *SAA*,...

Similarly, perform *SAA* on i-subtrees, $i = 1, 2, ...$

When N is unknown and T is an infinite tree, *SAA* might not terminate. In order to overcome the difficulty, an upper bound B, the estimate of depth N, may be chosen. If the search reaches the bound, then a new round of *SA* search starts.

On the other hand, in *SAA*, the chosen width of confidence intervals is $\delta = \frac{c}{4}$, where $c = u_1 - u_0$, but $c = u_1 - u_0$ is unknown beforehand generally. Thus, we may choose a monotonically decreasing series $\delta_1, \delta_2 \ldots$. At the beginning, δ_1 is chosen as the width of confidence intervals, if $I(T_0^1, \delta)$ (the left most one in *i*-subtrees) intersects with one of $I(T_0^j, \delta), j \neq 1$, then replace δ_1 by δ_2 and restart *ASM* test. In order to prevent the search from not being terminated, a lower bound δ_0 may be chosen. When $\delta_t < \delta_0$ if $I(T_0^1, \delta)$ still intersects with $I(T_0^j, \delta), j \neq 1$, the current search stops and a new round of *SAA* starts. Of course, at the beginning a proper δ_0 should be chosen as the width of confidence intervals and perform *SAA* search, where δ_0 is chosen according to previous experience and domain knowledge.

6.5.2 AND/OR Graph Search

The statistical inference methods can be applied to AND/OR graph search as well. Now, we take the combination of *ASM* test and *GBF* search (Pearl, 1984a, 1984b, 2000) as an example to show the *SA* search in AND/OR graphs.

G is an AND/OR graph and *G'* is a sub-graph generated from *G* when search reaches a certain stage. $B(n)$ is a sub-graph of *G'* and satisfies (1) $B(n)$ contains starting node s_0, (2) if an expanded *AND* node *p* is in $B(n)$, then all sub-nodes of *p* are in $B(n)$, (3) if an expanded *OR* node *p* is in $B(n)$, then just one of its sub-nodes is in $B(n)$, (4) there is no '*UNSOLVABLE*' node in $B(n)$, (5) *n* is a node in $B(n)$. In this case, $B(n)$ is called a solution base of *G* containing node *n*.

In *GBF* search, a graph evaluation function f_1 is used to judge the most promising solution base. Then the graph (base) is expanded according to node evaluation function f_2.

Assume that $B(n)$ is a solution base of *G* containing *n*. $G(n)$ is a sub-graph of *G* rooted at *n*. $G_k(n)$ is an expanded part of $G(n)$ and has *k* nodes. For $q \in G_k(n)$, let $f_1(q)$ be a graph evaluation function of a solution base containing node *q* (Fig. 6.9). Thus, $f_1(q)$ reflects some property of a set of solution graphs that potentially generated from $B(n)$.

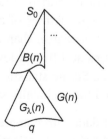

Figure 6.9: *AND/OR* **Graph Search**

$\alpha_k(B(n)) = F(f_1(q), q \in G_k(n))$, where F is a combination function of $f_1(q)$. Assume that G_0 is a unique optimal solution graph of G. For any solution base $B(n)$ containing n, when expanding $G(n)$ rooted at n in order to search G_0, the observation $\{\alpha_k(B(n))\}$ from subgraph $G_k(n)$ of $G(n)$ reflects the possibility of seeking out G_0. Thus, observation $\{\alpha_k(B(n))\}$ can be used as the statistic of *ASM* test for discriminating the most promising solution base. Therefore, we have a corresponding statistic *AND/OR* graph search algorithm-*SGBF*.

Assume that G is a $(2N, b)$ -game tree and has a unique optimal solution. Statistic $\alpha_k(B(n))$ satisfies a hypothesis similar to Hypothesis I. Using *ASM* as hypothesis testing method S, in the $2n$-th level let the confidence probability be $\gamma_n = 1 - \frac{\alpha}{b^n(n+1)^2}, 0 < \alpha < 1$, the width of confidence intervals be $\delta > 0$, where δ is a constant, and the threshold be $E = cn^2$, where c is a constant and independent of n. If the complexity of *SGBF* is defined as the average number of frontier nodes tested by the algorithm (Pearl, 1984a, 1984b), then we have the following theorem.

Theorem 6.14

When *SGBF* searches a $(2N, b)$ - double game tree, it can find the goal with probability one and its upper bound of complexity is $O(N^2, b^N)$.

Theorem 6.15

When *SGBF* searches a $(2N, b)$ - double game tree, if there is a *MAX* win strategy by letting the threshold be $E = C \ln^2 N$, c is a constant, in the $2n$-th level, then *MAX* will win with probability $(1 - \alpha), 0 < \alpha < 1$, and its upper bound of complexity is $O(N \ln^2 N)$.

6.6 Statistical Inference and Hierarchical Structure

Even search is performed on a tree (or graph) structure generally, the traditional search algorithms do not use the structural information, for example, in the best first search algorithm the node expansion only depends on the evaluation function of each single node. From granular computing point of view, only the finest grain-size information is used, i.e., the node evaluation functions. In statistical heuristic search, the hierarchical tree structure is used, since the search is carried through subtrees of a tree from top to down. While a subtree consists of a set of nodes and it is coarser than a single node. Therefore, *SA* is a multi-granular computing, since subtrees at different levels have different grain-sizes and compose a sequence of quotient spaces. So the statistical heuristic search is a perfect combination of statistical inference and hierarchically structural knowledge.

In web age, there is a huge amount of data with complex structures and strong noise. The statistical methods can handle big and noisy data effectively. While the quotient space model is a suitable model for representing complex structures. So the combination of both is in favor of processing big, noisy and complex data.

In fact, a tree corresponds to a sequence of monotonic quotient spaces. In *SA* search, when performing statistical inference on *i*-subtrees, each subtree is an equivalence class, the inference is implemented on a quotient space that composed by the subtrees, and the decision making does not depend on the single node evaluation function but the global evaluation function extracted from the whole nodes of each subtree. Due to the noise, incomplete knowledge, etc. uncertain factors, we are unable to make precise decisions generally. Statistical inference methods will ensure the decision-making reliability under a certain statistical sense.

CHAPTER 7

The Expansion of Quotient Space Theory

Chapter Outline

In this chapter, we extend the quotient space theory to general cases. It includes two aspects. First, the falsity- and truth-preserving principles are extended to a general quotient space approximation principle. Second, the quotient space theory based on equivalence relations is extended to that based on tolerant relations and closure operations.

7.1 Quotient Space Theory in System Analysis

In Chapter 5, we presented several examples to show how the falsity- and truth-preserving principles can be used to solve spatial planning. In order to use the principles, when transforming a solution in the original space to a solution in its quotient space, or vice versa, a precise quotient space should be constructed. Basically, this is a problem-dependent work. Now, we present a general principle, the quotient space approximation principle. By this principle, a set of quotient spaces is constructed to approximate the original space. Then the solution (or performance) of the original space is estimated from the solutions (or performances) of the quotient spaces. This is just the well-known multi-resolution system analysis (Zhang and Zhang, 2005a) and the multi-granular computing as well.

Now, we restate the quotient space theory from the multi-resolution system analysis perspective as follows.

7.1.1 Problems

Assume that (X, f, T) is a system, where f is its performance (attribute functions). We have a set $[X]_1, [X]_2, ..., [X]_n, ...$ of quotient spaces, where $[f]_i$ is the quotient performance of $[X]_i$. Then, the following quotient space approximation problem emerged. That is, when space $[X]_i$ approaches to X, whether its performance $[f]_i$ approaches f. If the answer is yes, the f is called quotient space approachable. In this section, we will use the quotient space approximation model to analyze systems' performances. We will discuss the necessary and sufficient conditions for quotient space approachable function f, and quotient space approximation methods.

For simplicity, the quotient function $[f]$ on $[X]$ is defined according to a certain convex closure rule, e.g., $[f](a) \in C(f(x)|x \in a)$, where $C(f(x)|x \in a)$ is the convex closure of point set $\{f(x)|x \in a\}$, a is an element on $[X]$, or an equivalence class on X.

7.1.2 Quotient Space Approximation Models

In order to establish the model, it's needed to solve the following three problems, (1) the description of performances, (2) the description of the performance approximation, and (3) the definition of the convergence of a set of quotient spaces.

1 The Performance Description

The performance of a system X is described by an attribute function f defined on X. So the performance approximation problem is that of the approximation of function f by a set of quotient spaces.

2 The Convergence of a Set of Quotient Spaces

Assume that the original space (X, d) is a metric one, and d is its distance function.

Definition 7.1

$A \subset X$, letting $d(A) = \sup_{x,y \in A} \{d(x, y)\}$, $d(A)$ is called the diameter of A.

Definition 7.2

R is an equivalence relation on X, and $[X]$ is its corresponding quotient space. Let $d(R) = \sup_{a \in [X]} \{d(a)\}$. $d(R)$ is called the fineness of R.

Definition 7.3

$R_1, R_2..., R_n, ...$ is a set of equivalence relations on X. If $d(R_n) \to 0$, then a set $[X]_1, [X]_2, ..., [X]_n, ...$ of the corresponding quotient spaces converges to X with respect to their grain-size, where $[X]_n$ is the corresponding quotient space of R_n.

3 Performance $f(x)$ of system X

Definition 7.4

Function $f(x)$ on (X, d) is defined as $f: (X, d) \to (Y, d_1)$. The corresponding function $[f]$ on $[X]$ is defined according to a specified convex closure principle, where $[X]$ is a quotient space of X. $[f](a)$ is the quotient function induced from $f(x)$. (X, d) and (Y, d_1) both are metric spaces. d and d_1 are metric functions.

Definition 7.5

Given a quotient function $[f](a)$, we define a function $[f]'(x)$ on X such that
$\forall x \in X, x \in a, [f]'(x) = [f](a)$.

Definition 7.6

Let $M(X)$ be a metric space composed by all bounded functions on X. Its distance is defined as $d_M(f_1, f_2) = \sup\{d(f_1(x), f_2(x)) | x \in X\}, \forall f_1, f_2 \in M(X)$.

Definition 7.7

$\{[X]_i\}$ is a series of quotient spaces on X. $\{[f]_i\}$ is its corresponding quotient performance functions. When the series $\{[X]_i\}$ of quotient spaces converges to X in accordance with their grain-size, if $\{[f]'_i\}$ (or simply $\{[f]_i\}$) on $M(X)$ converges to f, then f is called quotient space absolutely approachable.

Proposition 7.1

Assume that performance function $f(x)$ on metric space (X, d) is quotient space absolutely approachable; the necessary and sufficient condition is that function $f(x)$ on X is uniformly continuous.

Proof:

$\Rightarrow$: $\forall x_0 \in X, \varepsilon > 0, \exists \delta > 0$, when $d(x, x_0) < \delta$, have $d_1(F(x), F(x_0)) < \varepsilon$. Since $[X]_i$ converges to X, there exists i_0 such that when $i > i_0$ have $d(R_i) < \delta$. When $y_{a(x_0)} \in a, d(y_{a(x_0)}, x_0) < \delta$. Thus

$$d_1\left(f(x_0), [f]'_i(x_0)\right) = d_1\left(f(x_0), [f]_i(a)\right) = d_1\left(f(x_0), f\left(y_{a(x_0)}\right)\right) < \varepsilon$$

where, point $y_{a(x_0)}$ satisfies $x_0 \in a$, $[f]'_i(x_0) = f(y_{a(x_0)})$.

Again, $d_M(f, [f]_i') \leq \sup_{x_0}\{d_1(f(x_0), f(y_{a(x_0)}))\}\langle 2\varepsilon$, i.e., $\{[f]_i'\}$ on $M(X)$ converges to f.

$\Leftarrow$: Assume that $\{[f]_i'\}$ converges to f. By reduction to absurdity, assuming that $f(x)$ on X is not uniformly continuous, there exists ε_0 such that for any n,

$$\exists x_n, x_n', d(x_n, x_n')\langle 1/n, d_1(f(x_n), f(x_n'))>\varepsilon_0$$

Construct a set $[X]_n$ of quotient spaces such that their fineness satisfies $\frac{1}{n} < d(R_n) < \frac{2}{n}$, meanwhile x_n and x_n' belong to the same class a_n on $[X]_n$. Let $[f]_n(a_n) = f(x_n')$. Then, for $\forall n$, we have $d_1([f]_i'(x_n), f(x_n)) = d_1(f(x_n), f(x_n')) > \varepsilon_0$. When $n \to \infty$, $d(R) \to 0$. This contradicts with the definition that f is an absolutely approachable function.

Example 7.1

$f(x)$ is a continuous function on X, $X = [0, 1]$. $[0,1]$ is divided into i intervals equally. Letting each interval as an equivalence class, we have a quotient space $[X]_i$. According to the inclusion principle of gaining quotient functions, we construct a quotient function $[f]_i$. Since $[0,1]$ is a bounded close set, $f(x)$ is uniformly continuous on $[0,1]$. From Proposition 7.1, $[f]_i$ converges to f in accordance with their grain-size.

Definition 7.8

f is the performance of X. If there exists a series $\{[X]_i\}$ of finite quotient spaces such that when the series converges to X, then $\{[f]_i'\}$ on $M(X)$ converges to f, where $\{[f]_i'\}$ is the corresponding quotient performance functions. f is called quotient space approachable, and $\{[X]_i\}$ is called one of its approximate quotient space series, where 'a finite quotient space' means that the number of elements in the space is finite.

Proposition 7.2

$(X.d)$ is a metric space. $f : X \to R^N$ is a performance function (measurable function), the necessary and sufficient condition that f is quotient space approachable is that f on X is bounded.

Proof:

$\Rightarrow$: For simplicity, assume that $N=1$. If f is measurable and bounded, let its bound be m. For any n, let

$$a_i(n) = \left\{x \left| \frac{(i-1)m}{n} \leq f(x) < \frac{im}{n}\right.\right\}, i = 1, 2..., n-1$$

$$a_n(n) = \left\{x \left| \frac{(n-1)m}{n} \leq f(x) < m\right.\right\}$$

Construct a quotient space $[X]_n = \{a_1(n), ..., a_n(n)\}$, based on the inclusion principle, define a quotient function $[f]_n'$. Obviously, $[f]_n'$ converges to f.

$\Leftarrow$: By reduction to absurdity, assuming that $f(x)$ is unbounded, for a finite quotient space $[X]$, there at least exists an element a on $[X]$ such that $f(x)$ is unbounded at a. Namely, $\forall x \in a$, $d_1(f(x), [f]'_n(x)) < \varepsilon$ does not always hold.

Different from general function approximation, the quotient space approximation is to approximate a function on X by a series of functions on its quotient spaces rather than the original space X. Since quotient spaces have a small number of elements, it's easy to define their functions.

Moreover, in the quotient space approximation, the quotient spaces that we chose may have overlapped elements. This kind of quotient space is called a quasi-quotient space. The conclusions we made above are still available to a series of quasi-quotient spaces.

Definition 7.9

If a relation R on X satisfies reflexivity and symmetry, R is called a tolerance relation.

Definition 7.10

R is called a tolerance relation on X. Let $< x >= \{y | y R x, y \in X\}$, where $x R y$ indicates that x and y are R tolerant. Let $< X >= \{< x > | x \in X\}$. $< X >$ is a quasi-quotient space on X.

Accordingly, giving a corresponding definition of convergence of a series of quasi-quotient spaces with respect to their grain-size, we have the following proposition.

Proposition 7.3

Assume that $f : (X, d) \rightarrow (Y, d_1)$ is a uniformly continuous function. If a series $\{< X >_i\}$ of quasi-quotient spaces converges to X with respect to their grain-size, a series $\{[f]_i\}$ of the corresponding quotient functions converges to f with respect to the grain-size as well.

7.2 Quotient Space Approximation and Second-Generation Wavelets

Since the quotient space approximation is a multi-resolution analysis method, it is closely related to wavelets analysis. Now, we discuss their connection.

7.2.1 Second-Generation Wavelets Analysis

We can see the wavelet transform (WT) as a decomposition of a signal $f(x)$ onto a set of basis functions called wavelets to obtain a series expansion of the signal. So far there are two kinds of WT, the first-generation wavelets (Mallat, 1989; Rioul and Vetterli, 1991; Unser and Blu, 2003) and the second-generation wavelets (Sweldens, 1998). In the first-generation wavelets, the basis functions are obtained from a single mother wavelet by dilations and translations. Then, the signal $f(x)$ is directly projected onto the basis functions by taking the inner product between $f(x)$ and the functions. If a set of basis functions is obtained from dilating and translating the mother wavelet, the function becomes spread out in time, then the corresponding projection onto the set of basis functions takes only the coarse resolution structure of $f(x)$ into account. This implies that this set of basis functions composes a coarse space. Conversely, if a set of basis functions is obtained from contracting and translating the mother wavelet, the fine structure of $f(x)$ will be taken. It means that this set of basis functions composes a fine space.

Now, we introduce Haar wavelet as follows, where X is a measurable subset in an n-dimensional European space.

Definition 7.11

$\{S_{jk}|j,k \in K(j)\}$ is a family of measurable subsets on X. If each $S_j = \{S_{jk}|k \in K(j)\}$ is a finite partition of X and for $\forall i$, when $j > i$, S_j is finer than S_i, where $K(j)$ is a finite set of indices, $\{S_{jk}|j,k \in K(j)\}$ is called a series of hierarchical partitions, or a nested set of partitions.

General Haar Wavelet

Definition 7.12

$\{S_{jk}|j,k\}$ is a series of hierarchical partitions on X. Let the characteristic function of set S_{jk} be $\chi(S_{jk})$. Defining $\varphi_{jk} = \tilde{\varphi}_{jk} = \frac{\chi(S_{jk})}{\mu(S_{jk})}$, then φ_{jk} is a scaling function.

Definition 7.13

Define a subspace $V_i = closspan\{\varphi_{jk}|k \in K(j)\}, j = 0, 1, ...$

Definition 7.14

Assume that W_j is the orthogonal complement of V_j on V_{j+1}. $\{\psi_{jm}|j,m\}$ is an orthogonal base on W_j, $\{\psi_{jm}|j,m\}$ is called a general Haar wavelet.

Example 7.2

Divide $S_{j,k}$ into two equal parts $S_{j+1,2k+1}$ and $S_{j+1,2k}$, i.e., $\mu(S_{j+1,2k+1}) = \mu(S_{j+1,2k})$. Assume that $\mu(X) = 1$. Let the scaling function be

$$\varphi = \tilde{\varphi}_{jk} = \frac{\chi(X_{jk})}{\mu(X_{jk})} \tag{7.5}$$

Define a wavelet

$$\psi_{jm} = (\varphi_{j+1,2m+1} - \varphi_{j+1,2m})/2, j = 0, 1, ...; m = 0, ..., 2^j - 1 \tag{7.6}$$

The wavelet defined by Formulas (7.5) and (7.6) is called a general Haar (dyadic) wavelet.

7.2.2 Quotient Space Approximation

1 Introduction

(X, f, T) is a space. f is a performance function on X. $\{[X]_i\}$ is a set of hierarchical quotient spaces on X. $\{R_i\}$ is a set of corresponding equivalence relations.

Since equivalence relation and spatial partition are mutually equivalent, a set of hierarchical quotient spaces, a set of hierarchical equivalence relations and a set of hierarchical partitions are equivalent. Namely, a series of finite hierarchical partitions in the second-generation wavelet is equivalent to the above as well.

We will show below that the quotient space approximation of signal $f(x)$ corresponds to some sort of wavelet approximation.

2 Quotient Space Approximation

Recently, there are two forms for approximating (or decomposing) a signal $f(x)$, the limit form $f_i \to f$, and the series expansion $f = \sum_i f_i$. These two forms are equivalent. In wavelet transform, the signal is expanded into a series form. In the series expansion, only the increment of the signal values is represented at the high-resolution levels. The quotient space approximation of a given signal is based on the limit form. If transforming the limit form of quotient space approximation into the series expansion, we will have some sort of wavelet transforms.

Assume that f is an attribute function on X. $\{[X]_i\}$ is a set of hierarchical quotient spaces on X. Define a quotient function $[f](a) = E(\{f(x)|x \in a\})$, where $E(\cdot)$ denotes the mean of x. And we call the quotient function as a quotient function defined by the mean principle. Assume that $[X]_{i+1}$ is the (dyadic) quotient space of $[X]_i$.

As shown in Fig. 7.1, f_0 is the mean of f on $X(X = [X]_0)$. f_{10} and f_{11} are the means of f at elements a_{10} and a_{11} of $[X]_1$, respectively. For simplicity, assume that the measure of each equivalence class is the same, i.e., $\mu(a_{10}) = \mu(a_{11})$. We may use $\{f_{10}, f_{11}\}$ to describe $[f]_1$, or use the increment between $f_{10}(f_{11})$ and f_0 to describe $[f]_1$, for example, if $d_{00} = \frac{f_{11} - f_{10}}{2}$, then $f_{11} = f_0 + d_{00}$ and $f_{10} = f_0 - d_{00}$. We may use $\{f_0, d_{00}\}$ to describe $[f]_1$ as well.

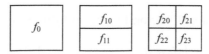

Figure 7.1: Dyadic Quotient Spaces

Assume that $[X]_2 = \{a_{20}, a_{21}, a_{22}, a_{23}\}$. For f_{10}, let $d_{10} = \frac{f_{21} - f_{20}}{2}$. For f_{11}, let $d_{11} = \frac{f_{23} - f_{22}}{2}$.
We have $f_{21} = f_{10} + d_{10}, f_{20} = f_{10} - d_{10}, f_{23} = f_{11} + d_{11}, f_{22} = f_{11} - d_{11}$.

Generally, there are 2^i equivalence classes in the i-th level and its corresponding mean is $f_{ik}, k = 0, 1, ..., 2^j - 1$. Let

$$d_{i-1,m} = \frac{f_{i,2m+1} - f_{i,2m}}{2} \tag{7.7}$$

We have

$$f_{i,2m+1} = f_{i-1,m} + d_{i-1,m}, f_{i,2m} = f_{i-1,m} - d_{i-1,m}, i = 1, ..., n; m = 0, 1, ..., 2^{i-1} - 1 \tag{7.8}$$

Definition 7.15

$\{f_{ik}\}$ is known. $\{d_{i-1,m}\}$ defined by Formula (7.7) is called the quotient incremental function of f in the i-th level.

The quotient space approximation process can also be described by the quotient incremental function.

3 The Relation between Two Quotient Space Approximation Forms

From Formula (7.7), we know that d_{im} can be computed from a known f_{im}. We will show below that f_{im} can be computed from the known d_{im} and f_0.

Definition 7.16

Assume that integer a is a binary number with n bits. $[a]_j$ is the first j bits of a.

Example 7.3

Assume that $a = (1, 0, 0, 1, 1)$. Then, $[a]_1 = (1) = 1$, $[a]_2 = (1, 0) = 2$,
$[a]_3 = (1, 0, 0) = 4$, $[a]_4 = (1, 0, 0, 1) = 9$, and $[a]_5 = a = 19$. Therefore, an element of quotient space $[X]_j$ can be represented by a j-dimensional vector $[a]_j$. Replacing each component with 0 value of $[a]_j$ by value -1, we have a new vector $< a >_j$.

Definition 7.17

Assume that $\{f_{jm}\}$ is known and $\{d_{jm}\}$ is defined by Formula (7.7). Now, define a vector as follows: $d_0 = (d_{00}), d_i = (d_{i0}, ..., d_{i,2^{i-1}-1}), i = 1, 2, ...$.

Definition 7.18

Assume that a is an n-dimensional vector. Define an i-dimensional vector:

$$d([a]_i) = \left(d_{0,0}, d_{1,[a]_1}, ..., d_{i-1,[a]_{i-1}} \right), i = 1, ..., n$$

Example 7.4

$$a = (1,0,0,1,1), \quad \text{thus}$$

$$d([a]_5) = \left(d_{0,0}, d_{1,[a]_1}, ..., d_{4,[a]_4}\right) = d\left(d_{0,0}, d_{1,1}, d_{2,2}, d_{3,4}, d_{4,9}\right)$$

$$d([a]_4) = \left(d_{0,0}, d_{1,[a]_1}, ..., d_{3,[a]_3}\right) = d\left(d_{0,0}, d_{1,1}, d_{2,2}, d_{3,4}\right)$$

Theorem 7.1

A function f on (X, d), $\mu(X) = 1$ and a set $\{S_{jm}\}$ of hierarchical (dyadic) partitions are given. $\{f_{jm}\}$ is a quotient function defined by the mean principle. $\{d_{jm}\}$ is a quotient incremental function defined by Formula (7.7). a is an n-dimensional binary vector. Then

$$[f]_i([a]_i) = f_0 + \sum <a>_{i,k} d([a]_i)_k, i = 1, ..., n \tag{7.9}$$

Proof:

By induction, when $i = 1$, from the definition of d_{00}, we have that Formula (7.9) holds. Assume that Formula (7.9) holds for $i - 1$, i.e.,

$$[f]_{i-1}([a]_{i-1}) = f_0 + \sum <a>_{i-1,k} d([a]_{i-1})_k$$

$$= [f]_{i-1}([a]_{i-1}) = f_{i-1,[a]_{i-1}} = f_0 + <a>_{i-1,1} d_{0,0} + ... + <a>_{i-1,i-1} d_{i-2,[a]_{i-2}} \tag{7.10}$$

Since

$$f_{i,[a]_i} = f_{i-1,[a]_{i-1}} + <a>_{i,i} d_{i-1,[a]_{i-1}} \tag{7.11}$$

Substituting Formula (7.10) into (7.11), and when $j \leq i - 1$, $<a>_{i-1,j} = <a>_{i,j}$, we have

$$[f]_i([a]_i) = f_0 + \sum <a>_{i,k} d([a]_i)_k, i = 1, ..., n$$

where, $<a>_{i,j}$ is the j-th component of $<a>_i$, $<a>$ is a vector obtained via replacing the '0' component of $[a]$ by '−1'.

Example 7.5

Find the f value of the 21st element at the 5th quotient space. Let $a = (1,-1,1,-1,1) = 21$. And find the f value of the equivalence class that a belongs to at the 4th level.

Solution:

$$[f]_5(a) = [f]_5((1, -1, 1, -1, 1)) = f_0 + d_{0,0} - d_{1,1} + d_{2,2} - d_{3,5} + d_{4,10}$$

$$[f]_4([a]_4) = [f]_4(1, -1, 1, -1) = f_0 + d_{0,0} - d_{1,1} + d_{2,2} - d_{3,5}$$

Theorem 7.2

Assume that $[X]_i$ converges to X with respect to its grain-size, and quotient function $[f]_i$ is constructed by the mean principle. If f is uniformly continuous on X, then $[f]_i$ converges to f with respect to the grain-size.

The theorem can be obtained from Proposition 7.1 directly.

Proposition 7.4

$\{f_{jm}\}$ and $\{d_{jm}\}$ are the coefficients of the expansion of performance function $f(x)$ with respect to scaling functions $\{\varphi_{jm}\}$ and wavelets $\{\psi_{jm}\}$ of general (dyadic) Haar wavelet, respectively.

Proof:

The coefficient of f with respect to φ_{jm} is

$$\int_X f(x)\varphi_{jm}dx = \frac{\int\limits_{X_{jm}} f(x)dx}{\mu(x_{jm})} = f_{jm}$$

The coefficient of f with respect to ψ_{jm} is

$$\int_X f(x)\psi_{jm}dx = \frac{\int\limits_{X_{j+1,2m+1}} f(x)dx - \int\limits_{X_{j+1,2m}} f(x)dx}{2\mu(x_{j+1,2m})} = \frac{f_{j+1,2m+1} - f_{j+1,2m}}{2} = d_{jm}$$

Theorem 7.3

If $\{[f]_i\}$ is a series of quotient functions approximating to f on (X, d), then

(1) The quotient function $[f]_i(\{f_{im}\})$ at the i-th level is the coefficient of the expansion of $f(x)$ on scaling function base $\{\varphi_{im}, m = 1, 2, ..., 2^i\}$ of the general Haar wavelet at the i-th level (multi-resolution).
(2) The quotient incremental function $\{d_{im}\}$ at the i-th level is the coefficient of the expansion of $f(x)$ on the general Haar wavelet base $\{\psi_{im}\}$.
(3) Formula (7.9) is the transformation relation between quotient functions $[f]$ and quotient incremental functions in the quotient space approximation.

It's noted that although Formula (7.9) is obtained under the dyadic assumption, the similar but more complex result can be got in general cases. In multi-resolution analysis, the dyadic wavelet with n levels has 2^n basis functions (wavelets), so the number of coefficients in the wavelet expansion of $f(x)$ is 2^n. But in Formula (7.9), the number of coefficients is only n simply. Of course, the total number of values in $\{d_{im}\}$ is $2^n - 1$.

7.2.3 The Relation between Quotient Space Approximation and Wavelet Analysis

7.2.3.1 The Meaning of Wavelet Analysis

We will explain the physical significance of wavelet analysis from the quotient space approximation point of view. From Section 7.3, $[f]_2$ is a quotient function obtained from refining space $[X]_1$, or from adjusting function $[f]_1$. It can also be represented by the quotient function on $[X]_2$ directly. If adding a quotient incremental function $[D]_1$, then we have $[f]_1 \oplus [D]_1 = [f]_2$. By recursion, we have a series form

$$f = [f]_1 \oplus [D]_1 \oplus [D]_2 \oplus ... \oplus [D]_n \oplus ...$$

where $\oplus$ indicates the 'sum' obtained from Formula (7.9).

Generally, $[f]_n = [f]_{n-1} \oplus [D]_{n-1}$.

From the multi-granular computing point of view, term $[D]_{n-1}$ represents the variation of f, when the grain-size changing from the n-1-th level to the n-th level, i.e., the rate of change (frequency) at each grain-size. The finer the grain-size, or the bigger the n, the higher the changing frequency of $\{[D_n]\}$. So $\{[D_n]\}$ is just the so-called 'wavelet'. From a mathematical view point, when replacing the sequential convergence-based quotient space approximation by the series convergence-based one, 'wavelet' is an inevitable product. 'Wavelet' is the description of the difference between two adjacent quotient space approximations.

7.2.3.2 The Comparison between Wavelet and Quotient Space Approximation

In wavelet analysis, it's needed to choose a set of complete, orthonormal basis functions in a functional space, and then a square-integrable function is represented by a wavelet series with respect to the base. The method allows the commonality across different applications. In quotient space approximation, for a given function, it's needed to choose a specific domain partition method, and then to approximate the quotient functions (or quotient incremental functions). In the domain partition process, when the incremental value d_{jm} of quotient functions in some equivalence class is rather large, the class is refined. When the value d_{jm} in some equivalence class is small enough, the partition stops. The partition can be adjusted dynamically. This 'customized' method is flexible and personalized. Therefore, in wavelet analysis, for a kind of functions, we need to choose a proper wavelet base that is difficult generally. In quotient space approximation, it's only needed to construct a proper quotient function for a specific function that is an easier task.

7.2.3.3 Different Forms of Quotient Functions

In the above discussion, the quotient functions are defined by the mean of values of the given original function. The quotient functions can also be defined by the sum of values of the given original function.

Assume that f is a performance function on X. $\{[X]_i\}$ is a set of hierarchical quotient spaces. The sequence of quotient spaces is required to be dimidiate, not necessarily halved. Let quotient functions be

$$\{g_{im}\}, i > 0, m = 0, 1, ... 2^{i-1} - 1$$

$$g_0 = \int f(x)dx$$

The corresponding quotient incremental functions $\{e_{im}\}$ are defined as

$$e_{i-1,m} = (g_{i,2m+1} - g_{,2m}), i > 0, m = 0, 1, ..., 2^{i-1} - 1 \tag{7.12}$$

We have

$$g_{i,2m+1} = (g_{i-1,m} + e_{i-1,m})/2$$
$$g_{i,2m} = (g_{i-1,m} - e_{i,m})/2, i > 0, m = 0, 1, ..., 2^{i-1} - 1 \tag{7.13}$$

Definition 7.19

Define an i-dimensional vector as

$$< \underline{a} >_i = (< a >_{i,1}/2^i, < a >_{i,2}/2^{i-1}, ..., < a >_{i,k}/2^{i-k+1}, ..., < a >_{i,i}/2)$$

Definition 7.20

Define an i-dimensional vector as

$$e([a]_i) = \left(e_{0,0}, e_{1,[a]_1}, ..., e_{i-1,[a]_{i-1}} \right)$$

Proposition 7.5

The quotient function and quotient incremental function defined by Formulas (7.12) and (7.13) have the following properties.

$$[g]_i(a) = g_0/2^i + \sum_k < \underline{a} >_{i,k} e([a]_i)_k \tag{7.14}$$

$$f_{ik} = g_k/\mu(S_{ik}), i = 1, ..., n, k = 0, 1, ..., 2^k - 1 \tag{7.15}$$

Proof:

Similar to the proof in Theorem 7.3, by recursion, the results can be obtained directly.

It's noted that when the partition is not halved, g_{ik} may be obtained by Formulas (7.12)–(7.14), and again f_{ik} and d_{ik} may be obtained from Formula (7.15).

We show that the series form of quotient space approximation is equivalent to the second-generation wavelets. This means that many mature tools in wavelet analysis can be transformed to quotient space-based granular computing, for example, lifting scheme, fast lifting wavelet transform, etc.

Further, other methods in the second-generation wavelets can also be applied to performance, stability, robustness, and convergence analysis of systems besides the attribute functions that we have discussed.

7.3 Fractal Geometry and Quotient Space Analysis

7.3.1 Introduction

A famous Sierpinski carpet is shown in Fig. 7.2. It's a typical fractal graph. From the quotient space view point, it's a chain of quotient spaces, where X_0 has one element, X_1 has four and X_2 has 13 elements. Therefore, the concepts of quotient space and fractal geometry have a close relation. We will discuss them using the quotient space approximation principle in the following sections.

7.3.2 Iterated Function Systems

In order to investigate fractal graphs from quotient space theory, the concept of quotient fractals is established first. Then, the quotient fractals are used to approximate fractal graphs. Its procedure is the following. An equivalence relation is defined through a mapping. A corresponding chain of hierarchical quotient spaces is built by the equivalence

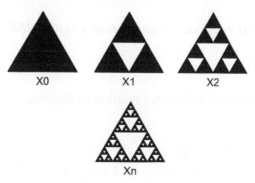

Figure 7.2: A Sierpinski Carpet

relation. Then, quotient mappings are set up on the quotient spaces. Finally, quotient fractals are obtained from the quotient mappings.

Definition 7.19

A set $\{w_i : (X, d) \to (X, d), i = 1, ..., n\}$ of compressed mappings on a compact metric space (X, d) is given, where compression factor $s_i < 1$. Let $s = \min\{s_i, i = 1, ...n\}$. It is called an iterated function system on X, simply denoted by $\{X, w_i, s_i, i = 1, ..., n\}$.

Definition 7.20

Assume that (X, d) is a complete metric space. $x \in X$, $B \in H(x)$, where $H(x)$ is a power set of X. Define $d(x, B) = \min\{d(x, y), y \in B\}$. $d(x, B)$ is called a distance from point x to set B.

Definition 7.21

Assume that (X, d) is a complete metric space. Sets $A, B \in H(x)$, define $d(A, B) = \max\{d(x, B), x \in A\}$. $d(A, B)$ is called a distance from set $A \in H(x)$ to set $B \in H(x)$.

Definition 7.22

(X, d) is a complete metric space. The Hausdorff distance between points A and B on $H(x)$ is defined as $h(A, B) \leq d(A, B) \vee d(B, A)$.

The main theorem in iterated function systems is the following.

Theorem 7.4 (Attractor Theorem)

Assume that $\{X, W_i, s, i = 1, 2, \cdots, n\}$ is an iterated function system on X. W is a fractal mapping on X. Then, $h(W(A), W(B)) \leq sh(A, B)$ holds on $(H(x), h(d))$. Namely, there exists a unique fixed point P on $H(x)$, i.e.,

$$P = W(P) = \bigcup_{i=1}^{n} W_i(P)$$

P is a corresponding fractal graph on iterated function system $IFS = W$.

7.3.3 Quotient Fractals

A mapping is used to define an equivalence relation as follows.

Definition 7.23

An iterated function system $IFS = \{X, w_i, s_i, i = 1, 2, \cdots, n\}$ on X is given. Construct $B_i = w_i(X), i = 1, ..., n$ and $B_0 = X - \bigcup_{i=1}^{n} B_i$. Letting $X_1 = \{B_i, i = 0, 1, ..., n\}$, then X_1 is a quotient space of X.

Now, X_1 is partitioned as follows, i.e., B_i is partitioned as B_{ij}. Let

$$B_{i,j} = W_i(B_j) = W_i W_j(X), i = 1, ..., n, j = 1, ..., n \quad \text{and} \quad B_{i0} = W_i(B_0), i = 1, 2, ..., n$$

We obtain

$$B_i = \bigcup_{j=0}^{n} B_{ij}, i = 1, 2, ..., n \tag{7.16}$$

Set B_0 remains unchanged.

Then, we have a partition of X denoted by X_2. From Formula (7.16), it's known that X_1 is a quotient space of X_2.

By induction, assume that X_{k-1} is a known quotient space. For its elements, the partition procedure is the following. Let

$$B_{i_1 i_2 ... i_k} = W_{i_1} W_{i_2} ... W_{i_k}(X), i_1, i_2, ..., i_{k-1}, i_k = 1, ..., n$$
$$B_{i_1 i_2 ... i_{k-1} 0} = W_{i_1} W_{i_2} ... W_{i_{k-1}}(B_0), i_1, i_2, ..., i_{k-1} = 1, ..., n$$

We obtain

$$X_k = \left\{ B_{i_1 i_2 ... i_k}, i_1, i_2, ..., i_{k-1}, i_k = 1, ..., n \text{ and } B_{i_1 i_2 ... i_{j-1} 0}, i_1, i_2, ..., i_{j-1} = 1, ..., n, j = 2, ... k \right\}$$

Obviously, $X_1, ... X_k, ... X$ compose a chain of hierarchical quotient spaces. For simplicity, the element $B_{i_1, ..., i_k}$ of X_k is denoted by its subscript $(i_1, ..., i_k)$ in the following discussion.

Definition 7.24

Define a mapping W_i^k on X_k as $\forall a \in X_k$, $W_i^k(a) = p_k(W_i(a)), i = 1, ..., n$, where $p_k : X \rightarrow X_k$ is a nature projection and $W_i(a) = \{ W_i(x) | x \in a \}$.

Definition 7.25

Define $P_k = p_k(P)$ on X_k, where P is an invariant subset on X corresponding to mapping W, i.e., a fractal graph.

Definition 7.26

$\{ (X_k, W^k, P_k), k = 1, 2, ... \}$ is called a quotient fractal model of iterated function system (X, W, P).

Theorem 7.4

If an iterated function system *IFS* on X is given, then it corresponds to a chain of hierarchical quotient sets on X.

Proof:

Assume that mapping $W_i, i = 1, ..., n$. Let $B_i = W_i(X), i = 1, ..., n$ and $B_0 = X - \cup_{i=1}^{n} B_i$.

(1) Assume that $B_i \cap B_j = \varnothing, j \neq i$. Then, $\{B_0, B_1, ..., B_n\}$ compose a partition of X. Its corresponding quotient space is denoted by X_1. Again, let $B_{i,j} = W_i(B_j) = W_i W_j(X), i = 0, 1, ..., n, j = 1, ..., n$ and $B_{i0} = B_i - \cup_{j=1}^{n} B_{ij}$. Then, $\{B_{ij}\}$ compose a partition of X denoted by X_2. Obviously, X_1 is a quotient space of X_2.

By induction, define

$$B_{i_1 i_2 ... i_k} = W_i W_i ... W_{i_k}(X), i_1, i_2, ..., i_{k-1} = 0, 1, ..., n; i_k = 1, ..., n$$

Let

$$B_{i_1, i_2, ..., i_{k-1}, 0} = B_{i, i, ..., i_{k-1}} - \overset{n}{\underset{j=1}{\cup}} B_{i, i, ..., i_{k-1}, j}$$

Obviously, $\{B_{i, i, ..., i_k}\}$ compose a partition of X denoted by X_k. It's easy to show that X_{k-1} is a quotient space of X_k.

Therefore, $\{X_1, X_2, ...\}$ is a chain of quotient sets of X or a chain of quotient spaces corresponding to an iterated function system.

(2) When some B_i and B_j are overlapping, i.e., $B_i \cap B_j \neq \varnothing, j \neq i$. An abstract space $X_1 = \{0, 1, ..., n\}$ can be constructed, where element i corresponds to set B_i. Define an abstract space $X_2 = \{(i,j), i, j = 0, 1, ..., n\}$, where element (i,j) corresponds to set B_{ij}, i.e., $X_2 = \{0, 1, ..., n\}^2$.

Generally, define $X_k = \{0, 1, ..., n\}^k$, where element $(i_1, i_2, ..., i_k)$ corresponds to $B_{i_1, i, ..., i_k}, 0 \leq i_j \leq n, j = 1, 2, ..., k$. Let $X = \{0, 1, ..., n\}^{\infty}$. The point on X is an infinite sequence composed by 0,1,...,n, i.e., $x \in X, x = (x_1, x_2, ...)$.

Similarly, we may have a chain $\{X_1, X_2, ..., X_n, ...\}$ of quotient sets.

We have a profound relation between quotient fractals and fractal graphs as follows.

Theorem 7.5 (Quotient Fractal Approximation Theorem)

We have the following properties.

Property 1

$$x = (x_1, ..., x_k), x \in P_k \Leftrightarrow \forall j, x_j \neq 0$$

Property 2

P_k is an invariant subset on X_k corresponding to mapping $W^k = (W_1^k, ..., W_n^k)$.

Property 3

$IFS = \{X, w_i, s_i, i = 1, 2, \cdots, n\}$ is an iterated function system on X. Then, $\lim_{k \to \infty} P_k = P$, its convergence is based on the Hausdorff distance defined on the power set of X.

Property 4

$$x \in X, \ x = (x_1, ..., x_k, ...), x \in P \Leftrightarrow \forall j, x_j \neq 0$$

7.3.4 Conclusions

Property 3 in Section 7.3.3 is the quotient fractal approximation theorem of fractal graphs. It means that in fractal geometry we can still use a set of simple quotient spaces to approximate the original space so that the computational complexity is reduced. This is just the basic principle of quotient space approximation method and the multi-granular computing as well.

7.4 The Expansion of Quotient Space Theory

7.4.1 Introduction

The quotient space theory we have discussed so far is based on the following two main assumptions. (1) The domain structure is limited to topology. (2) The domain granulation is based on equivalence relations, i.e., classification without overlap. Now, we will relax the two restrictions. First, we consider the structures formed by closure operations that are broader than topological ones. Second, domain granulation will be extended from equivalence relations to tolerance relations.

7.4.2 Closure Operation-Based Quotient Space Theory

There is a variety of closure operations, so different structures can be defined by the operations. The domain structures described by closure operations are broader than topological ones generally. For example, the pre-topology defined by closure operations under the Cech's sense is more universal than well-known topology defined by open sets (Cech, 1966). But the topology defined by Kuratowski closure operation is equivalent to well-known topology.

Now, we introduce some basic concepts about closure space (see Addenda A for more details).

Definition 7.27

Assume that X is a domain. If mapping $cl : 2^X \to 2^X$ satisfies the following axioms, where 2^X is a power set of X,

$$(\mathbf{cl1})cl(\varnothing) = \varnothing$$

$$(\mathbf{cl2})\forall A \subseteq X,\ A \subseteq cl(A)$$

$$(\mathbf{cl3})\forall A \subseteq X,\ \forall B \subseteq X,\ cl(A \cup B) = cl(A) \cup cl(B)$$

cl is called a closure operation on X, correspondingly (X, cl) is called a closure space, $cl(A)$ is a $cl-$ closure of A, and for simplicity, $cl(A)$ is indicated by $\overline{A}$.

Proposition 7.6

Assume that (X, cl) is a closure space, then

(1) $cl(X) = X$
(2) $\forall A \subseteq X, \forall B \subseteq X$, if $A \subseteq B$, then $cl(A) \subseteq cl(B)$
(3) For any family $X_i (i \in \mathcal{I})$ of subsets on X, $cl(\bigcap_{i \in \mathcal{I}} X_i) \subseteq \bigcap_{i \in \mathcal{I}} cl(X_i)$.

Definition 7.28

$C(X)$ is a set of whole closure operations defined on X, i.e., $C(X) = \{\mu | \mu$ is the closure operation on $X\}$. Define a binary relation $\leq$ on $C(X)$ as

$$\forall \mu, \nu \in C(X),\ \nu \leq \mu \Leftrightarrow \forall A \subseteq X,\ \nu(A) \subseteq \mu(A)$$

If $\nu \leq \mu$, then μ is called coarser than ν, or ν is finer than μ.

Proposition 7.7

Binary relation $\leq$ is a semi-order relation on $C(X)$. $(C(X), \leq)$ has the greatest element μ_1 and the least element μ_0. For $\forall A \subseteq X$, if $A \neq \varnothing$ then $\mu_1(A) = X$, otherwise $\mu_1(\varnothing) = \varnothing$. And for $\forall A \subseteq X$, $\mu_0(A) = A$. Furthermore, any subset $\{\mu_i | i \in I\}$ on $C(X)$ and $\forall A \subseteq X$, $(\sup\{\mu_i | i \in \mathcal{I}\})(A) = \cup \{\mu_i(A) | i \in \mathcal{I}\}$ holds, i.e., $C(X)$ is order complete with respect to '$\leq$'.

7.4.2.1 The Construction of Quotient Closure and its Property

(X, cl, f) is a triplet, where cl is a closure operation on X, f is a set of attribute functions. Assume that R is an equivalence relation on X, $[X]$ is its corresponding quotient set, and $p : X \to [X]$ is a nature projection. $[cl]$ on $[X]$ is a closure operation induced from projection p with respect to closure operation cl, i.e.,

$$\forall U \subseteq [X], [cl](U) = p\big(cl\big(p^{-1}(U)\big)\big)$$

Especially, when cl is a topological closure operation, the structure decided by $[cl]$ is a corresponding quotient topology on $[X]$.

Assume that $R_1, R_2 \in \mathcal{R}$ and $R_2 < R_1$, $p_i : X \rightarrow [X]_i$ is a nature projection, and $([X]_i, [cl]_i), i = 1, 2$, is a quotient space having a closure structure, or simply a quotient closure structure. Since $R_2 < R_1$, $p_{12} : [X]_1 \rightarrow [X]_2$ is a nature projection from $[X]_1$ to its quotient set $[X]_2$. $[cl]_{12}$ on $[X]_2$ is a closure operation induced from projection p_{12} with respect to closure operation $[cl]_1$. Thus, $[cl]_2 = [cl]_{12}$ (Cech, 1966). Generally, the similar result can be obtained for a chain of equivalence relations. Then we have the following proposition.

Proposition 7.8

Assume that $R_n < R_{n-1} < \cdots < R_2 < R_1$ is a chain of equivalence relations on (X, cl). $p_i : X \rightarrow [X]_i$ is a nature projection. $([X]_i, [cl]_i)$, $i = 1, 2, \cdots, n$, is a corresponding quotient closure space. $\{([X]_i, [cl]_i) | i = 0, 1, ..., n\}$ composes a hierarchical structure, where $([X]_0, [cl]_0) = (X, cl)$.

The similar falsity-preserving principle in closure spaces is the following (Chen, 2005).

Proposition 7.9

If $A \subseteq X$ is a connected subset on (X, cl), the image $p(A)$ of A under the projection p is a connected subset on $([X], [cl])$.

Theorem 7.6 (Falsity-Preserving Principle)

P is a problem on the domain of (X, cl). $[P]$ is the corresponding problem on the domain of $([X], [cl])$. If $[P]$ has no solution on $[X]$, then P also has no solution on X.

From Chapter 1, it's known that a semi-order relation under the quotient mapping only maintains the reflexivity and transitivity but does not necessarily maintain anti-symmetry generally. For the closure spaces, we will prove that the quasi-semi-order structures are invariant under the quotient mapping (projection), with the help of the continuity of the mapping, but the semi-order structure cannot maintain unchanged under the mapping generally.

Proposition 7.10

Assume that $(X, \leq)$ is a quasi-semi-order space. R is an equivalence relation on X, and $[X]$ is the corresponding quotient set. Then, there exists a quasi-semi-order $[\leq]$ on $[X]$ such that the nature projection is order-preserving, i.e., $\forall x, y \in X$, we have

$$x \leq y \Rightarrow p(x)[\leq]p(y)$$

Proof:

Since $\leq$ is a quasi-semi order on X, define an operation induced from $\leq$ as follows

$$cl(U) = \{y \in X \mid \exists x \in U, \ s.t. \ y \leq x\}, \forall U \subseteq X$$

It's easy to prove that cl is a closure operation on X. In fact, cl is a topologic closure operation with the Alexandroff property. If from closure space (X, cl) define a quasi-semi-order $\leq^*$ as $x \leq^* y \Leftrightarrow x \in cl(\{y\})$, then $\leq^*$ is the same as $\leq$. This means that closure operation cl and quasi-semi order $\leq$ are interdependent.

If $\mu = [cl]$ is a quotient closure operation on $[X]$ with respect to cl, then $([X], \mu)$ is a topologic closure space. Define a quasi-semi-order $\leq_\mu$ on $[X]$ as

$$\forall a, b \in [X], a \leq_\mu b \Leftrightarrow a \in \mu(\{b\})$$

Finally, we show that $\forall x, y \in X, x \leq y \Rightarrow p(x) \leq_\mu p(y)$. In fact, we have

$$x \leq y \Leftrightarrow x \in cl(\{y\})$$
$$\Rightarrow p(x) \in \mu(p(\{y\})) = \mu(p(y)) \ (p \text{ is continuous on } x)$$
$$\Leftrightarrow p(x) \leq_\mu p(y)$$

In summary, there exists a quasi-semi-order relation on the quotient structure of a quasi-semi-order space such that the corresponding nature projection is order-preserving.

The order-preserving processing processes of quotient closure spaces are shown in Fig. 7.3, where $cl_\leq$ indicates the closure topology induced from $\leq$, $[cl_\leq]$ is its corresponding quotient topology, $[\leq]$ is a quasi-semi-order on $[X]$ induced from $\leq$, $\leq_\mu$ is a quasi-semi-order induced from topology μ, and $[cl]$ on $[X]$ is a topology induced from cl.

The whole quasi-semi-order relations satisfying reflexivity and transitivity on a domain and the whole Alexandroff topologies on the domain are one—one correspondence. Especially, the whole semi-order relations, i.e., the quasi-semi-order satisfying anti-symmetry as well, and whole Alexandroff topologies satisfying T_0-separation axiom are one—one correspondence. So the order structure may be regarded as a specific topological structure, and a specific closure structure spontaneously.

Since T_0-separation axiom does not satisfy divisibility, the order relation $[\leq]$ on quotient space $[X]$ of semi-order space $(X, \leq)$ that is constructed by the above method does not

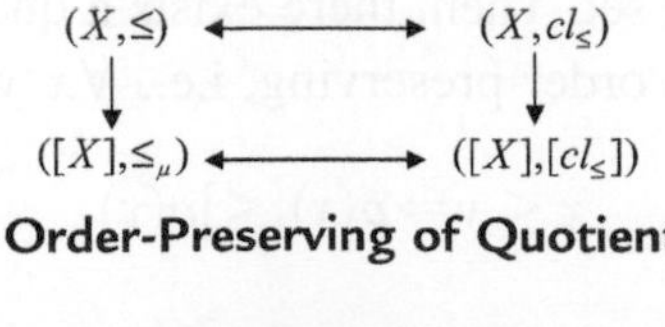

$$
\begin{array}{ccc}
(X, \leq) & \longleftrightarrow & (X, cl_\leq) \\
\downarrow & & \downarrow \\
([X], \leq_\mu) & \longleftrightarrow & ([X], [cl_\leq])
\end{array}
$$

Figure 7.3: The Order-Preserving of Quotient Closure Spaces

have anti-symmetry generally, although its nature projection is an order-preserving mapping. As in Chapter 1, by merging and decomposing, the original equivalence relation R can be changed to $R*$ such that corresponding relation $[\leq]$ satisfies the anti-symmetry in space $([X]^*, [\leq])$.

7.4.2.2 The Synthesis of Different Grained Worlds

So far we have shown that a new space can be constructed from given spaces through synthesis methods, when their structure is topologic. We also show that the synthetic space is the least upper bound one, and the projection from the synthetic space on the given spaces plays an important role. In fact, the synthetic principle can be represented as an optimization problem with respect to $p_i \circ Z = Z_i$, where $p_i : X \to X_i$ is a projection from the original to quotient spaces, Z and Z_i represent the domain, topological structure, or attribute function of the original and quotient spaces, respectively. The synthetic space is either the least upper bound, or the greatest lower bound space among the given spaces. In this section, we will consider the synthetic problem under the closure structures.

$(X_i, cl_i, f_i), i = 1, 2$ are two different grain-size descriptions of a problem. R_i, cl_i and f_i are the corresponding equivalence relation, closure operation, and attribute function, respectively. $(X^\triangle, cl^\triangle, f^\triangle)$ and $(X_\triangledown, cl_\triangledown, f_\triangledown)$ are the least upper bound and the greatest lower bound spaces constructed from spaces $(X_i, cl_i, f_i), i = 1, 2$, respectively.

Define $R^\triangle = R_1 \cap R_2$. $X^\triangle$ is a quotient set corresponding to $R^\triangle$, and the least upper bound of X_1 and X_2 in partition lattice $\mathcal{P}$. Both X_1 and X_2 are quotient sets of $X^\triangle$. $p^i : X^\triangle \to X_i$ $i = 1, 2$ are their corresponding projections. It's easy to show that for each i, there exists $p^i \circ X^\triangle = X_i$ such that $X^\triangle$ is projected onto X_i by projection p^i, and quotient space $X^\triangle$ satisfies the synthetic principle, i.e., $X^\triangle$ is the coarsest partition among all partitions that satisfy $p^i \circ X^\triangle = X_i$. Dually, define $R_\triangledown = tr(R_1 \cup R_2)$, where $tr(X)$ denotes the set obtained after implementing transitive operation on elements of X. Quotient space $X_\triangledown$ corresponding to $R_\triangledown$ is the greatest lower bound of X_1 and X_2 in partition lattice $\mathcal{P}$. For $i = 1, 2$, $X_\triangledown$ is the quotient set of X_i, and its corresponding projection is $p_i : X_i \to X_\triangledown$. It's easy to show that $X_\triangledown$ satisfies the synthetic principle, i.e., $X_\triangledown$ is the finest partition among all partitions that satisfy $p_i \circ X_i = X_\triangledown$.

According to the synthetic principle, $f^\triangle$ should be defined as the solution of a set $p^i \circ f_i = f^\triangle, i = 1, 2$, of equations. If their solution is not unique, some optimization criteria should be added in order to have an optimal one. Dually, $f_\triangledown$ should be defined as the solution of a set $p_i \circ f_i = f_\triangledown, i = 1, 2$, of equations which similar to solving $f^\triangle$.

A new closure operation can be constructed in the following way, i.e., a new closure operation (or a set of closure operations) can be generated projectively, or inductively by a known mapping (or a set of mappings), respectively. The following proposition shows the relation between the two generation methods.

Proposition 7.11 (Cech, 1966)

f is a surjection from closure space $(\mathcal{Y}, \mu)$ onto closure space $(\mathcal{Z}, \nu)$. If mapping f : $\mathcal{Y} \rightarrow (\mathcal{Z}, \nu)$ projectively generates closure operation μ with respect to closure operation ν, then mapping $f : (\mathcal{Y}, \mu) \rightarrow \mathcal{Z}$ inductively generates closure operation ν with respect to closure operation μ. Dually, g is an injection from closure space $(\mathcal{Y}, \mu)$ to closure space $(\mathcal{Z}, \nu)$. If mapping $g : (\mathcal{Y}, \mu) \rightarrow \mathcal{Z}$ inductively generates closure operation ν with respect to closure operation μ, then mapping $g : \mathcal{Y} \rightarrow (\mathcal{Z}, \nu)$ projectively generates closure operation μ with respect to closure operation ν.

First, we consider the construction of closure operation $cl^{\triangle}$. ν_i is a closure operation on $\mathcal{U}^{\triangle}$ that generated projectively by $p^i : X^{\triangle} \rightarrow X_i$ with respect to closure operation cl_i. Since p^i is a surjection, cl_i is generated inductively by p^i with respect to closure operation ν_i. Space (X_i, cl_i) is a quotient closure space of $(X^{\triangle}, \nu_i)$ with respect to equivalence relation R_i. Defining closure operation $cl^{\triangle}$ as $cl^{\triangle} = inf\{\nu_i | i = 1, 2\}$, then $cl^{\triangle}$ on $X^{\triangle}$ is the coarsest one among all closure operations that make each $p^i (i = 1, 2)$ continuous. Closure space $(X^{\triangle}, cl^{\triangle})$ is the least upper bound of synthetic spaces $(X_i, cl_i), i = 1, 2$, but an explicit expression of $cl^{\triangle}$ cannot be obtained generally.

Dually, the construction of closure operation $cl_{\triangledown}$ is as follows. μ_i is a closure operation on $X_{\triangledown}$ that generated inductively by $p_i : X_i \rightarrow X_{\triangledown}$ with respect to closure operation cl_i, i.e., μ_i is the finest one on $X_{\triangledown}$ among all closure operations that make each p^i $(i = 1, 2)$ continuous. Defining closure operation $cl_{\triangledown}$ as $cl_{\triangledown} = sup\{\mu_i | i = 1, 2\}$, then $cl_{\triangledown}$ is the finest one on $X_{\triangledown}$ among all closure operations that make each $p^i (i = 1, 2)$ continuous. Closure space $(X_{\triangledown}, cl_{\triangledown})$ is the greatest lower one of synthetic spaces (X_i, cl_i) $(i = 1, 2)$. The expression of $cl_{\triangledown}$ is the following.

$$\forall U \subseteq X_{\triangledown}, cl_{\triangledown}(U) = U \cup \left\{ p_i \left(cl_i \left((p_i)^{-1}(U) \right) \right) \middle| i = 1, 2 \right\}$$
$$= \bigcup_i p_i \left(cl_i \left((p_i)^{-1}(U) \right) \right)$$

The synthetic process of quotient closure spaces can intuitively be shown in Fig. 7.4.

7.4.3 Non-Partition Model-Based Quotient Space Theory

The quotient space theory that we have discussed so far is based on a partition model, i.e., a complete lattice composed by all equivalence relations on a domain, or a partition lattice. The quotient space theory based on the partition model that we called traditional theory is too rigorous. Many real problems do not necessarily meet the requirement, for example, classification with overlap, or with incomplete knowledge, etc. If abandoning the transitivity condition in an equivalence relation, then we have a tolerance relation. Tolerance relation is a broader binary relation than the equivalence one, but still has good

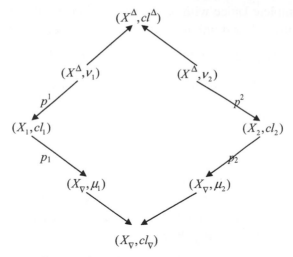

Figure 7.4: The Synthetic Process of Quotient Closure Spaces

attributes. So the tolerance relation-based quotient space theory is a very useful extension of the traditional one.

7.4.3.1 Tolerance Relations

Definition 7.29

R is a binary relation on X. If relation R satisfies reflexivity and symmetry, then it is called tolerance relation (Zuo, 1988).

Definition 7.30

For $\forall x \in X$, define $\langle x \rangle_R$ as a R-relevant class of x, i.e., $\langle x \rangle_R = \{y \in X | xRy\}$. The whole $\langle x \rangle_R$ is denoted by $\langle X \rangle_R$, where $\langle X \rangle_R = \{\langle x \rangle_R | x \in X\}$, for simplicity, $\langle x \rangle_R$ and $\langle X \rangle_R$ are denoted by $\langle x \rangle$ and $\langle X \rangle$ respectively, if it does not cause confusion.

Proposition 7.12

If and only if tolerance relation R satisfies transitivity, then $\langle X \rangle_R$ is a partition of X.

Theorem 7.7

Assume that $\mathcal{S} = \{R_i | i \in \mathcal{I}\}$ is the whole tolerance relations on X, and $\mathcal{I}$ is a set of subscripts.

(1) $\bigcap_{i \in \mathcal{I}} R_i$ and $\bigcup_{i \in \mathcal{I}} R_i$ are tolerance relations on X.

(2) Define a binary relation $\leq$ on $\mathcal{S}$ as

$$\forall i, j \in \mathcal{I}, \forall x, y \in X, R_j \leq R_i \text{ iff } xR_iy \Rightarrow xR_jy$$

S composes a complete lattice with respect to relation $\leq$, denoted by $(S, \leq)$. The intersection operation $\wedge$ and union operation $\vee$ on lattice S are defined as follows.

$$\forall i, j \in \mathcal{I}, \ R_i \wedge R_j = R_i \cup R_j, \ R_i \vee R_j = R_i \cap R_j$$

where $\cap$ and $\cup$ are set intersection and union operations, respectively.

(3) $\forall x \in X, \forall \mathcal{J} \subseteq \mathcal{I}, \ \langle x \rangle_{\underset{i \in \mathcal{J}}{\cap} R_i} = \cap \{ \langle x \rangle_{R_i} | i \in \mathcal{J} \}, \ \langle x \rangle_{\underset{i \in \mathcal{J}}{\cup} R_i} = \cup \{ \langle x \rangle_{R_i} | i \in \mathcal{J} \}$

The proof of the theorem is obvious.

A complete lattice S, composed by all tolerance relations on a domain, is similar to a complete lattice $\mathcal{R}$, composed by all equivalence relations on the domain or a partition lattice $\mathcal{P}$. Both can be used to describe multi-granular worlds but they are different. In partition, the classes are mutually disjointed. In classification based on tolerance relations the classes do not necessarily mutually disjoint.

7.4.3.2 Tolerance Relation-Based Quotient Space Theory

(X, f, T) is a triplet, where T and f are topological structure and attribute function on X, respectively. $R \in S$ is a tolerance relation. We will discuss three basic problems, i.e., projection, property preserving, and the synthesis of multi-granular worlds, under tolerance relations.

Definition 7.31

t is a mapping from set X to set Y. An equivalence relation $\equiv_f$ on X can be induced from t as follows

$$\forall x_1, x_2 \in X, x_1 \equiv_f x_2 \Leftrightarrow t(x_1) = t(x_2)$$

For simplicity, $\equiv_f$ is denoted by $\equiv$. $[x]$, $x \in X$, is an equivalence class with respect to equivalence relation $\equiv$. $[X]$ is the corresponding quotient set, and $p : X \rightarrow [X]$ is a nature projection.

Definition 3.30

X and Y are topologic spaces. $t : X \rightarrow Y$ is a quotient mapping. If

(1) t is a surjection
(2) for $A \subseteq Y$, $t^{-1}(A)$ is an open set on X

then, A is an open set on Y. Accordingly, the topology on Y is called quotient topology with respect to mapping t (Xiong, 1981; You, 1997).

Proposition 7.13

t is a quotient mapping from topologic space (X, T) to topologic space Y. $\equiv$ is an equivalence relation on $[X]$ induced from t. $([X], [T])$ is a quotient topologic space with respect to nature projection $p : X \to [X]$. Then, topologic spaces $([X], [T])$ and Y are homeomorphism, where homeomorphous mapping $h : [X] \to Y$ satisfies $h \circ p = t$, equivalently, $h^{-1} \circ t = p$.

The proposition shows that when $t : X \to Y$ is a quotient mapping, Y can be regarded as a quotient space of X. t is just the corresponding pasting mapping. In fact, quotient spaces and quotient mappings are closely related concepts. The nature projection discussed in Chapter 1 is a specific quotient mapping that satisfies the conditions (1) and (2) in Definition 7.32.

Definition 7.33

t is a surjection from (X, T) onto $\langle X \rangle$. For $\forall x \in X, t(x) = \langle x \rangle$, define a topology on $\langle X \rangle$ as $\langle T \rangle = \{ A \subseteq \langle X \rangle | t^{-1}(A) \in T \}$. That is, $\langle T \rangle$ is the finest among topologies that make the surjection t from topologic space (X, T) onto $(\langle X \rangle, \langle T \rangle)$ continuous.

Proposition 7.14

t is a quotient mapping from space (X, T) to $\langle X \rangle$. Topologic spaces $(\langle X \rangle, \langle T \rangle)$ and $([X], [T])$ are homeomorphism, where $([X], [T])$ is a pasting space induced from t.

Although R is not an equivalence relation, i.e., $\langle X \rangle$ cannot compose a partition on X, since there is no distinction among homeomorphous spaces in some sense, from Proposition 3.17 it's shown that the traditional quotient space theory is still available to the tolerance relation. But since the elements on $\langle X \rangle$ as subsets on X are no longer mutually disjointed, the computational complexity discussed in Chapter 2 will not hold, likely increases.

The construction of quotient attribute $\langle f \rangle$ is the same as that of a traditional one. Therefore, if tolerance relation R and space (X, f, T) are given, the quotient space $(\langle X \rangle, \langle f \rangle, \langle T \rangle)$ can be constructed.

Similar to the traditional theory, we have the following property.

Proposition 7.15

If $U \subseteq X$ is a connected subset on X, then $t(U)$ is a connected subset on $\langle X \rangle$.

Now, we consider the order preserving property. Assume that $\leq$ on $(X, \leq)$ is a quasi-semi-order structure. T on (X, T) is an Alexzandroff topology determined by the quasi-semi-order $\leq$. $\langle T \rangle$ on $(\langle X \rangle, \langle T \rangle)$ is a quotient topology with respect to quotient mapping $t : X \to \langle X \rangle$. Define a binary relation $\leq_{<T>}$ on $\langle X \rangle$ as follows

$$\forall a, b \in \langle X \rangle, a \leq_{<T>} b \Leftrightarrow \forall u(a), \ b \in u(a)$$

where $u(a)$ is an open neighborhood of a.

Relation $\leq_{<T>}$ is just a specified quasi-semi-order determined by $\langle T \rangle$. Since $(\langle X \rangle, \langle T \rangle)$ and $([X], [T])$ are homeomorphism, from Proposition 3.13, there exists a quasi-semi-order $[\leq]$ on $[X]$ such that $\forall x, y \in X$, if $x < y$ then $[x] \leq [y]$. The following proposition shows that quasi-semi-order relation $\leq_{<T>}$ has the order preserving property.

Proposition 7.16

If $x, y \in X$ and $x \leq y$, then $\langle x \rangle \leq_{<T>} \langle y \rangle$.

Proof:

Since $([X], [T])$ and $(\langle X \rangle, \langle T \rangle)$ are homeomorphous, the quasi-semi-order $[\leq]$ on $[X]$ induced from $[T]$ and the quasi-semi-order $\leq_{<T>}$ on $\langle X \rangle$ induced from $<T>$ are equivalent.

Again from the order preserving of $[\leq]$, $\leq_{<T>}$ on $\langle X \rangle$ has order-preserving as well.

The order-preserving property in tolerance relation-based quotient spaces can be shown in Fig. 7.5 intuitively.

$(X, \leq)$ is a semi-order structure. T on (X, T) satisfies T_0-separation axiom. $(\langle X \rangle, \langle T \rangle)$ is a quotient topology on $\langle X \rangle$ corresponding to quotient mapping $t : \mathcal{U} \to \langle \mathcal{U} \rangle$. $\leq_{<T>}$ is a quasi-semi-order induced from $\langle T \rangle$. In general, $\leq_{<T>}$ does not satisfy the anti-symmetry.

When we discuss the order-preserving property, the homeomorphism of topologic spaces $(\langle X \rangle, \langle T \rangle)$ and $([X], [T])$ plays an important role. Similarly, the above homeomorphous relation can still play a significant role in the synthetic problem.

7.4.4 Granular Computing and Quotient Space Theory

Quotient space-based problem-solving theory is a multi-granular computing model under the framework of set theory. We have dealt with the following problems. First, the projection problem is that given a quotient set, to find the representations of attribute and structure on the set, i.e., the descriptions of the coarse-grained world and the relation to the original one. Second, the synthesis problem is that given different views of the world, to find a new understanding of the world based on the known knowledge. Third, the reasoning problem is the reasoning over different grain-size worlds. The final problem is

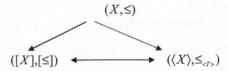

Figure 7.5: The Order-Preserving Property in Tolerance Relation

how to choose a proper grain-size world in order to reduce the computational complexity of multi-granular computing.

Now, we discuss granulation and granular computing from the quotient space theory view point.

7.4.4.1 Granule, Granulation and Granular World

In quotient space theory, a 'granule' is defined as a subset in a space (domain). In the partition model, the subset is an equivalence class and an element in its quotient space, whose inner structure is determined by the corresponding partition. Each subset can be represented by a complete graph. For example, in a grained level $\{[1],[4]\}=\{\{1,2,3\},\{4,5\}\}$, element [1] has three components (elements) $\{1,2,3\}$ and can be represented by a complete graph. Similarly, element [4] has two components $\{4,5\}$ and can be represented by a complete graph as well. Any two elements are mutually disjointed. In the tolerance relation model, the subset consists of all elements that have tolerance relations. They may have a center that can be represented by a stellate graph. They may have several centers that can also be represented by a stellate graph, when the centers are regarded as a whole. For example, in a grained level $\{<1>,<2>,<4>,<5>\}=\{\{\mathbf{1},2\},\{\mathbf{1},2,3,4\},\{2,\mathbf{3},\mathbf{4},5\},\{\mathbf{3},\mathbf{4},5\}\}$, where 'bold' Arabic numerals indicate 'centers'. Element $<1>$ is a graph with component '1' as a center. Element $<4>$ is a graph with components $\{\mathbf{3},\mathbf{4}\}$ as centers, while components '2' and '5' do not have any connected edge.

In quotient space theory, the granulation criterion is equivalence or tolerance relation. The relation may be induced from attributes, or relevant to them. This is different from the rough set theory. When an equivalence or tolerance relation is given, we have a coarse-grained world. In the world, each element can be regarded as independent; while as subsets in the original domain, they may be mutually disjointed or have an overlapping portion. In addition, a coarse-grained world may have a structure, for example, topologic, closure or order structure. The structure is obtained by a quotient mapping from the original world. The continuity of the quotient mapping plays an important role that we have discussed in previous sections adequately.

7.4.4.2 The Multi-Granular Structure

When a granulation criterion is given, we have a grained world. When several granulation criteria are given, then we have a multi-grained world. What relation exists within the multi-granular world? In other words, what structure the multi-granular world has? In partition model, all equivalence relations compose a complete lattice. Correspondingly, all partitions compose a complete lattice as well. In the tolerance relation model, all tolerance relations compose a complete lattice. Specially, a chain of equivalence relations or tolerance relations is chosen, we have a hierarchical structure. In addition, the existence of complete lattice guarantees the closeness of the newly constructed grained worlds.

7.4.4.3 Granular Computing

In granular computing, the computational and inference object is 'granules'. Quotient space theory deals with several basic problems of granular computing. For example, considering the computation of quotient attribute functions in a certain grained level, since the arguments of the functions are 'granules', their values may adopt the maximum, minimum, or mean of the attribute functions of all elements in the granule. If an algebraic operation is defined on a domain, it's needed to consider the existence and uniqueness of its quotient operation on a certain grained level. We have discussed this problem in Chapter 4.

The descriptions of a problem in several grain-size worlds are given, how to choose a proper grain-size world to carry out the problem solving? Quotient space theory deals with the problem by information synthesis that mirrors the characteristics of human problem solving, i.e., viewing the same problem from different granularities, translating from one abstraction level to the others freely, and solving the problem at a proper grained level. Information synthesis includes domain, structure and attribute function. Here, the homomorphism principle plays an important role.

Falsity-preserving property is very important in the inference over a multi-granular world. With the help of the continuity of quotient mappings and the connectivity of sets, and considering the structure of domain, the computational complexity can be reduced by multi-granular computing based on quotient space theory.

7.4.5 Protein Structure Prediction — An Application of Tolerance Relations

In the section, we will use the binary relation satisfying anti-reflexivity and symmetry, i.e., equivalent to a tolerance relation, to define the sequence adjacency and topology adjacency in the amino acid sequence folding. Furthermore, we will explain the enhancement method for estimating the lower bound of energy of a protein obtained by the folding of its amino acid sequence, using the concept of tolerance relations.

7.4.5.1 Problem

Protein structure prediction is the prediction of the three-dimensional structure of a protein from its amino acid sequence that is a hot topic in bioinformatics (Martin, 2000). Generally, there are three methods to dealing with the problem, molecular dynamics, protein structure prediction and homology modeling. Different protein models may be established depending on the ways of describing the protein molecular and treating the interaction between amino acid residues and solution. The experimental result for small proteins implies that the primary state of proteins approaches the minimum of free energy. This widely accepted assumption becomes the foundation of protein structure prediction from a given amino acid sequence by means of computation.

Due to the complexity and large scale of protein structure, the simple models are adopted generally. A lattice model is one of the well-known models (Dill et al., 1995). In lattice models, each amino acid residue is represented as an equal size and is confined to regular lattices, the connection between them is assumed to be the same length. For simplicity, *2D* rectangle or *3D* cuboid lattice point representation of lattice models is adopted. We will only discuss the *2D* lattice model below.

HP lattice model is a representative one (Lau and Dill, 1989, 1990). In the model, amino acids are divided into two categories: hydrophobic (*H*) and hydrophilic (*P*). The hydrophilic force is the important driving force behind the folding process. Under the impact of the force, after the folding of the amino acid sequence, the hydrophobic amino acids will concentrate in the center of the protein as far as possible in order for them to keep out of water. In Fig. 7.6(a) the inappropriate folding, (b) the appropriate folding of amino acid sequences are shown.

A sequence $S = s_1 s_2 \cdots s_n$ of amino acids is given, where $\forall k \in \{1, 2, \cdots, n\}$, $s_k \in \{H, P\}$. After the folding of S, we have protein P represented in a *2D-HP* model as follows. Amino acids s_1 and s_2 are confined in coordinates $(0, 0)$ and $(0, 1)$, respectively. For $\forall k \in \{3, 4, \cdots, n\}$, the coordinate of s_k is represented by the directions of $\overrightarrow{s_{k-1}s_k}$ relative to $\overrightarrow{s_{k-2}s_{k-1}}$, i.e., forward, towards the left, and towards the right, respectively. Assume that the interaction of amino acids happens inside a topology adjacent pair, i.e., the amino acids in a pair are adjacent in their lattice but are not adjacent in their sequence. The interaction (e_{ij}) of amino acid pair (s_i, s_j) with type $H - H, H - P$, or $P - P$, is defined as follows respectively.

$$e_{HH} = -1.0, \ e_{HP} = 0.0, \ e_{PP} = 0.0$$

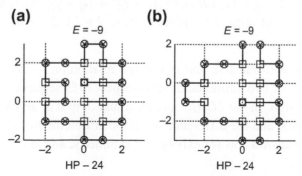

Figure 7.6: Amino Acid Sequence with Length 24 and Energy -9, where '□'-Hydrophobic (*H*) 'o'-Hydrophilic (*P*)

The energy of protein obtained by the folding of its amino acid sequence is defined as $E(P) = \sum e_{ij}\Delta_{ij}$, where if and only if s_i and s_j are topology adjacent, $\Delta_{ij} = 1$, otherwise $\Delta_{ij} = 0$.

An amino acid sequence $\mathbb{S}$ with length n is given. Let $\mathcal{P} = \{P|P$ obtained by the folding of $\mathbb{S}$ and the hydrophobic amino acids concentrate in the center of $P\}$. Under the widely accepted assumption, the protein-folding problem can be represented as follows.

$$\arg\min\{E(P)|P \in \mathcal{P}\}$$

It has been shown in Nayak et al. (1999) that this is a NP-hard problem. There exists an (or several) optimal solution, or only several sub-optimal solutions.

7.4.5.2 The Estimation of the Lower Bound of Energy

Each anti-reflexive relation corresponds to a reflexive relation uniquely, and vice versa. Correspondingly, each anti-reflexive and symmetric binary relation corresponds to a tolerance relation uniquely. Therefore, in the isomorphism sense, there is no distinction between an anti-reflexive and symmetric binary relation and a tolerance relation.

Assume that $S = s_1 s_2 \cdots s_n, i \in \{1, 2, \cdots, n\}, s_i \in \{H, P\}$ is an amino acid sequence. Protein P is obtained from the folding of S, and represented in $2D$ HP lattice model. For simplicity, $\{s_1, s_2, \cdots, s_n\}$ is indicated by $\mathbb{U}$.

Definition 7.34

Define $R \subseteq \mathbb{U} \times \mathbb{U}$ as $s_i R s_j \Leftrightarrow i = j - 1$, or $i = j + 1$.

Definition 7.35

Define $R_\mathbb{P} \subseteq \mathbb{U} \times \mathbb{U}$ as $\forall s_i, s_j \in \mathbb{U}, s_i R_\mathbb{P} s_j \Leftrightarrow |x_i - x_j|^2 + |y_i - y_j|^2 = 1$, where x_k and y_k represent the horizontal and vertical coordinates of $s_k, k \in \{1, 2, \cdots, n\}$, in the 2D HP lattice model, respectively.

Binary relation R is an anti-reflexive and symmetric relation on $\mathbb{U}$ induced from $\mathbb{S}$. It indicates the adjacency of two amino acids with respect to $\mathbb{S}$ sequence, and is called a sequence adjacent relation. In the 2D HP model, if and only if s_i and s_j satisfy that one of their coordinates is equal and the difference of the other coordinates is 1 unit, then $s_i R_\mathbb{P} s_j$ holds. Obviously, $R_\mathbb{P}$ satisfies anti-reflexivity and symmetry, and is called a structure adjacent relation.

Now, we define a topology adjacent relation in 2D HP lattice model as follows.

Definition 7.36

Define $T_\mathbb{P} \subseteq \mathbb{U} \times \mathbb{U}$ as $\forall s_i, s_j \in \mathbb{U}$, $s_i T_\mathbb{P} s_j \Leftrightarrow s_i R_\mathbb{P} s_j$ and $s_i R s_j$.

Obviously, the topology adjacent relation is the difference between the structure and sequence adjacent relations, as they can be regarded as a subset on $\mathbb{U} \times \mathbb{U}$. In other words, $T_\mathbb{P} = R_\mathbb{P} \cap R^C$, where R^C is a complement set of R.

From the widely accepted assumption, the energy of primary state of a protein approaches the minimum. While in the 2D *HP* lattice model, the hydrophobic amino acids is required to concentrate in its center as far as possible after the folding. Assume that protein P is located in the 2D lattice model with length l and width m, after the folding of an amino acid sequence with length n. In the ideal situation, an amino acid is placed in each lattice point, and the hydrophobic ones are placed in the center lattice points as far as possible. Let $n = lm$ and $|*|$ be the number of elements in set '$*$'. Then, $R_\mathbb{P}$ satisfies

$$\frac{|R_\mathbb{P}|}{2} \leq (l-1)m + l(m-1) = 2lm - (l+m) = 2n - (l+m)$$

While

$$l + m \geq 2\sqrt{lm} = 2\sqrt{n}$$

we have

$$\frac{|R_\mathbb{P}|}{2} \leq 2n - (l+m) \leq 2n - 2\sqrt{n} - 2(n - \sqrt{n})$$

Since

$$\frac{|R|}{2} = n - 1$$

$$\frac{|R_P|}{2} - \frac{|R|}{2} \leq n - 2\sqrt{n} + 1 = (\sqrt{n} - 1)^2 \qquad (7.17)$$

From $E(P) = \sum e_{ij} \Delta_{ij}$ and the definition of Δ_{ij}, if and only if s_i and s_j are topology adjacent, $\Delta_{ij} = 1$, otherwise $\Delta_{ij} = 0$. Therefore, the Formula (7.17) is the estimation of the lower bound of $E(P)$, i.e., $E(P) \geq (\sqrt{n} - 1)^2$. The estimation does not eliminate topology adjacent that consists of amino acid pairs with $P-P$ or $H-P$ type. While the interaction among the amino acid pairs either with $P-P$ type or $H-P$ type is zero, and has no effect on the $E(P)$. The lower bound obtained above is not satisfactory. It's known that only the topology adjacent amino acid pairs with $H-H$ type play a part in $E(P)$. In more ideal cases, the topology adjacent amino acid pairs with $H-H$ type only appear on the rectangle $(l-2) * (m-2)$ that within the rectangle lm. Now, the number of topology adjacent amino acids with $H-H$ type is at most

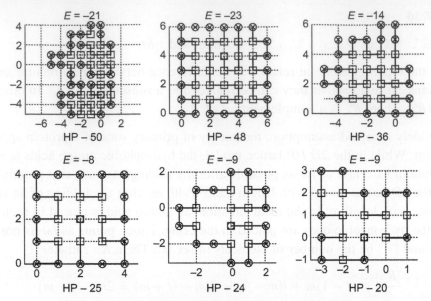

Figure 7.7: The Results of Benchmark Sequence via GA

$$(l-2)(m-3) + (l-3)(m-2) = 2lm - 5(l+m) + 12 = 2n - 5(l+m) + 12$$

And, $2lm - 5(l+m) + 12 \leq 2(n - 5\sqrt{n} + 6)$.

Let f be the number of amino acid pairs with $H-H$ type in sequence $\mathbb{S}$, including the head and the end amino acids of the sequence are H type. We have

$$E(P) \geq f - 2(n - 5\sqrt{n} + 6) \tag{7.18}$$

This is also a lower bound estimation of $E(P)$.

Fig. 7.7 shows the results that are obtained by the folding of HP benchmark sequences in Unger and Moult (1993) via genetic algorithms (GA). The results of the lower bound of energy obtained by genetic algorithms (GA) are shown in Table 7.1.

Table 7.1: The Results of the Lower Bound of Energy via GA

Name	Length	Sequence	f	LB1	LB2	E
HP-20	20	$HPHP_2H_2PHP_2HPH_2P_2HPH$	3	-12	invalid	-9
HP-24	24	$H_2P_2(HP_2)_6H_2$	3	-16	3-12=-9	-9
HP-25	25	$P_2HP_2 (H_2P_4)_3H_2$	4	-16	4-12=-8	-8
HP-36	36	$P_3H_2P_2H_2P_5H_7P_2H_2P_4H_2P_2H \ P_2$	10	-25	10-24=-14	-14
HP-48	48	$P_2H (P_2H_2)_2P_5H_{10}P_6(P_2H_2)_2HP_2H_5$	17	-36	17-40=-23	-23
HP-50	50	$H_2(PH)_3PH_4P(PH_3)_3P(HP_3)_2HPH_4(PH)_4H$	17	-48	17-41=-24	-21

The experimental results indicated in Table 7.1 show that the estimation of the lower bound by Formula (7.18) is better than (7.17). The reason may be that the estimation by Formula (7.18) is related to the whole sequence, but Formula (7.17) only considers the length of sequence.

7.4.6 Conclusions

In the section, we extend the quotient space theory from the aspects of the structure and granulation of a domain. That is, further consider the structure produced by closure operations, and the granulation by tolerance relations. The domain structure plays an important role in quotient space theory, and also is one of the characteristics of the theory. With the help of the continuity of mappings and the connectivity of sets, we have the falsity-preserving property that is very useful in reasoning. The order relation is a specific topological structure. We pay attention to the order-preserving property that is also very useful in reality. Fortunately, these good properties still maintain under the expansion.

7.5 Conclusions

As the expansion of the falsity- and truth-preserving principles, in Section 7.1, the general principle of quotient space approximation method is presented. In Section 7.2, its relation to the second-generation wavelet multi-resolution analysis is discussed. So quotient space approximation can seek out new mathematical tools from wavelet analysis. It is also the expansion of information synthesis in some sense. In Section 7.3, the relation between quotient space approximation method and fractal geometry is discussed. In Section 7.4 the theory is extended to structures induced from closure operations and the tolerance relations. We also show that many useful properties in traditional theory are still available under the expansion. As an application of tolerant relation-based quotient space theory, a protein structure prediction task is presented.

ADDENDA A

Some Concepts and Properties of Point Set Topology

A.1 Relation and Mapping

A.1.1 Relation

Definition 1.1.1

X and Y are any two sets. $\{(x,y)|x \in X, y \in Y\}$ is called a Cartesian product of X and Y, denoted by $X \times Y$, where (x,y) is a pair of ordered elements. x is the first coordinate of (x,y), and y is the second coordinate of (x,y). X is a set of the first coordinates of $X \times Y$, and Y is a set of the second coordinates of $X \times Y$.

Definition 1.1.2

X and Y are two sets. For any $R \subset X \times Y$, R is called a relation from X to Y.

Assume that R is a relation from X to Y. If $(x,y) \in R$, then x and y are R−relevant, denoted by xRy.

Set $\{x|\exists y, (x,y) \in R\}$ is called the domain of R, denoted by $D(R)$.

Set $\{y|(x,y) \in R, x \in D(R)\}$ is called the range of R, denoted by $R(R)$.

For $A \subset X$, letting $\{y|\exists x \in A, (x,y) \in R\} = R(A)$, $R(A)$ is called a set of images (or image) of A.

For $B \subset Y$, letting $\{x|\exists y \in B, (x,y) \in R\} = R^{-1}(B)$, $R^{-1}(B)$ is called the preimage of B.

Definition 1.1.3

For $R \subset X \times Y, S \subset Y \times Z$, letting $T = \{(x,z)|\exists y \in Y, (x,y) \in R, (y,z) \in S\}$, T is called the composition of R and S, denoted by $T = S \circ R$.

For $R \subset X \times Y$, letting $R^{-1} = \{(y,x)|(x,y) \in R\} \subset Y \times X$, R^{-1} is called the inverse of R.

Proposition 1.1.1

For $R \subset X \times Y, S \subset Y \times Z$ and $T \subset Z \times U$, we have

(1) $(R^{-1})^{-1} = R$
(2) $(S \circ R)^{-1} = R^{-1} \circ S^{-1}$
(3) $T \circ (S \circ R) = (T \circ S) \circ R$
(4) $\forall A, B \subset X, R(A \cup B) = R(A) \cup R(B)$ and $R(A \cap B) \subset R(A) \cap R(B)$
(5) $(S \circ R)(A) = S(R(A))$

Note that in (4) $R(A \cap B) \subset R(A) \cap R(B)$ rather than $R(A \cap B) = R(A) \cap R(B)$.

A.1.2 Equivalence Relation

Definition 1.2.1

Assume that R is a relation from X to X (or a relation on X) and satisfies

(1) $\Delta(X) = \{(x, x) | x \in X\} \subset R$ (Reflexivity)
(2) $R = R^{-1}$ (Symmetry)
(3) $R \circ R \subset R$ (Transitivity)

R is called an equivalence relation on X.

Assume that R is an equivalence relation on X. For $\forall x \in X$, letting $[x]_R = \{y | yRx, y \in X\}$, $[x]_R$ is an R–equivalent set of x.

Definition 1.2.2

For $\forall \alpha, A_\alpha \subset X$, if $A_\alpha \cap A_\beta = \varnothing, \alpha \neq \beta$ and $\underset{\alpha}{\cup} A_\alpha = X$, then $\{A_a\}$ is a partition of x.

Proposition 1.2.1

R is an equivalence relation on X. Then, $\{[x]_R | x \in X\}$ is a partition of X.

A.1.3 Mapping and One–One Mapping

Definition 1.3.1

F is a relation from X to Y. For $\forall x \in X$, if there exists a unique $y \in Y$ such that $(x, y) \in F$, then F is called a mapping from X to Y, denoted by $F : X \rightarrow Y$.

If $R(F) = Y$, F is called surjective, where $R(F)$ is the range of F.

For $x_1, x_2 \in X$, if $x_1 \neq x_2 \Rightarrow F(x_1) \neq F(x_2)$, F is called 1-1 mapping.

Proposition 1.3.1

$f : X \rightarrow Y$ is a mapping. For $\forall A, B \subset X$, we have

$$f(A \cup B) = f(A) \cup f(B)$$
$$f(A \cap B) = f(A) \cap f(B)$$
$$A \subset f(f^{-1}(A))$$

If $A \subset B$, then $f(A) \subset f(B)$.

For $\forall A, B \subset Y$, we have

$$f^{-1}(A \cup B) = f^{-1}(A) \cup f^{-1}(B)$$
$$f^{-1}(A \cap B) = f^{-1}(A) \cap f^{-1}(B)$$
$$f(f^{-1}(A)) \subset A, f^{-1}(A^C) = f^{-1}(A)^C$$

If $A \subset B$, then $f^{-1}(A) \subset f^{-1}(B)$.

If f is surjective, then $\forall A \subset X, f(A^C) \supset f(A)^C$.

If f is a 1-1 mapping, then $f(A^C) \subset f(A)^C$.

Where, A^C is the complement of A. f^{-1} is the inverse of f.

If f is surjective and 1-1 mapping, then $A = f^{-1}(f(A))$ and $f(A^C) = f(A)^C$.

Definition 1.3.2

Assume that X is a Cartesian product of $X_1, X_2, \cdots, X_n$. Let $x = (x_1, x_2, \cdots, x_n) \in X$. Define $p_i : X \rightarrow X_i, p_i(x) = x_i$. p_i is the projection of X on X_i, or a set of the i-th coordinates.

A.1.4 Finite Set, Countable Set and Uncountable Set

Definition 1.4.1

A and B are two sets. If there exists a 1-1 surjective mapping from A to B, A and B are called equinumerous.

Any set that is not equinumerous to its proper subsets is a finite set.

A set that is equinumerous to the set N of all natural numbers is a countable set.

An infinite set that is not equinumerous to the set N of all natural numbers is an uncountable set.

Theorem 1.4.1 (Bernstein)

If A and the subset of B are equinumerous, and B and the subset of A are also equinumerous, A and B are equinumerous.

A.2 Topology Space

A.2.1 Metric Space

X is a non-empty set. $d : X \times X \rightarrow R$ is a mapping, where R is a real set. $\forall x, y, z \in X, d$ satisfies:

(1) $d(x, y) \geq 0$ and $d(x, y) = 0 \Leftrightarrow x = y$

(2) $d(x, y) = d(y, x)$

(3) $d(x, z) \leq d(x, y) + d(y, z)$

Then, d is a distance function on X and (X, d) is a metric space.

Definition 2.1.2

(X, d) is a metric space. For $x \in X$, $\forall \varepsilon > 0$, $\{y | d(x, y) < \varepsilon, y \in X\} = B(x, \varepsilon)$. $B(x, \varepsilon)$ is called a spherical neighborhood with x as its center and ε as its radius, or simply $\varepsilon-$ neighborhood.

Proposition 2.1.1

(X, d) is a metric space. Its spherical neighborhoods have the following properties.

(1) $\forall x \in X$, there is one neighborhood at least. $\forall B(x, \varepsilon)$, have $x \in B(x, \varepsilon)$.

(2) $x \in X$, for any two spherical neighborhoods $B(x, \varepsilon_1)$ and $B(x, \varepsilon_2)$, there exists $B(x, \varepsilon_3)$ such that $B(x, \varepsilon_3) \subset B(x, \varepsilon_1) \cap B(x, \varepsilon_2)$.

(3)   If $y \in B(x, \varepsilon)$, then there exists $B(y, \varepsilon_1) \subset B(x, \varepsilon)$.

A.2.2 Topological Space

Definition 2.2.1

X is a non-empty set. $\mathcal{T}$ is a family of subsets of X. If $\mathcal{T}$ satisfies the following conditions

(1) $X, \varnothing \in \mathcal{T}$

(2) $A, B \in \mathcal{T}, A \cap B \in \mathcal{T}$

(3) $\mathcal{T}_1 \subset \mathcal{T}, \underset{A \in \mathcal{T}_1}{\cup} A \in \mathcal{T}$

then $\mathcal{T}$ is a topology of X. $(X, \mathcal{T})$ is a topologic space. Each member of $\mathcal{T}$ is called an open set on $(X, \mathcal{T})$.

(X, d) is a metric space. For $A \subset X$ and $\forall x \in A$, if there exists $B(x, \varepsilon) \subset A$, then A is an open set on X. Let $\mathcal{T}_d$ be a family of all open sets on X. It can be proved that $\mathcal{T}_d$ is a topology on X. $(X, \mathcal{T}_d)$ is called a topologic space induced from d.

Definition 2.2.2

$(X, \mathcal{T})$ is a topologic space ($(X, \mathcal{T})$ always indicates a topologic space below). For $x \in X$ and $U \in \mathcal{T}$, if $x \in U$, then U is called a neighborhood of x denoted by $U(x)$.

For $x \in X$, the set of all neighborhoods of x is called a system of neighborhoods of x, denoted by U_x.

Proposition 2.2.1

(X, d) is a topologic space. For $x \in X$, U_x is a neighborhood system of x. We have

(1) $\forall x \in X$, $U_x \neq \varnothing$ and $\forall u \in U_x$, then $x \in u$.

(2) If $u, v \in U_x$, then $u \cap v \in U_x$.

(3) If $u \in U_x$, there exist $v \subset u$, $v \in U_x$ such that for $\forall y \in v$ have $v \in U_y$.

A.2.3 Induced Set, Close Set and Closure

Definition 2.3.1

For $A \subset (X, \mathcal{T})$, $x \in X$, if $\forall u \in U_x$, $u \cap (A/\{x\}) \neq \varnothing$, then x is called an accumulation (limit) point of A.

Set A' of all accumulation points of A is called an induced set of A.

Proposition 2.3.1

For $\forall A, B \subset (X, \mathcal{T})$, we have

(1) $\varnothing' = \varnothing$

(2) $A \subset B$ $A' \subset B'$

(3) $(A \cup B)' = A' \cup B'$

(4) $(A')' \subset A \cup A'$

Definition 2.3.2

For $A \subset (X, \mathcal{T})$, if all accumulation points of A belong to A, then A is a close set.

Proposition 2.3.2

A is close $\Leftrightarrow A^c$ is open.

Proposition 2.3.3

Assume that $\mathcal{F}$ is a family of all close sets on $(X, \mathcal{T})$. We have

(1) $X, \varnothing \in \mathcal{F}$

(2) If $A, B \in \mathcal{F}$, then $A \cup B \in \mathcal{F}$.

(3) If $\mathcal{F}_1 \subset \mathcal{F}$, then $\underset{A \in \mathcal{F}_1}{\cap} A \in \mathcal{F}$.

Definition 2.3.3

For $A \subset (X, \mathcal{T})$, letting $\overline{A} = A \cup A'$, $\overline{A}$ is called a closure of A.

Proposition 2.3.4

For $\forall A, B \subset (x, \mathcal{T})$, we have

(1) $\overline{\varnothing} = \varnothing$

(2) $A \subset \overline{A}$

(3) $\overline{\overline{A} \cup \overline{B}} = \overline{A} \cup \overline{B}$

(4) $\overline{\overline{A}} = \overline{A}$

Definition 2.3.4

For $A \subset (X, d), x \in X$, define $d(x, A) = \inf\{d(y, x) | y \in A\}$.

Proposition 2.3.5

For $A \subset (X, d)$, we have

(1) $x \in A' \Leftrightarrow d(x, (A - \{x\})) = 0$

(2) $x \in \overline{A} \Leftrightarrow d(x, A) = 0$

A.2.4 Interior and Boundary

Definition 2.4.1

For $A \subset (X, \mathcal{T})$, letting $A^0 = \{x | \exists u \in U, x \in u \subset A\}$, A^0 is called the interior (core) of A.

Proposition 2.4.1

For $A \subset (X, \mathcal{T})$, we have

(1) A is open $\Leftrightarrow A^0 = A$

(2) $(A^0)^c = \overline{(A^c)}, (A^c)^0 = (\overline{A})^c$

(3) $X^0 = X$

(4) $A^0 \subset A$

(5) $(A \cap B)^0 = A^0 \cap B^0$

(6) $(A^0)^0 = A^0$

Definition 2.4.2

For $A \subset (X, \mathcal{T}), x \in X$, if $\forall u \in U_x, u \cap A \neq \varnothing$ and $u \cap A^c \neq \varnothing$, x is called a boundary point of A. The set of all boundary points of A is called boundary of A, denoted by ∂A.

Proposition 2.4.2

For $A \subset (X, \mathcal{T})$, we have

(1) $\overline{A} = A \cup \partial A$

(2) $A^0 = A - \partial A$

(3) $\partial A = \overline{A} \cap \overline{(A^c)}$

(4) $\partial A^0 \subset \partial A, \partial(\overline{A}) \subset \partial A$

(5) $\partial(A \cup B) \subset \partial A \cup \partial B, \partial(\partial B) \subset \partial B$

A.2.5 Topological Base and Subbase

Definition 2.5.1

$(X, \mathcal{T})$ is a topologic space. For $\mathcal{B} \subset \mathcal{T}$ and $\forall u \in \mathcal{T}$, if there exists $\mathcal{B}_1 \subset \mathcal{B}$ such that $u = \underset{v \in \mathcal{B}_1}{\cup} v$, then $\mathcal{B}$ is a base of $\mathcal{T}$.

Proposition 2.5.1

(X, d) is a space. $(X, \mathcal{T}_d)$ is a topologic space induced from d. Then, $\mathcal{T}_1 = \{$all spherical neighborhoods of x, $\forall x \in X$ $\}$ is a base of $\mathcal{T}_d$.

Proposition 2.5.2

$\mathcal{B}$ is a family of open sets on $(X, \mathcal{T})$. Then, $\mathcal{B}$ is a base $\Leftrightarrow \forall u \in \mathcal{T}$ and $x \in u$, there is $v \in \mathcal{B}$ such that $x \in v \subset u$.

Proposition 2.5.3

$\mathcal{B}$ is a family of subsets of X and satisfies

(1) $X = \underset{u \in \mathcal{B}}{\cup} u$

(2) If $B_1, B_2 \in \mathcal{B}$, for $\forall x \in B_1 \cap B_2$, there exists $B(x) \in \mathcal{B}$ such that $x \in B(x) \subset B_1 \cap B_2$.

Then, let $\mathcal{T} = \{A | A = \underset{u \in \mathcal{B}_1}{\cup} u, \forall \mathcal{B}_1 \subset \mathcal{B}\}$ be a topology of X and $\mathcal{B}$ be a base of $\mathcal{T}$.

Definition 2.5.2

$(X, \mathcal{T})$ is a space. φ is a sub-family of $\mathcal{T}$. If $s_i \in \varphi, i = 1, 2, \dots, n, n \in N$, letting $s_1 \cap s_2 \cap \dots \cap s_i \in \mathcal{B}$, i.e., $\mathcal{B}$ is a family of sets composed by the intersections of any finite number of elements in φ, then $\mathcal{B}$ is a base of $\mathcal{T}$, and φ is a subbase of $\mathcal{T}$.

A.2.6 Continuous Mapping and Homeomorphism

Definition 2.6.1

$f : (X, \mathcal{T}_1) \rightarrow (Y, \mathcal{T}_2)$ is a mapping. If $\forall u \in \mathcal{T}_2, f^{-1}(u) \in \mathcal{T}_1$, then f is a continuous mapping.

If $x \in X$, $\forall w \in \mathcal{T}_2$ and $f(x) \in w$, have $f^{-1}(w) \in \mathcal{T}_1$, then f is continuous at x.

Proposition 2.6.1

For $f : (X, \mathcal{T}_1) \rightarrow (Y, \mathcal{T}_2)$, the following statements are equivalent.

(1) f is a continuous mapping
(2) If $\mathcal{B}$ is a base of Y, then $\forall u \in \mathcal{B}, f^{-1}(u) \in \mathcal{T}_1$.
(3) $f^{-1}(F)$ is a preimage of any close set F in Y; $f^{-1}(F)$ is close in X.

(4) φ is a subbase of Y; $\forall u \in \varphi$, have $f^{-1}(u) \in \mathcal{T}_1$.
(5) $\forall A \subset X$, have $f(\overline{A}) \subset \overline{(f(A))}$.
(6) $\forall B \subset Y$, have $f^{-1}(\overline{B}) \supset \overline{(f^{-1}(B))}$.

Proposition 2.6.2

For $f : (X, \mathcal{T}_1) \to (Y, \mathcal{T}_2), x \in X$, the following statements are equivalent.

(1) f is continuous at x.
(2)   For all neighborhoods $u(f(x))$ of $f(x)$, there exists $u(x) \in U$ such that $f(u(x)) \subset u(f(x))$.

Proposition 2.6.3

If $f : (X, \mathcal{T}_1) \to (Y, \mathcal{T}_2)$ and $g : (Y, \mathcal{T}_2) \to (Z, \mathcal{T}_3)$ are continuous, then $g \circ f : (X, \mathcal{T}_1) \to (Z, \mathcal{T}_3)$ is continuous.

Definition 2.6.3

$(X, \mathcal{T}_1)$ and $(Y, \mathcal{T}_2)$ are two spaces. If there exists $f : (X, \mathcal{T}_1) \to (Y, \mathcal{T}_2)$, where f is a 1-1 surjective and bicontinuous mapping, i.e., both f and f^{-1} are continuous, then f is called a homeomorphous mapping from X to Y, or X and Y are homeomorphism.

A.2.7 Product Space and Quotient Space

Definition 2.7.1

$\mathcal{T}_1$ and $\mathcal{T}_2$ are two topologies on X. If $\mathcal{T}_1 \subset \mathcal{T}_2$, $\mathcal{T}_1$ is called smaller (coarser) than $\mathcal{T}_2$.

$\{\mathcal{T}_a, a \in I\}$ is a family of topologies on X. If there exists $\mathcal{T}_{a_0}$ such that $\forall \mathcal{T}_a, \mathcal{T}_{a_0} \subset \mathcal{T}_a$, then $\mathcal{T}_{a_0}$ is called the smallest (coarsest) topology in $\{\mathcal{T}_a\}$.

Similarly, we may define the concept of the largest (finest) topology.

Proposition 2.7.1

Assume that $\forall a \in I, f_a : X \to (Y_a, \mathcal{T}_a)$. There exists the smallest (coarsest) topology among topologies on X that make each f_a continuous.

Proposition 2.7.2

Assume that $\forall a \in I, f_a : X \to (Y_a, \mathcal{T}_a)$. There exists the largest (finest) topology among topologies on X that make each f_a continuous.

Corollary 2.7.2

Assume that $f : (X, \mathcal{T}) \to Y$. There exists the largest (finest) topology among topologies on Y that make f continuous. The topology is called the quotient topology with respect to $\mathcal{T}$ and f.

Definition 2.7.2

For $A \subset (X, T)$, letting $T_A = \{u | u = A \cap v, v \in \mathrm{T}\}$, (A, T_A) is called the subspace of (X, T).

Definition 2.7.3

Assume that $X = \prod_{\alpha \in I} X_\alpha, I \neq \varnothing$, where $\prod_{\alpha \in I} X_\alpha$ indicates the product set. $\{(X_\alpha, T_\alpha), \alpha \in I\}$ is a family of topologic spaces. Let $p_\alpha : X \to X_\alpha$ be a projection. T is the smallest topology among topologies on X that make $p_\alpha (\forall \alpha \in I)$ continuous. (X, T) is called the product topologic space of $\{(X_\alpha, T_\alpha)\}$, denoted by $(X, T) = \prod_{\alpha \in I} (X_\alpha, T_\alpha)$.

Proposition 2.7.3

Assume that (X, T) is a product topologic space of $\{(X_\alpha, T_\alpha), \alpha \in I\}$. Letting $\varphi = \{p_\alpha^{-1}(u_\alpha) | u_\alpha \in T_\alpha \ \ \forall \alpha \in I\}$, φ is a subbase of T.

Proposition 2.7.4

Assume that (X, T) is a product topologic space of $\{(X_\alpha, T_\alpha), \alpha \in I\}$. $f : (Y, T') \to (X, \mathrm{T})$ is continuous $\Leftrightarrow \forall \alpha \in I$, $p_\alpha \circ f : (Y, T') \to (X_\alpha, T_\alpha)$ is continuous.

Proposition 2.7.5

Assume that (X, T) is a product topologic space of $\{(X_\alpha, T_\alpha), \alpha \in I\}$. Then, series $\{x^i\}$ on X converges to $x^0 \in X \Leftrightarrow \forall \alpha \in I$, series $p_\alpha(x^i)$ on X_α converges to $p_\alpha(x^0)$.

Where, the definition of convergence is that for $\{x^i\} \subset (X, T), x \in X$, if $\forall u \in U_x$, there exists n_0 such that when $n > n_0$, $x^n \in u$. Then $\{x^i\}$ is called to be converging to x, denoted by $\lim_{n \to \infty} x^n = x$.

Definition 2.7.4

R is an equivalence relation on (X, T). Let p be a nature projection $X \to X/R$ ($p(x) = [x]$), and $[T]$ be the finest topology that makes p continuous. $(X/R, [T])$ is called the quotient space of (X, T) with respect to R. Where, X/R may be indicated by $[X]_R$, or $[X]$.

Proposition 2.7.6

Assume that $([X], [T])$ is a quotient topologic space of (X, T) with respect to R. Then, $[T] = \{u | u \subset [X], p^{-1}(u) \in \mathrm{T}, p : X \to [X]\}$.

Definition 2.7.5

For $f : (X, T) \to Y$, letting $T/f = \{u | u \subset Y, f^{-1}(u) \in T\}$, T/f is called the quotient topology of (X, T) with respect to f. We have a topologic space $(Y, T/f)$ and $(Y, T/f)$ is a congruence space of T and f.

Proposition 2.7.7

$f : (X, \mathcal{T}_1) \to (Y, \mathcal{T}_2)$ is an open (close) surjective mapping. Then, $\mathcal{T}_2 = \mathcal{T}_1/f$.

Proposition 2.7.8

$(Y, \mathcal{T}_2)$ is an congruence space of $\mathcal{T}$ and f. Assume that $f : (X, \mathcal{T}_1) \to (Y, \mathcal{T}_2)$ and $g : (Y, \mathcal{T}_2) \to (Z, \mathcal{T}_3)$. Then, g is continuous $\Leftrightarrow g \circ f$ is continuous.

A.3 Separability Axiom

A.3.1 T₀, T₁, T₂ Spaces

Definition 3.1.1

$(X, \mathcal{T})$ is a space. For $\forall x, y \in X, x \neq y$, there is $u \in U_x$ such that $y \notin u$, or there is $u \in U_y$ such that $x \notin u$, X is called T_0 space.

Definition 3.1.2

$(X, \mathcal{T})$ is a space. For $\forall x, y \in X, x \neq y$, there must be $u \in U_x, v \in U_y$ such that $y \notin u, x \notin v$, X is called T_1 space.

Definition 3.1.3

$(X, \mathcal{T})$ is a space. For $\forall x, y \in X, x \neq y$, there must be $u \in U_x, v \in U_y$ such that $u \cap v = \varnothing$, X is called T_2 space, or Hausdorff space.

Proposition 3.1.1

X is a T_0 space $\Leftrightarrow \forall x, y \in X, x \neq y$, $\overline{\{x\}} \neq \overline{\{y\}}$, where $\overline{\{x\}}$ is the closure of singleton $\{x\}$. It means that the closures of any two different singletons are different.

Proposition 3.1.2

$(X, \mathcal{T})$ is a topologic space. The following statements are equivalent.

(1) X is a T_1 space.
(2) Each singleton on X is a close set.
(3) Each finite set on X is a close set.

Proposition 3.1.3

$(X, \mathcal{T})$ is a T_1 space $\Leftrightarrow \forall x \in X$, the intersection of all neighborhoods containing x is just $\{x\}$.

Proposition 3.1.4

$A \subset (X, \mathcal{T})$, X is a T_1 space. Then, $\forall x \in A' \Leftrightarrow \forall u \in U_x$, $u \cap (A - \{x\})$ is an infinite set.

Proposition 3.1.5

$(X, \mathcal{T})$ is a T_2 space. Then, the convergent series on X has only one limit point.

Proposition 3.1.6

$(X, \mathcal{T})$ is a T_2 space $\Leftrightarrow$ the diagonal $\Delta = \{(x, x) | x \in X\}$ of product topologic space on $X \times X$ is a close set.

3.2 T₃, T₄, Regular and Normal Space

Definition 3.2.1

In space $(X, \mathcal{T}), \forall A \subset X$, A is close. For $x \notin A$, if there exist open sets u and v, $u \cap v = \emptyset$, such that $x \in v, A \subset u$, then X is called a T_3 space.

Definition 3.2.2

In space $(X, \mathcal{T})$, for $\forall A, B \subset X$, if there exist open sets u and v such that $A \subset u, B \subset v, u \cap v = \emptyset$, then X is called a T_4 space.

Proposition 3.2.1

$(X, \mathcal{T})$ is a T_3 space $\Leftrightarrow \forall x \in X$ and $u \in U_x$, there exists $v \in U_x$ such that $\bar{v} \subset u$.

Proposition 3.2.2

$(X, \mathcal{T})$ is a T_4 space $\Leftrightarrow$ for any close set A in X and any open set u that contains A, i.e., $A \subset u$, there exists open set v such that $A \subset v \subset \bar{v} \subset u$.

Proposition 3.2.3

$(X, \mathcal{T})$ is a T_4 space $\Leftrightarrow$ For close sets $A, B \subset X$, $A \cap B = \emptyset$, there exists a continuous mapping f such that $(X, \mathcal{T}) \rightarrow [0, 1]$ and $f(A) = 0, f(B) = 1$.

Proposition 3.2.4 (Tietz Theorem)

$(X, \mathcal{T})$ is a T_4 space $\Leftrightarrow$ For any close set $\forall A \subset X$ and any continuous function $f_0 : A \rightarrow [0, 1]$ on A, there exists a continuous expansion $f : X \rightarrow [0, 1]$ of f_0 on X.

Definition 3.2.3

If $(X, \mathcal{T})$ is a T_1 and T_3 space, then X is called a regular space.

Definition 3.2.4

If $(X, \mathcal{T})$ is a T_1 and T_4 spaces, then X is called a normal space.

Proposition 3.2.5

$(X, \mathcal{T})$ is a normal space $\Rightarrow X$ is a regular space $\Rightarrow X$ is a T_2 space $\Rightarrow X$ is a T_1 space $\Rightarrow X$ is a T_0 space.

A.4 Countability Axiom

A.4.1 The First and Second Countability Axioms

Definition 4.1.1

If $(X, \mathcal{T})$ has countable base, then X is said to satisfy the second countability axiom.

Definition 4.1.2

If in $(X, \mathcal{T})$, for $\forall x \in X$, there exists countable local base, then X is said to satisfy the first countability axiom.

Proposition 4.1.1

Real space R satisfies the second countability axiom.

Proposition 4.1.2

If (X, d) is a metric space, then X satisfies the first countability axiom.

Proposition 4.1.3

If $(X, \mathcal{T})$ satisfies the second countability axiom, then X satisfies the first countability axiom.

Proposition 4.1.4

$f : (X, \mathcal{T}_1) \rightarrow (Y, \mathcal{T}_2)$ is a continuously open and surjective mapping. If X satisfies the second (or first) countability axiom, then Y will satisfy the second (or first) countability axiom.

Definition 4.1.3

If $(X, \mathcal{T})$ has property P and any sub-space of X also has the property P, property P is called having heredity.

If for $\forall X_i$ has property P and their product space $X = \prod_{i \in I} X_i$ also has property P, then P is called having integrability.

The relation among separation axiom, countability axiom, heredity and integrability is shown in Table 4.1.1.

Table 4.1.1

	T_0	T_1	T_2	T_3	T_4	A_1	A_2	Separable	Distance
heredity	√	√	√	√	×	√	√	×	√
integrability	√	√	√	√	×	√	√	√	√(countable)

Where, A_1 and A_2 are the first and second countability axioms, respectively.
√ (countable) means that the product space of the countable number of metric spaces is metrizable.

Proposition 4.1.5

For $f : (X, \mathcal{T}_1) \rightarrow (Y, \mathcal{T}_2)$, if X is countable, then f is continuous at $x \in X \Leftrightarrow \forall x_i \rightarrow x$, have $f(x_i) \rightarrow f(x)$.

A.4.2 Separable Space

Definition 4.2.1

If $D \subset (X, \mathcal{T})$ and $\overline{D} = X$, then D is called dense in X, or D is a dense subset of X.

Proposition 4.2.1

Assume that D is a dense subset in $(X, \mathcal{T})$. $f : X \rightarrow R$ and $g : X \rightarrow R$ are two continuous mappings. Then, $f = g \Leftrightarrow f = g$ on D.

Definition 4.2.2

If $(X, \mathcal{T})$ has dense countable subsets, X is called a separable space.

Proposition 4.2.1

If $(X, \mathcal{T})$ satisfies A_2, then X is separable.

Proposition 4.2.2

If a separable metric space satisfies A_2, then it must be A_1.

The relation among A_1, A_2 and metric spaces is shown below.

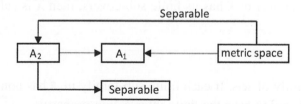

Where, $A \underset{B}{\rightarrow} C$ indicates that property A with the addition of property B infers property C.

A.4.3 Lindelof Space

Definition 4.3.1

$\mathcal{A}$ is a family of sets and B is a set. If $B \subset \underset{A \in \mathcal{A}}{\cup} A$, then $\mathcal{A}$ is called a cover of set B. When $\mathcal{A}$ is countable or finite, $\mathcal{A}$ is called a countable or finite cover.

If a family $\mathcal{A}$ of sets covers B and sub-family $\mathcal{A}_1$ of $\mathcal{A}$ also covers B, then $\mathcal{A}_1$ is called a sub-cover of $\mathcal{A}$.

If each set of cover $\mathcal{A}$ is open (closed), then $\mathcal{A}$ is called an open (closed) cover.

Definition 4.3.2

In $(X, \mathcal{T})$, for any open cover of X, there exists countable sub-cover, X is called a Lindelof space.

Proposition 4.3.1

If $(X, \mathcal{T})$ satisfies A_2, then X is a Lindelof space.

Corollary 4.3.1

An n-dimensional Euclidean space R^n is a Lindelof space.

Proposition 4.3.2

If (X, d) is a Lindelof space, then X satisfies A_2.

Proposition 4.3.3

If any sub-space in $(X, \mathcal{T})$ is a Lindelof space, then each uncountable subset A of X must have accumulation points of A.

A.5 Compactness

A.5.1 Compact Space

Definition 5.1.1

In $(X, \mathcal{T})$, if each open cover of X has its finite sub-covers, then X is called a compact space.

Definition 5.1.2

Assume that $\mathcal{A}$ is a family of sets. If each finite sub-family in $\mathcal{A}$ has non-empty intersection, then $\mathcal{A}$ is said to have the finite intersection property.

Proposition 5.1.1

$(X, \mathcal{T})$ is compact $\Leftrightarrow$ each family of close sets that has the finite intersection property in X has non-empty intersection.

Proposition 5.1.2

$f : (X, \mathcal{T}_1) \to (Y, \mathcal{T}_2)$ is a continuous mapping. If X is compact, then $f(X)$ is also compact.

Proposition 5.1.3

Each close subset of a compact set is compact.

Proposition 5.1.4

If $X_i, i \in I$, is compact, then their product space is compact as well.

A.5.2 Relation between Compactness and Separability Axiom

Proposition 5.2.1

A compact subset in T_2 is close.

Proposition 5.2.2

A compact T_2 space is a normal space.

Proposition 5.2.3

$f : (X, T_1) \to (Y, T_2)$ is a continuous mapping. If X is compact and Y is T_2, then f is a close mapping, i.e., mapping a close set to a close set.

Proposition 5.3.4

$f : (X, T_1) \to (Y, T_2)$ is a continuous and 1-1 surjective mapping. If X is compact and Y is T_2, then f is homeomorphous.

Proposition 5.2.5

If $A \subset R^n$ and R^n is an n-dimensional Euclidean space, then A is compact $\Leftrightarrow$ A is a bounded close set.

Proposition 5.2.6

$f(X, T) \to R$ is a continuous mapping. If X is compact, there exist $x_0, y_0 \in X$ such that $\forall x \in X, f(x_0) \leq f(x) \leq f(y_0)$.

A.5.3 Some Relations in Compactness

Definition 5.3.1

A topological space (X, T) is countably compact if every countable open cover has a finite subcover.

Definition 5.3.2

A topological space (X, T) is said to be limit point compact if every infinite subset has a limit point.

Definition 5.3.3

A topological space (X, T) is sequentially compact if every infinite sequence has a convergent subsequence.

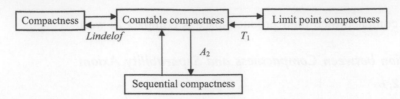

In metric space, especially in n-dimensional Euclidean space, the four concepts of compactness, limit point compactness, countable compactness, and sequential compactness are equivalent.

A.5.4 Local Compact and Paracompact

Definition 5.4.1

In $(X, \mathcal{T})$, for each point on X there exists a compact neighborhood, and X is called a local compact space.

Definition 5.4.2

Assume that $\mathcal{A}_1$ and $\mathcal{A}_2$ are two covers of X. If each member of $\mathcal{A}_1$ is contained by some member of $\mathcal{A}_2$, then $\mathcal{A}_1$ is called the refinement of $\mathcal{A}_2$.

Definition 5.4.3

In $(X, \mathcal{T})$, $\mathcal{A}$ is a cover of subset A. If $\forall x \in A$, there exists $u(x) \in U$ such that $u(x)$ only intersects with the finite number of members in $\mathcal{A}$, then $\mathcal{A}$ is called a the local finite cover of A.

Definition 5.4.4

In $(X, \mathcal{T})$, for each open cover of $\mathcal{A}$ on X, there exists local finite cover $\mathcal{A}_1$, where $\mathcal{A}_1$ is the refinement of $\mathcal{A}$, then X is called a paracompact space.

Proposition 5.4.1

Each locally compact and T_2 space are normal spaces.

Proposition 5.4.2

Each paracompact normal space is a regular space.

The relation among compactness, paracompactness and local compactness is shown below.

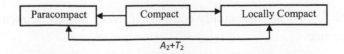

A.6 Connectedness

A.6.1 Connected Space

Definition 6.1.1

Assume that $A, B \subset (X, \mathcal{T})$. If $(A \cap \overline{B}) \cup (\overline{A} \cap B) = \varnothing$, then A and B are separate subsets.

Definition 6.1.2

In $(X, \mathcal{T})$, if there exist non-empty separate subsets A and B on X such that $X = A \cup B$, then X is said to be disconnected. Non-disconnected spaces are called connected spaces.

Proposition 6.1.1

In $(X, \mathcal{T})$, the following conditions are equivalent.

(1) X is disconnected
(2) X can be represented by the union of two non-empty and mutually disjoint close sets, i.e., $X = A \cup B$, $A \cap B = \varnothing$, where A and B are non-empty close sets
(3) X can be represented by the union of two non-empty and mutually disjoint open sets.
(4) There exists non-empty both open and close proper subset on X.

Definition 6.1.3

For $A \subset (X, \mathcal{T})$, if A is regarded as a sub-space of X, then it's connected; A is called a connected subset of X.

Proposition 6.1.2

$Y \subset (X, \mathcal{T})$ is disconnected $\Leftrightarrow$ there exist non-empty separate subsets A and B on X and $Y = A \cup B$.

Proposition 6.1.3

Assume that Y is a connected subset on $(X, \mathcal{T})$. If A and B are separate subsets on $X, Y = A \cup B$, then $Y \subset A$ or $Y \subset B$.

Proposition 6.1.4

Assume that $A \subset (X, \mathcal{T})$ is a connected subset. Let $A \subset B \subset \overline{A}$. Then, B is a connected subset, especially $\overline{A}$ is connected.

Proposition 6.1.5

Assume that $\{A_{\alpha, \alpha \in I}\}$ is a family of connected sets on $(X, \mathcal{T})$ and $\bigcap_{\alpha \in I} A_\alpha \neq \varnothing$. Then, $\bigcup_{\alpha \in I} A_\alpha$ is connected.

Proposition 6.1.6

$f : (X, \mathcal{T}_1) \to (Y, \mathcal{T}_2)$ is a continuous mapping. If X is connected, then $f(X)$ is connected on Y.

Proposition 6.1.7

If $X_1, X_2, \cdots X_n$ are connected spaces, then their product space $X = \prod_{1}^{n} X_i$ is also connected.

From R^1 is connected, R^n is connected.

Proposition 6.1.8

If $f : (X, \mathcal{T}) \to R$ is continuous, X is connected, and there exist $a, b \in X$ such that $f(a) < f(b)$, then for $\forall f(a) < r < f(b)$, there must have $c \in X$ such that $f(c) = r$.

Proposition 6.1.9

If $f : S^1 \to R$ is a continuous mapping, where S^1 is a unit circle, then there exists $z \in S^1$ such that $f(z) = f(z')$, where $z' = -z$.

A.6.2 Connected Component and Local Connectedness

Definition 6.2.1

Assume that x and y are two points on topologic space $(X, \mathcal{T})$. If there exists a connected set $A \subset X$ such that $x, y \in A$, then x and y are called connected.

The connected relation among points on $(X, \mathcal{T})$ is an equivalence relation.

Definition 6.2.2

Each equivalent class with respect to connected relations on $(X, \mathcal{T})$ is called a connected component of X.

Definition 6.2.3

For $A \subset (X, \mathcal{T})$, if A is regarded as a sub-space, its connected component is called a connected component of subset A of X.

Definition 6.2.4

In $(X, \mathcal{T})$, for each neighborhood u of $x \in X$, there exist connected neighborhood v such that $x \in v \subset u$, then X is called local connected at point x. If for $\forall x \in X$ X is local connected at x, then X is called a local connected space.

Proposition 6.2.1

In $(X, \mathcal{T})$, C is a connected component of X, then

(1) If Y is a connected subset on X and $Y \cap C \neq \emptyset$, then $Y \subset C$.
(2) C is a connected subset.
(3) C is a close set on X.

Proposition 6.2.2

In $(X, \mathcal{T})$, the following statements are equivalent.

(1) X is a local connected space.
(2) Any connected component of any open set of X is open.
(3) There exists a base on X such that its each member is connected.

Proposition 6.2.3

$f : (X, \mathcal{T}_1) \to (Y, \mathcal{T}_2)$ is a continuous mapping. X is local connected. Then, $f(X)$ is also local connected.

Proposition 6.2.4

If $X_1, X_2, \cdots X_n$ are local connected spaces, then their product space is also local connected.

Proposition 6.2.5

If $A \subset (X, \mathcal{T})$ is a connected open set, then A must be a connected component of $(\partial A)^c$.

A.6.3 Arcwise Connected Space

Definition 6.3.1

$f : [0, 1] \to (X, \mathcal{T})$ is a continuous mapping and is called an arc (or path) that connects points $f(0)$ and $f(1)$ on $(X, \mathcal{T})$, where $f(0)$ and $f(1)$ are called start and end points of arc f, respectively. If $f(0) = f(1)$, then f is called a circuit.

If f is an arc on X, then $f([0, 1])$ is called a curve on X.

For $\forall x, y \in X$, if there exists an arc $f : [0, 1] \to (X, \mathcal{T})$ such that $f(0) = x$ and $f(1) = y$, then X is an arcwise connected space.

For $A \subset (X, \mathcal{T})$, regarding A as a sub-space, if A is arcwise connected, then A is an arcwise connected subset of X.

Definition 6.3.2

For $x, y \in (X, \mathcal{T})$, if there is an arc on X that connects x and y, then x and y are arcwise connected.

All points on X are an equivalent relation with respect to arcwise connected relations.

Definition 6.3.3

The points on $(X, \mathcal{T})$ that belong to an equivalent class with respect to arcwise connected relations are called an arcwise connected component of X.

Proposition 6.3.1

If $(X, \mathcal{T})$ is arcwise connected, then X is connected.

Proposition 6.3.2

$f : (X, \mathcal{T}_1) \to (Y, \mathcal{T}_2)$ is a continuous mapping. If X is an arcwise connected space, then $f(X)$ is also an arcwise connected space.

Proposition 6.3.3

If $X_1, X_2, \cdots X_n$ are arcwise connected spaces, then their product space is also an arcwise connected space.

Corollary 6.3.3

R^n is an arcwise connected space.

Proposition 6.3.4 (Bond Lemma)

Assume that $A, B \subset (X, \mathcal{T})$ are close sets and $X = A \cup B$. $f_1 : A \to (Y, \mathcal{T}_2)$ and $f_2 : B \to (Y, \mathcal{T}_2)$ are continuous mappings. $f_1 | A \cap B = f_2 | A \cap B$, i.e., f_1 and f_2 are the same on $A \cap B$. Let $f(x) = \begin{cases} f_1(x), x \in A \\ f_2(x), x \in B \end{cases}$. Then, $f : (X, \mathcal{T}_1) \to (Y, \mathcal{T}_2)$ is continuous.

Proposition 6.3.5

For $A \subset R^n$, if A is an open connected set, then A is arcwise connected.

Definition 6.3.4

In $(X, \mathcal{T})$, $\forall x \in X$ for any neighborhood $u(x)$ of x, if there exists a connected neighborhood $v(x)$ such that $x \in v(x) \subset u(x)$, then X is called local arcwise connected.

Proposition 6.3.6

If $A \subset (X, \mathcal{T})$ is local arcwise connected and A is connected, then A is arcwise connected.

Proposition 6.3.7

If $(X, \mathcal{T})$ is local arcwise connected and $A \subset X$ is an open connected subset, then A is arcwise connected.

Proposition 6.3.8

The continuous image of a local arcwise connected space is also local arcwise connected.

Proposition 6.3.9

If $X_1, X_2, \cdots X_n$ are local arcwise connected, then their product space is also local arcwise connected.

Definition 6.3.5

(X, d) is a metric space. For $x, y \in X$ and $\forall \varepsilon > 0$, if there exist a set of points $x_0 = x, x_1, x_2, \cdots, x_n = y, x_i \in X$ such that $d(x_i, x_{i+1}) < \varepsilon, i = 0, 1, 2, \cdots, n - 1$, then $(x_0, x_1, \cdots, x_n)$ is called a ε−chain that connects points x and y.

The above materials are from [Xio81]. The interested readers can also refer to [Eis74].

A.7 Order-Relation, Galois Connected and Closure Space

A.7.1 Order-Relation and Galois Connected

Definition 7.1.1

Assume that '$\leq$' is a binary relation on $\mathcal{U}$ and satisfies reflexivity and transitivity properties, i.e., $\forall x \in \mathcal{U}, x \leq x$ and $\forall x, y, z \in \mathcal{U}$, if $x \leq y$ and $y \leq z$, then $x \leq z$, '$\leq$' is called a pre-order or quasi-order on $\mathcal{U}$.

Especially, if '$\leq$' satisfies transitivity and anti-reflexivity, i.e., for $\forall x \in \mathcal{U}, x \leq x$ does not hold, then '$\leq$' is a strict pre-order on $\mathcal{U}$ denoted by '$<$' generally.

Definition 7.1.2

If a pre-order relation satisfies anti-symmetry, i.e., $\forall x, y \in \mathcal{U}, x \leq y, y \leq x \Rightarrow x = y$, then $\leq$ is called a partial order relation on $\mathcal{U}$. $(\mathcal{U}, \leq)$ is called a partial ordered set.

If a pre-order relation $\leq$ satisfies symmetry, i.e., $\forall x, y \in \mathcal{U}, x \leq y \Rightarrow y \leq x$, then $\leq$ is called an equivalence relation on $\mathcal{U}$. Symbol $\leq$ is not used to denote equivalence relations generally.

Definition 7.1.3

Assume that $\leq$ is a semi-order (partial-order) relation on $\mathcal{U}$. For any two elements $x, y \in \mathcal{U}$, if their supremum $sup\{x, y\}$ and infimum $inf\{x, y\}$ exist, then $(\mathcal{U}, \leq)$ is a lattice. For a lattice $(\mathcal{U}, \leq)$, $x \vee y$ and $x \wedge y$ are used to represent the supremum and infimum of two elements x and y generally.

Especially, if for any $\mathcal{V} \subseteq \mathcal{U}, sup\{x | x \in \mathcal{V}\}$ and $inf\{x | x \in \mathcal{V}\}$ exist, then $(\mathcal{U}, \leq)$ is called a complete lattice.

Definition 7.1.4

$(\mathcal{U}, \leq)$ is a semi-order set. $\forall x, y \in \mathcal{U}$, if self-mapping $\varphi : \mathcal{U} \rightarrow \mathcal{U}$ satisfies the following conditions

(1)　$x \leq \varphi(x)$ (increasing property)
(2)　$x \leq y \Rightarrow \varphi(x) \leq \varphi(y)$ (order-preserving)
(3)　$\varphi(x) = \varphi(\varphi(x))$ (idempotent)

Then, φ is a closure operator on $(\mathcal{U}, \leq)$. Correspondingly, if a self-mapping $\phi : \mathcal{U} \rightarrow \mathcal{U}$ on $\mathcal{U}$ satisfies order-preserving, idempotent and decreasing property, i.e., $\phi(x) \leq x$, then ϕ is called an interior operator on $(\mathcal{U}, \leq)$.

Note 7.1.1

φ is a closure operator on $(\mathcal{U}, \leq)$. A set $\varphi(\mathcal{U}) \triangleq \{x \in \mathcal{U} | \exists y \in \mathcal{U} \text{ s.t. } \varphi(y) = x\}$ of images is just a set composed by all fixed points of φ, i.e., $\varphi(\mathcal{U}) = \{x \in \mathcal{U} | \varphi(x) = x\}$. Elements of $\varphi(\mathcal{U})$ are called to be closed under the mapping φ. Especially, if $(\mathcal{U}, \leq)$ is a complete lattice, then $\varphi(\mathcal{U})$ is also a complete lattice.

Note 7.1.2

Assume that φ is a closure operator on a complete lattice $(2^{\mathcal{U}}, \subseteq)$, where $\mathcal{U}$ is any given set and $2^{\mathcal{U}}$ is a power set of $\mathcal{U}$. Then, φ uniquely corresponds to a family $\Omega \subseteq 2^{\mathcal{U}}$ of subsets of $\mathcal{U}$ and Ω satisfies (1) $\mathcal{U} \in \Omega$, (2) $\forall \Omega^* \subseteq \Omega$, $\cap \Omega^* \in \Omega$, Ω is called a Moore family on $\mathcal{U}$, and two-tuple $(\mathcal{U}, \varphi)$ is a closure system.

Please refer to Davey and Priestley (1992) for more details.

Galois Connection (Davey and Priestley, 1992)

Definition 7.1.5

Assume that $(\mathcal{U}, \leq_{\mathcal{U}})$ and $(\mathcal{V}, \leq_{\mathcal{V}})$ are a pair of semi-order structures. $f : \mathcal{U} \rightarrow \mathcal{V}$ and $g : \mathcal{V} \rightarrow \mathcal{U}$ are a pair of mappings. The domains of f and g are $\mathcal{U}$ and $\mathcal{V}$, respectively. If f and g satisfy

For $\forall x \in \mathcal{U}$ and $\forall y \in \mathcal{V}$, $x \leq_{\mathcal{U}} g(y) \Leftrightarrow f(x) \leq_{\mathcal{V}} y$.

Then, (f, g) is called a Galois connection between $(\mathcal{U}, \leq_{\mathcal{U}})$ and $(\mathcal{V}, \leq_{\mathcal{V}})$ as shown below,

$$(\mathcal{U}, \leq_{\mathcal{U}}) \quad (\mathcal{V}, \leq_{\mathcal{V}})$$

Proposition 7.1.1

(f, g) is a Galois connection between $(\mathcal{U}, \leq_{\mathcal{U}})$ and $(\mathcal{V}, \leq_{\mathcal{V}})$, where $f : \mathcal{U} \rightarrow \mathcal{V}$ and $g : \mathcal{V} \rightarrow \mathcal{U}$. If $x, x_1, x_2 \in \mathcal{U}$ and $y, y_1, y_2 \in \mathcal{V}$, then we have the following conclusions.

(1)　$x \leq_{\mathcal{U}} g(f(x)), f(g(y)) \leq_{\mathcal{V}} y$
(2)　$x_1 \leq_{\mathcal{U}} x_2 \Rightarrow f(x_1) \leq_{\mathcal{V}} f(x_2), y_1 \leq_{\mathcal{V}} y_2 \Rightarrow g(y_1) \leq_{\mathcal{U}} g(y_2)$

(3) $f(g(f(x))) = f(x), g(f(g(y))) = g(y)$

Conversely, assume that f and g are a pair of mappings between $(\mathcal{U}, \leq_{\mathcal{U}})$ and $(\mathcal{V}, \leq_{\mathcal{V}})$. For $\forall x, x_1, x_2 \in \mathcal{U}$ and $\forall y, y_1, y_2 \in \mathcal{V}$, the above two conditions (1) and (2) hold. Then, f and g are a Galois connection between $(\mathcal{U}, \leq_{\mathcal{U}})$ and $(\mathcal{V}, \leq_{\mathcal{V}})$.

Proposition 7.1.2

Assume that (f, g) is a Galois connection between $(\mathcal{U}, \leq_{\mathcal{U}})$ and $(\mathcal{V}, \geq_{\mathcal{V}})$, where $f : \mathcal{U} \rightarrow \mathcal{V}$ and $g : \mathcal{V} \rightarrow \mathcal{U}$. Then the combination mapping $g \circ f$ is a closure operator on $(\mathcal{U}, \leq_{\mathcal{U}})$, and $f \circ g$ is an interior operator on $(\mathcal{V}, \leq_{\mathcal{V}})$.

A.7.2 Closure Operation and Closure Space

The concept of closure operation that we previously introduced is under the order theory sense. The terms of closure operation, closure space and related properties that we will introduce below have the topologic sense, especially under E. Cech sense, i.e., based on set theory and always assuming that there does not appear paradox (Cech, 1966).

Definition 7.2.1

$\mathcal{U}$ is a domain. If mapping $cl : 2^{\mathcal{U}} \rightarrow 2^{\mathcal{U}}$ satisfies the following three axioms, where $2^{\mathcal{U}}$ is a power set of $\mathcal{U}$,

(cl1) $cl(\emptyset) = \emptyset$
(cl2) $\forall X \subseteq \mathcal{U}, X \subseteq cl(X)$
(cl3) $\forall X \subseteq \mathcal{U}$ and $\forall Y \subseteq \mathcal{U}, cl(X \cup Y) = cl(X) \cup cl(Y)$

then, cl is called a closure operation on $\mathcal{U}$. Correspondingly, two-tuples $(\mathcal{U}, cl)$ is a closure space, and $cl(X)$ is a $cl-$ closure of subset X. If not causing confusion, the closure $cl(X)$ of subset X is denoted by $\overline{X}$.

Proposition 7.2.1

If $(\mathcal{U}, cl)$ is a closure space, then

(1) $cl(\mathcal{U}) = \mathcal{U}$
(2)   For $\forall X \subseteq \mathcal{U}$ and $\forall Y \subseteq \mathcal{U}$, if $X \subseteq Y$, then $cl(X) \subseteq cl(Y)$
(3)   For any family $X_i (i \in \mathcal{I})$ of subsets of $\mathcal{U}$, have $cl(\bigcap_{i \in \mathcal{I}} X_i) \subseteq \bigcap_{i \in \mathcal{I}} cl(X_i)$

Definition 7.2.2

$C(\mathcal{U})$ is a set composed by all closure operations on $\mathcal{U}$, i.e., $C(\mathcal{U}) = \{\mu | \mu$ is a closure operation on $\mathcal{U}\}$. Define a binary relation $\leq$ on $C(\mathcal{U})$ as

$$\forall \mu, \nu \in C(\mathcal{U}), \nu \leq \mu \Leftrightarrow \forall X \subseteq \mathcal{U}, \nu(X) \subseteq \mu(X)$$

If $v \leq \mu$ holds, then closure operation μ is said to be coarser than v. Equivalently, v is said to be finer than μ.

Theorem 7.2.1

Binary relation $\leq$ is a semi-order relation on $C(\mathcal{U})$. $(C(U), \leq)$ has a greatest element μ_1 and a least element μ_0. That is, for $\forall X \subseteq U$, if $X \neq \varnothing$, then $\mu_1(X) = \mathcal{U}$, otherwise $\mu_1(\varnothing) = \varnothing$; and $\mu_0(X) = X$. Furthermore, for any subset $\{\mu_i | i \in I\}$ of $C(U)$ and $\forall X \subseteq U$, we have $(\sup\{\mu_i | i \in \mathcal{I}\})(X) = \cup \{\mu_i(X) | i \in \mathcal{I}\}$, i.e., $C(U)$ is order complete with respect to $\leq$.

Definition 7.2.2

(U, cl) is a closure space. Mapping $int_{cl} : 2^{\mathcal{U}} \rightarrow 2^{\mathcal{U}}$, induced by closure operation cl, is called an interior operation, denoted by int. Its definition is as follows

$$\forall X \subseteq \mathcal{U}, \ int(X) = \mathcal{U} - cl(\mathcal{U} - X)$$

Correspondingly, $int(X)$ is called $cl-$interior of X, or simply interior.

Proposition 7.2.3

$(\mathcal{U}, cl)$ is a closure space. If int is defined by Definition 7.2.2, then

(int1) $int(\mathcal{U}) = \mathcal{U}$
(int2) $\forall X \subseteq \mathcal{U}, \ int(X) \subseteq X$
(int3) $\forall X \subseteq \mathcal{U}$ and $\forall Y \subseteq \mathcal{U}, \ int(X \cap Y) = int(X) \cap int(Y)$

Assume that $int \ 2^{\mathcal{U}} \rightarrow 2^{\mathcal{U}}$ satisfies axioms **int1** $\sim$ **int3**. Define an operation cl as follows

$$\forall X \subseteq \mathcal{U}, \ cl(X) = \mathcal{U} - int(\mathcal{U} - X)$$

It can be proved that cl is a closure operation on $\mathcal{U}$ and $int_{cl} = int$. If $I(\mathcal{U})$ is a set of mappings int on $\mathcal{U}$ that satisfy axioms **int1** $\sim$ **int3**, then there exists one-one correspondence between $C(\mathcal{U})$ and $I(\mathcal{U})$. Or a closure operation and an interior operation are dual.

Definition 7.2.3

$(\mathcal{U}, cl)$ is a closure space. int is a dual interior operation of cl. For $\forall X \subseteq \mathcal{U}$, if $cl(X) = X$, then X is called a close set. If $cl(\mathcal{U} - X) = \mathcal{U} - X$, or equivalently, $int(X) = X$, then X is called an open set.

Proposition 7.2.4

$(\mathcal{U}, cl)$ is a closure space. int is a dual interior operation of cl. We have

(1) $int(\varnothing) = \varnothing$

(2) For $\forall X \subseteq \mathcal{U}$ and $\forall Y \subseteq \mathcal{U}$, if $X \subseteq Y$, then $int(X) \subseteq int(Y)$.

(3) For any family $X_i (i \in \mathcal{I})$ of subsets of $\mathcal{U}$, have $\underset{i \in \mathcal{I}}{\cup} int(X_i) \subseteq int(\underset{i \in \mathcal{I}}{\cup} X_i)$

Definition 7.2.4

A topological closure operation on $\mathcal{U}$ is a closure operation cl that satisfies the following condition

$$(cl4) \, \forall X \subseteq \mathcal{U}, \; cl(cl(X)) = cl(X)$$

If cl is a topological closure operation, then closure space $(\mathcal{U}, cl)$ is a topological space.

Proposition 7.2.5

If $(\mathcal{U}, cl)$ is a closure space, then each condition shown below is the necessary and sufficient condition that $(\mathcal{U}, cl)$ is a topological space.

(1) The closure of each subset is a close set

(2) The interior of each subset is an open set

(3) The closure of each subset equals to the intersection of all close sets that include the subset

(4) The interior of each subset equals to the union of all open sets that include the subset.

Theorem 7.2.2

Assume that $\tilde{O}$ is a family of subsets of set $\mathcal{U}$ that satisfies the following conditions

(o1) $\varnothing \in \tilde{O}, \mathcal{U} \in \tilde{O}$

(o2) $\forall \tilde{O}_1 \subseteq \tilde{O}, \cup \{A | A \in \tilde{O}_1\} \in \tilde{O}$, i.e., $\tilde{O}$ is closed for any union operation

(o3) $\forall A, B \in \tilde{O}, A \cap B \in \tilde{O}$, i.e., $\tilde{O}$ is closed for finite intersection operation.

Let $C_{\tilde{O}} = \{cl | cl$ is a closure operation on $\mathcal{U}$ and the set composed by all open sets of $(\mathcal{U}, cl)$ is just $\tilde{O}\}$.

Then, there just exists a topological closure operation cl_T on $C_{\tilde{O}}$ such that cl_T is the roughest element on $C_{\tilde{O}}$.

Theorem 7.2.3

Assume that $\tilde{C}$ is a family of subsets of set $\mathcal{U}$ that satisfies the following conditions

(c1) $\varnothing \in \tilde{C}, \mathcal{U} \in \tilde{C}$

(c2) $\forall \tilde{C}_1 \subseteq \tilde{C}, \cap \{A | A \in \tilde{C}_1\} \in \tilde{C}$, i.e., $\tilde{C}$ is closed for any union operation

(c3) $\forall A, B \in \tilde{C}, A \cup B \in \tilde{C}$, i.e., $\tilde{C}$ is closed for finite intersection operation.

Then, there just exists a topological closure operation cl_T on $\mathcal{U}$ such that $\tilde{C}$ is just a set that composed by all close sets on $(\mathcal{U}, cl_T)$.

Using open set as a language to describe topology, axioms **(o1)** ∼ **(o3)** are used. However, conditions **(cl1)** ∼ **(cl4)** are called axioms of Kuratowski closure operator. Kuratowski closure operator, interior operator that satisfies axioms **(int1)** ∼ **(int3)** and **(int4)**: $\forall X \subseteq \mathcal{U}$ $int(int(X)) = int(X)$, open set and neighborhood system are equivalent tools for describing topology. For describing non-topologic closure spaces, only closure operations, interior operations and neighborhood systems can be used, but open set or close set cannot be used as a language directly. In some sense, closure spaces are more common than topologic spaces. We will discuss continuity, connectivity and how to construct a new closure space from a known one below.

A closure operation *cl* on a domain set $\mathcal{U}$ is defined as a mapping from $2^{\mathcal{U}}$ to itself, where domain $Dom(cl) = 2^{\mathcal{U}}$ and codomain $Ran(cl) \subseteq 2^{\mathcal{U}}$. Closure operation *cl* is completely defined by binary relation $R \subseteq \mathcal{U} \times 2^{\mathcal{U}}$, i.e., $\forall x \in \mathcal{U}$ and $\forall X \subseteq \mathcal{U}$, $xRX \Leftrightarrow x \in cl(X)$. Obviously, we have $cl(X) = R^{-1}(X) \triangleq \{y \in \mathcal{U} | yRX\}$.

Compared to *cl*, relation *R* more clearly embodies the intuitive meaning of closure operation, i.e., what points are proximal to what sets. Naturally, the intuitive meaning of continuous mappings is the mapping that remains the '*x* is proximal to subset *X*' relation.

Definition 7.2.5

f is a mapping from closure space $\mathcal{U}$ to closure space $\mathcal{V}$. For $x \in \mathcal{U}$ and $\forall X \subseteq \mathcal{U}$, if $x \in \overline{X}$, have $f(x) \in \overline{f[X]}$ holds, then *f* is called continuous at *x*. If *f* is continuous at any *x*, then *f* is called continuous.

Theorem 7.2.4

f is a mapping from closure space $\mathcal{U}$ to closure space $\mathcal{V}$. The following statements are equivalent.

(1) *f* is a continuous mapping
(2) For $\forall X \subseteq \mathcal{U}, f[\overline{X}] \subseteq \overline{f[X]}$ holds.
(3) For $\forall Y \subseteq \mathcal{V}, \overline{f^{-1}[Y]} \subseteq f^{-1}[\overline{Y}]$ holds.

Definition 7.2.6

f is an 1-1 correspondence (bijective mapping) from closure space $\mathcal{U}$ to closure space $\mathcal{V}$. Both *f* and f^{-1} are continuous mappings. Then, *f* is called a homeomorphous mapping from $\mathcal{U}$ to $\mathcal{V}$, or $\mathcal{V}$ is a homeomorph of $\mathcal{U}$.

Definition 7.2.7

If there exists a homeomorphous mapping from closure space $\mathcal{U}$ to $\mathcal{V}$, then $\mathcal{U}$ and $\mathcal{V}$ are called homeomorphous closure spaces.

Definition 7.2.8

If a closure space $\mathcal{U}$ has property **P** such that all spaces that homeomorphous to $\mathcal{U}$ have the property, then **P** is called the topological property.

Obviously, the homeomorphous relation is an equivalent relation on the set composed by all closure spaces.

Definition 7.2.9

$(\mathcal{U}, \mu)$ is a closure space. For $X \subseteq \mathcal{U}$, if there exist subsets X_1 and X_2 on $\mathcal{U}$ such that $X = X_1 \cup X_2$, and if $(\mu(X_1) \cap X_2) \cup (X_1 \cup \mu(X_2)) = \varnothing$, then $X_1 = \varnothing$ or $X_2 = \varnothing$, then X is called a connected subset of $(\mathcal{U}, \mu)$.

Definition 7.2.10

f is a continuous mapping from closure space $(\mathcal{U}, \mu)$ to closure space $(\mathcal{V}, \nu)$. If $X \subseteq \mathcal{U}$ is a connected subset, then $f(X)$ is a connected subset on $(\mathcal{V}, \nu)$.

Below we will discuss how to generate a new closure operation from a known closure operation, or a set of closure operations. Two generated approaches are discussed, the generated projectively and generated inductively. The product topology and quotient topology discussed in point topology are special cases of the above two generated approaches in closure operation.

Definition 7.2.11

$\{(\mathcal{U}_i, \mu_i) | i \in \mathcal{I}\}$ is a set of closure spaces. For any $i \in \mathcal{I}$, the closure operation on $\mathcal{V}$ generated inductively by mapping $f_i : \mathcal{U}_i \to \mathcal{V}$ is defined as follows

$$\forall X \subseteq \mathcal{V}, \ \nu_i(X) = X \cup f_i\big(\mu_i\big(f_i^{-1}(X)\big)\big)$$

The above closure operation is the finest one among all closure operations that make f_i continuous.

The closure operation on $\mathcal{V}$ generated inductively by a set $\{f_i | i \in \mathcal{I}\}$ of mappings is defined as follows

$$(\sup\{\nu_i | i \in \mathcal{I}\})(X) = X \cup \big\{f_i\big(\mu_i\big(f_i^{-1}(X)\big)\big) \big| i \in \mathcal{I}\big\}$$

The above closure operation is the finest one among all closure operations that make each f_i, $i \in \mathcal{I}$ continuous.

Proposition 7.2.6

$(\mathcal{U}, \mu)$ is a closure space. R is an equivalence relation on $\mathcal{U}$, and its corresponding quotient set is $[\mathcal{U}]$, where $p : \mathcal{U} \to [\mathcal{U}]$, $p(x) = [x]$. The closure operation ν generated inductively by p is defined as a quotient closure operation on $[\mathcal{U}]$. And for $\forall X \subseteq [\mathcal{U}]$,

$$\nu(X) = X \cup p\big(\mu\big(p^{-1}(X)\big)\big) = p\big(\mu\big(p^{-1}(X)\big)\big)$$

Definition 7.2.12

$\{(\mathcal{U}_i, \mu_i) | i \in \mathcal{I}\}$ is a set of closure spaces. For any $i \in \mathcal{I}$, the closure operation on $\mathcal{V}$ generated projectively by $f_i : \mathcal{V} \to \mathcal{U}_i$ is defined as follows

$$\forall X \subseteq \mathcal{V}, \ \nu_i(X) = f_i^{-1}\big(\mu_i(f_i(X))\big)$$

The above closure operation is the coarsest one among all closure operations that make f_i continuous. The closure operation on $\mathcal{V}$ generated projectively by a set $\{f_i | i \in \mathcal{I}\}$ of mappings is defined by $inf\{\nu_i | i \in \mathcal{I}\}$. It is the coarsest one among all closure operations that make each f_i, $i \in \mathcal{I}$ continuous.

Note that $(inf\{\nu_i | i \in \mathcal{I}\})(X)$ is not necessarily the $\cap \{f_i^{-1}(\mu_i(f_i(X))) | i \in \mathcal{I}\}$. And the latter is not necessarily a closure operation, unless a set $\{(\mathcal{U}_i, \mu_i) | i \in \mathcal{I}\}$ of closure spaces satisfies a certain condition (Cech, 1966).

A.7.3 Closure Operations Defined by Different Axioms

Two forms of closure that we mentioned previously are denotes by closure operator and closure operation, respectively. The former is under order theory sense and the latter is under topologic sense. In fact, the term of closure does not have a uniform definition. In different documents it might have different meanings. We introduce different definitions of closure, quasi-discrete closure space, Allexandroff topology, etc. below.

$\mathcal{U}$ is a domain. Assume that $Cl : 2^{\mathcal{U}} \to 2^{\mathcal{U}}$ is a given mapping. For $\forall X \subseteq \mathcal{U}$, $Cl(X)$ is called the closure of subset X. $(\mathcal{U}, Cl)$ is called the most general closure space. $Int : 2^{\mathcal{U}} \to 2^{\mathcal{U}}$ is a dual mapping of Cl, i.e., $Int(X) \triangleq \mathcal{U} - Cl(\mathcal{U} - X)$. $Int(X)$ is called the interior of subset X. For convenience, for $\forall X, Y \in 2^{\mathcal{U}}$, the following axioms are introduced (Table 7.3.1).

Table 7.3.1

	(CL0)	(CL1)	(CL2)	(CL3)	(CL4)	(CL5)
Neighborhood space	◆	◆	◆			
Closure space	◆	◆	◆		◆	
Smith space	◆	◆		◆		
Cech closure space	◆	◆	◆	◆		
Topological space	◆	◇	◆	◆	◆	
Alexandroff space	◆	◇	◆	◇		◆
Alexandroff topology	◆	◇	◆	◇	◆	◆

◆: the axiom satisfied by definition ◇: the property induced by definition.

(CL0) $\quad Cl(\varnothing) = \varnothing$

(CL1) $\quad X \subseteq Y \Rightarrow Cl(X) \subseteq Cl(Y)$

(CL2) $\quad X \subseteq Cl(X)$

(CL3) $\quad Cl(X \cup Y) \subseteq Cl(X) \cup Cl(Y)$

(CL4) $\quad Cl(X) = Cl(Cl(X))$

(CL5) $\quad$ for any family $\{X_i | i \in \mathcal{I}\}$ of subsets on $\mathcal{U}$, $\bigcup_{i \in \mathcal{I}} Cl(X_i) = Cl(\bigcup_{i \in \mathcal{I}} X_i)$.

where, **(CL1)**+**(CL3)** are equivalent to axiom **(CL3)'**: $Cl(X \cup Y) = Cl(X) \cup Cl(Y)$.

Using the dual interior operation *Int* of *Cl*, we have the following equivalent axioms **(CL0)** $\sim$ **(CL5)**. For $\forall X, Y \in 2^{\mathcal{U}}$, we have

(INT0) $\quad Int(U) = U$

(INT1) $\quad X \subseteq Y \Rightarrow Int(X) \subseteq Int(Y)$

(INT2) $\quad Int(X) \subseteq X$

(INT3) $\quad Int(X) \cap Int(Y) \subseteq Int(X \cap Y)$

(INT4) $\quad Int(X) = Int(Int(X))$

(INT5) $\quad$ for any family $\{X_i | i \in \mathcal{I}\}$ of subsets on $\mathcal{U}$, $\bigcap_{i \in \mathcal{I}} Int(X_i) = Int(\bigcap_{i \in \mathcal{I}} X_i)$.

where, **(INT1)**+**(INT3)** are equivalent to **INT3'**: $Int(X \cap Y) = Int(X) \cap Int(Y)$.

Note 7.3.1

Under the general order theory sense, the closure space is defined by axioms **(CL1)**, **(CL2)** and **(CL4)**. For example, the closure operation defined by Definition 7.1.4 is called closure operator. When considering the inclusion relation between a power set and a subset, the axiom **(CL0)** may be or may not be satisfied.

Note 7.3.2

Under the Cech's sense, the closure space is called pre-topology and is defined by axioms **(CL0)** $\sim$ **(CL3)**. In Definition 7.1.4, axioms **(CL0)** and **(CL3)** are replaced by **(CL3)'**. The topology described by the Kuratowski closure operator that satisfies axioms **(CL0)**, **(CL2)**, **(CL3)'** and **(CL4)** is equivalent to the above description, since axiom **(CL3)'** may induce axiom **(CL3)**, and **(CL4)**+**(CL3)** may induce **(CL3)'**. The distinction between the closure space in the Cech's sense and the topologic space in general sense is the satisfaction of the idempotent axiom or not. So the former is the extension of the latter.

Note 7.3.3

Axiom **(CL5)** is called Alexandroff property. The topologic space that satisfies the Alexandroff property is called Alexandroff topology. In Cech (1966) and Galton (2003), axiom **(CL5)** is called quasi-discrete property. The Cech closure space that satisfies quasi-discrete property is called quasi-discrete closure space.

Note 7.3.4

To describe the closure space, except closure and interior operations, the neighborhood and the filter convergent sequence can be used equivalently. In Table 7.3.1, the neighborhood and Smith spaces (Kelly, 1955; Smith, 1995) originally are described by neighborhood language; we use the equivalent closure axioms.

Some Concepts and Properties of Integral and Statistical Inference

B.1 Some Properties of Integral

B.1.1 Functions of Bounded Variation

Definition B.1.1

$f(x)$ is a finite function on $[a, b]$. Points of division on $[a, b]$ are
$x_0 = a < x_1 < x_2 < \cdots < x_n = b$. Define

$$V = \sum_{0}^{n-1} |f(x_{i+1}) - F(x_i)|$$

The supremum of V is called total variation of $f(x)$ on $[a, b]$ denoted by $V_a^b f(x)$.

When $V_a^b f(x) < \infty$, $f(x)$ is called a function of bounded variation on $[a, b]$, or $f(x)$ has a bounded variation on $[a, b]$.

Proposition B.1.1

A monotonic function is a function of bounded variation.

Proposition B.1.2

A function of bounded variation is bounded.

Proposition B.1.3

The sum, difference and product of two functions of bounded variation are still functions of bounded variation.

Proposition B.1.4

If both $f(x)$ and $g(x)$ have a bounded variation and $|g(x)| \geq \delta > 0$, then $f(x)/g(x)$ is still a function of bounded variation.

Proposition B.1.5

If $f(x)$ is a finite function on $[a, b]$ and $a < c < b$, then $V_a^b(f) = V_a^c(f) + V_c^b(f)$.

Proposition B.1.6

The necessary and sufficient condition that function $f(x)$ has a bounded variation is that $f(x)$ can be represented by the difference of two increasing functions.

Proposition B.1.7

If $f(x)$ has a bounded variation on $[a, b]$, then $f'(x)$ is finite almost everywhere on $[a, b]$, and is integrable on $[a, b]$, where $f'(x)$ is the differential of $f(x)$.

Proposition B.1.8

Any function of bounded variation can be represented by the sum of its jump function and a continuous function of bounded variation.

Proposition B.1.9 (Herlly' Principle of Selection)

Define an infinite number $f_\alpha(x)$ of functions of bounded variation on $[a, b]$, and denoted by $F = \{f_\alpha(x)\}_{\alpha \in I}$. If there is a constant c such that $\forall \alpha \in I$, $|f_\alpha(x)| < c$ and $V_a^b(f_\alpha) < c$, then a sequence $\{f_n(x)\}$ of everywhere convergent functions on $[a, b]$ can be selected from F and its limit function $\varphi(x)$ still has a bounded variation.

B.1.2 LS Integral

Definition B.2.1

$f(x)$ and $g(x)$ are two finite functions on $[a, b]$. Points of division on $[a, b]$ are $x_0 = a < x_1 < x_2 < \cdots < x_n = b$. Choose any point ξ_k from each interval $[x_k, x_{k+1}]$ and construct a sum as follows

$$\sigma = \sum_0^{n-1} f(\xi_k)[g(x_{k+1}) - g(x_k)]$$

When $\lambda = \max(x_{k+1} - x_k) \to 0$, if the sum converges to the same limit I independent of the selection of ξ_k, then limit I is called S–integral of $f(x)$ with respect to $g(x)$ denoted by

$$\int_a^b f(x)dg(x), \text{ or } (S) \int_a^b f(x)dg(x)$$

Proposition B.2.1

If $f(x)$ is continuous on $[a, b]$ and $g(x)$ has a bounded variation on $[a, b]$, then $\int_a^b f(x)dg(x)$ exists.

Proposition B.2.2

If $f(x)$ is continuous on $[a, b]$, $g(x)$ has differential $g'(x)$ everywhere and $g'(x)$ is $(R)-$ integrable (Riemann integrable), then

$$(S) \int_a^b f(x)dg(x) = (R) \int_a^b f(x)g'(x)dx$$

Proposition B.2.3

$f(x)$ is continuous on $[a, b]$ and $g(x)$ has a bounded variation, then

$$\left| \int_a^b f(x)dg(x) \right| \le M(f) \overset{b}{\underset{a}{V}}(g)$$

where $M(f) = \max|f(x)|$.

Proposition B.2.4

If $g(x)$ is a function of bounded variation on $[a, b]$, $f_n(x)$ is a sequence of continuous functions on $[a, b]$ and uniformly converges to a continuous function $f(x)$, then

$$\lim_{n \to \infty} \int_a^b f_n(x)dg(x) = \int_a^b f(x)dg(x).$$

Proposition B.2.5

$f(x)$ is a continuous function on $[a, b]$. $g_n(x)$ on $[a, b]$ converges to a finite function $g(x)$. If

$$\forall n, \ V_a^b(g_n) \le K < \infty, \text{ then } \lim_{n \to \infty} \int_a^b f_n(x)dg_n(x) = \int_a^b f(x)dg(x).$$

Definition B.2.2

If $\forall e \subset [a, b]$, e is measurable set and has its corresponding value $\phi(e)$, then $\phi(\cdot)$ is called a set function on $[a, b]$. Given e, when $me \to 0$ have $\phi(e) \to 0$, then $\phi(\cdot)$ is called an absolutely continuous function, where me is the measure of e.

For countable mutually disjoint measurable sets $e_1, e_2, \cdots, e_n, \cdots$, have $\phi(\sum_1^\infty e_k) = \sum_1^\infty \phi(e_k)$, then $\phi(\cdot)$ is called a completely additive set function.

Definition B.2.3

$f(x)$ is a bounded measurable function on $[a, b]$. $g(x)$ is a completely additive set function on $[a, b]$. Assume that $A < f(x) < B$. Interval $[A, B]$ is partitioned as follows

$$y_0 = A < y_1 < y_2 < \cdots < y_n = B$$

Define $e_k = E(y_k \leq f(x) < y_{k+1})$ on $[y_k, y_{k+1}]$ and construct a sum as

$$s = \sum_0^{n-1} y_k g(e_k), \quad S = \sum_0^{n-1} y_{k+1} g(e_k)$$

If s and S have the same limit I independent of the selection of y_k, then I is called $LS-$integral (Lebesgue-Stieltjes integral) of $f(x)$ with respect to $g(\cdot)$.

B.1.3 Limit Under Integral Symbol

Proposition B.3.1

$f_1(x), f_2(x), \cdots, f_n(x), \cdots$ is a sequence of measurable functions on E and converge in measure to $F(x)$. If there exists integrable function $\phi(x)$ such that $\forall n, |f_n(x)| \leq \phi(x), x \in E$, then

$$\lim_{n \to \infty} \int_E f_n(x)dx = \int_E F(x)dx$$

Definition B.3.1

Assume that $M = \{f(x)\}$ is a family of integrable functions on E. If for $\forall \varepsilon > 0$, there exists $\delta > 0$, when $e \subset E$ and $me < \delta$, for all $f(x) \in M$, $|\int_e f(x)dx| < \varepsilon$ uniformly holds, M is called absolutely equicontinous integral on E.

Proposition B.3.2 (Vitali Theorem)

A sequence $f_1(x), f_2(x), \cdots, f_n(x), \cdots$ of functions converges in measure to $F(x)$ on E, $f_n(x)$ is integrable on E and $\{f_n(x)\}$ has absolutely equicontinuous integral on E, then $F(x)$ is integrable on E and

$$\lim_{n \to \infty} \int_E f_n(x)dx = \int_E F(x)dx$$

Proposition B.3.3

$\{f_n(x)\}$ is a sequence of integrable functions on a measurable set E. For $\forall e \in E$, e is measurable, if $\lim_{n \to \infty} \int_e f_n(x)dx = 0$ holds, then $\{f_n(x)\}$ has absolutely equicontinuous integral.

Corollary B.3.1

Assume that $\{f_n(x)\}$ is a sequence of integrable functions and $F(x)$ is an integrable function on a measurable set E. For any measurable set $e \subset E$, if

$$\lim_{n \to \infty} \int_e f_n(x)dx = \int_e F(x)dx,$$

then $\{f_n(x)\}$ has absolutely equicontinuous integral on E.

Proposition B.3.4

$\{f_n(x)\}$ is a sequence of integrable functions on E and converges in measure to an integrable function $F(x)$, then $\forall e \subset E$ (e is measurable), we have

$$\lim_{n \to \infty} \int_e f_n(x)dx = \int_e F(x)dx$$

The necessary and sufficient condition of the above result is that $\{f_n(x)\}$ has absolutely equicontinuous integral on E.

Proposition B.3.5 (Vallee-Poussin Theorem)

$M = \{f_\alpha(x)\}_{\alpha \in I}$ is a family of measurable functions on a measurable set E. If there is a positive increasing function $\phi(u)$, $u \geq 0$, such that $\lim_{u \to \infty} \phi(u) = \infty$ and for $\forall f_\alpha(x) \in M$, have $\lim_{n \to \infty} \int_E |f_\alpha(x)| \phi(|f_\alpha(x)|)dx < A$, where A is a constant independent of $f(x)$, then each $f_\alpha(x)$ is integrable on E and $M = \{f_\alpha(x)\}_{\alpha \in I}$ has absolutely equicontinuous function.

Proposition B.3.6

If $M = \{f_\alpha(x)\}$, $\alpha \in I$, is a family of functions on E having absolutely equicontinuous integral, then there exists a monotonically increasing function $\phi(u)(u \geq 0)$ such that $\lim_{u \to \infty} \phi(u) = \infty$ and $\forall \alpha \in I$, $\int_a^b |f_\alpha(x)| \phi(|f_\alpha(x)|)dx \leq A < \infty$, where A is a constant independent of $f_\alpha(x)$.

Proposition B.3.7

$f(x)$ is an integrable function on $[a, b]$. If $\forall c \in [a, b]$, have $\int_a^c f(x)dx = 0$, then $f(x) \sim 0$ ($f(x)$ is zero almost everywhere).

B.2 Central Limit Theorem

$x_1, x_2, \cdots, x_n, \cdots$ are independently random variables. Let

$$a_k = E(x_k), b_k^2 = D(x_k), B_n^2 = \sum_1^n b_k^2$$

Proposition B.2.1

$\{x_n\}$ is an independently random variable. If $\forall \tau > 0$, the following formula is satisfied

$$\lim_{n \to \infty} \frac{1}{B_n^2} \sum_1^n \int_{|x-a_k|>\tau B_n} (x - a_k)^2 dF_k(x) = 0$$

where $F_k(x)$ is the distribution function of x_k, then when $n \to \infty$, for x the following formula uniformly holds

$$P\left\{\frac{1}{B_n}\sum_1^n (x_k - a_k) < x\right\} \to \frac{1}{\sqrt{2\pi}}\int_{-\infty}^x \exp(-t^2/2)\,dt$$

Corollary B.2.1

x_k is *i.i.d* and has a non-zero variance, then when $n \to \infty$, for x the following formula uniformly holds

$$P\left\{\frac{1}{B_n}\sum_1^n (x_k - a) < x\right\} \to \frac{1}{\sqrt{2\pi}}\int_{-\infty}^x \exp(-t^2/2)\,dt$$

where, a is its mean and $B_n = \sqrt{n}b$, b is its variance.

Proposition B.2.2

$\{x_k\}$ is an independently random variable. If there exists a positive constant $\delta > 0$ such that when $n \to \infty$,

$$\frac{1}{B_n^{2+\delta}}\sum_1^n E(x_k - a_k)^{2+\delta} \to 0$$

then when $n \to \infty$, for x, the following formula uniformly holds

$$P\left\{\frac{1}{B_n}\sum_1^n (x_k - a_k) < x\right\} \to \frac{1}{\sqrt{2\pi}}\int_{-\infty}^x \exp(-t^2/2)\,dt$$

Definition B.2.1

x is a discrete random variable. If there exist constants $a, h > 0$ such that all possible values of x can be represented by form $a + kh$, where $k : (-\infty < k < \infty)$, then x is called having sieve distribution, or x is a sieve variable.

Proposition B.2.3

$\{x_n\}$ is an i.i.d. sieve random variable. If it has finite mean and variance, then when $n \to \infty$, for x $(-\infty < k < \infty)$ the following formula uniformly holds

$$\frac{B_n}{h}P_n(k) - \frac{1}{\sqrt{2\pi}}\exp(-Z(n,k)^2/2) \to 0$$

where, $Z(n, k) = (an + kh - A_n)/B_n, A_n = E(y_n), B_n^2 = D(y_n), y_n = x_1 + x_2 + \cdots + x_n.$

Proposition B.2.4

$\{x_n\}$ is *i.i.d* and has finite mean and variance. When $n > n_0$ (n_0 is a fixed integer) let the distribution density function of $S_n = \frac{1}{\sqrt{nDx_1}} \sum_1^n (x_k - a_k)$ be $P_n(x)$. Then, the necessary and sufficient condition that $n \to \infty$, for $x \in (-\infty, \infty)$ the formula $P_n(x) - \frac{1}{\sqrt{2\pi}} \exp(-x^2/2) \to 0$ uniformly holds, is that there exists an integer n_1 such that $n \geq n_1$ function $P_n(x)$ is bounded.

B.3 Statistical Inference

B.3.1 SPRT Method

Definition 3.1.1

$\{x_k\}$ is *i.i.d* and its distribution depends on parameter θ, denoted by $f(x; \theta)$.

A hypothesis testing problem: the simple null hypothesis $H_0 : \theta = \theta_0$ and the simple alternative hypothesis $H_1 : \theta = \theta_1$. Let

$$f_{jn} = \prod_{i=1}^n f(x_i; \theta_j), j = 0, 1$$

$$\lambda_n(x) \triangleq \lambda_n(x_1, x_2, \cdots, x_n) \triangleq \frac{f_{1n}(x)}{f_{0n}(x)}$$

The testing procedure is the following

Given constants A and B. Assume that x_1 is the first observation of the subsample. Calculate $\lambda_1(x_1)$.

If $\lambda_1(x_1) \geq A$, then stop the observation and reject the null hypothesis H_0.

If $\lambda_1(x_1) \leq B$, then stop the observation and accept the null hypothesis H_0.

If $B < \lambda_1(x_1) < A$, then continue to get the second observation x_2.

Generally, if from the $n - 1$-th observation the 'stopping decision' cannot be made, then continue to get the n-th observation x_n and calculate $\lambda_n(x_1, x_2, \cdots, x_n)$.

If $\lambda_n(x_1, x_2, \cdots, x_n) \geq A$, then stop sampling and reject H_0.

If $\lambda_n(x_1, x_2, \cdots, x_n) \leq B$, then stop sampling and accept H_0.

If $B < \lambda_n(x_1, x_2, \cdots, x_n) < A$, then continue sampling.

The above testing procedure is called Sequential Probability Ratio Test denoted by *SPRT*. Constants A and B are called the stopping boundaries of *SPRT*.

Proposition 3.1.1

If *SPRT* stops with probability 1, its stopping boundaries are constants A and B, and significance level is (α, β), then

$$A \leq \frac{1-\beta}{\alpha}, B \geq \frac{\beta}{1-\alpha}, 0 < \alpha, \beta > 1$$

Proposition 3.1.2

If *SPRT* stops with probability 1, stopping boundary $A = \frac{1-\beta}{\alpha}, B = \frac{\beta}{1-\alpha}$ and significance level (α', β'), then $\alpha' \leq \frac{\alpha}{1-\beta}, \beta' \leq \frac{\beta}{1-\alpha}$.

Let

$$z \triangleq \log \frac{f(x; \theta_1)}{f(x; \theta_0)}, z_i \triangleq \log \frac{f(x_i; \theta_1)}{f(x_i; \theta_0)}$$

$$a \triangleq \log A, b \triangleq \log B$$

$$\log \lambda_n(x_1, x_2, \cdots, x_n) = \sum_1^n z_i = S_n$$

The stopping rule of *SPRT* is the following.

If $S_n \geq a$, then reject H_0.

If $S_n \leq b$, then accept H_0.

If $b < S_n < a$, then continue sampling.

Proposition 3.1.3

If for a given parameter θ, have $P_\theta(Z = 0) < 1$, where $Z = \log(f(x; \theta_1)/f(x; \theta_0))$, then there exist ρ, $0 < \rho < 1$, n_0 and c, $0 < c < \infty$ such that

$$P_\theta(N > n) \leq c\rho^n, \forall n \geq n_0$$

where, N is the stopping variable of *SPRT*.

Proposition 3.1.4

Assume that $Z = \log(f(x; \theta_1)/f(x; \theta_0))$. If for $f(x; \theta)$, have $P_\theta(|Z| > 0) > 0$, then $P_\theta\{N < \infty\} < 1$.

Proposition 3.1.5

$\{x_n\}$ is *i.i.d.*, $g(x)$ is a measurable function and $E(|g(x)|) < \infty$. Let N be a stopping variable and $S_N \triangleq \sum_1^n g(x_i)$. If $E(N) < \infty$, then

$$E(S_N) = E(g(x))E(N)$$

Especially, if $E_{\theta i}(|Z|) < \infty, E_{\theta i}(|Z|) \neq 0, i = 0, 1$, then

$$E_{\theta_0}(N) \approx \frac{\alpha a + (1 - \alpha)b}{E_{\theta_0}(Z)}$$

$$E_{\theta_1}(N) \approx \frac{(1 - \beta)a + \beta b}{E_{\theta_1}(Z)}$$

Proposition 3.1.6

Assume that $E_{\theta_0}(|Z|) < \infty, E_{\theta_0}(Z) \neq 0$. For a *SPRT* with stopping probability one and significance level (α, β), the following formula holds

$$E_{\theta_0}(N) \approx \frac{(1 - \alpha)\log\frac{\beta}{1-\alpha} + \alpha \log\frac{1-\beta}{\alpha}}{E_{\theta_0}(Z)}$$

Or approximately,

$$E_{\theta_0}(N) \approx \frac{(1 - \alpha)b + \alpha a}{E_{\theta_0}(Z)}$$

Proposition 3.1.7

For simple null hypothesis $H_0 : \theta = \theta_0$ and simple alternative hypothesis $H_1 : \theta = \theta_1$ testing, among the testing methods, including sequential and non-sequential, that have P_{θ_0} (reject H_0) $\leq \alpha$, P_{θ_1} (accept H_0) $\leq \beta$ and $E_{\theta_i}(N) < \infty (i = 0, 1)$, the *SPRT* with significance level (α, β) has the minimums of $E_{\theta_0}(N)$ and $E_{\theta_1}(N)$.

B.3.2 ASM Method

3.2.1 Normal Distribution

$\{x_n\}$ is *i.i.d* and its distribution function is $N(\mu; \sigma^2)$, $-\infty < \mu < \infty, 0 < \sigma < \infty$. Given credibility probability $\gamma(0 < \gamma < 1)$. When δ^2 is known, there exists a fixed size of samples $n_0 \equiv n_0(\delta, \sigma)$, where $n_0(\delta, \sigma)$ is the minimal integer satisfying the following formula

$$n \geq \frac{\alpha^2 \sigma^2}{\delta^2}$$

where $\alpha = \Phi^{-1}\left(\frac{1+\gamma}{2}\right)$, $\Phi(x)$ is a normal function, i.e., $\Phi(x) = \frac{1}{\sqrt{2\pi}} \int_{-\infty}^{x} \exp(-t^2/2)dt$. Then $\forall (\mu, \sigma)$, have

$$P\{\mu \in (\overline{X}_{n_0} - \delta, \overline{X}_{n_0} + \delta)\} \geq \gamma \tag{II.1}$$

where

$$\overline{X}_{n_0} = \frac{1}{n_0} \sum_1^{n_0} x_i$$

When δ^2 is unknown, define a sampling process and assume that $N(\delta)$ is its stopping variable (when sampling stops Formula (II.1) holds). If $N(\delta)$ satisfies the following formula

$$\lim_{\delta \to \infty} \frac{n_0(\delta, \sigma)}{E_{\mu,\sigma}\{N(\delta)\}} \geq 1, \forall (\mu, \sigma)$$

Then the process is called asymptotically efficient. The corresponding method is called asymptotically efficient testing method with fixed width of the mean confident interval, denoted by *ASM*. The distribution of x_i is assumed to be $N(\mu; \delta^2)$.

Definition 3.2.1

Let $n_1, n_2 \geq 2$. For each $n \geq n_1$, calculate $S_n^2 = \frac{1}{n-1} \sum_1^n (x_i - \overline{x}_n)^2$. Define stopping variable $N(\delta)$ as the minimal integer satisfying the following formula

$$n \geq \left\{ n_1, \frac{\alpha_n^2 S_n^2}{\delta^2} \right\} \tag{II.2}$$

where, α_n is a series of positive constants and converges to α, $\alpha = \Phi^{-1}\left(\frac{1+\gamma}{2}\right)$.

Proposition 3.2.1

Assume that $N(\delta)$ is a stopping variable defined by Formula (II.2). Then, we have the following properties.

(1) $\forall (\mu, \sigma), P(N(\delta) < \infty) = 1$
(2) If $\delta_1 < \delta_2$, then $N(\delta_1) \geq N(\delta_2), a.s$ and $\lim_{\delta \to \infty} N(\delta) = \infty, a.s$
    where, symbol *a.s* means almost everywhere.
(3) $E_\sigma\{N(\delta)\} < \infty, \forall \sigma \in (0, \infty), \delta \in (0, \infty)$ holds
(4) $\lim_{\delta \to \infty} \frac{N(\delta)}{n_0(\delta,\sigma)} = 1, a.s \forall \sigma \in (0, \infty)$
(5) $\lim_{\delta \to \infty} \frac{E_\sigma\{(N(S)\}}{n_0(\delta,\sigma)} = 1, a.s \forall \sigma \in (0, \infty)$
(6) $P_\sigma\{(N(\delta) > n\} \sim O\left(n^{-\frac{3}{2}} \exp\left(-\frac{1}{2}n^2\right)\right)$

Proposition 3.2.2

In Formula (II.2), letting $\alpha_n \equiv \alpha$ and assuming that $N(\delta)$ is the corresponding stopping variable, then $\forall n \geq n_1$, have

$$E_\sigma\{N(\delta)\} \leq n_0(\delta, \sigma) + n_1 + 1, \forall \delta > 0, 0 < \sigma < \infty$$

Proposition 3.2.3

In Formula (II.2), letting $\alpha_n \equiv \alpha$, $n_1 \geq 3$, then for a finite $k \geq 0$ such that for $\forall (\mu, \sigma), \delta > 0$, $P_{\mu,\sigma}\{|\bar{x}_{N+k} - \mu| < \delta\} \geq \gamma$.

B.3.2 General Cases

Definition 3.2.2

Define $N(\delta)$ as the minimal integer satisfying the following formula

$$n \geq \frac{\alpha_n^2}{\delta^2} \left\{ \frac{1}{n} \left(1 + \sum_{i=1}^{n} (x_i - x_n)^2 \right) \right\} \tag{II.3}$$

where, α_n a series of positive constants and converges to α, $\alpha = \Phi^{-1}\left(\frac{1+\gamma}{2}\right)$.

Proposition 3.2.4

Assume that $\{v_n, n = 1, 2, \cdots\}$ is a series of positive random variables $a.s$ and $\lim_{n \to \infty} v_n = 1, a.s.$ Let $f(n)$ be a series of constants satisfying the following condition

$$f(n) > 0, \quad \lim_{n \to \infty} \frac{f(n)}{f(n-1)} = 1$$

For $\forall t, t > 0$, define $N(t)$ as the minimal integer satisfying the following formula

$$f(k) \geq t v_k, k \geq 1$$

Then, $N(t)$ is a non-decreasing stopping variable of t and

(1) $P(N(t) < \infty) < 1$
(2) $\lim_{t \to \infty} N(t) = \infty$
(3) $\lim_{t \to \infty} E(N(t)) = \infty$
(4) $\lim_{t \to \infty} \frac{f(N(t))}{t} = 1, a.s.$

If $E_P\left\{ \sup_{n \geq 1} v_n \right\} < \infty$ again, then $\lim_{t \to \infty} E_F\left\{ \frac{f(N(t))}{t} \right\} = 1$, $\forall F \in \mathcal{T}$.

Proposition 3.2.5 (Chow-Robbins Theorem)

Assume that $N(\delta)$ is a stopping variable defined by Formula (II.3). Then,

(1) $P(N(\delta) < \infty) = 1$
(2)   When $\delta \to 0$ monotonically, $N(\delta) \to \infty$ monotonically $a.s.$
(3) $\lim_{\delta \to \infty} \frac{\delta^2 N(\delta)}{\alpha^2 \sigma^2(F)} = 1, a.s, \forall F \in \mathcal{T}$

   If $E\left\{ \sup_{n \geq 1} S_n^2 \right\} < \infty$ again, then

(4) $\lim_{\delta \to \infty} \frac{\delta^2(N(\delta))}{\alpha^2 \sigma^2(F)} = 1$

where, $\sigma^2(F)$ is the variance of F and $\mathcal{T}$ is a set of all distribution functions having finite second moments.

Proposition 3.2.6

$\{x_n\}$ is *i.i.d.*, $E(x_1) = 0$ and $E(x_1^2) = 1$. Let $S_n = \sum_1^n x_i$. $N(t)$ is a positive random integer, $t > 0$, and satisfies

$$p \lim_{t \to \infty} \frac{N(t)}{t} = c, 0 < c < \infty$$

Then, we have

$$\lim_{t \to \infty} P\left\{ \frac{1}{\sqrt{N(t)}} S_{N(t)} \leq x \right\} = \Phi(x), -\infty < x < \infty$$

where, $p \lim_{t \to \infty}$ is a convergent in measure limit and $\Phi(x) = \frac{1}{\sqrt{2\pi}} \exp(-t^2/2) dt$.

The above proposition is the extension of common central limit theorem. In the common theorem N is a constant variable but $N(t)$ is a random variable.

Proposition 3.2.7

Let $\{x_n\}$ be a sequence of random variables satisfying the following properties

(1)   There exist real number θ, distribution function $F(x)$ and a series $\{\omega_n\}$ of real such that for all continuous points of F the following formula holds

$$\lim_{n \to \infty} P\{x_n - \theta \leq \omega_n x\} = F(x)$$

(2) $\forall \varepsilon > 0, \eta > 0$, there exists a sufficiently large n_0 and sufficient small positive number c such that when $n > n_0$ have

$$P\{|x_{n'} - x_n| < \varepsilon \omega_n \text{ and } n', |n' - n| < cn\} > 1 - \eta$$

Let $\{n(t)\}$ be a sequence of ascending integers and $n(t) \to \infty$. Let $N(t)$ be a stopping variable, $P(N(t) < \infty) < 1$ and $\lim_{t \to \infty} \frac{N(t)}{n(t)} = 1$, *a.s.* Then, for all continuous points of $F(x)$, we have

$$\lim_{t \to \infty} P\left\{ x_{N(t)} - \theta \leq \omega_{n(t)} x \right\} = F(x)$$

The materials of Addenda B are from Hogg (1977), Gnedenko (1956), and Natanson (1955).

References

Allen, J. F. (1981). An interval-base representation of temporal knowledge. *IJCAI-81*, 221–226.

Allen, J. F. (1983). Planning using a temporal world model. *IJCAI-83*, 741–747.

Allen, J. F. (1984). Toward a general theory of action and time. *Artificial Intelligence*, 123–154.

Benjio, Y., Lamblin, P., Popovici, D., & Larochelle. (2007). Greedy layer-wise training of deep networks. In *Advances in Neural Information Processing Systems, 19 (NIPS'06)* (pp. 153–160). MIT Press.

Bhaskar, R., & Simon, H. A. (1977). Problem solving in semantically rich domains: an example from engineering thermodynamics. *Cognitive Science, 1*, 193–215.

Bobrow, D. G., & Winograd, T. (1977). A knowledge representation language. *Cognitive Science, 1*(1), 3–46.

Bredeweg, B., & Struss, P. (2003). Current topics in qualitative reasoning. *AI Magazine, 24*(no.4). Winter, pp13.

Brooks, R. A., & Lozano-Perez, T. (1982). A subdivision algorithm in configuration space for findpath with rotation, *M.I.T. Artificial Intelligence Laboratory Report*. AIM-684. Dec.

Brooks, R. A. (1983). Solving the find-path problem by good representation of free space. *IEEE Transactions on SMC, SMC-13*(No.3), 190–197.

Cech, E. (1966). *Topological Space*. New York: Wiley.

Cheeseman, P. (1986). *Probabilistic Versus Fuzzy Reasoning, in Uncertainty in Artificial Intelligence*. North Holland.

Chen, W. (2005). *The model of granular computing based on quotient space and rough set theories, doctoral dissertation (in Chinese)*. Anhui University.

Chien, R. T., Zhang, L., & Zhang, B. (1984). Planning collision-free paths for robotic arm among obstacles. *IEEE Transactions On PAMI-6* (no.1). January, $91-96$ $d(i) = d(0) \in D$.

Cohen, P. R. (1985). *Heuristic Reasoning about Uncertainty: an Artificial Intelligence Approach*. Marshfield, MA, USA: Pitman Publishing, Inc.

Davey, B. A., & Priestley, H. A. (1992). *Introduction to Lattice and Order*. Cambridge: Cambridge University Press.

Dijkstra, E. W. (1959). A note on two problems in connection with graphs. *Numerische Mathematik, 1*, 269–271.

Dill, K. A., Bromberg, S., Yue, K., Fiebig, K. M., Yee, D. P., Thomas, P. D., & Chan, H. S. (1995). Principle of protein folding—a perspective from simple exact models. *Protein Science, (4)*, 561–602.

Doyle, J. (1979). A truth maintenance system. *AI, 12*, 231–272.

Dubois, D., & Prade, H. (2001). Possibility theory, probability theory and multiple-valued logics: a clarification. *Annals of Mathematics and Artificial Intelligence, 32*, 35–66.

Duda, R. O. (1978). *Development of the prospector consultation system for mineral exploration*. Final Report, SRI International.

Eisenberg, M. (1974). *Topology*. Holt, Rinehart and Winston, Inc.

Field, R., et al. (1984). An investigation of dynamic weighting in heuristic search. *Proceedings of 6th ECAI*, 277–278.

Floyd, R. (1962). Algorithm 97: shortest path. *Communications of the ACM, 5*, 345.

Forbus, K. D. (1981). Qualitative reasoning about physical process. In *Proc. of IJCAI-7* (pp. 326–330).

Forbus, K. D. (1984). Qualitative process theory. *AI, 24*, 85–168.

Galton, A. (1966). A generalized topological view of motion in discrete space. *Theoretical Computer Science, 305*, 111–134.

Gnedenko, B. V. (1956). *A Course in Probability Theory, People's Education Press (Chinese Version)*.

Hinton, G. E., Osindero, S., & The, Yee-Whye (2006). A fast learning algorithm for deep belief nets. *Neural Communication, 18*, 1527–1554.

Hand, D., Mannila, H., & Smyth, P. (2001). *Principles of Data Mining*. Cambridge, MA: MIT Press.

He, Fugui. (2011). *The application of quotient space theory to network path analysis, doctoral dissertation*. Hefei, China: Anhui University.

Hobbs, J. R. (1985). Granularity. In *Proc. of IJCAI*. Los Angeles, USA, 432–435.

Hogg, R. V., et al. (1977). *Probability and Statistical Inference*. Macmillan Publishing Co. Inc.

Hu, Xiaolin, Qi, Peng, & Zhang, Bo (2012). *Hierarchical K-means algorithm for modeling visual area V2 neurons*. Doha, Qatar: 19th International Conference on Neural Information Processing. Nov. 12–15.

Kak, A. C., & Slaney, M. (2001). *Principles of Computerized Tomographic Imaging, Society of Industrial and Applied Mathematics*.

Kashyap, R. L., & Mittal, M. C. (1975). Picture reconstruction for projections. *IEEE Transactions Computing, 24*(no.9), 915–923.

Kelly, J. L. (1955). *General Topology*. Princeton: N. J., Van Nostrand Co.

Kolmogorov, A. N. (1950). *Foundations of the theory of probability*. Oxford, England: Chelsea Publishing Co.

Kowalski, R. (1979). *Logic for Problem Solving*. New York: North Holland.

Kuipers, B. (1988). Using incomplete quantitative knowledge in qualitative reasoning. *Proceedings of AAAI-88*, 324–329.

Lau, K. F., & Dill, K. A. (1989). A lattice statistical mechanics model of the conformational and sequence space of proteins. *Macromolecules, 22*, 3986–3997.

Lau, K. F., & Dill, K. A. (1990). Theory for protein mutability and biogenesis. *Proceedings of the National Academy of Sciences USA, 87*, 683–642.

Liang, P., & Song, F. (1996). what does a probabilistic interpretation of fuzzy sets mean? *IEEE Transactions on Fuzzy Systems, 4*(2), 200–205.

Lin, T. Y. (1988). Neighborhood systems and approximation in relational databases and knowledge bases. *Proceedings of the 4th International Symposium on Methodologies of Intelligent Systems*.

Lin, T. Y. (1992). Topological and fuzzy rough sets. In R. Slowinski (Ed.), *Decision Support by Experience—Application of the Rough Sets Theory* (pp. 287–304). Kluwer Academic Publishers.

Lin, T. Y. (1996). A set theory for soft computing. In *Proceeding of 1996 International Conference on Fuzzy Systems* (pp. 1140–1146). New Orleans: Louisiana. Sept. 8-11.

Lin, T. Y. (1997). Neighborhood systems—application to qualitative fuzzy and rough sets. In P. P. Wang (Ed.), *Advances in Machine Intelligence and Soft-Computing* (pp. 132–155). Durham, North Carolina, USA: Department of Electrical Engineering, Duke University.

Lin, T. Y. (1998). *Granular computing on binary relations I: data mining and neighborhood systems, manuscript*. San Jose, California, USA: Department of Mathematics and Computer Science, San Jose State University.

Lin, T. Y., & Tsumoto, S. (2000). Qualitative fuzzy sets revisited; granulation on the space of membership functions. In *The 19th International Meeting of North American Fuzzy Information Processing Society* (pp. 331–337). July 1-15, Atlanta.

Lin, T. Y. (2001a). Granular fuzzy sets and probability theories. *International Journal of Fuzzy Systems, 3*(2), 373–381.

Lin, T. Y. (2001b). Qualitative fuzzy sets: a comparison of three approaches. In *Proceeding of Joint 9th IFSA World Congress and 20th NAFIPS International Conference* (pp. 2359–2363). Vancouver: Canada. July 25–28.

Lozano-Perez, T., & Wesley, M. A. (1979). An algorithm for planning collision-free paths among polyhedral obstacles. *Communication Association Computing Math, ACM-22*, 560–570.

Lozano-Perez, T. (1983). Spatial planning: A configuration space approach. *IEEE Transactions Computing, C-32*. Feb, 108−120.

Mallat S. G., 1989. A theory for multiresolution signal decomposition: the wavelet representation, IEEE *Transaction on PAMI, 11*(no.7), July, 674−693.

Martin, T. (2000). *Computational molecular biology lecture*. Winter: University of Washington.

McCarthy, J. (1980). Circumscription - a form of non-monotonic reasoning. *AI, 13*, 27−39.

McDermott, D., & Doyle, J. (1980). Non-monotonic logic I. *AI, 13*, 41−72.

Mello, L. S. H., & Sanderson, A. C. (1989a). A correct and complete algorithm for the generation of mechanical assembly sequences. *Proceedings of IEEE International Conference on Robotics and Automation*, 56−61.

Mello, L. S. H., & Sanderson, A. C. (1989b). Representation of assembly sequences. *Proceedings of IJCAI-89*, 1035−1040.

Mitchell, T. (1997). *Machine Learning*. McGraw Hill.

Mitsuishi, T., Endou, N., & Shidama, Y. (2000). The concept of fuzzy set and membership function and basic properties of fuzzy set operation. *Journal of Formalized Mathematics, 12*. Released 2000, Published 2003.

Murthy, S. S. (1988). Qualitative reasoning at multiple resolutions. *Proceedings of AAAI-88*, 296−300.

Natanson, I. P. (1955). *Real Function Theory*. Beijing (Chinese): Renmin Educational Publishing Press.

Nayak, A., Sinchair, A., & Zwick, U. (1999). Spatial codes and the hardness of string folding problem. *Journal of Comparative Biology, 6*, 13.

Newell, A., & Simon, H. A. (1972). *Human Problem Solving*. Englewood Cliffs, NJ: Prentice-Hall.

Nilsson, N. J. (1980). *Principle of Artificial Intelligence*. Tioga Publishing Co.

Nutter, J. T. (1987). Uncertainty and probability. *Proceedings 10th IJCAI-87*, 373−379.

Pawlak, Z. I. (1982). Rough sets. *International Journal of Parallel Programming, 11*(5), 314−356.

Pawlak, Z. I. (1991). *Rough Sets Theoretical Aspects of Reasoning about Data*. Dordrecht, Boston, London: Kluwer Academic Publishers.

Pawlak, Z. I. (1998). Granularity of knowledge, indiscernibility and rough sets. *Proceedings of IEEE World Congress on Computational Intelligence, 1*, 106−110.

Pearl, J. (1984a). *Heuristics, Intelligent Search Strategies for Computer Problem Solving*. Addison-Wesley Publishing Company.

Pearl, J. (1984b). Some recent results in heuristic search theory. *IEEE Transactions PAMI-6, 1*, 1−12.

Pearl, Judea (2000). *Causality: Models, Reasoning, and Inference*. Cambridge University Press.

Reif, J. H. (1979). *Complexity of the mover's problem and generalizations*. 20th Annual IEEE Symposium on Foundations of Computer Science. San Juan, Puerto Rico. October, pp. 421−427.

Reif, J. H., & Sharir, M. (1985). *Motion planning in the presence of moving obstacles*. Portland, OR: 26th Annual IEEE Symposium on Foundations of Computer Science. October, pp. 144−154.

Reiter, R. (1980). A logic for default reasoning. *Artificial Intelligence, 13*, 81−132.

Rioul, O., & Vetterli, M. (1991). Wavelets and signal processing. *IEEE Signal Processing Magazine, 8*. Oct. 14−38.

Schwatz, J. T., & Shatic, M. (1983a). On the 'piano movers' problem I, the case of a two-dimensional rigid polygonal body moving admist polygonal barriers. *Communications on Pure and Applied Mathematics, 36*, 345−398.

Schwatz, J. T., & Shatic, M. (1983b). On the 'piano movers' problem II, general technique for computing topological properties of real algebraic manifolds. *Advances in Applied Mathematics, 4*, 298−351.

Serra, J. (1982). *Image Analysis and Mathematical Morphology*. London Academic Pr.

Serre, T., Oliva, A., & Poggio, T. (2007). A feed-forward architecture accounts for rapid categorization. *Proceedings of the National Academy of Sciences (PNAS), 104*(No. 15), 6424−6429.

Shafer, G. (1976). *A Mathematical Theory of Evidence*. Princeton University Press.

Shapiro, Stuart C. (1979). *Techniques of Artificial Intelligence*. D. Van Nostrand Company.

Shortiffe, E. H. (1976). *Computer-based Medical Consultations: MICIN*. American Elsevier Publishing Co. Inc.

Sims, B. T. (1976). *Fundamental of Topology*. New York, London.

Smith, M. B. (1995). Semi-metrics, closure space, and digital topology. *Theoretical Computer Science, 151*, 157–276.

Sweldens, W. (1998). The lifting scheme: a construction of second generation wavelets. *SIAM Journal on Mathematical Analysis, 29*(no.2). March, 511–546.

Toussaint, G. T. (Ed.). (1985). *Computational Geometry.* North-Holland: Elsevier Science Publishers B.V.

Unger, R., & Moult, J. (1993). Genetic algorithms for protein folding simulations. *J. Mol. Biol., 231*, 75–81.

Unser, M., & Blu, T. (2003). wavelet theory demystified. *IEEE Transactions on Signal Processing, 51*(no.2). Feb. 2003, 470–483.

Verkuilen, J. (2001). *Measuring fuzzy set membership functions: a dual scaling approach, prepared for presentation at annual meeting of the APSA.* San Francisco, CA. August 30-September 2.

Williams, B. C. (1988). A symbolic approach to qualitative algebraic reasoning. *Proceedings of AAAI-88*, 264–269.

Wolter, J. D. (1989). On the automatic generation of assembly plans. *Proceedings of IEEE ICRA*, 62–68.

Xiong, J. C. (1981). *Point Set Topology (in Chinese).* Higher Education Press.

Yao, Jingtao, Vasilakos, A. V., & Pedryez, W. (2012). Granular computing: perspectives and challenges, will appears. In *IEEE Trans. on Cybernetics*.

Yao, Y. Y., & Chen, X. C. (1997). Neighborhood based information systems. In *Proceedings of the 3rd Joint Conference on Information Sciences* (Vol. 3) Rough Set & Computer Science Research (pp.154–157). Triangle Park, North Carolina, USA. March 1–5.

Yao, Y. Y., & Zhong, N. (1999). Potential applications of granular computing in knowledge discovery and data mining. *Proceedings of World Multi-conference on Systemics, Cybernetics and Informatics*, 573–580.

You, C. Y. (1997). *The Foundation of Topology (Chinese).* Peking University Press.

Zacks, S. (1971). *The Theory of Statistic Inference.* New York: Wiley.

Zadeh, L. A. (1965). Fuzzy sets. *Information and Control, 3*(8), 338–353.

Zadeh, L. A. (1979). Fuzzy sets and information granularity. In M. Gupta, R. Ragade, & R. Yager (Eds.), *Advances in Fuzzy set Theory and Applications* (pp. 3–18). Amsterdam: North-Holland.

Zadeh, L. A. (1997). Towards a theory of fuzzy information granulation and its centrality in human reasoning and fuzzy logic. *Fuzzy Sets and Systems, 19*, 111–127.

Zadeh, L. A. (1998). Some reflections on soft computing, granular computing and their roles in the conception, design and utilization of information/intelligent systems. *Soft Computing, 2*(1), 23–25.

Zadeh, L. A. (1999). From computing with number to computing with word - from manipulation of measurements to manipulation of perceptions. *IEEE Transactions on Circuit and system, 45*(No.1), 105–120.

Zhang, B., & Zhang, L. (1982a). The collision-free path planning of a manipulator under obstacles (in Chinese). *Chinese Journal of Artificial Intelligence, 3*, 56–68.

Zhang, B., & Zhang, L. (1982b). The collision detection of coordinate operation of two arms (in Chinese). *The Journal of Anqing Normal College, 1*, 6–12.

Zhang, L., & Zhang, B. (1984). The successive SA search and its computational complexity. In *Proc. of 6-th ECAI* (pp. 249–258).

Zhang, B., & Zhang, L. (1985). A weighted technique in heuristic search. In *Proc. of 9-th IJCAI* (pp. 1037–1039).

Zhang, B., & Zhang, L. (1987). Statistical heuristic search. *Journal of Computer Science and Technology, 2*(1). Jan. 1–11.

Zhang, B., Zhang, L., et al. (1988a). An algorithm for findpath with rotation. In *Proc. of IEEE on SMC-88.* Beijing, 795–798.

Zhang, B., Zhang, L., et al. (1988b). A findpath algorithm for a manipulator by finite division of configuration space, Robotics and Manufacturing. In M. Jamshidi (Ed.), *Recent Trends in Research, Education and Applications* (pp. 99–106). New York: ASME Press.

Zhang, B., & Zhang, L. (1988c). *Path planning based on topologic method.* Paris: The Second France-Sino International Conference on Robotics. Dec.

Zhang, B., & Zhang, L. (1988d). The dimension reduction method for collision-free path planning (in Chinese). *Robot*, (no. 6), 32—38.

Zhang, L., & Zhang, B. (1988e). Motion planning of multi-joint arm (in Chinese). *Pattern Recognition and Artificial Intelligence, 2*, 22—29.

Zhang, B., & Zhang, L. (1989a). Statistical heuristic search. In Ci Yungui (Ed.), *Research on Frontier in Computing.* Tsinghua University Press.

Zhang, B., & Zhang, L. (1989b). The comparison between the statistical heuristic search and A*. *Journal of Computer science and Technology, 4*(No. 2), 126—132.

Zhang, L., & Zhang, B. (1989c). The quotient space model of qualitative reasoning I (in Chinese). *Journal of Anqing Normal College, 8*(no. 1—2), 1—8.

Zhang, B., Zhang, L., et al. (1990a). Motion planning of multi-joint robotic arm with topological dimension reduction method. In *Proc. of 11th IJCAI* (pp. 1024—1034).

Zhang, L., & Zhang, B. (1990b). The quotient space model of qualitative reasoning II (in Chinese). *Journal of Anqing Normal College, 9*(no.1).

Zhang, B., & Zhang, L. (1990c). The automatic generation of mechanical assembly plans. In *Proc. of PRICAL* (pp. 480—485).

Zhang, L., & Zhang, B. (1990d). The computational complexity of quotient space based problem solving model. *The Journal Anqing Normal College, 9*(no.2), 1—7.

Zhang, B., & Zhang, L. (1992). *Theory and Application of Problem Solving.* North- Holland Elsevier Science Publishers B.V.

Zhang, L., & Zhang, B. (1997a). Statistical genetic algorithms (in Chinese). *Journal of Software, 8*(no.5), 335—344.

Zhang, L., & Zhang, B. (1997b). The application of statistical heuristic search method to function optimization (in Chinese). *Chinese Journal of Computers, 20*(no.8), 673—680.

Zhang, L., & Zhang, B. (2003a). The quotient space theory of problem solving. *Proceedings of International Conference on Rough Sets, Fuzzy Set, Data Mining and Granular Computing (RSFDGrC'2003).* October 19—22, Chongqing, China: 11—15.

Zhang, L., & Zhang, B. (2003b). Fuzzy quotient space theory (fuzzy granular computing). *Chinese Journal of Software (in Chinese), 14*(4), 770—776.

Zhang, L., & Zhang, B. (2003c). Quotient space theory and granular computing. In *Proc. of Chinese Conference on Rough Set and Soft Computing, CRSSC'2003.* Chongqing, 1—3.

Zhang, Ling, & Zhang, Bo (2003d). Fuzzy reasoning model under quotient space structure (Invited Lecture). *International Conference on Fuzzy Information Processing—Theories and Applications.* March 1—4, Beijing China.

Zhang, Ling, & Zhang, Bo (2004a). The quotient space theory of problem solving. *Fundamenta Informaticae, 59*(2,3), 2004:287—298.

Zhang, Ling, & Zhang, Bo (2005a). A quotient space approximation model of multi-resolution signal analysis. *Journal of Computer Science & Technology.* Jan. 20(1):90—94.

Zhang, Ling, & Zhang, Bo (2005b). Fuzzy reasoning model under quotient space structure. *Information Sciences, 173*(4), 353—364. June.

Zhang, Ling, & Zhang, Bo (2005c). The structural analysis of fuzzy sets. *Journal of Approximate Reasoning, 40*, 92—108.

Zhang, Weixiong (1988). The weighted technique in heuristic search (in Chinese). *The Chinese Journal of Computers, 11*(no. 8), 500—504.

Zuo, X. L. (1988). *Discrete Mathematics (Chinese).* Shanghai Science Press.

Index

Note: Page numbers with "*f*" denote figures; "*t*" tables.

Printed and bound by CPI Group (UK) Ltd, Croydon, CR0 4YY

03/10/2024

01040323-0003